D1568934

Medieval Narratives of Alexander the Great

Studies in Medieval Romance

ISSN 1479-9308

General Editor
Corinne Saunders

Editorial Board
Siobhain Bly Calkin
Rhiannon Purdie
Robert Allen Rouse

This series aims to provide a forum for critical studies of the medieval romance, a genre which plays a crucial role in literary history, clearly reveals
medieval secular concerns, and raises complex questions regarding social
structures, human relationships, and the psyche. Its scope extends from the
early Middle Ages into the Renaissance period, and although its main focus is
on Enlish literature, comparative studies are welcomed.

Proposals or queries should be sent in the first instance to one of the addresses
given below; all submissions will receive prompt and informed consideration.

Professor Corinne Saunders, Department of English, University of Durham,
Durham DH1 3AY

Boydell & Brewer Limited, PO Box 9, Woodbridge, Suffolk IP12 3DF

Previously published volumes in the series
are listed at the back of this book

Medieval Narratives of Alexander the Great

Transnational Texts in England and France

VENETIA BRIDGES

D. S. BREWER

First published 2018
D. S. Brewer, Cambridge

ISBN 978 1 84384 502 7

D. S. Brewer is an imprint of Boydell & Brewer Ltd
PO Box 9, Woodbridge, Suffolk, IP12 3DF, UK
and of Boydell & Brewer Inc.
668 Mount Hope Ave, Rochester, NY 14620–2731, USA
website: www.boydellandbrewer.com

A CIP catalogue record for this book is available
from the British Library

The publisher has no responsibility for the continued existence or accuracy
of URLs for external or third-party internet websites referred to in this book,
and does not guarantee that any content on such websites is, or will remain,
accurate or appropriate.

This publication is printed on acid-free paper

For my family, past and present,
but particularly for Edmund

Contents

Acknowledgements

Thanking all those who have helped during the gestation of this book is an impossible task, since so many have contributed so much in a huge variety of ways; the following list is merely the tip of the iceberg, and I apologize for any omissions. The universities of Cambridge, York, Leeds, Surrey, and Durham have all been stimulating homes, and I am particularly in debt to my colleagues at each institution for their willingness to hear yet more about Alexander. I am also extremely grateful to the research seminars at the universities of Cambridge, Cardiff, Leeds, Oxford, and York, where many of the ideas developed here were first tentatively aired. Thanks are also due to the staffs of Bodleian Library, the British Library, and Cambridge University Library, where much of the research was carried out, and to the Arts and Humanities Research Council for the doctoral funding that enabled the book's first stages. My PhD supervisor, Professor Philip Ford, has been greatly missed during its writing, although his influence is very much present in chapters 2 and 3.

I owe an especially large debt to the Centre for Medieval Literature at the universities of York and Southern Denmark (Odense), funded by the Danish National Research Foundation, and its leaders Christian Høgel, Lars Boje Mortensen, and Elizabeth M. Tyler for providing both financial support in the form of a postdoctoral research fellowship and also an intellectually vibrant context that has informed the book throughout. Elizabeth Tyler's generosity in particular has been crucial, although of course she bears no responsibility for the results. Neil Cartlidge's support has been a constant encouragement, as has that of Elizabeth Archibald, Julia Boffey, Helen Cooper, Rita Copeland, Tony Edwards, Jane Gilbert, Jill Mann, Eric Stanley, and David Wallace. Caroline Palmer has, as ever, maintained an unflagging optimism that was vital: my editorial and personal gratitude to her is manifold. Tamara Atkin, Joanna Bellis, Aisling Byrne, Alexandra Coghlan, Victoria Flood, Peter Foggitt, Rachel Gubbins, Sara Harris, Shazia Jagot, Gavin Kirk, Megan Leitch, Jessica Lockhart, Catherine Pope, Emily Wingfield, and George Younge have been of special importance, intellectually, practically, and in terms of much valued (and hopefully not too much tested) friendship. Finally, thanks beyond words are due to my family, especially to my siblings Camilla, Drusilla, and Edmund: *faire sans dire*.

List of Abbreviations

AM	*Of Arthour and of Merlin*
ANTS	Anglo-Norman Text Society
B	Oxford, Bodleian Library, MS Laud misc. 622
BnF	Bibliothèque nationale de France
CCCM	Corpus Christianorum Continuatio Medievalis
CSEL	Corpus Scriptorium Ecclesiasticorum Latinorum
EETS	Early English Text Society
FRETS	French of England Translation Series
L	London, Lincoln's Inn, MS 150
MED	Middle English Dictionary
MJ	*Mittellateinisches Jarbuch*
PMLA	*Proceedings of the Modern Languages Association*
RTC	*Roman de toute chevalerie*
SBT	*The Seege or Batayle of Troye*
STS	Scottish Text Society

Note on Names and Titles

For ancient material, I have cited the most usual translated or transliterated form of a name or text (e.g. Plutarch, *Parallel Lives*; Arrian, *Anabasis Alexandri*; Quintus Curtius Rufus, *Histories of Alexander*); all texts' titles are listed in Appendix 1 in English alongside their Latin or Greek original. For medieval material, I have used the most frequently encountered version of a name, whether in English, French, or Latin (e.g. Marie de France, Peter of Blois), and kept texts' titles in the original language (e.g. *Roman de Troie*, *Alexandreis*). I have also opted for the spelling 'Nectanebus' throughout, as it is the most familiar Anglicized version of the name, although it is found in various forms across the texts discussed.

Introduction

Epic, which was invented after memory and before history, occupies a third space in the human desire to connect the present to the past: it is the attempt to extend the qualities of memory over the reach of time embraced by history. Epic's purpose is to make the distant past as immediate to us as our own lives, to make the great stories of long ago beautiful and painful now.[1]

Appropriating Adam Nicholson's quotation describing Homeric epic and applying it to twelfth- and thirteenth-century literature, material that is frequently defined by its distance from classical epic, may seem a deliberately provocative way to begin a study of Alexander narratives of the High Middle Ages. For Alexander the Great is the hero of no classical epic poem: no Homer or Virgil chose to immortalize him in prestigious verse, despite his extraordinary personal qualities and his imperial domination of the known world. Indeed, Alexander's self-proclaimed medieval Virgil, Walter of Châtillon, gleefully points out this glaring deficiency on the part of his classical rivals in his own twelfth-century treatment of the Macedonian.[2] So Alexander would appear to be an unlikely participant, interpolated more by the academic need for a starting point rather than for his strict relevance, in Nicolson's memorable discussion of classical epic poetry.

Yet the elevated purpose that Nicolson here ascribes to epic surely transcends not only this particular poetic form but also the classical age that produced it. The idea of poetry making 'the distant past as immediate to us as our own lives … the great stories of long ago beautiful and painful now' describes, in far more inspiring terms than those habitual in academic analysis, the explicitly stated function of much medieval poetry focusing on the stories of the past, stories retold in and for different times but connected to that past via the act of *translatio studii*. Romance narratives of Troy, for example, frequently begin with the idea that hearing stories of the past will benefit the audience from a moral perspective, an attitude simultaneously found to justify the reading of pre-Christian classical poetry like the works

---

[1]   Adam Nicolson, *The Mighty Dead: Why Homer Matters* (London, 2014), p.xix.

[2]   'nullus ueterum poetarum … ausus fuit aggredi perscribendam [materiam]', *Alexandreis*, Prologue, 35–6, in *Galteri de Castellione Alexandreis*, ed. M. L. Colker (Padua, 1979).

1

of Ovid in medieval centres of learning.[3] Romance is one of the medieval heirs of classical epic, in that it becomes a dominant narrative medium of 'great stories' of both the ancient and more recent pasts from the twelfth century onwards. Alexander, Aeneas, Charlemagne, Roland, Arthur: all are epic, battle-hardened heroes, occupying both romance narratives and also those of *chansons de geste*, and in doing so demonstrating the slipperiness of generic classification and distinction in general but during the twelfth and thirteenth centuries in particular.[4] So medieval Alexanders of all narratives and genres may surely assert their relevance, and importance, in the role ascribed here to classical epic of 'connect[ing] the [medieval] present to the past'.[5]

The major questions I pose in this book coalesce around this connection, the 'third space' of Nicolson's description, which in my terms is the interaction (interruption?) of Alexander with (or into) several connected medieval 'presents'. What is the range of meanings in which Alexander participates in literary contexts during the twelfth and thirteenth centuries? How do these meanings relate to cultural identities as they form and re-form in this period of swift change and innovation? These broad questions in turn invite us to consider connections between literatures and contexts not usually juxtaposed in academic analysis but which are brought into being by the ubiquitous, if not unifying, figure of Alexander the Great.

The study that follows considers these questions in the context of Alexander literature, predominantly narratives of his life and achievements rather than exemplary or philosophical texts, composed between the mid-twelfth and mid-fourteenth centuries. It focuses on northern France and parts of the British Isles, an area that for much of this period was divided by not one but two common languages, French in various forms (which I will discuss in more detail below) and Latin. The book begins accordingly, after a survey of the available material up to the twelfth century (chapter 1), by considering three Alexander texts in these languages, the *Alexandreis*, the *Roman d'Alexandre*, and the

---

[3] For examples of this attitude, see *Medieval Literary Theory and Criticism c. 1100–c. 1375: The Commentary Tradition*, ed. A. J. Minnis and A. B. Scott with David Wallace, rev. edn (Oxford, 1998), and for discussion J. B. Allen, *The Ethical Poetic of the Later Middle Ages* (Toronto, 1982).

[4] On the vexed question of the distinction between 'romance' and *chanson de geste* in French, see Sarah Kay, *The Chansons de Geste in the Age of Romance: Political Fictions* (Oxford, 1995), which argues for dialogue between the two, as does the more recent article by Melissa Furrows, '*Chanson de Geste* as Romance in England', in *The Exploitations of Medieval Romance*, ed. Laura Ashe, Ivana Djordjević, and Judith Weiss (Cambridge, 2010), pp.57–72. One of the Alexander romances discussed in this book, the *Roman de toute chevalerie*, is often thought to have elements from *chanson de geste*: see *Le Roman d'Alexandre ou le roman de toute chevalerie*, trans. and introd. Catherine Gaullier-Bougassas and Laurence Harf-Lancner, Moyen Âge (Paris, 2003), pp.xxxiii–xxxviii.

[5] Nicolson, *The Mighty Dead*, p.xix.

Roman de toute chevalerie (in chapters 2, 3, and 4) before moving on to English material in *Kyng Alisaunder* (in chapter 5), proceeding chronologically.

The key aims of this Alexander research, however, transcend the conqueror's histories. I hope to set his texts in dialogue not just with one another but also with contemporary material to which they are connected via literary, political, and social networks. In order to achieve this, in each chapter after the first I compare these Alexander narratives with others, both Latin and vernacular, to illuminate their individual but also potentially their collective impact upon literary culture/s. So my study is multilingual and wide-ranging, acknowledging historical, political, and linguistic boundaries but not restricted by them. It is also defined by the concept of *translatio studii* mentioned above, a vital medieval tool in authorizing and justifying narratives of past non-Christian eras and a crucial idea for modern critics' understanding of the period. Finally, the book seeks to investigate a tumultuous and vital period for literary studies that is still sometimes not given due credit as important in its own right rather than simply as a source for later, more interesting centuries, especially in English studies. These aims inevitably flow from, and may also help to create, a sense that medieval studies in general needs to become much more wide-ranging, linguistically and politically, in order more accurately to understand and represent medieval literary realities. Alexander the Great, in his dominance of European culture over so many centuries, is an inspirational if intimidating subject for such a study.

Alexander Narratives: Continuities and Changes

Moving on (or back) from Nicolson's wonderful if romantic idea of epic's importance to the words of Chaucer's *Canterbury Tales* demonstrates Alexander's almost tedious ubiquity by the late fourteenth century, the end point of this book. The Monk's moralizing list of 'popes, emperours, [and] kynges' brought low by Fortune inevitably includes 'worthy, gentil Alisandre',[6] but more interesting than this already well-worn trope is the idea that the Macedonian's history itself has become a cliché:

> The storie of Alisaundre is so commune
> That every wight that hath discrecioun
> Hath herd somwhat or al of his fortune.[7]

Perhaps Chaucer is here gently mocking the Monk's prolixity – his lugubrious and long-winded presentation of Fortune's fickleness, supported by over one hundred tragedies he claims to have in his cell, does not argue for his

---

[6]   'The Monk's Prologue', 1986, and 'The Monk's Tale', 2658, in *The Riverside Chaucer*, gen. ed. Larry D. Benson, 3rd edn (Boston, MA, 1987), p.241 and p.250.

[7]   'The Monk's Tale', 2631–3, in *The Riverside Chaucer*, ed. Benson, p.250.

'discrecioun', in literary terms at least[8] – but the wider point that Alexander's 'storie' is almost universal is clearly made by the adjective 'commune'. The adjective is surely deliberately chosen to make the point that not only is Alexander widely known, but that he is also 'common' in one of the word's modern as well as medieval senses, that is, ordinary, usual, and (by extrapolation) not particularly interesting.[9] Alexander, the world's great conqueror, has been reduced to an entry in a morality tale because he is such a common figure in the British literary landscape of the fourteenth century.

One reason that Chaucer can describe Alexander's 'storie' as 'commune' by the later 1300s is because the Macedonian has become a literary as well as a historical colossus. Looming large over medieval cultures, the controversial king, conqueror, explorer, and pupil of Aristotle was the subject of histories, romances, epic poetry, satires, and sermons in most of the languages of Europe and the Middle East. Alexander's popularity in early Greek, Georgian, Armenian, and Syriac narratives from late antiquity was matched if not surpassed by accounts of his wanderings in Western European languages of the later Middle Ages, both vernaculars and transnational *linguae francae* such as Latin: from the Greek *Alexander Romance* (in a version from the third century AD but circulating earlier) to the tenth-century Latin of Leo the Archpriest and its descendent the *Historia de preliis* (in three main versions) and the Castilian *Libro de Alexandre* (after 1200), Alexander is found across the continent throughout the medieval era.[10]

This medieval ubiquity is important beyond the Middle Ages themselves, since it has had a large impact on modern studies of medieval Alexander literature, and therefore on the wide-ranging questions posed above about Alexander's meanings and their relationships to cultural and political identities. Alexander literature appears to move from East to West chronologically, geographically, and linguistically, following a well-known formulation of *translatio studii*.[11] This attractive literary-historical arc suggests that there is a fundamental continuity, despite differences of language, time, place, and even genre, between Alexander in Greece and Alexander in the Iberian peninsula, or in the British Isles, or in Iceland. It has therefore been relatively easy to

---

[8] 'The Monk's Prologue', 1971–2, in *The Riverside Chaucer*, ed. Benson, p.241.

[9] 'commune', adj., *MED*, <http://quod.lib.umich.edu/cgi/m/mec/med-idx?-type=id&id=MED8618> [accessed 1 August 2016]. The idea of 'commune' as 'common, usual, ordinary' is the fifth of eleven meanings listed.

[10] *The Greek Alexander Romance*, trans. and introd. Richard Stoneman (London, 1991); *Der Alexanderroman des Archipresbyters Leo*, ed. Friedrich Pfister (Heidelberg, 1913); *Libro de Alexandre*, ed. Francisco Marcos Marín (Madrid, 1987).

[11] The opening of the twelfth-century Arthurian romance *Cligès* by Chrétien de Troyes is the classic description of this, with learning moving from Greece to Rome and then France: *Cligès*, lines 33–5, ed. Claude Luttrell and Stewart Gregory, Arthurian Studies, 28 (Cambridge, 1993).

place Alexander at the centre of an apparently ready-formed medieval literary canon, a tradition of material translated between a wide variety of languages but that ultimately flows from the earliest Greek texts.[12] Vital critical study, in particular that of George Cary, supports this view by placing material from different languages in thematic or intellectual categories, enabling connections to be made between the various works.[13]

Yet this appealing emphasis on connections and continuity is only one aspect of Alexander's literary history, or histories. Returning to Nicolson's description of epic in the quotation above reveals that the relationship between 'then' and 'now' is constructed by our own need to see the one reflected in the other, or, in his words, 'the *human desire* to connect the present to the past' (my italics).[14] This desire to connect past with present, or languages with each another, is surely a major factor in the formation of the Alexander canon, a literary problem of concupiscence. However, an important result of this desire to see similarities is that moments of disjunction and discontinuity can be overlooked. One such moment, the later twelfth century, which is at the heart of the questions about Alexander literature posed in this book, is described as follows by Francine Mora:

> Au XIIᵉ siècle la réception de l'Antiquité était loin d'être sereine: elle suscitait des polémiques et déclenchait des passions, à la mesure des enjeux mis en oeuvre par sa redécouverte et son assimilation.[15]

Mora identifies a debate about how to rewrite/adapt/translate (none of these modern words alone comprises the range of the French word 'translater' used by medieval authors[16]) in the later twelfth century, with reference to the Troy story. In her acute analysis, there is a far-from-serene battle over ownership of this prestigious material being fought between authors writing in Latin, like Joseph of Exeter (fl.1180s), and those adapting it 'en romanz', initially meaning

---

12 On these authors, who include Plutarch and Arrian as well as less well-known writers, see chapter 1.

13 George Cary, *The Medieval Alexander*, ed. D. J. A. Ross (Cambridge, 1956). Cary's book is still the standard collection and description of medieval Alexander material.

14 Nicolson, *The Mighty Dead*, p.xix.

15 F. Mora, 'L'*Ylias* de Joseph d'Exeter: une réaction cléricale au *Roman de Troie* de Benoît de Saint-Maure', in *Progrès, réaction, décadence dans l'occident médiéval*, ed. E. Baumgartner and L. Harf-Lancner, Publications Romanes et Françaises, 231 (Geneva, 2003), pp.199–213 (p.213).

16 See for example the Prologue to the *Roman de Troie*, 33–7, which describes the process of 'en romanz metre' as encompassing (in modern terms) both translation and free adaptation (*Le Roman de Troie par Benoît de Sainte-Maure*, ed. Léopold Constans, 6 vols (Paris, 1904–12), i).

the French vernacular, such as Benoît de Sainte-Maure.[17] I think that this is also happening more widely in the same area of northern France with reference to Alexander literature, as I have discussed elsewhere.[18] The idea that the supposedly tranquil flow of Alexander's *translatio studii* is fiercely interrupted in the 1180s highlights the necessity of seeing discontinuities as well as connections as part of his literary history, keeping both in view as far as possible.

This point about discontinuity, of change both violent and subtle, is important for Alexander literature beyond the immediate context of the 1180s. Although the thirteenth-century works discussed in the later chapters, the *Roman de toute chevalerie* and *Kyng Alisaunder*, occupy different geographical, literary, and linguistic contexts from that described by Mora, they may still be marked by change rather than by continuity in their *translatio*. Asking questions about the nature of any such change in *translatio* means thinking about the effects of these different contexts. As I discuss in more detail below in the 'Language, Nation, Identity' section, a constant theme in the analysis of insular medieval literature is the importance of 'Englishness' (whether expressed in English, Anglo-Norman, or other languages), which is assumed to be a significant motivation in rewriting and composing material at this later time.[19] However, the movement of narratives from one language to another, from one cultural framework to another, may not always be governed by so dominant a sense of cultural nationalism; other factors may also be at play that affect the performance of *translatio studii*. To adapt Mora's idea in this insular context, there may also be various kinds of *translatio* involved in these Anglo-Norman and English Alexander narratives, *translatio* that is not solely focused on 'Englishness'.

This idea of variety in contexts, languages, and *translatio* suggests that medieval Alexander narratives, despite their focus on an individual figure, are multiple and multivalent. This is the basis of my analysis throughout the book, and underpins the discussions of networks, language, scholarship, and terminology in the rest of this introduction.

---

[17] Joseph of Exeter composed his poem the *Ylias* in the 1180s, in Mora's view as a response to Benoît de Sainte-Maure's *Roman de Troie* (c. 1165): see 'L'*Ylias* de Joseph d'Exeter'.

[18] Venetia Bridges, '"L'estoire d'Alixandre vos veul par vers traitier [...]": Passions and Polemics in Latin and Vernacular Alexander Literature of the Later Twelfth Century', *Nottingham Medieval Studies*, 58 (2014), pp.87–113.

[19] For more detailed discussion of 'Englishness' in both languages, see chapters 4 and 5. Thorlac Turville-Petre, *England the Nation: Language, Literature, and National Identity, 1290–1340* (Oxford, 1996), is an important study of insular literature from this perspective.

Networks

Invoking continuities and differences in this way presupposes that texts can be connected to one another, directly and/or indirectly. One important aspect of my approach is therefore a focus on networks, or webs of connections. I use this term fluidly, since its precise configuration alters depending on circumstances, many of which can be unknown or indefinable in medieval contexts. However, my usage encompasses people, places, institutions (formal but also familial, such as households), and books that come into contact, cohabit, and/or converge. Movement is therefore a crucial aspect of networks, movement not just of people and objects but the transference of ideas. This emphasis on movement, in both concrete and abstract terms, of course makes it difficult to say just where one network begins and another ends. It also highlights geographical issues, since although some aspects of networks may relate to a particular location (such as Paris), the cultural and intellectual webs connecting individuals and ideas do not necessarily map easily on to geographical or political co-ordinates. Yet geography is a necessary part of networks, as David Wallace's recent work *Europe: A Literary History, 1348–1415* shows clearly how trade routes and ideas do undoubtedly move together.[20] So my use of the concept 'network' is of necessity based in the geography (physical and political) of northern France and the British Isles, but seeks not to be limited by it. Constant J. Mews and John N. Crossley's description of 'communities of learning' is useful here:

> Invoking communities of learning as a paradigm moves away from a strict focus on specific texts or specific masters, or even specific locations. It allows us to obtain a more realistic picture of the development of learning and the way that interactions – between individuals and between communities, which may have been widely distributed – affected that development, than heretofore. Some of these communities may cross boundaries that are national, cultural, religious, or linguistic; some may be intangible, sharing either spiritual traditions or a common philosophy.[21]

Although my networks do focus as far as possible on 'specific texts … specific masters … [and] specific locations', Mews' and Crossley's idea that communities of learning transcend physical location to some extent is also helpful when considering the histories of Alexander material. Especially important

---

[20] David Wallace (ed.), *Europe: A Literary History, 1348–1415*, 2 vols (Oxford, 2016). The description of the book is suggestive, covering 'ten sequences of places linked by trade, travel, topography, language, pilgrimage, alliance, disease, and artistic exchange' <https://global.oup.com/academic/product/europe-9780198735359?cc=g-b&lang=en&#> [accessed 2 August 2016].

[21] *Communities of Learning: Networks and the Shaping of Intellectual Identity in Europe, 1100–1500*, ed. Constant J. Mews and John N. Crossley, Europa Sacra, 11 (Turnhout, 2011), p.4.

here is the final point in this quotation, the idea that networks ('communities of learning' in Mews' and Crossley's terms) are not delimited by boundaries, 'national, cultural, religious, or linguistic'. For my purposes, this means that thinking about networks necessitates multilingual and cross-disciplinary research, which here means considering texts in Latin, varieties of French and English. The concept of networks, then, also emphasizes the need to approach Alexander narratives with variety in mind.

Language, Nation, Identity

Undertaking multilingual and cross-disciplinary Alexander research means addressing modern questions of nation and identity. This is because Alexander scholarship, despite the wide-ranging linguistic nature of his medieval narratives and hence his variety, still tends to be defined by monolingual studies with a national focus (as discussed in more detail below). Although 'nation' in its generally understood sense is a post-medieval concept, national identity, particularly in relation to language, has been at the heart of medieval studies in Europe at least since the field became a defined area in the nineteenth century.[22] Newly emergent (or resurgent) nation states sought their literary origins in *Ur*-texts composed in the vernacular language that they identified as ethnically and culturally definitive. For English studies, the connection of language and national identity can be seen even earlier, in Archbishop Matthew Parker's collection and use of manuscripts to bolster the Protestant Church's claims to ancient indigenous authority, often conveyed in English, against the demands of Rome;[23] the subsequent rediscovery and canonization of *Beowulf*

---

[22] The literature on the vexed question of when national identities of various kinds become apparent is substantial, but a keystone work remains Benedict Anderson, *Imagined Communities: Reflections on the Origin and Spread of Nationalism*, 2nd edn (London, 1991), which firmly locates this development in the early modern era. Anderson's work has been influential for medievalists seeking ideas of the nation before this era, for example Geraldine Heng, 'The Romance of England: *Richard Coeur de Lyon*, Saracens, Jews and the Politics of Race and Nation', in *The Postcolonial Middle Ages*, ed. Jeffrey Jerome Cohen (Basingstoke, 2000), pp.135–71, especially pp.150–2, who engages explicitly with Anderson's work. For a different perspective on medieval states and the nation, see Robert M. Stein, *Reality Fictions: Romance, History, and Governmental Authority, 1025–1180* (Notre Dame, IN, 2006), who observes that 'for most of medieval Europe, the nation is simultaneously too small and too large to be a useful analytic unit' (p.5).

[23] On Parker's hunt for manuscripts (both Old English and Latin), see Timothy Graham and Andrew G. Watson, *The Recovery of the Past in Early Elizabethan England: Documents by John Bale and John Goscelin from the Circle of Matthew Parker*, Cambridge Bibliographical Society, 13 (Cambridge, 1998), especially pp.55–9, which is a list of sources for Anglo-Saxon history drawn up by Parker's secretary John Joscelyn between 1565 and 1567. It includes six copies of the *Anglo-Saxon Chronicle*. Parker's research was printed as *De antiquitate Britannicae ecclesiae* in 1572.

made the collocation of linguistic and national identities even stronger. The same applies to the French poem *La Chanson de Roland*, with the fact that the oldest manuscript is copied in Anglo-Norman an inconvenient truth for French literature.[24] I am discussing texts from northern and western Europe here, but medievalists working on material from the east and the south have highlighted the same connection between language and nation, if anything even stronger because of recent political developments.[25] What all these medievalists, and others, have noted is that this prevailing connection of language with nation and national identity is pernicious, since it encourages prioritizing a particular language or languages over others because of modern, rather than medieval, concerns.[26] My Alexander study attempts to unpick this dangerous modern connection in order to consider questions of *translatio* from a more truly historicist perspective. This may not sound a particularly dramatic or controversial aim, but the following examples of Anglo-Norman and Latin, both major features of this book, demonstrate how embedded this modern connection is in contemporary medieval studies, and how difficult it is to escape.

The fight to include Anglo-Norman material within the remit of English literature is ongoing, since the attitude that such texts are somehow not important in British literary history because they are not English linguistically can still be found, despite the efforts of several current scholars.[27] Yet this material is vital not just as a source for later English-language texts but also as a significant literary culture of its own time, both in its own right and as inspiration for other authors composing in other languages.[28] Anglo-Norman

---

[24] Oxford, Bodleian Library, MS Digby 32 (part 2). See for example Robert Bossuat's claim that 'le poème de *Roland* est plus que tout autre la veritable épopée française', in I: *Le Moyen Âge, Histoire de la littérature française*, gen. ed. Jean Calvet (Paris, 1955), p.25. For an overview of this issue in French literary history more widely, see Simon Gaunt, 'French Literature Abroad: Towards an Alternative History of French Literature', *Interfaces: A Journal of Medieval European Literatures*, 1 (2015), pp.25–66, especially pp.25–8.

[25] The articles in the first issue of *Interfaces* provide very useful snapshots of this connection in a variety of fields. As well as the introduction, 'What is Medieval European Literature?' by Paolo Borsa, Christian Høgel, Lars Boje Mortensen, and Elizabeth M. Tyler, pp.7–24, and Gaunt, 'French Literature Abroad', the articles on Byzantine and Czech literature are particularly relevant: see Panagiotis A. Agapitos, 'Contesting Conceptual Boundaries: Byzantine Literature and Its History', pp.62–91, and Pavlína Rychterová, 'Genealogies of Czech Literary History', pp.110–41.

[26] See also Stein, *Reality Fictions*, who talks of 'the enormous weight of the nation in our contemporary disciplinary structures', p.5.

[27] See for example the essays collected in *Language and Culture in Medieval Britain: The French of England, c.1100–c.1500*, ed. Jocelyn Wogan-Browne et al. (York, 2009).

[28] The *Roman de Troie*, possibly composed in Henry II's circles, is important both in its own right, surviving in over forty manuscripts, and also as a source for later works such as the *Histoire ancienne jusqu'à* César: for discussion of *Troie*, see chapter 3.

(or Anglo-French, or the French of England[29]) is not just an embarrassing malaise suffered during a couple of uncouth centuries after the humiliation of the Norman Conquest and before the rescue of English by Chaucer. It is the era of *Ivanhoe*, which was published in the aftermath of the battle of Waterloo in 1815, which bears a lot of responsibility for this lingering anti-French attitude, rather than these medieval centuries themselves.[30] Anglo-Norman texts have effectively been denied their place within medieval British literary history because of distaste surely engendered in great part by the British–French conflicts of the nineteenth century.

There is an important related point to be made here. Where Anglo-Norman material has been brought into English literary conversations, it has often had to justify its existence by means of the same approaches and terms used for English texts. So Anglo-Norman romances, for example, are seen as contributing to a nascent sense of 'Englishness' or 'insularity' despite their linguistic status, which distinguishes them in a cultural sense from French romances composed elsewhere.[31] Effectively, they have to be even more culturally 'English', or 'insular', than English-language works in order to justify their inclusion in the literary canon. Whilst I do not deny that many Anglo-Norman romances do naturally reflect the particular insular circumstances of their composition,[32] seeing them only or primarily via the lens of insular exceptionalism restricts the kind of comparative work that enables scholars to set them in a wider and more plural context. This is particularly important for Alexander material, given its European linguistic and geographical spread; seeing its variety on this broader stage is predicated not only upon crossing national and linguistic boundaries, as mentioned above, but also disciplinary and terminological ones.

---

[29] The terminology used for this particular kind of French is a vexed question that I shall address later in this introduction.

[30] Sir Walter Scott, *Ivanhoe* (Edinburgh, 1820): the attitudes to 'Normans' and 'Saxons' are strongly negative and positive respectively at the start of the novel. Ardis Butterfield reflects upon the same situation in genealogical terms: 'French is part of the paternity of English through the "Norman yoke" but finally English overthrows and transcends its continental father in an Oedipal blow that liberates English into a new national condition' (*The Familiar Enemy: Chaucer, Language, and Nation in the Hundred Years War* (Oxford, 2009), p.xxv). I am indebted to her book for much of my perspective here.

[31] See recently Laura Ashe, *History and Fiction in England, 1066–1200*, Cambridge Studies in Medieval Literature, 68 (Cambridge, 2007). A pioneering study remains Susan Crane, *Insular Romance: Politics, Faith, and Culture in Anglo-Norman and Middle English Literature* (Berkeley, CA, 1986).

[32] See for example Rosalind Field's analysis in 'Children of Anarchy: Anglo-Norman Romance in the Twelfth Century', in *Writers of the Reign of Henry II: Twelve Essays*, ed. Simon Meecham-Jones and Ruth Kennedy (Basingstoke, 2006), pp.249–62, which focuses on features like the establishment of justice, inheritance, and baronial power.

Studying Alexander material from a multilingual perspective, then, brings into sharp focus ongoing problems with current models for research in medieval studies, particularly as these relate to questions of vernacular languages. However, there is another connected linguistic issue that even multilingual studies that pave the way for truly integrated research often overlook, namely Latin. Ardis Butterfield, in her masterly study *The Familiar Enemy: Chaucer, Language and Nation in the Hundred Years War*, bemoans the fact that space and time have not allowed her to include Latin material in her analysis of 'the story of English if we do not isolate it from French, England's other vernacular':

> An even longer and better book would bring Latin properly into the picture as well, since in a sense this is the most important linguistic perspective of all.[33]

Butterfield does not explain why she thinks Latin's 'linguistic perspective' is 'the most important of all', going on to say that despite her valuation of Latin 'it seems worth starting at least with the vernacular, our own starting point'.[34] It seems probable that her view of Latin's importance arises from the language's long history as the medium of learning and its pan-European spread: it is, and remains, the *lingua franca* or cosmopolitan language of western Europe for intellectual, ecclesiastical, and diplomatic affairs even as vernaculars begin to take on some of these functions in the later period on which Butterfield focuses.[35] Yet medieval Latin, a non-national or transnational medium, is now a language without a disciplinary home, one consequence of the nationalistic interest in vernaculars as markers of cultural identity. Latin literature, because it is everywhere, is paradoxically nowhere. For literary scholars, based in language-defined departments, Latin has become primarily a documentary resource in support of the study of vernacular texts: the reading of Latin charters to identify scribes also copying Chaucerian material, the most prestigious of English-language canonical works, is a good example.[36] And when Latin *is* read as literature rather than as supporting documentary evidence, it often suffers from the same issues affecting the study of vernacular languages, namely a lack of multilingual interaction on equal terms.[37] As

---

[33] Butterfield, *Familiar Enemy*, p.xxiv.

[34] Ibid., p.xxiv.

[35] Henry III confirmed the Provisions of Oxford in English and French in 1258, a moment rightly seen as a milestone in the English language's functions but also a reminder of the ongoing currency of French: see Heng, 'The Romance of England', p.155.

[36] See for example Linne R. Mooney and Estelle Stubbs, *Scribes and the City: London Guildhall Clerks and the Dissemination of Middle English Literature, 1375–1425* (York, 2013).

[37] Very few scholars address Latin and, for example, French texts of similar dates together: Francine Mora is an unusual example ('L'*Ylias* de Joseph d'Exeter').

11

I will argue in chapters 2 and 3, this has had significant consequences for the study of Alexander literature of the twelfth century in particular. A single but potent example demonstrates the impact of this disciplinary and linguistic problem: Walter of Châtillon, the now little-known author of the highly popular Latin *Alexandreis* (c. 1180), very probably came into contact with the romance author (and dominant figure in the modern literary canon) Chrétien de Troyes at the court of Henry I and Marie of Champagne in the 1160s and 1170s. Latin and French, epic and romance, intellectual and 'popular' culture, are intriguingly intertwined in this multilingual and multicultural space, with the potential for both of these significant poets to be profoundly affected, yet there is no trace of what is surely an important contact in any scholarship that I have read on either author's work. This is because French and Latin poetic specialists of this era do not frequently venture into one another's perceived areas, with some ground-breaking exceptions like Francine Mora.[38] The issues of nation and identity that have driven vernacular multilingual study, and the correspondingly narrow focus on which they tend to rely and to promote, have therefore had an even more stark effect when it comes to Latin. The major European transnational language of literature has effectively been sidelined as a literary language of equal import in modern research, reducing its interpretative possibilities and once again disallowing plural perspectives.

Alexander Scholarship: Approaches and Absences

These scholarly perspectives tied up with ideas about national language and identity have had a profound impact on the study of medieval literature, as the examples of Latin and Anglo-Norman demonstrate: texts are often read in a restricted interpretative framework dominated by vernacular and nationalist imperatives. Of course, not all scholarship takes this approach: the work of Elizabeth Salter is an especially useful and inspiring model for the sort of multilingual and transnational study I am attempting.[39] Yet these perspectives have been dominant for Alexander narratives, which are widespread in almost all European and Middle Eastern languages and therefore very easily co-opted into this frequently anachronistic approach. Linguistically-focused studies, such as David Maddox and Sara Sturm-Maddox's work on Alexander in medieval French, or area-based analyses that also tend to focus on literature

---

[38] See e.g. Mora, 'L'*Ylias* de Joseph d'Exeter'.

[39] The introduction and first three chapters of Salter's posthumously published book *English and International: Studies in the Literature, Art and Patronage of Medieval England*, ed. Derek Pearsall and Nicolette Zeeman (Cambridge, 1988) have been crucial (pp.1–100). These chapters discuss the twelfth and thirteenth centuries. The chapter 'Chaucer and Internationalism' (pp.239–44) extends this range, and ends with the still-provocative phrase that Chaucer's 'use of English is the triumph of internationalism' (p.244): for more discussion of this, see chapter 5.

in one language, like Gerrit H. V. Bunt's overview of Alexander literature in medieval Britain, are the usual result.[40] Much of the scholarship on Alexander is therefore essentially 'local', focusing on his literary *translatio studii* in a single language and/or location, and frequently separates the conqueror's narratives from contemporary material. This scholarship is of course extremely useful and valuable work, but it does not of itself help in comparative analysis. Other Alexander studies do take a more wide-ranging view, encompassing many different languages and regions, but they too are often compiled from essays based on the same linguistic and nationalistic principles as these more local studies. For example, *The Companion to Alexander Literature of the Middle Ages* edited by Z. David Zuwiyya, which covers much of Europe and the Middle East, is divided into chapters based primarily on texts in individual languages.[41] So even in wide-ranging and multilingual scholarship the same attitudes, and the same separation of material, often persist.

Some scholarship does take a different approach. George Cary's book *The Medieval Alexander* first surveys sources of knowledge about the Macedonian and then discusses 'the medieval conception of Alexander' as he is depicted in moral, theological, exemplary, and secular authors.[42] Cary's main focus is on Latin material, although he does discuss vernacular writers in two country-focused chapters at the book's end.[43] Although Cary's aim is rather a broad survey than minute analysis, his approach enables non-nationalizing comparisons to be drawn across various boundaries. Yet it too has limitations. An unintended consequence of Cary's approach is that Alexander becomes ubiquitous without being locatable, a free-floating, ahistorical figure whose relevance to individual times and places is lost. This effect mostly stems from Cary's overall aim, but I think it is significant that it occurs in a discussion of primarily Latin material. As discussed in 'Language, Nation, Identity', one

---

40 *The Medieval French Alexander*, ed. David Maddox and Sara Sturm-Maddox (Albany, NY, 2002); Gerrit H. V. Bunt, *Alexander the Great in the Literature of Medieval Britain*, Mediaevalia Groningana, 14 (Groningen, 1994). Bunt's work, despite the potentially multilingual implications of its title, primarily discusses works in Middle English and Scots.

41 *A Companion to Alexander Literature in the Middle Ages*, ed. Z. David Zuwiyya, Brill's Companions to the Christian Tradition, 29 (Leiden, 2011). Representative chapters are 'The Arabic Alexander Tradition' by Z. David Zuwiyya and 'Medieval French Alexander Romance I' by Laurence Harf-Lancner (pp.73–112, pp.201–39). The same applies to publications of the MythAlexandre project, *L'historiographie médiévale d'Alexandre le Grand*, ed. C. Gaullier-Bougassas (Turnhout, 2011) and *Alexandre le Grand à la lumière des manuscrits et des premiers imprimés en Europe (XIIᵉ-XVIᵉ siècle)*, ed. C. Gaullier-Bougassas (Turnhout, 2015).

42 'The Medieval Conception of Alexander' is the title of Part B of Cary's book.

43 'The Late Medieval Conception of Alexander in England, France, and Germany', pp.226–59, and 'The Conception of Alexander in Late Medieval and Renaissance Italy', pp.260–72.

result of Latin's modern lack of a disciplinary home is the opposite of the current scholarly situation for vernacular texts: Latin is frequently *not* localized via nation or any other context, but is assumed to transcend boundaries and areas.[44] Scholarship on the *Alexandreis* in particular demonstrates this clearly, since the poem is generally studied for its relationship to intellectual trends that, whilst usually derived from northern French schools, are rightly perceived to move far beyond these locations.[45] This intellectual, wide-ranging *translatio studii* is of course, like the 'local' approach to vernaculars, absolutely valid, but again it results in a partial perspective, since frequently Latin literature is assumed not to interact with immediate local contexts. So despite the *Alexandreis'* connection with William of Champagne, the archbishop of Reims, the poem is rarely if ever read against the specific backdrop of the literary and political context of that city in the later 1170s and 1180s.[46]

Finally, there is a contemporary approach to Alexander literature inspired less by language or intellectual history than by political interpretation. Alexander's status as ruler of the known world inspired medieval authors to use him as an example for kings and princes, as detailed in chapter 1, so elements of Alexander scholarship have always had a political angle. However, recent work has focused more explicitly on the Macedonian in literary-political terms. A collection of essays edited by Markus Stock combines political approaches with language-based studies to focus on 'these remarkable legends not merely as stories of conquest and discovery, but also as representations of otherness, migration, translation, cosmopolitanism, and diaspora'.[47] This is

---

[44] Peter Dronke's scholarship is a good example of this trend: he is much more interested in large trans-European themes and connections than in historicist analysis. See for example his monumental book *Medieval Latin and the Rise of European Love-Lyric*, 2 vols (Oxford, 1965 and 1966). Tellingly, a contemporary review by Charles Witke praises Dronke for 'shift[ing] critical attention away from social criticism', by which I assume he means biographical readings of lyric poetry, but which of course presupposes a historicist perspective (*Modern Philology*, 64.4 (1967), pp.326–31). Peter Godman is an unusual example of a medieval Latinist with literary interests who is also a historicist critic: see for example *The Archpoet and Medieval Culture* (Oxford, 2014).

[45] See for example the most recent monograph on the work by Maura K. Lafferty, *Walter of Châtillon's* Alexandreis: *Epic and the Problem of Historical Understanding*, Publications of the Journal of Medieval Latin, 2 (Turnhout, 1998), which discusses the poem primarily in terms of its relationship with classical literature rather than with medieval literary or political contexts.

[46] Jean-Yves Tilliette briefly discusses Reims as a literary centre for the *Alexandreis* and the *Ylias* in *L'Iliade: épopée du XIIᵉ siècle sur la guerre de Troie*, trad. and notes under direction of Francine Mora, introd. Jean-Yves Tilliette, Miroir du Moyen Âge (Turnhout, 2003), p.16.

[47] *Alexander the Great in the Middle Ages: Transcultural Perspectives*, ed. Markus Stock (Toronto, 2016). The quotation is from the book's abstract, available online at < https://utorontopress.com/us/alexander-the-great-in-the-middle-ages-3> [accessed 14 November 2017].

a welcome and timely addition to Alexander scholarship, and to some extent provides a model for my study since it seeks to combine multilingual and historicist interpretations. Yet, inevitably perhaps given the impressive scope of the book and its essays, connections between different languages and contexts are again left to be drawn by the reader rather than made explicitly by the authors; this is a counsel of perfection, but ideas about how these different interpretations might compare or diverge are less obvious here.

This overview of the research situation has highlighted the importance of local and transnational perspectives for both vernacular languages and Latin as a balance for often nationalistic approaches to multilingual study, and again underlines the need for a scholarly approach that takes account of both kinds of perspectives, trying to contextualize Alexander works whilst also highlighting their features that transcend local contexts and connect them to larger, transnational trends.

Terminology

The last few paragraphs have started to use terms such as 'local' and 'transnational' in attempts to describe both the scholarly situation of Alexander literature and also my own approach. Terminology is always a problematic issue, since describing medieval concepts in modern terms inevitably involves both linguistic and conceptual anachronism, but it is especially difficult when we consider the interactions of languages and locations. The word 'nation' seems to be unavoidable, despite its post-medieval implications.[48] Even describing concepts that transcend 'nation' necessitates using the word in compounds like 'international' or 'transnational', so that ostensibly non-national concepts are still implicitly defined by the term. Alternatives are also unsatisfactory: 'global' naturally tends to be used to refer to the whole world, and 'cosmopolitan', a suggestive and intriguing possibility that is beginning to gain academic traction, seems to me still too much of a covert value judgement that connects a non-national perspective to sophistication and culture and is therefore subtly pejorative about more local contexts.[49] 'Cosmopolitan' is also used as

[48] The medieval Latin 'natio' has various different meanings, of which 'nation' in the modern sense is not primary. The first meaning given in *Glossarium,* ed. Charles du Fresne (du Cange), 10 vols (Paris, 1882–87), v, part 2, p.573 (col. 203) is 'nativitas, generis et familiae conditio', citing the Lex Longobardia; the fourth and final entry is 'patria'. The *Revised Medieval Latin Word-List*, ed. R. E. Latham (Oxford, 1965) gives a date of 'nascio' for 'nation' of 1227, but again this is a subsidiary meaning, following 'territory, habitation' and 'group of students' (col.1, p.311).

[49] The 'Global Chaucers' initiative, which has 1945 as a starting point, has a worldwide scope, as is shown by its master list of materials: < https://globalchaucers.wordpress.com/resources/translations-and-adaptations-listed-by-country/> [accessed 8 August 2016]. On 'cosmopolitan' as a developing cultural term, see *Cosmopolitanism,* ed.

a specific term to denote languages like Latin, Arabic, and Sanskrit that are prestigious (and therefore potentially elitist) as well as wide-ranging, and is therefore problematic for my stated aim of discussing both cosmopolitan and vernacular languages.[50] I have therefore opted *faute de mieux* for 'transnational', as even though it has 'nation' as one of its components the prefix 'trans-' suggests a perspective that acknowledges boundaries and simultaneously looks beyond them, which matches my attempt to consider both 'local' and wider perspectives. Simon Gaunt's important recent study of French outside France coins the term 'supralocal', which I find useful, but for me its implications are less obviously comparative than 'transnational', so that for this particular study it is less helpful than the latter term.[51] Using 'transnational' has the additional benefit of suggesting connections with modern postcolonial and global literary scholarship where the term is more frequently used, areas in which conversations about language, nation, and cultural identity may have useful insights for medieval studies.[52]

'Transnational' is a term that has been current in modern historiography more than in literary studies, so my use of it in the latter context requires some further explanation since it differs somewhat from its use in the former. In historiographical terms, it is used to define 'an approach that emphasizes what works between and through the units that humans have set up to organize their collective life'.[53] It therefore has a systemic and structural focus, interested in societal features such as religion, race, and technology, among others.[54] Although these features include the movement of ideas, what 'transnational' does not seem frequently to describe are the relationships between languages across political and geographical boundaries (actual or imagined). This is a crucial difference between my use of the concept in this book and its current

---

Carol A. Breckenridge, Homi K. Bhabha, Sheldon Pollock, and Dipesh Chakrabarty (Durham and London, 2002), and the more recent *Cosmopolitanism and the Middle Ages*, ed. John M. Ganin and Shayne Aaron Legassie, The New Middle Ages (Basingstoke, 2013).

[50] On 'cosmopolitan' in this sense see Sheldon Pollock, *The Language of the Gods in the World of Men* (Berkeley, CA, 2006), who focuses on Sanskrit with some comparisons to Latin, and Karla Mallette, 'Cosmopolitan Philology', in *Postmedieval*, 5.4 (2014), pp.414–27, who discusses Arabic.

[51] Gaunt, 'French Literature Abroad', p.25.

[52] Postcolonial studies have had an impact on medievalists for at least fifteen years (see for example *The Postcolonial Middle Ages*, ed. Jeffrey Jerome Cohen (New York, 2001)), although at the time of writing (August 2016) it is notable that a search for 'transnational' on the International Medieval Bibliography only produces four results, ranging from 2004 to 2014.

[53] Pierre-Yves Saunier, *Transnational History*, Theory and History (Basingstoke, 2013), p.2. I am grateful to Constance Bantman for this reference.

[54] Ibid., especially chapters 4 and 5, 'Relations' and 'Formations' (pp.80–98 and p.99–116 respectively).

formulation in historiography. In addition, using 'transnational' to refer to pre-modern periods is a point over which historians disagree, on account of the potential danger of introducing 'an essentialist understanding of nation that the transnational perspective wants to avoid'.[55] However, as this book does not engage with nationhood as a useful concept in any case, I hope that my use of 'transnational' is distant enough from ideas of nation in the modern sense to avoid this particular pitfall.

I have chosen to use 'local' as the converse of 'transnational', since even if less comparative it conveys a sense of immediate relevance to a particular context that can be both geographical and intellectual. 'Insular', which is sometimes effectively a synonym for 'local' in English literary studies, is another difficulty, since although it is in common scholarly use to denote literature of the British Isles it often has a negative meaning in most modern non-academic contexts. It also implicitly restricts the literature of the British Isles to the islands themselves, and in practice often to England, which does not represent either the circulation of material or political situations during the twelfth and thirteenth centuries.[56] I use it here to refer to literature or culture of the British Isles only. The term 'regional' is a little less troubled, since it is more neutral (certainly more so than 'provincial', which overlaps in modern usage with 'insular'). I use it on occasion in this study to refer to areas that are larger than those denoted by 'local' but which are not large 'transnational' areas, and which may also have distinct political or intellectual cultures; the Champagne area is a good example.

The issue of nation raises its complicated hydra-like heads again with particular reference to French. 'Cosmopolitan', when referring to a language, tends to imply sacrality, prestige, and standardization, which means that the term does not fit the situation of French in the period under discussion.[57] The variety of written French (or Frenches) across modern France and Europe is well documented, so it makes sense that the language has generally been described using geographically defined terms.[58] Thus we have created

---

[55] Kiran Klaus Patel, cited in ibid., p.6.

[56] I am thinking here for example of the *Roman de Troie*, which although an 'insular' romance in that it was probably composed for Henry II and Eleanor of Aquitaine's court may well have come to life in the Angevin territories of mainland Europe rather than the British Isles; one of its earliest extant manuscripts, Milan, Biblioteca Ambrosiana, MS D 55, was potentially copied by a Provençal scribe in the Veneto (see *Troie*, ed. Constans, VI, p.5).

[57] Mallette defines it as 'the learned language of formal culture', which is not a mother tongue, nor confined by sovereignty, nor 'link[ed] ... to contemporaneity' ('Cosmopolitan Philology', pp.415–16).

[58] See for example Ian Short, *Manual of Anglo-Norman*, 2nd edn (Oxford, 2013). For a wide-ranging philological survey of medieval French, see Frédéric Duval, *Le français médiéval* (Turnhout, 2009), part 1, especially pp.39–52. For a general overview of French in Europe, see Ad Putter and Keith Busby, 'Introduction: Medieval

'Anglo-Norman' to refer to the French language as found in the areas of Britain and France under Norman control after 1066. This is ostensibly fairly neutral, but in practice it tends to be equated with 'insular', although technically Anglo-Norman can also refer to the areas of continental France under Angevin control in the twelfth and thirteenth centuries.[59] So this term is less neutral in its usage than its name would suggest, since the effect of using it tends to contribute to insular exceptionalism. Another label given to this French is 'the French of England', which I find more problematic than Anglo-Norman since it is even more explicitly insular, ignoring for example the issue of French used in Ireland after the Henrician invasions of 1169 onwards.[60] This has gained currency in scholarly circles, but given that I want to emphasize connections between different locations I think it again has too insular a focus for my purposes. Ardis Butterfield uses 'Anglo-French' in order to highlight such cross-Channel connections, but, as Jocelyn Wogan-Browne points out, this was also the term used in the nineteenth century to refer to 'textual imports from the continent into England and to contacts between England and the continent in the later 14th and early 15th centuries', rather than to indigenous works, and as such fosters unhelpful divisions between the two kinds of works.[61] Butterfield's use of the term is still unusual in British literary studies. I have opted for 'Anglo-Norman' in this study where I have not been able simply to use 'French' in context, since it is at least the recognized philological term for a particular variety of the language, even though it is often accompanied by unhelpful cultural assumptions.

However, a significant caveat is that defining Frenches in this way, certainly for texts that travel outside their area of linguistic origin (if definable), often becomes actively unhelpful when we consider that linguistically Anglo-Norman works are often recopied into different kinds of French. This is important for one of the Alexander texts in this study, the *Roman de toute chevalerie*. The most complete manuscript, Paris, BnF, MS français 24364 (late thirteenth or early fourteenth century), is not the prime witness used for the modern scholarly text because its revision 'by a Continental redactor makes it

---

Francophonia', in *Medieval Multilingualism: The Francophone World and its Neighbours*, ed. Christopher Kleinhenz and Keith Busby, Medieval Texts and Cultures of Northern Europe, 20 (Turnhout, 2010), pp.1–13.

[59] See for example Field, 'Children of Anarchy'.

[60] See Jocelyn Wogan-Browne, 'What's in a Name? The French of England', introduction to *Language and Culture in Medieval Britain*, ed. Wogan-Browne et al., pp.1–13. Wogan-Browne is concerned to integrate French into insular literary culture, which is a necessary prequel to the kinds of transnational connections I intend to make. The Irish question is particularly relevant to my discussion of the *Roman de Horn* in chapter 4.

[61] Ibid., p.1. See Butterfield, *Familiar Enemy*, p.2 and discussion at pp.55–6.

unsuitable for use as the basis of an edition'.[62] In addition, the Anglo-Norman work is only found now with interpolations from the 'continental' *Roman de Alexandre* created by Alexandre de Paris, which starkly shows how artificial dividing Anglo-Norman from other kinds of French can be in practice.[63] So when I use 'Anglo-Norman', I do so meaning a particular incarnation of a text composed (as far as we can tell) or copied in that specific variety of French, without intending to define the work's history in cultural or linguistic terms after that distinct moment.

Translatio studii

Finally, I want briefly to discuss the concept of *translatio studii*, which underpins both this study's approach and also the material that it discusses. Frequently discussed in medieval prologues in this period, *translatio studii* combines linguistic, political, and geographical movement of key narratives and ideas, as Serge Lusignan's recent study of the phenomenon in terms of the development of French as a literary language makes clear.[64] Lusignan's study is especially valuable because it reminds us that *translatio studii* is not simply an extremely useful theoretical concept for modern medievalists to describe the transmission of material in general terms, but that it is also a historical practice, a method rooted in cultural requirements that alter over time. Lusignan highlights the differences between twelfth-century formulations of the trope, using Chrétien de Troyes' famous preface to *Cligès*, and those constructed in the fourteenth century, seeing each as a response to different contexts.[65] This historicizing of the phenomenon demonstrates that large, transnational theoretical concepts are also inflected at a local level, in individual texts and places, and that *translatio studii* itself performs the task of connecting the two.

---

[62] *The Anglo-Norman Alexander* (Le Roman de Toute Chevalerie), ed. Brian Foster and Ian Short, 2 vols, ANTS, 29–33 (London, 1976 and 1977), II, p.10. The title makes the editors' insular as well as linguistic priorities clear.

[63] Foster's and Short's edition omits these lines, presumably in the attempt to create 'the Anglo-Norman Alexander'. Tellingly, they describe this omission in terms of a return to an original and therefore a 'pure' text; 'shorn of the borrowings from RAlex, there remains a work of just over 8,000 lines ... which may well approximate to the original work of Thomas of Kent' (ibid., II, p.2).

[64] Serge Lusignan, '*Translatio studii* and the Emergence of French as a Language of Letters in the Middle Ages', *New Medieval Literatures*, 14 (2012), pp.1–19. I am grateful to Rita Copeland for this reference.

[65] 'In the twelfth century, Chrétien de Troyes harnessed it [*translatio studii*] to promote a French *clergie* invested with the same authority as its Latin counterpart. Nicole Oresme took up the theme in the fourteenth century to challenge Latin's monopoly on learned discourse, arguing that French could develop and progress vis-à-vis Latin just as Latin had done in Antiquity vis-à-vis Greek', ibid., p.16.

Lusignan's essay focuses on Chrétien's preface as a moment in which *translatio studii* gains a 'linguistic dimension', a dimension that is a large part of the debate about 'ownership' of classical material described earlier:

> Rather than dwelling … on the relationship between a French text and its Latin source, Chrétien connects an entire vernacular literate culture – audaciously termed *clergie* – to its Greek and Latin antecedents. Chrétien pleads the case of a Romance *clergie* the equal of its Greek or Latin counterparts, vindicating the language itself rather than a particular text.[66]

This linguistically-focused analysis reminds us that it is vital not to elide differences when seeking to connect texts in different languages, particularly differences of function. Lusignan goes on immediately to say that despite his passionate promotion of *romanz* as a language of authority and truth, Chrétien 'does not seem entirely convinced of the literary status he claims for the French language', indicating that there is a gap regarding function and prestige between French and Latin.[67] A similar situation is found at the opposite chronological end of this study in the early fourteenth-century Middle English romance *Of Arthour and of Merlin*, whose prologue vehemently asserts the greater appropriateness of that vernacular for the author's narrative rather than Latin or French, again suggesting unease about the literary qualities of 'Inglisch'.[68] So, whilst *translatio studii* is a useful theoretical concept used by both modern and medieval authors to justify connections perceived between texts or to support the act of translation in its infinite variety, in the period under discussion this act of connection is frequently grounded upon perceptions of *difference* between languages. This is an important historical corrective to my scholarly desire to juxtapose texts in languages of differing status, as this kind of multilingual research, which I have shown is extremely important for Alexander and other texts, still needs to take into account the varying cultural weight of the languages in question.

Lusignan's sensitive historicism also highlights the fact that despite the undoubted importance of Chrétien's formulation, most *translatio studii* of this era is still monolingual and academically-focused.[69] Admittedly Lusignan is discussing Paris' intellectual output, but given that many Alexander texts seem

---

[66] Ibid., p.6.

[67] Ibid., p.6.

[68] *Of Arthour and of Merlin*, lines 19–30, ed. O. D. Macrae-Gibson, 2 vols, EETS, o.s., 268 and o.s. 279 (Oxford, 1973 and 1979), I, p.3 and p.5. See chapter 5 for more detail on this text. The prologue has been much analyzed by critics: for a recent and valuable discussion, see Patrick Butler, 'A Failure to Communicate: Multilingualism in the Prologue to *Of Arthour and of Merlin*', in *The Auchinleck Manuscript: New Perspectives*, ed. Susanna Fein (York, 2016), pp.52–66.

[69] 'In the eyes of every author who addressed the subject, the learning relayed from Rome to Paris remained essentially Latin. The schoolmen's *translatio studii* entailed no linguistic translation': Lusignan, '*Translatio studii*', p.5.

to be influenced by, if not derived from, the literary trends of that city, this academic perspective is a crucial one.[70] If this seems potentially contradictory in light of the importance of linguistic difference just discussed, I think that is because once again scholars have tended to emphasize *translatio studii* in terms of its relevance to Latin–vernacular rather than intra-Latin transference. The point is rather that *translatio studii* is a plural phenomenon, occurring between Latin texts as well as between Latin and vernacular ones; as a formulation, it describes a fluid, adaptable concept rather than a dogmatic practice. Like the debate over ownership of the classics so intriguingly posited by Mora and of which it is a significant feature, *translatio studii* in this period is varied and potentially contested. My use of *translatio studii* therefore seeks both to reflect this pluralism and also to highlight *translatio*'s particular historical inflections where applicable.

Following the lead of the authors whose work I analyze, including Chrétien, Alexandre de Paris, and Benoît de Sainte-Maure, who all proclaim theoretical adherence to their prestigious sources whilst in practice using material created by themselves, *translatio studii* in this book encompasses stylistic and hermeneutic perspectives as well as language difference. This awareness of *translatio* broadens the practice beyond comparisons of source texts with 'new' material in terms of subject matter (although this is still an important feature of the study), and allows for important intellectual trends which are not immediately obvious from that kind of intertextual research but that are still vital. A good example is the insistent historicism of the *Alexandreis*, which I argue is a hostile reaction to contemporary Latin and French texts' habits of eliding historical chronologies to recreate narratives as 'modern', and which is related to twelfth-century debates about classical literature that are rarely connected to imaginative literature by critics. This allows me to acknowledge both the monolingual nature of the *Alexandreis* itself and its source materials, which is the context in which the poem is usually studied, and also its relationships to other medieval texts in both Latin and French that are connected to it via various networks, which has not to date been a frequent feature of scholarship discussing the work.[71] Additionally, thinking about *translatio studii* in this wider, historically informed context allows me to query the frequent assumptions made by critics concerning the inevitable direction of movement from Latin to vernaculars; considering the *Alexandreis* as a response to French material reminds us that inspiration also travels the other way. I hope in this to allow for mono- and multilingual influences, and

---

[70] Walter of Châtillon may well have been educated at Paris, and the author of the *Roman d'Alexandre* named himself 'de Paris': see chapters 2 and 3 respectively.

[71] As discussed earlier with reference to Lafferty, *Epic and the Problem of Historical Understanding*.

also for local and more regional or even transnational perspectives, all from a sensitive and historically aware starting point.

In discussing the hermeneutics that underpin acts of *translatio*, I also attempt to allow for variety as well as to identify important dominant narratives. When discussing ethical interpretations, for example, I assume that ethical *translatio* is itself an umbrella practice, incorporating moral ideas that may derive from and be applicable to different philosophical and religious practices (such as classical ideas about moral character and Christian confessionally driven perspectives). Similarly, when describing historically focused *translatio*, the concept may include a spectrum of ideas about history and historiography. So when an act of translation or adaptation is identified as 'ethical' or 'historical', that label does not imply a simplistic or one-dimensional perspective, but rather an approach that itself contains varied ideas and practices clustered together.

Conclusion

The aims of this book therefore transcend the immediate subject of Alexander the Great, since they are to contribute to important conversations about approaches to medieval studies in the twenty-first century. Yet Alexander is far from being simply a case study for modern scholarly debate. His ubiquity, tedious or otherwise, in the Middle Ages makes his narratives just as vital to literary histories in European languages as tales of Arthur or of Troy, a point this study highlights by explicitly comparing the Macedonian's stories with these latter tales. Before analyzing examples of Alexander's medieval *translatio*, however, we must consider the narratives inherited by the Middle Ages from antiquity, since these texts and the interpretative traditions they reveal may be instructive for medieval works. These antique texts and traditions are the subject of the first chapter.

1

Alexander in Antiquity

What could medieval authors have read or heard about Alexander the Great? This is a vital question, since understanding the nature of the literary and cultural material to which writers in the Middle Ages had access helps us to identify their intellectual inheritance (both texts and also interpretative traditions) and thus to analyze their *translatio studii* more perceptively. To address this large question, I shall discuss the main narratives focusing on Alexander in the period between his life in the fourth century BC and the twelfth century AD, the point at which my analysis of medieval texts begins.[1] I shall focus on the ways in which antique and early medieval authors engage with the narrative of Alexander's life and conquests, highlighting their preoccupations and approaches in order to characterize their performance of *translatio*. This allows me to identify similarities between texts that do not relate to one another directly but that may still share themes and interpretations.

The Alexander materials inherited by twelfth-century and later medieval authors were a complex mixture derived from a wide variety of direct and indirect sources. This complexity and variety may be one reason for the freedom with which high medieval authors treated Alexander, since there was no single prestigious account of the Macedonian king looming in the background to restrict their poetic imagination.[2] Yet there was also an awareness of Alexander as a historical figure with a long and convoluted literary history, as demonstrated by Chaucer's Monk in the late fourteenth century.[3] This history is important for later medieval Alexander works even if only in the sense of 'known unknowns', that is, material and/or authors that medieval poets

---

[1] This chapter will not address Alexander's impact upon philosophical writings, partly for reasons of space, but mainly because my focus throughout the book is on his narratives. On attitudes to Alexander in philosophy, see for example J. Rufus Fears, 'The Stoic View of the Career and Character of Alexander the Great', *Philologus*, 118 (1974), pp.113–30.

[2] In contrast to the Aeneas story, for example, which was also adapted *en romanz* in the twelfth century as the *Roman d'Eneas*: see chapter 3, 'Anxious Romance', for a short discussion of this.

[3] See the discussion in the introduction: the reference is 'The Monk's Tale', 2631–3, in *The Riverside Chaucer*, gen. ed. Larry D. Benson, 3rd edn (Boston, MA, 1987).

knew about but to which they had no access. So this chapter will not only discuss works that were definitely used (directly or indirectly) by such poets, but also some important texts and authors who were mere names in the high Middle Ages. It will also analyze works and writers, such as Arrian, that were unknown in the medieval period but whose approach contextualizes other antique works.

There are eight major works that are now extant: in probable chronological order, these are the *Alexander Romance* (and its descendants), Diodorus Siculus' account in his *Bibliotheke*, Valerius Maximus' anecdotes in his *Memorable Deeds and Sayings*, Plutarch's *Life of Alexander* (part of the *Parallel Lives*), Quintus Curtius Rufus' *Histories of Alexander*, Arrian's *Anabasis Alexandri*, Justin's *Epitome* of Pompeius Trogus' *Philippic Histories*, and Orosius' narrative in the *Seven Books of History against the Pagans*.[4] The majority of these texts, which form the direct and indirect background to the medieval works analyzed later in this book, are the product of the first and second centuries AD, some four to five hundred years after the Macedonian's life. This period, characterized in particular by the Roman Empire, is often described as the 'Second Sophistic' era.[5] However, these works have their roots in literature of the earlier 'Hellenistic' period, which usually refers to the centuries between Alexander's death in 323 BC and the battle of Actium in 31 BC, when accounts of Alexander's life were written that are now only preserved in other narratives, and when the tales that form the compendium known as the *Alexander Romance* were first collected.[6] The final work in chronological terms (although one of the most important for the Middle Ages), Orosius' early fifth-century account, is composed in a different context, in which the

---

[4] I give these texts' names in their most frequently cited forms; for translations and original titles, see Appendix 1. The historian Polybius also apparently discusses Alexander, but only in a few scattered references. Richard Billows claims that these show Polybius was interested in 'five basic themes concerning Alexander' (p.289), namely the destruction of Thebes, comparison with contemporary kings, his character and military leadership, the role of his generals in his successes, and the importance of Fortune ('Polybius and Alexander Historiography', in *Alexander the Great in Fact and Fiction*, ed. A. B. Bosworth and E. J. Baynham (Oxford, 2000), pp.286–306).

[5] For overviews of this era, see Graham Bowersock, *Hellenism in Late Antiquity* (Cambridge, 1990), and Tim Whitmarsh, *The Second Sophistic*, New Surveys in the Classics, 35 (Oxford, 2005). For greater detail, see Tim Whitmarsh, *Greek Literature and the Roman Empire: The Politics of Imitation* (Oxford, 2001) and Simon Swain, *Hellenism and Empire* (Oxford, 1996). Whitmarsh, *Greek Literature*, discusses the approaches of Swain's and Bowersock's works at pp.2–3.

[6] On the term 'Hellenistic', see Graham Shipley, *The Greek World after Alexander 323–30 BC*, Routledge History of the Ancient World (London, 2000), pp.1–5. On the *Alexander Romance*, see *The Greek Alexander Romance*, trans. and introd. Richard Stoneman (London, 1991), pp.8–11, for a useful overview of the *Romance*'s formation, and the section on the *Romance* later in this chapter.

intellectual inheritance of ancient Greece and Rome is being actively interrogated and reworked in a newly Christian imperial world. Orosius' narrative is a crucial link between antiquity and the Middle Ages, reinterpreting received material in a new philosophical and religious framework; it is therefore both an appropriate finale for this chapter and also a suitable introduction to the medieval texts discussed in the rest of the book.

Analyzing the Alexander literature of late antiquity, then, means considering the Hellenistic era as well as the early centuries AD. Before considering the texts themselves, I shall briefly outline some key historical and literary features of this period in order to provide a historical and cultural framework for what may be unfamiliar territory. My aim is to identify the kinds of factors – political, cultural, literary – that may affect Alexander's *translatio* during these centuries.

Hellenism (323 BC–c. AD 200)

Both the Hellenistic and Second Sophistic periods are strongly marked by interest in the productions of classical Greek antiquity. More precisely, the two periods are connected by the idea that Greek linguistic ability (and hence the production and consumption of written texts) defined literary culture; such 'Hellenism', or 'Greekness', particularly in education (*paideia*), was a cultural narrative current throughout these five centuries.[7] The role of Greek, linguistic and cultural, is thus a vital factor in considering Alexander literature in this era.

The importance of a single language and its canonical literature across the Hellenistic world suggests a cultural and linguistic hegemony, perhaps uniformity. Yet Hellenism is a concept that, whilst defined by Greek linguistically for most of its history, did not give rise to 'a distinctive, unified hellenistic world-culture'.[8] Certainly in the first centuries after Alexander, 'Hellenization' was 'a variegated picture of co-existence, interaction, and sometimes confrontation between newly settled Greeks and indigenous populations', taking place 'in a dynamic rather than static social context'.[9] However, this interaction and expansion did not lead to cultural fusion, certainly not in modern, multilingual terms. With some exceptions, such as the city of Alexandria, and despite the fact that interaction between Greeks and indigenous populations of Egypt and Asia was a two-way process, the focus of literary Hellenism was on 'the maintenance of Greekness, not the creation of a new hybrid', certainly in the sense of generic forms.[10] Prose fiction, such as the *Alexander Romance*,

---

[7]   See Whitmarsh, *Greek Literature*, p.7.
[8]   Shipley, *Greek World after Alexander*, p.1.
[9]   Ibid., p.1.
[10] Ibid., p.270.

might be the product of 'genuine cross-cultural hybridity, fusing Greek, Egyptian, and Western Asian elements into something recognizably new', but although literature in Egyptian and Aramaic was produced alongside material in Greek this cross-cultural interaction is not the dominant feature of Hellenism.[11] Hellenism was a predominantly monolingual, elite culture, operating in urban centres, which nevertheless was far from being uniform.[12]

The transfer of power to Rome during the later period continued to promote Hellenism as Greek in a broad sense even as Latin literary culture developed, since elite literature still remained rooted in Greek traditions and the Greek language; the mimetic relationship of Virgil to Homer, despite the language difference, is a good example of this.[13] However, the relationship between Greek and Roman culture was far from being a straightforward, transactional one, as Tim Whitmarsh notes:

> Not only was the relationship between 'Greece' and 'Rome' (these terms conceived of as imaginary rather than geopolitical entities) fluid and oscillatory, but also the very concepts of 'Greek' and 'Roman' were under constant definition, scrutiny, review, and redefinition.[14]

This 'oscillatory' relationship meant that Roman attitudes towards Greece and Hellenism occupied the full spectrum between 'acquiescence' and 'dissent', and were usually far more ambivalent than these terms suggest.[15] Plutarch's *Parallel Lives*, explicitly connecting and comparing Romans and Greeks and composed in Greek by an ethnic Greek who became a Roman citizen, are a fascinating example of the multiple possibilities of literary-cultural *translatio*: in Simon Goldhill's words, 'Plutarch is intimately engaged with a Roman cultural (and political) world, which is itself engaged with Greek cultural value'.[16] Greekness at this point is refracted through Roman cultural ideas, which in turn are refracted through ideas about Greek antiquity. So Hellenism, already

---

[11] James J. Clauss and Martine Cuypers, 'Introduction', in *A Companion to Hellenistic Literature*, ed. James J. Clauss and Martine Cuypers, Blackwell Companions to the Ancient World (Oxford, 2010), pp.1–14 (p.11).

[12] On the generally urban nature of Hellenistic literature, see Shipley, *Greek World after Alexander*, pp.269–70.

[13] See Whitmarsh, *Greek Literature*, pp.26–9, where he discusses this phenomenon in terms of *mimesis*. He also points out that Arrian called himself 'the new Xenophon', a clear example of Hellenistic literary aspiration.

[14] Ibid., p.2.

[15] The terms 'acquiescence' and 'dissent' are those used by Graham Bowersock, *Greek Sophists in the Roman Empire* (Oxford, 1969), p.1; see the discussion in Whitmarsh, *Greek Literature*, p.2. On reactions to Hellenism, see ibid., pp.7–17, where Whitmarsh describes the Augustan period's engagement with Hellenization as 'civilization/luxurious decline', illustrating two possible reactions to Greek culture (p.9).

[16] Simon Goldhill, *Who Needs Greek? Contests in the Cultural History of Hellenism* (Cambridge, 2002), p.261.

a complex phenomenon before the Roman imperial period, became yet more multifaceted in the early centuries AD as Rome's own varied literary and political cultures engaged in the process of *translatio imperii et studii*.

This fascinating and multi-layered context is the broad framework within which the Alexander literature discussed in this chapter is produced and experienced. Its complexities should make it clear that, while it is probable that Alexander narratives' *translatio studii* will engage with questions of cultural identity in general terms, any simple replacement of 'Greek' with 'Roman' is unlikely, even naïve. Writing about Alexander during these centuries so marked by Hellenism is certainly to tell a narrative that is Greek (both in its origins and potentially also in its later cultural context) in an increasingly Roman world, but the multivalent and slippery nature of all these categories precludes any easy *translatio*. We need to bear this in mind when reading Alexander literature throughout this period.

The Early Literature: Ambiguity and Absence

To complicate matters further, the historical Alexander was of course not a Greek but a Macedonian. This has important implications for the earliest works about him, which needed to portray him as truly Greek and thus the rightful ruler of both traditional Greece and Macedonia. Although most of these early texts are now fragmentary (of which more shortly), it is clear from what is extant that they were keen to present an Alexander who was culturally Greek, an image the historical king himself wanted to promote by emulating canonical Greek heroes like Achilles, for example.[17] Official accounts, which can be assumed to portray the Macedonian king in a flattering light since they were in effect approved by him, reveal this; as Eugene Borza notes, 'reports of the king's activities … would convince the Hellenes that their ruler was not a backwoods Macedonian boar'.[18] From the beginning, then, Alexander's literary existence consciously muddied the waters in terms of cultural identity, constructing the dubiously hybrid king as a pure Greek. This might seem to go against the disclaimers just made about the complexities of *translatio*, since Alexander the Macedonian appears to have become Greek without any trouble, but in fact the need to proclaim him so strongly as such surely highlights the fact that he was in many ways an outsider.[19] Although their loss makes it

---

[17] Clauss and Cuypers, 'Introduction', p.1. Alexander also famously travelled with his own copy of the *Iliad*.

[18] Eugene N. Borza, 'The Nature of the Evidence', in *The Impact of Alexander the Great: Civilizer or Destroyer?*, ed. Eugene N. Borza, European Problem series (Hinsdale, IL, 1974), pp.21–5 (p.23).

[19] Tim Whitmarsh describes the Greek-Macedonian question in terms of 'struggle': 'on the margins between the world of the Greek *poleis* and the non-Greek North, and hence on the imaginary boundaries between Hellenism and barbarism, Macedonia constitutes

mostly an educated guess, these texts may therefore have displayed traces of anxiety about Alexander's own Greekness,[20] an ambivalence that in turn may be important more generally for the later works that draw on these accounts. Whether this unverifiable ambivalence is the case or not, the concern about Alexander as a Greek cultural figure highlights the crucial point that his narrative is politicized from the very start: there is no such thing as a historical, factual, neutral Alexander.

Assessing Alexander literature from his life and immediately after his death is made hard, if not impossible, by its almost complete loss. Borza notes that 'there survive more than four hundred fragments from nearly thirty lost writers whose works were written between Alexander's death and our earliest account, that of Diodorus [Siculus, first century BC]'.[21] It is easy as a non-specialist to think that this is confined to the Macedonian's histories. In fact, loss is a common theme across the whole corpus of Hellenistic literature, especially for prose works concerning oratory (rhetoric), philosophy, and historiography, for epic poetry, and for drama (particularly tragedy).[22] What is extant, especially for prose literature, is often as a result of incorporation into later texts or the act of creating epitomes. As a result, the term 'fragment', when applied to Hellenistic material, often means 'a quotation or summary of a lost author in the works of a surviving author' rather than a physical portion of a manuscript or inscription.[23] This means intertextuality is a vital theme not just in Hellenistic literature itself but in its transmission, with the inevitable questions about context, appropriation, and meaning that this raises. Once again, this point demonstrates the impossibility of a neutral, historical Alexander, since the original works have been subsumed into material that may have a strikingly different set of priorities.

Writing about Alexander during his life and in the immediate aftermath of his death seems to have been a popular activity. Alexander himself was anxious that his exploits should be recorded, especially since he modelled himself on heroes as described by Homer. He took writers with him on his expedition

---

an intellectual testing-ground for the idea of Greekness' ('Alexander's Hellenism and Plutarch's Textualism', *Classical Quarterly*, n.s., 52 (2002), pp.174–92 (p.175)).

[20] The disapproval displayed by Macedonians over Alexander's adoption of Persian customs, which is a feature that seems to go back to the earliest accounts, makes sense in this context of concern over Greek identity. Although the early texts are lost, Plutarch and Arrian, both of whom probably had access to them, discuss the vexed issue of Persian customs: see Plutarch, *Life of Alexander*, ch. 47, in *The Age of Alexander: Ten Greek Lives by Plutarch*, ed. and trans. Ian Scott-Kilvert and Timothy E. Duff, rev. ed. (London, 2011), pp.329–30; Arrian, *Anabasis* IV.8–12, in *The Campaigns of Alexander*, trans. Aubrey de Selincourt and introd. J. R. Hamilton, rev. ed. (London, 1971), pp.214–23.

[21] Borza, 'The Nature of the Evidence', p.23.

[22] See Clauss and Cuypers, 'Introduction', p.4, pp.7–11.

[23] Shipley, *Greek World after Alexander*, p.6.

for this purpose, including Chares of Mytilene (his chamberlain), Medeius of Larissa, Polyclitus of Larissa, Ephippus of Olynthus, and Callisthenes of Olynthus, Aristotle's close relative.[24] In addition, accounts were written by a number of men who travelled with Alexander: the Cynic philosopher Onesicritus of Astypalaea, the fleet commander Nearchus, Aristobulus the technical expert, Ptolemy, later king of Egypt, and Cleitarchus (although it is uncertain whether the last actually accompanied Alexander or not).[25] There were also the royal diaries, or *Ephemerides*, supposedly written by Alexander's secretary Eumenes, but these may not be genuine.[26] However, virtually none of this material survives in more than occasional fragments and citations by later authors.[27] Yet it is still hugely important, since it appears to have influenced these later authors in terms of style and approach, as well as information.[28] These writers have often been categorized on historiographical grounds, with the 'more reliable tradition' led by Ptolemy and Aristobulus, who in turn relied on Callisthenes (Alexander's official historian), and the '"vulgate" tradition' based on Cleitarchus, who likewise used first-hand accounts.[29] However, it should be clear from the concern about Alexander's Greekness discussed above that these accounts, despite their early date, do not provide a historical picture, but are politically and culturally revisionist narratives.[30]

Facts and Fictions

This division of the early accounts into two categories highlights another point that is vital for Alexander literature throughout the whole period and into the Middle Ages, namely genre. The 'vulgate tradition', 'deriving perhaps from popular traditions written down not long after the king's death', is

[24] Richard Stoneman, *Alexander the Great* (London, 1997), p.3.
[25] Ibid., p.4.
[26] Ibid., p.3. For the debate over their authenticity, see Edward M. Anson, 'The *Ephemerides* of Alexander the Great', *Historia: Zeitschrift für Alte Geschichte*, 45.4 (1996), pp.501–54. For a discussion of the practice of keeping personal accounts in context, see Cinzia Beartot, 'Royal Autobiography in the Hellenistic Age', in *Political Autobiographies and Memoirs in Antiquity*, ed. Gabriele Marasco (Leiden, 2011), pp.37–85 (pp.47–53).
[27] Borza, 'The Nature of the Evidence', p.21. For an overview of the lost accounts, see Lionel Pearson, *The Lost Histories of Alexander the Great* (London, 1960).
[28] Shipley, *Greek World After Alexander*, notes that 'works written about Alexander during the early part of the period were influential in important ways, both on contemporary culture and on the writing of history' (p.6).
[29] Ibid., p.6.
[30] The fact that some of them were written for Alexander himself, such as that of Callisthenes, should give us pause in any case, since of course they would have praised his exploits.

often thought of as more 'fictional' (in modern terms) than historical.[31] This fictional perspective is furthered by the fact that the *Alexander Romance* uses many of the same materials as the 'vulgate' tradition.[32] There is in effect a division between the 'traditions' (and I use the term conscious of its monolithic nature) that equates to a generic distinction between fiction, or 'romance', and history. This is deeply problematic, not just because of Alexander literature's non-historical nature from its inception, but because such ideas about fictional versus historic genres are modern, not antique. Not only was Hellenistic literature generically diverse, but boundaries between different modes of literary discourse, modes that were themselves not the same as those current in modern times, were being consciously blurred.[33] Despite this difference, in modern discussions questions concerning historical accuracy have predominated, probably since most scholarship on Alexander literature of this period has been undertaken by historians.[34] This has had the effect of so-called historical works not being read alongside material like the *Alexander Romance*, further perpetuating this problematic generic distinction.

This focus on history has implications that go beyond genre to affect literary analysis more widely. James Davidson identifies Alexander historians' concern for factual accuracy, 'what really happened', as obscuring our understanding of the stylistic, not simply historical-political, imperatives behind Alexander's literary *translatio*. In a vivid account of why 'what really happened' is the wrong question to be asking, based on his analysis of the motivations and, crucially, the style of ancient historians, Davidson argues that early Alexander material from the Hellenistic period became both politically and stylistically abhorrent to later writers and was therefore classicized:

> The lost histories of Alexander [from the period of his life and immediately afterwards] weren't mislaid, therefore, they were consigned to oblivion ... The replacement of the early histories by ones written centuries after the events was not so much an exercise in historiographical recension as an

---

[31] Shipley, *Greek World After Alexander*, p.7.

[32] Ibid., p.7.

[33] See for example the discussion of hymns, *encomiae*, and *epyllia* in Clauss and Cuypers, 'Introduction', p.5 (and passim). Clauss and Cuypers also cite Whitmarsh's chapter in the same volume on the generic issues of Alexander material, which he apparently describes as 'various ill-demarcated literary categories of the Hellenistic period ... in which history and myth, fact and fiction, Greek and non-Greek were closely interwoven', (p.11). I could not find this quotation in Whitmarsh's chapter ('Prose Fiction', pp.394–411).

[34] A. B. Bosworth and N. L. G. Hammond are particularly important scholars in this context.

act of translation. At all costs, Great Alexander had to be rescued from the trivial indecencies of Alexandrian style.[35]

In other words, it is not (lack of) factual accuracy or political necessity as much as changing literary tastes that led to the loss of the early Alexander material in later centuries. From Davidson's admittedly provocative perspective, so-called 'histories' (referring predominantly to Arrian and Plutarch), although conforming more to modern ideas about historiography than these early lost texts, are driven as much by literary-stylistic concerns in their *translatio* as by a desire for factual accuracy. Modern assumptions about genre and historical accuracy have led to a greater focus on the historical-political contexts of Alexander than upon literary-stylistic ones, and a crucial aspect of Alexander's *translatio* in this period of five hundred years has therefore been under-emphasized.

Of course, distinguishing between the historical and literary qualities of texts is frequently a misplaced effort, since the two are so often inextricably linked. However, focusing on more literary features such as interpretative approaches to material and generic interplay provides context for still-important questions of historiography, questions that are more about political refashioning than about 'what really happened'. This perspective is extremely helpful for any medievalist venturing into this little-known late antique territory, since prioritizing the literary qualities of the texts (even in translation) allows non-specialists some access to the period without in-depth historical knowledge. Thinking about Alexander narratives in this way also resembles medieval approaches to such material as was available, which would of necessity have been via texts (and therefore fluid qualities such as style) rather than through such factual knowledge. To reiterate the observation made at the start of this chapter, then, in the following analysis, I shall consider the works in terms of their literary nature rather than their historical accuracy, focusing on their individual performance of Alexander narratives' *translatio* (for example in terms of hermeneutics, genre, and historiography). This may seem a redundant point, since this book takes just such an approach overall, but given the predominantly historical focus of late antique scholarship on Alexander, perhaps stating the obvious here is excusable.[36]

---

[35] James Davidson, 'Bonkers about Boys', *London Review of Books*, 1 November 2001, <www.lrb.co.uk/v23/n21/james-davidson/bonkers-about-boys> [accessed 4 January 2017].

[36] Davidson describes the historicism of 'Alexanderland' in memorable terms: 'some great beasts, having wandered in, can still be found here decades later, well beyond the forces of evolution … secluded behind the high, impassable peaks of prosopography, military history, and, above all, *Quellenforschung*' ('Bonkers about Boys').

The following sections on individual texts and authors are arranged in chronological order, as far as this can be ascertained.[37]

Alexander Texts and Authors

Alexander Romance *(from the third century BC)*

The term 'romance' has slightly different connotations for medievalists than for specialists in late antiquity, although as will become clear romance works in both eras have shared features. Medievalists tend to use 'romance' to refer to a specific genre, whereas for late antique scholars it appears to be a less generic and more descriptive term (although this distinction may of course be a slight one).[38] The material known under the title of the *Alexander Romance* is not a single text but a collection (in fact several collections) of tales that developed over many centuries. Although its initial genre is often described as the ancient Greek novel, it is best envisaged as a text network that connected readers across the Mediterranean, Levant, and into Asia, an 'open text' that is 'identified not by its genre but by the way in which the literary work is produced'.[39] Originating in Greek, it was translated and adapted into dozens of languages in antiquity, and in its Latin incarnation inspired many medieval vernacular Alexander narratives. Because of this linguistic and textual diversity, it is difficult to discuss any one individual version or manuscript tradition as representative: we are dealing with a textual phenomenon that is multi-headed from its origins. Bearing this caveat in mind, I shall nevertheless consider two linguistic traditions in the *Alexander Romance*'s history that provide important perspectives on other antique and medieval Alexander material, the Hellenistic Greek versions and the various Latin narratives composed between the fourth and tenth centuries AD. The Latin narratives are especially important, since they underpin the majority of medieval Alexander works.

The Greek *Romance* survives in three recensions, which differ markedly from one another and appear to derive from different centuries, and which

[37] I am predominately using English translations of these works, but where I quote from a Latin or Greek text, I provide details of an edition in the original language.

[38] For example, 'romance' is not a separate genre in Clauss and Cuyper's 'Introduction' which surveys different genres and forms. In comparison, see *A Companion to Romance: From Classical to Contemporary*, ed. Corinne Saunders, Blackwell Companions to Literature and Culture, 27 (Oxford, 2014); despite its title, only one chapter covers the ancient world (Elizabeth Archibald, 'Ancient Romance', pp.10–25). The two books are published by the same press and follow similar formats.

[39] Daniel L. Selden, 'Mapping the Alexander Romance', in *The Alexander Romance in Persia and the East*, ed. Richard Stoneman, Kyle Erickson, and Ian Netton (Eelde, 2012), pp.19–59. The quotations are from David Konstan, 'The "Alexander Romance": The Cunning of the Open Text', *Lexis*, 16 (1998), pp.123–38 (p.123).

give rise to further versions that on occasion borrow from one another.[40] The earliest version, A, is now found in a single manuscript of the third century AD, but the origins of the *Romance* are much earlier: Stoneman argues that the essential elements were already circulating in Ptolemaic Alexandria and that 'they were combined into a single narrative by the end of the third century BC'.[41] This would mean that 'the main outlines of the narrative could have been fully formed as early as 50–100 years after Alexander's death'.[42] This third-century Alexandrian context makes sense of the prominence of Nectanebus in the narrative, since it appears that despite the Greek-language nature of much Hellenism, there was some cross-fertilization between Greek and demotic Egyptian literature in Alexandria, particularly in 'popular' works involving folk tales.[43] Alexander's conception by the Egyptian pharaoh Nectanebus in the *Alexander Romance* also demonstrates a contemporary Alexandrian political context, since making Alexander Nectanebus' son emphasizes the legitimacy both of his own and also of then-current Ptolemaic rule over Egypt.[44] This Alexandrian location is a reminder then that the Greek origins of the *Alexander Romance*, and the language of the collection, do not prevent non-Greek influences from being a significant feature within it, demonstrating its multilingual and multicultural nature even if this is occluded by the dominant language and cultural traditions of Hellenism.

As discussed above, the Hellenistic Greek *Alexander Romance* is often separated from the supposedly historical accounts of Alexander. However, Stoneman shows that parts of the *Romance* can be traced back to the historians Onesicritus and Cleitarchus and that some elements (such as the Nectanebus story) are shared with Plutarch, so it seems likely that the Greek *Romance* was drawing on similar sources to those used by the first-century BC and AD historians, a claim also made by Elizabeth Baynham.[45] This is supported by the mistaken idea that the philosopher Callisthenes was the author of the Greek *Romance*, since his account and that of Cleitarchus are important for the so-called 'vulgate tradition' used by these historians.[46] This potential reliance on

---

[40] For a succinct overview of the textual history of the Greek *Alexander Romance*, see Stoneman, *Greek Alexander Romance*, pp.28–32.

[41] Ibid., p.10. See p.20 for a useful summary of this process.

[42] Ibid., p.14.

[43] Ibid., p.14–17. See also Z. Dukat, 'The Romance of Alexander: A Specimen of the Ancient Popular Literature', *Ziva antika*, 26 (1976), pp.463–86. However, B. J. B. Berg disagrees to some extent about the role of third-century Alexandria in the *Romance*'s formation: see 'An Early Source of the Alexander Romance', *Greek, Roman and Byzantine Studies*, 14 (1973), pp.381–7.

[44] Clauss and Cuypers, 'Introduction', p.11.

[45] Stoneman, *Greek Alexander Romance*, p.12, p.13; Elizabeth Baynham, 'Who Put the "Romance" in the Alexander Romance? The Alexander Romances within Alexander Historiography', *Ancient History Bulletin*, 9 (1995), pp.1–13.

[46] Stoneman, *Greek Alexander Romance*, p.9.

the same sources, often themselves as interested in legends as in verifiable events, again highlights the difficulty of distinguishing between history and romance in terms of facts. This also demonstrates the important related point that history and fiction are intertwined from the starting point of Alexander's written accounts; it is not the case that early history is corrupted by later fictions.[47] So the Greek *Romance* needs to be read in the context of these other works, not separated from them by modern ideas of genre.

The Latin accounts are the product of later eras, and confusingly do not come from any single one of the Greek traditions. The work of Julius Valerius, which is based on A, was produced in the fourth century AD and then epitomized in the ninth century; it is the epitome that was prevalent during the later Middle Ages.[48] A Latin prose work, the epitome includes the Nectanebus story, the encounter of Alexander and queen Candace, and a brief mention of the Amazons, but is less focused on Alexander's Eastern adventures than the Greek material or its own source, Julius Valerius.[49] The tenth-century work of Leo the Archpriest (now lost) does not come from A but from another version, and was itself the basis for the better-known *Historia de preliis*. The *Historia de preliis* itself occurred in three main versions (J1, J2, and J3), each more expansive than the last, which date from the tenth to the early thirteenth centuries.[50] In addition, there are several episodes that are sometimes included

---

[47] The earliest or A version of the Greek *Romance* in particular 'most closely resembles a conventional historical work', again relating it to the so-called 'historical' accounts (Stoneman, *Greek Alexander Romance*, p.28), but nevertheless contains many fictional narratives.

[48] Ibid., p.28. According to D. J. A. Ross, the epitome 'came near to obliterating the memory of the full text', with only three near-complete MSS plus some fragments surviving of the latter in contrast with sixty-eight of the epitome ('A Check-List of Manuscripts of Three Alexander Texts: The *Julius Valerius Epitome*, the *Epistola ad Aristotelem* and the *Collatio cum Dindimo*', *Scriptorium*, 10.1 (1956), pp.127–32 (p.127)). Ross later added one more manuscript for a total of sixty-nine (*Studies in the Alexander Romance* (London, 1985), pp.83–8). The epitome is often known as the 'Zacher epitome' after its nineteenth-century editor. On Julius Valerius, see Robin J. Lane Fox, 'The "Itinerary of Alexander": Constantius to Julian', *Classical Quarterly*, n.s., 47 (1997), pp.239–52, and Richard Stoneman, 'The Latin Alexander', in *Latin Fiction: The Latin Novel in Context*, ed. Heinz Hofmann (London, 1999), pp.167–86 (pp.167–8).

[49] The latter two episodes mentioned are significantly abbreviated when the Zacher epitome is compared with Julius Valerius' Latin text: see III.19–25 in *Julii Valerii Epitome*, ed. Julius Zacher (Halle, 1867), pp.55–61, and *Julius Valère, Roman d'Alexandre*, trans. and comm. Jean-Pierre Callu (Turnhout, 2010), III.18–26, pp.180–203. The Amazons encounter in the epitome is a single sentence, whereas in Julius Valerius' work it is an exchange of letters.

[50] Richard Stoneman, *Legends of Alexander the Great*, 2nd edn (London, 2012), p.x. A useful table of texts and dates is at p.xxix. For an overview of the *Historia de preliis*, see *The History of Alexander's Battles*: Historia de preliis – *The J1 Version*, trans. and introd. R. Telfryn Pritchard, Medieval Sources in Translation, 34 (Toronto, 1992), pp.1–12. The J2 version uses Orosius, *Historiarum adversum paganos libri VII (Seven*

with the Latin *Romance* narrative but that also circulated separately, such as the *Letter of Alexander to Aristotle* (part of the Greek *Romance* but only extant now in Latin versions of the seventh and tenth centuries), Palladius' fifth-century *On the Brahmins*, and the *Collatio Alexandri et Dindimi* (current by AD 700).[51] The Latin *Letter of Alexander to Aristotle* seems to have been particularly popular, surviving in seventy-two manuscripts; in addition to this wide-spread Latin version, it was the first Alexander work to be translated into a medieval language (Old English).[52] It is this complex network, too diverse and intertwined a body of texts to be defined using terms like 'tradition' or 'transmission', that brings Alexander's narratives, occupying the entire spectrum from history to fiction, to the later Middle Ages. Given this complexity, for practical purposes I am basing the following brief discussion of the *Romance* on the only full-length modern English translation of the oldest A version of the Greek *Alexander Romance*, which includes material from the other Greek recensions.[53] Although the Latin versions of the *Historia de preliis* are both separate from one another and also different from the Greek, many of the narratives characteristic of the Greek *Romance* are often seen in them as well.[54] Likewise, the *Epitome* of Julius Valerius' text is another independent version, but contains similar (if abbreviated) material. This broad discussion therefore uses the Greek *Alexander Romance* to illustrate tendencies of *translatio* in its narratives, narratives which are shared by this complex web of Latin material.

The outline of the *Alexander Romance* follows the narrative of Alexander's historical deeds, but expands existing episodes and adds new ones, especially during the section based in India. Many of these episodes are described in letters from Alexander to others (for example his mother, Olympias), which both connects the *Romance* to the ancient epistolary novel in generic terms and also adds to the multifaceted nature of the work, since the narratorial voice/s alter; the *Romance* is 'patched together from several different pre-existing literary fabrics'.[55] The stories are frequently dramatic and fantastical.

Books of History Against the Pagans); see *Orosius: Seven Books of History Against the Pagans*, trans. and introd. A. Fear (Liverpool, 2010), p.25, n.144.

[51] Stoneman, *Legends of Alexander the Great*, p.x.

[52] Ibid., p.xxiii.

[53] This is Stoneman, *Greek Alexander Romance*.

[54] J2 and J3 are independent reworkings of J1: see the useful English outline of the versions in *History of Alexander's Battles,* trans. and introd. Telfryn Pritchard, pp.1–12 (p.8). The modern editions of the three versions have confusingly similar titles: *Historia Alexandri Magni (Historia de Preliis) Rezension J1*, ed. Alfons Hilka and Karl Steffens (Meisenheim am Glan, 1979); *Historia Alexandri Magni (Historia de Preliis) Rezension J2 (Orosius-Rezension)*, ed. Alfons Hilka, 2 vols (Meisenheim am Glan, 1976 and 1977); and *Die* Historia de preliis Alexandri Magni *Rezension J3*, ed. Karl Steffens (Meisenheim am Glan, 1975).

[55] Tim Whitmarsh, 'Addressing Power: Fictional Letters between Alexander and Darius', in *Epistolary Narratives in Ancient Greek Literature*, ed. Owen Hodkinson, Patricia A.

The begetting of Alexander by the Egyptian Nectanebus is described in detail, with the pharaoh depicted as a magician. In addition, Alexander's travels in the Far East see him finding the spring of immortality, exploring the depths of the sea in a glass jar, flying in the air lifted by birds, visiting and tricking a beautiful queen (Candace), and corresponding with the Amazons. The reason for these episodes' inclusion is primarily surely due to their marvels and therefore fascinating plots, but they also serve to illustrate Alexander's greatness and the importance of wisdom (chiefly in recognizing the limits of enquiry).[56] For example, during the aerial episode in the Greek *Romance*, Alexander is approached by 'a flying creature in the form of a man' who tells him to return to earth, which he has not yet wholly conquered, rather than exploring the heavens, 'or you will become food for these birds'.[57] The Amazons, despite their power, write to Alexander pledging obedience because 'we have heard of your bravery and generosity; we dwell beyond the edges of the world, but still you have come to be our lord'.[58] So these episodes frequently highlight the importance of wisdom and philosophy; they thus have an intellectual and pedagogical purpose, admittedly in the broadest of terms. This educational and ethical purpose is combined with (and perhaps sweetened by) the *Romance*'s use of folk-tale motifs, such as magic, disguise, deception, and triadic schemes, which Grammatiki A. Karla sees as a unifying technique throughout the whole narrative.[59] In addition, such fanciful episodes, which may seem entirely fictional and hence wholly related to romance composition, may be based on historical possibilities. As Stoneman notes, 'though the episodes in these letters are quite unhistorical in character, they still derive their inspiration from matters of historical record'.[60] Alexander's travels in the east are the factual starting-point for the imaginative histories these episodes describe, once again problematizing the easy separation of history and fiction.

In some of the later Greek versions, Christian and Jewish influences can potentially be seen. The emphasis on the need for wisdom and humility is easily consonant with Christian perspectives; in addition, Stoneman draws intriguing parallels between elements of the apocryphal lives of the Apostles – such as the wanderings of the hero, miracles, monsters, dreams, and

---

Rosenmeyer, and Evelien M. J. Bracke (Leiden, 2013), pp.169–86 (pp.171–2).

[56] These two potentially opposed ideas of greatness but also the limits of enquiry may be a sign of the tension between Alexander's historical achievements and his empire's subsequent fragmentation, and thus an indication of the *Romance*'s chronological development over a long period of time; see Stoneman, *Greek Alexander Romance*, pp.21–2.

[57] Stoneman, *Greek Alexander Romance*, II.41, p.123.

[58] Ibid., III.27, p.145.

[59] Grammatiki A. Karla, 'Folk Narrative Techniques in the "Alexander Romance"', *Mnemosyne*, series 4, 65 (4–5) (2012), pp.636–55. See also Dukat, 'Romance of Alexander'.

[60] Stoneman, *Greek Alexander Romance*, p.11.

divine aid – and the *Romance*, observing that 'the development of Hellenistic romance in the Christian period has in turn influenced the successive rewritings of the [Greek] *Romance*'.[61] These Christian possibilities are surely one aspect of the *Romance*'s appeal in the Middle Ages, and an important factor behind its many Latin versions.[62] The *Romance*, by the early Christian era and certainly by the time of its appearance in Latin, proffered a narrative based on ancient history yet broadly consonant with Christian ideas, one that featured motifs recognizable from hagiography in vivid and memorable episodes that could easily stand alone if necessary for didactic purposes.

In conclusion, the work's use of history and fiction, wonder and pedagogy demonstrates the complex possibilities of *translatio* in Alexander narratives. It also shows that these varied approaches to Alexander, both generic and hermeneutic, are intertwined. Given the *Romance*'s huge medieval influence, this antique textual variety and co-existence may be an important precursor to the *translatio* performed in works of the Middle Ages.

Diodorus Siculus (late first century BC)

The Greek historian Diodorus Siculus probably composed his work, a huge history called *Bibliotheke* that narrates events in Greece, Rome, Sicily, and their environs from the Trojan War until 60 BC as well as non-Greek myths, in the last years of the Roman Republic and the early imperial era while based in Rome itself.[63] It is formed of forty books, of which only fifteen are complete; book XVII covers the exploits of Alexander. The *Bibliotheke* is a consciously composite work, hence its title. Diodorus was an admirer of the earlier Hellenistic historian Polybius, whose forty-book work is the only history to survive at all (even incomplete) between the fourth and first centuries BC,[64] so he sought to place himself in an established historiographical tradition by composing on such a scale. He was probably a contemporary of Pompeius Trogus, whose Latin *Philippic Histories* that discuss Alexander survived into

---

[61] Ibid., p.20. Stoneman lists motifs common to both traditions.

[62] Prologues in some manuscripts of the *Historia de preliis'* versions demonstrate an explicitly Christian perspective: a prologue to the J1 text cites the psalms and St Augustine in justification for reading Alexander's story (*Rezension J1*, ed. Hilka and Steffens, pp.xii–xiv), and an introduction to the J3 text claims that 'que bene gesta perleguntur, imitantes possint honestis moribus informari' (*Rezension J3*, ed. Steffens, p.2).

[63] K. S. Sacks, *Diodorus Siculus and the First Century* (Princeton, NJ, 1991), p.3. It seems that Diodorus altered the end point of his work from 46/45 BC, potentially because of the political difficulties that would be involved in writing about those years: Catherine Rubincam, 'How Many Books Did Diodorus Siculus Originally Intend to Write?', *Classical Quarterly*, n.s., 48.1 (1998), pp.229–33, argues that Diodorus originally planned forty-two books in a hexad structure (six sets of seven books), but wrote forty, in line with the work of Polybius.

[64] Clauss and Cuypers, 'Introduction', p.10.

the Middle Ages in the second-century AD epitome by Justin, and it is possible that Diodorus and the first-century AD writer Quintus Curtius Rufus drew on the same main source, given parallels between their two narratives.[65] As a Greek author based in Rome but originally from Sicily, writing in Greek but in contact with Latin texts and contemporaries, Diodorus is therefore a striking literary embodiment of the cultural complexities of this period.

As with all the late Hellenistic works discussed in this chapter, Diodorus draws on earlier Alexander material that is now lost, but does not name his sources at all.[66] Modern scholarly opinion about Diodorus' use of his sources has moved from seeing him as uncritical and careless to viewing him as a more skilful writer, who, whilst sometimes preserving the 'attitudes of his sources', was 'influenced by contemporary political and aesthetic considerations, [was] responsible for much of the nonnarrative material and determined the overall shape and main themes of the history'.[67] His *Bibliotheke* is therefore 'a document substantially reflecting the intellectual and political attitudes of the late Hellenistic period'.[68]

Diodorus begins his account of Alexander by describing his achievements and courage (I.3) and explicitly linking these to his pedigree: 'on his father's side Alexander was a descendant of Heracles and on his mother's he could claim the blood of the Aeacids, so that from his ancestors on both sides he inherited the physical and moral qualities of greatness'.[69] Alexander is thus a Greek hero through his blood, underlining his status as the legitimate instigator of political and cultural Hellenism. Diodorus was of course writing as a Greek, and one seemingly unafraid to criticize Rome where necessary, unlike many Greek immigrants to Rome;[70] his depiction of Alexander's bloodline

---

[65] *Diodorus Siculus, VIII: Books XVI.66–XVII*, trans. C. B. Welles, Loeb Classical Library, 422 (Harvard, MA, 1963), p.13, p.12. Welles also thinks that Diodorus, Curtius Rufus, and Justin (and Pompeius Trogus?) share a common source, p.19. For detailed analysis of the relationships between the three extant authors, see N. G. L. Hammond, *Three Historians of Alexander the Great: The So-Called Vulgate Authors, Diodorus, Justin and Curtius* (Cambridge, 1983).

[66] There is a single reference to Cleitarchus in book II: see *Diodorus Siculus*, trans. Welles, p.6.

[67] V. J. Gray, 'The Value of Diodorus Siculus for the Years 411–386 BC', *Hermes*, 115 (1987), pp.72–89, proposes the older view of Diodorus as careless; Catherine Rubincam, 'Did Diodorus Siculus Take Over Cross-References from his Sources?', *American Journal of Philology*, 119.1 (1998), pp.67–87, promotes the author as more skilful, as does Sacks, *Diodorus Siculus*. The quotation is taken from Sacks, *Diodorus Siculus*, p.5.

[68] Sacks, *Diodorus Siculus*, p.5.

[69] *Bibliotheke* XVII.1.5, in *Diodorus Siculus*, trans. Welles, pp.120–1.

[70] Sacks claims that the author criticized newly imperial Rome 'by slanting the narrative of his sources', in contrast to most Greek immigrants who were keen to praise the ruling power (Sacks, *Diodorus Siculus*, p.6).

is therefore likely to be more in terms of clear praise than would potentially be the case for an indigenous Roman author. This description of Alexander's descent suggests Diodorus' concern for Alexander's Greekness to be a positive phenomenon in an age of Roman ambivalence towards Hellenism. Despite the seemingly universal nature of his narrative, the historian is far from neutral. This Roman politico-cultural context, whilst implicit, also underpins Diodorus' interest in Alexander's greatness from an ethical perspective, which is a consistent theme throughout book xvii. His 'broadly moralistic' approach enables Alexander's narrative in turn to be interpreted more politically, as its 'central feature … is its call to peoples and nations to act clemently and with moderation';[71] ethical behaviour and politics are intertwined. In general terms, then, Diodorus' approach to Alexander's narrative uses an ethical hermeneutic in constructing an implicitly political history.

This ethical-political approach to Alexander is evident in Diodorus' first-person commentary on the king's actions towards Darius' female relatives.

> In general I would say that of many good deeds done by Alexander there is none that is greater or more worthy of record and mention in history than this [his protection of the women]. Sieges and battles and the other victories scored in war are due for the most part either to Fortune or valour, but when one in a position of power shows pity for those who have been overthrown, this is an action due only to wisdom.[72]

Here Diodorus extrapolates a general ethical principle from Alexander's kindness: mercy in victory is a sign of wisdom. Read against the *Bibliotheke*'s historical context (the civil wars at the end of the Roman Republic), however, this passage has a much more political flavour to it. Certainly the emphasis here on mercy in victory displays at the least a fear, if not a criticism, of imperial Macedonian/Roman power; it is not hard to read first-century AD anxiety into this account of a fourth-century BC victory. A similar fear, this time concerning the impact of war upon a city, becomes clear in his account of the siege and destruction of Thebes, where the defeated Thebans' futile yet brave resistance is described as rash yet courageous; Diodorus' empathy with the conquered Thebans (also of course Greeks) here may reflect the situation of many Romans and Greeks in the immediate aftermath of the late Republic's civil wars, as well as the wider situation of Greeks under Roman rule.[73]

Diodorus' Alexander history, then, uses ethical emphasis for historiopolitical effect. This demonstrates the multivalent possibilities of Alexander

---

[71] Ibid., p.6.

[72] *Bibliotheke* xvii.38.4, in *Diodorus Siculus*, trans. Welles, pp.226–7.

[73] See the brief discussion of this in the 'Hellenism' section above: for more detail, see Goldhill, *Who Needs Greek?*, pp.247–55, and Whitmarsh, *Greek Literature*, passim.

'history' in antiquity, in particular the refraction of his narrative via contemporary events. Despite the *Bibliotheke*'s lack of direct transmission to the Middle Ages in the West, these strategies of *translatio* are important for medieval Alexander works, since such *translatio* is also a feature of these texts.[74] In addition, the *Bibliotheke*'s interest in geography, and especially in historical synthesis (as displayed in the long explanation of Persian politics that forms the prequel to the struggle between Alexander and Darius in book XVII chapter 5), is paralleled in medieval universal chronicles.[75] Diodorus Siculus' *Bibliotheke*, then, is much more than simply the first extant Hellenistic Alexander history: its hermeneutic approaches and interests may be the indirect ancestors of those seen in the Middle Ages.

Valerius Maximus (active AD 14–37)

Valerius Maximus' approach to Alexander is very different from that of the *Bibliotheke*. He includes some tales of Alexander in his Latin collection of nearly one thousand stories called *Nine Books of Memorable Deeds and Sayings*, which was composed in the early years of the first century AD.[76] These stories are organized thematically, with each book covering a broad topic that in turn discusses related subjects.[77] These themes demonstrate Valerius' fundamentally ethical approach. In his preface, addressed to the emperor Tiberius, he claims to have collected these 'facta simul ac dicta memoratu digna' ('deeds and sayings worthy of memorial') for those people 'documenta sumere volentibus' ('wishing to take examples').[78] This idea of 'examples' suggests a 'practical utility' that is not explicitly ethical, but is certainly consonant with such an approach.[79] However, Valerius then goes on to praise Tiberius as the promoter of virtues and punisher of vice, linking the idea of historical examples to ethics under the new imperial order. So historical

[74] On ethical *translatio*, see chapter 3, 'Anxious Romance', and on historically informed writing, see chapter 2, '*Sic et Non*'.

[75] Matthew Paris' *Chronica majora*, begun around 1240, is a good example: see the discussion in chapter 4, 'Insular Alexander?', in the section 'Matthew Paris and the *RTC*'.

[76] He apparently finished the work in AD 31: see Valerius Maximus, *Memorable Deeds and Sayings: One Thousand Tales from Ancient Rome*, trans. and introd. Henry John Walker (Indianapolis, IN, 2004), p.xiii. D. R. Shackleton Bailey points to internal evidence that Valerius was still in the process of writing in AD 30 (Valerius Maximus, *Memorable Doings and Sayings*, ed. and trans. D. R. Shackleton Bailey, 2 vols, Loeb Classical Library, 492 and 493 (Cambridge, MA, 2000), I, p.2).

[77] These are I. religion; II. ancient customs; III. human characteristics; IV. moderation and related topics; V. compassion and related topics; VI. chastity and justice; VII. fortune and strategy; VIII. crime and eloquence; IX. negative characteristics such as greed, avarice, and violence.

[78] Valerius Maximus, *Memorable Sayings and Doings*, I, trans. Shackleton Bailey, p.12 and p.13.

[79] See the commentary on this preface in ibid., p.3, from where this quotation is taken.

examples, ethical values, and the Roman Empire are strongly connected from the outset in Valerius' indicated *translatio*, even though it is the ethical focus that is most dominant from the titles of the books.

This overt moral interpretation is also found in the Alexander episodes, which occur in books III and VII.[80] The anecdotes in book III come under the general theme of 'courage', and that in book VII under 'fortune and strategy', suggesting the specific ethics of Valerius' *translatio*. The first one is less about Alexander than a courageous young servant who endured burns from a coal so as not to disturb the king's sacrifice to the gods; Alexander sees the pain and prolongs the sacrifice to test the youth. Valerius interprets this anecdote as a sign of indomitable Macedonian valour. The second episode is the story of Alexander's doctor, who is accused of planning to poison the king, but whom Alexander chooses to trust. Valerius glosses this as a sign of Alexander's 'tam constanti … iudicio' ('so resolute … a confidence') in his doctor, namely an indication of trust. Finally, the story in book VII is interpreted by Valerius as a sign of Alexander's 'great cunning' ('summa in hoc [mansuetudo calliditas]'). Here Alexander is warned by an oracle to kill the first being ('primus') he meets; he encounters a donkey driver and arrests him, but the man declares his innocence and tells Alexander that in fact it is his donkey that the king encountered first, so the animal should die instead. Whilst admitting Alexander's cunning, Valerius points out that the donkey driver's cunning was just as great, and also describes the king as being 'ab errore revocatus' ('called back from error'): Alexander is implicitly fallible here.

These episodes, probably drawn from Pompeius Trogus' *Philippic Histories* (if anywhere), are an intriguing mixture of historically attested events (the doctor episode) and the kinds of material seen in the *Romance* (the donkey story), again underlining the cross-fertilization of 'history' and 'fiction'. As just demonstrated, Valerius gives them each an ethical twist, making each narrative illustrative of moral qualities regardless of its source. It might seem, then, that Valerius' *translatio* is wholly morally focused despite his connection of ethics to imperial rule in the *Preface*. However, it is important to notice Alexander's role and status in these short scenes. First and foremost, he is a king, an obvious point but one that Valerius emphasizes by his frequent use of the word 'rex' in place of Alexander's name.[81] In his commentary on the donkey episode, the author concludes that Alexander's great cunning is matched by that of another king's servant – 'par in alterius regis equisone calliditas' ('equal [was] the cunning of another monarch's groom')[82] – making

---

[80] III.3.ext.1 and III.8.ext.6; VII.3.ext.1, in Valerius Maximus, *Memorable Sayings and Doings*, trans. Shackleton Bailey, I, p.274 and p.275, p.334 and p.335; II, pp.136–9.

[81] See for example ibid., III.3.ext.1, 'rex, quo patientia pueri magis delectatus est…', p.274 and p.275.

[82] Ibid., II, VII.3.ext.1, p.136 and p.137.

an explicit comparison of this virtue in a regal context. This insistence on Alexander as a king may seem to be simply a reminder of his historical status, but Valerius' *Preface*, addressed to Tiberius, is a stark reminder that kingship, recently returned to the Romans after the years of the Republic, was being emphasized afresh: 'Augustus had been a very subtle tyrant, but the new emperor, Tiberius … made it abundantly clear to his subjects that they were now living under a monarchy and that the days of the Roman Republic … were gone forever'.[83] References to kingship, especially emphatic ones such as in the donkey episode, are therefore unlikely to be neutral, especially since Romans of this era 'hated but were fascinated by kingship', and frequently had an 'ambivalent' attitude.[84] This may be one reason for Tiberius' need to insist upon its acceptance. For Valerius, praise of Alexander's ethics is seen through the lens of his role as a king, connecting his moral worth with his kingly status in a similar (if implicit) performance of *translatio* to that of the *Preface*.

Valerius' ethical reading of Alexander, then, is affected by the resurgent state of monarchy in the first century AD under Tiberius, resulting in an additional emphasis on kingship. It is also important to note that most of the tales in the *Memorable Deeds and Sayings* concern Romans, rather than Greeks or others; this too is a result of first-century politics. Valerius' work 'was tailored to meet the social anxieties and insecurities of the people who belonged to [a] new administrative class' after the death of so many of the nobility at the end of the Republic,[85] and his stories enabled these often provincial men promoted by the new regime to model themselves on ancient Roman examples, again giving the ethical values he promotes a historical context. So Alexander's presence in this Roman-dominated work, as a non-Roman, Macedonian king, demonstrates the ability of Roman writers to absorb Greek history into their own. Perhaps Valerius' insistence on Alexander's kingship is an implicit acknowledgement of the need to depict the Macedonian in terms that first-century Romans would understand, and thus of some concealed anxiety about his non-indigenous origins. In any case, Valerius' combination of ethics and historically refracted kingship is another important moment in Alexander narratives' *translatio*.

This *translatio* is particularly vital for the Middle Ages, since Valerius Maximus' work was very widely read, especially the abridged version of Julius Paris produced in the fourth century.[86] It was apparently important even

---

[83] Valerius Maximus, *Memorable Deeds and Sayings*, trans. and introd. Walker, p.xx.

[84] Elizabeth J. Baynham, *Alexander the Great: The Unique History of Quintus Curtius Rufus* (Ann Arbor, MI, 1998), p.11, p.23.

[85] Valerius Maximus, *Memorable Deeds and Sayings*, trans. and introd. Walker, p.xxi.

[86] On manuscripts of Valerius Maximus' text in the Middle Ages, see *Texts and Transmission: A Survey of the Latin Classics*, ed. L. D. Reynolds (Oxford, 1982), pp.428–30; for Paris' epitome, see pp.290–2.

more for its moral *exempla* than for its information about Roman history, highlighting the form of *translatio* particularly appealing for medieval readers.[87] The *Memorable Deeds and Sayings* was therefore inspired by the needs of first-century readers, but its hermeneutic approach to Alexander and its Roman material transcended this immediate historical context.

Plutarch (c. AD 45–120)

The first-century AD Greek author Plutarch immediately presents a paradox, since 'more of his work survives than of almost any other author from Classical antiquity', yet he was little known (if at all) by the early Middle Ages in the European West.[88] He wrote over seventy treatises, usually known under the collective title *Moralia* ('ethical works'), and various biographies including the *Parallel Lives*, a series of paired biographies of Greek and Roman figures in which Alexander is paired with Caesar. Plutarch's Greek-language Alexander narrative in the *Parallel Lives* (on which my analysis focuses) was of course not available to medieval authors in its original form in the European West. However, his name was known to the Middle Ages from Jerome's translation of Eusebius' *Chronicon*, in which the author was inaccurately described as a philosopher active under Nero.[89] It also appears that Macrobius had read at least some of Plutarch's work.[90] Seven centuries later, John of Salisbury seems to have encountered some version of a Plutarchan text, although it is unclear whether it was indeed by the Greek author and which work it may have been.[91] This scattered acquaintance with Plutarch, mostly via his name alone, serves only to emphasize the near-universal lack of knowledge about him and his works in the medieval period.

Despite this lack of direct textual influence, however, Plutarch is still important for the Middle Ages, since his *Life of Alexander* demonstrates two modes of discourse concerning Alexander that are adopted and adapted by

---

[87] Valerius Maximus, *Memorable Deeds and Sayings*, trans. and introd. Walker, pp.xxi–xxii.
[88] His *Life of Alexander* is translated in *Age of Alexander*, ed. and trans. Scott-Kilvert and Duff. The quotation is at p.xv. All English quotations are taken from this text.
[89] Marianne Pade, 'The Reception of Plutarch from Antiquity to the Italian Renaissance', in *A Companion to Plutarch*, ed. Mark Beck, Blackwell Companions to the Ancient World (Oxford, 2014), pp.531–43 (p.535).
[90] Ibid., p.535.
[91] John uses a supposed letter from Plutarch to Trajan, the *Institutio Trajani*, in books v and vi of his *Policraticus*, although he probably invented this: see H. Liebeschütz, 'John of Salisbury and Pseudo-Plutarch', *Journal of the Warburg and Courtauld Institutes*, 6 (1943), pp.33–9, and Janet Martin, 'John of Salisbury as Classical Scholar', in *The World of John of Salisbury*, ed. Michael Wilkes, Studies in Church History, Subsidia, 3 (Oxford, 1984), pp.179–201.

other relevant material. He is explicit about his method and motivation in the Prologue to the *Lives of Alexander and Julius Caesar*:

> If I do not record all their most celebrated achievements or describe any of them exhaustively ... I ask my readers not to regard this as a fault. For I am writing Lives not history, and the truth is that the most brilliant exploits often tell us nothing of the virtues or vices of the men who performed them, while on the other hand a chance remark or a joke may reveal far more of a man's character [ἔθος] than battles where thousands die ... it is my task to dwell upon those details which illuminate the workings of the soul, and to use these to create a portrait of each man's life.[92]

The aim here is moral (ἔθος, 'character, habits', has an ethical meaning in late antiquity suggested by the semantic connection with the English 'ethics'): it is 'an exercise in cultural and biographical comparison' that encourages the reader to look beyond differences of historical context to potentially transcendent ethical values.[93] This aligns his work (in broad hermeneutic terms) particularly with that of Valerius Maximus. Plutarch's approach, stated so explicitly here, is instantly recognisable to medievalists as the justification for reading literature (such as non-religious and/or classical works) so frequently summed up in the phrase 'ethice supponitur'.[94] So even though Plutarch's *Parallel Lives* appears to have been mostly lost to the Middle Ages, the approach he applies to Alexander is inherited by that era. Plutarch's *Life of Alexander*, then, is related thematically to important medieval hermeneutics even if the text itself is not influential.

Plutarch's Alexander narrative runs from his conception and birth to his military triumphs and death, although as the end of this *Life* is probably missing it may have continued beyond this point.[95] However, his approach, in line with his ethical objective stated in the Preface, is not primarily that of historical chronology. Plutarch alters chronology for thematic emphasis, so that the episodes of Philotas' supposed treachery and the killing of Cleitus are juxtaposed (instead of being two years apart) in order to highlight aspects of

---

92   Plutarch, *Life of Alexander*, in *Age of Alexander*, ed. and trans. Scott-Kilvert and Duff, p.279. For the Greek text, see *Plutarch's Lives*, trans. Bernadotte Perrin, Loeb Classical Library (Cambridge, MA, 1919), VII: *Demosthenes and Cicero: Alexander and Caesar*, p.224.

93   Ibid., p.xviii.

94   As is well known, medieval *accessus* to classical texts frequently categorized classical material, especially poetry, as relevant to philosophy because it taught ethical values. See A. Minnis and A. B. Scott with D. Wallace, *Medieval Literary Theory and Criticism c.1100–1475: The Commentary Tradition*, 2nd edn (Oxford: Clarendon Press, 1991): 'Grammar ... was an art of living as well as an art of language, and the single method of instruction was the explication of the poets (*enarratio poetarum*)' (p.14).

95   See C. B. R. Pelling, 'Plutarch, *Alexander* and *Caesar*: Two New Fragments', *Classical Quarterly*, n.s., 23 (1973), pp.343–4.

Alexander's character:[96] this is perhaps one reason that historians have criticized his work. He also draws on ancient genres such as tragedy and epic in order to depict Alexander in relation to his ancestor and inspiration Achilles, an 'Iliadic parallelism' desired by the historical Alexander himself (as mentioned earlier).[97] 'Interweaving and contrasting epic and tragic elements' are also used to highlight the 'tension … between Alexander's hot temper and his self-control' throughout the *Life*.[98] So the examination of ἔθος that Plutarch constructs uses generic expectations and techniques drawn from a wide range of material. This diversity again underlines the need to read his work from a literary-stylistic perspective as well as for its historical facts.

However, Plutarch is still extremely interested in questions of sources and authority, questions characteristic of historiography. He used a wide range of early Hellenistic Alexander authors, including Aristobulus, Callisthenes, and Cleitarchus among others.[99] Throughout his narrative, but particularly at key points (such as at Alexander's conception, his visit to the temple at Ammon where he is allegedly acknowledged as the god's son, and his death), Plutarch cites the differing, sometimes opposing, accounts of various writers. At Alexander's death, for example, he writes:

> According to some writers, it was Aristotle who advised Antipater to arrange the murder … they cite a man named Hagnothemis as their authority: he claimed to have heard the details from Antigonus … But most authorities consider that this tale of poisoning is pure invention.[100]

What might seem to be simply virtuous historiographical practice, however, has more profound an impact. The effect of this citation is not primarily historiographical accuracy: it is not necessary to mention a story that is 'pure invention', for example. What this, and other similar references to multiple sources, do is to demonstrate a fictionalizing process in action by highlighting the complexities and possibilities of Alexander's narrative. Including possible differences between tales allows Plutarch to depict his own version of Alexander as authoritative yet multifaceted, informed by a wide range of historical accounts but ultimately focused on the ethical development of his ἔθος. In effect, Plutarch exposes the problem of a historical Alexander using his source

[96] Plutarch, *Life of Alexander*, chs 48–52, in *Age of Alexander*, ed. and trans. Scott-Kilvert and Duff.

[97] J. M. Mossman, 'Tragedy and Epic in Plutarch's *Alexander*', *Journal of Hellenic Studies*, 108 (1988), pp.83–93; repr. in B. Scardigli (ed.), *Essays on Plutarch's* Lives (Oxford, 1995), pp.209–28 (p.211).

[98] Ibid., p.213.

[99] See the overview of sources given in *Age of Alexander*, ed. and trans. Scott-Kilvert and Duff, p.278.

[100] Plutarch, *Life of Alexander*, ch.77, in *Age of Alexander*, ed. and trans. Scott-Kilvert and Duff, p.361.

citations; these are less about history or historiography than its implausibility, enabling Plutarch implicitly to demonstrate his own, more ethical approach's superiority. At this stage of Alexander's literary histories, fiction, and awareness of fiction as a process, is clearly present. Plutarch's *translatio* of his inherited Alexander narrative focuses on ἔθος and ethics (the near-tautology of this phrase demonstrates the connection between character and ethics clearly), but is also informed by a sophisticated awareness of the problems of historiography, an awareness that has so far not been paralleled in the other texts.

This concern for ἔθος and ethics in general is developed in greater detail in the comparison of Alexander and Caesar. The two men, whom Plutarch connects not just because of their conquests but through ambition, differ in terms of their attitude towards philosophy. Alexander, in contrast to Caesar, is depicted as a philosopher, or at least a lover of that discipline.[101] The suggestion is that Alexander is able to some extent to restrain his ambition because of his philosophical interests, unlike Caesar. Ethical ἔθος here is explicitly developed through learning, not a feature of Alexander narratives discussed so far.

The pairing of the two also relates to Plutarch's historical context. Tim Whitmarsh notes that 'in Roman contexts, Alexander was both a positive paradigm of military success and a negative paradigm of immoral excess', so pairing Alexander with the dictator for life who paved the way for the Empire was an inevitably polemical act.[102] Depicting Alexander as the more ethically engaged and restrained character is a revisionist attitude, therefore, and one that paints Caesar in yet darker colours. This favourable portrayal of the Macedonian in comparison with Caesar locates Plutarch's consideration of ἔθος even more firmly in a first-century AD Roman political context. Casting Caesar in negative terms as a figure of unrestrained ambition allowed Plutarch implicitly to ascribe the tumult and bloodshed at the end of the Republic to his individual character, making the events Caesar supposedly inspired unrepeatable if later emperors acted with less ambition, a potentially reassuring perspective for Romans living under imperial rule.

In cultural terms, Alexander's positive portrayal in contrast to Caesar highlights Plutarch's engagement with first-century Hellenism. It is perhaps unsurprising that, as a Greek writing under the aegis of the Roman Empire, 'much of Plutarch's writing smoothly assimilates Greek and Roman aspiration, expectation and moral precept'.[103] Yet it is not a straightforward act of *translatio*, since the terms of comparison under which Plutarch is writing are themselves Greek, as Simon Goldhill points out: the 'shared perspective' enshrined in

---

[101] See B. Buszard, 'Caesar's Ambition: A Combined Reading of Plutarch's *Alexander–Caesar* and *Pyrrhus–Marius*', *Transactions of the American Philological Association*, 138 (2008), pp.185–215.

[102] Whitmarsh, 'Alexander's Hellenism', p.175, p.177.

[103] Goldhill, *Who Needs Greek?*, p.254.

the *Parallel Lives* is itself 'distinctively Greek' and 'formed through a Greek tradition' of *paideia*.[104] In a crude sense, it is more that Romans are translated into Greeks rather than vice versa. Plutarch's ethical focus, therefore, which is shared by medieval readers and writers, 'draws on the long tradition of ethical writing formalized in the Hellenistic schools'. His narrative's *translatio* is itself inherited from (or at least inspired by) a prestigious antique context, something that his concern for Alexander's learning also suggests.[105] This is not something that other texts considered so far have made as clear, and is an important distinction between them and Plutarch's work.

In conclusion, Plutarch's *Life of Alexander* shares aspects of its approach with both late antique and medieval authors, but its interest in the problems of historiography and its classically derived study of ethics as exhibited in individual ἔθος connect it just as much with ancient Greek literature. As such, it is an important reminder of the power of the pre-Hellenistic period for Alexander texts composed much later.

Quintus Curtius Rufus (active c. AD 41–79)

Quintus Curtius Rufus' ten-book Latin *Histories of Alexander* demonstrates the oddities and accidents of literary transmission, since unlike Pompeius Trogus, Diodorus Siculus, Plutarch, and Arrian it was not quoted by any ancient commentator, yet appears to have been copied (and potentially read) widely in the Middle Ages, as 123 medieval manuscripts survive.[106] Because of this ancient silence, the work's exact date is hard to determine, but critical consensus based on internal references places its composition in the middle to late first century AD, most probably under the rule of either Claudius or Vespasian, making the author roughly contemporary with Plutarch.[107] The *Histories* are an oddity for another reason, in that Curtius Rufus is the only Latin historian we have extant between Livy and Tacitus (with the exception of Velleius Paterculus), and that his narrative is the sole Latin history devoted to Alexander alone (as

---

[104] Ibid., p.254.

[105] Ibid., pp.254–5. Shipley also highlights Plutarch's 'devotion to the ideals of classical Greece' more generally (*Greek World After Alexander*, p.13).

[106] Baynham, *Unique History of Quintus Curtius Rufus*, pp.1–2. See also Quintus Curtius Rufus, *The History of Alexander*, trans. John Yardley and introd. Waldemar Heckel, rev. edn (London, 2001), p.1.

[107] Baynham, *Unique History of Quintus Curtius Rufus*, pp.7–8, and appendix, pp.201–19, which provides a concise summary of the issues and possibilities. Baynham inclines towards Vespasian (p.213, p.218); Yardley opts for Claudius (*History of Alexander*, trans. Yardley and introd. Heckel, p.2), as does G. R. Hamilton, who considers that Seneca may have used Curtius Rufus as a source for his epistles 56 and 59 in 'The Date of Quintus Curtius Rufus', *Historia*, 37 (1988), pp.445–56 (p.456).

opposed to a universal history in which the Macedonian features).[108] However, it is likely that Curtius Rufus shared a primary material source with Diodorus Siculus, and that he had read Pompeius Trogus' work, connecting him at least indirectly with earlier Alexander authors.[109] Unfortunately, Curtius' text is no longer complete, so comparison with other works is inevitably a partial process: the whole of the first two books and parts of others are missing. In stylistic terms, he is influenced unsurprisingly by Virgil, but much more so by Livy, creating 'an Alexander whose history is permeated with Roman colouring'.[110] So although we have virtually no extra-textual knowledge about Curtius or his work, he was 'a Roman writing for Romans', specifically the 'well-to-do strata of Roman society' that was marked by an increasing interest in literary matters as an indication of culture.[111] (As we have already seen, however, this Roman identification is likely to be more complex than this phrase suggests, especially when writing about the alien, ancient Alexander.) Curtius' work, then, stands both at a distance from contemporary Roman literary fashions and yet is also embedded within the imperial society that produced such fashions.

I have already suggested that Diodorus Siculus' *Bibliotheke* reflects anxieties about imperial Rome in the immediate aftermath of the civil wars, so the idea that Curtius was 'a Roman writing for Romans' may similarly have a political dimension. The thematic influence of Livy is important here, given Curtius' stylistic relationship to the former's *Ab urbe condita*. For Livy, 'both Hannibal and Alexander were eclipsed by Rome', which was the culmination of worldly power.[112] Baynham considers Curtius' interest in *regnum*, the character of Alexander's kingship, to be informed by Livy's depiction of Roman kingly history in the latter's early books: 'Alexander's *vis* (force) … may recall the *vis* of Romulus … one may also note a similarity between Curtius' Alexander and Livy's Romulus in the former's slaying of Cleitus and the latter's murder of his brother, Remus'.[113] As discussed earlier, Romans of this era 'hated but were fascinated by kingship', and both Livy and Curtius would have been conscious of this 'ambivalent' attitude.[114]

---

[108] Baynham, *Unique History of Quintus Curtius Rufus*, p.8, p.7, and *History of Alexander*, trans. Yardley and introd. Heckel, p.1.

[109] *Diodorus Siculus*, trans. Welles, p.19; Baynham, *Unique History of Quintus Curtius Rufus*, pp.30–5.

[110] R. B. Steele, 'Quintus Curtius Rufus', *American Journal of Philology*, 36 (1915), pp.402–23 (p.409), cited in *History of Alexander*, trans. Yardley and introd. Heckel, p.8. On Livy's influence, see also Baynham, *Unique History of Quintus Curtius Rufus*, pp.20–5.

[111] Baynham, *Unique History of Quintus Curtius Rufus*, pp.15–16, citing S. Dosson, Étude *sur Quinte-Curce, sa vie et son œuvre* (Paris, 1887), p.218.

[112] Baynham, *Unique History of Quintus Curtius Rufus*, p.20.

[113] Ibid., p.21.

[114] Ibid., p.11, p.23.

This ambivalence needs to be borne in mind when reading Curtius' supposed paean to the Roman emperor (Claudius or Vespasian) who has recently saved the Roman people, 'a new star in the night that was almost our last' ('qui noctis quam paene supremam habuimus novum sidus illuxit').[115] This extra-narrative moment occurs just before Alexander's death, and introduces an explicit parallel between the civil wars over his kingdom and the conflicts over control of the Roman Empire, in which 'an empire that might have stood firm under a single man collapsed while it rested on the shoulders of a number' ('imperium sub uno stare potuisset, dum a pluribus sustinetur, ruit').[116] Crucially, it appears to be the personal cost to 'the people of Rome' ('populus Romanus'), who 'owe their salvation to their emperor' ('salutem se principi suo debere'), rather than the political effect on the empire, which is foremost here.[117] The implication of potential human suffering modifies this praise for the imperial saviour of Rome into an implicit warning about civil war. This political point is therefore made using an ethical perspective, a collocation of moral and political viewpoints that is reminiscent of Diodorus' *Bibliotheke*, with which the *Histories* may have shared a source.

Curtius takes this connection between ethical and political interpretation further, however. Given the depiction of Alexander as declining morally (discussed in greater detail below), and in light of Livy's analysis of Roman kings as tyrants, Curtius here is perhaps warning not just about civil war but implicitly about the tyranny that can be its cause. The experience of imperial rule in the mid to late first century AD would only have reinforced this connection between tyranny and war, with the tumultuous *regnum* of Nero (AD 54–68), the Pisonian conspiracy that tried to overthrow him (AD 65), and the chaotic Year of the Four Emperors (AD 69) all highlighting the civil dangers of absolute rule. Admittedly this is drawing a broad parallel between Curtius' text and wider Roman politics, but since Curtius himself explicitly relates Alexander to his own Roman emperor it seems a plausible one. So the historical and political background to the *Histories*' treatment of Alexander is first-century unease and ambivalence about kingship, civil war, and the position of Rome, factors that need to be borne in mind when reading the text.

Curtius' work has been criticized in recent times (mainly by historians) for being 'sensational and emotive', 'careless, overblown, flowery, and

---

[115] *Historiae* x.9.3, in *History of Alexander*, trans. Yardley and introd. Heckel, p.254. For the original Latin, see *Quintus Curtius Rufus, History of Alexander*, ed. and trans. John C. Rolfe, 2 vols, Loeb Classical Library, 368 and 369 (Cambridge, MA, 1946), II, p.546.

[116] *Historiae* x.9.2, in *History of Alexander*, trans. Yardley and introd. Heckel, p.254; *History of Alexander*, ed. and trans. Rolfe, II, p.546.

[117] *Historiae* x.9.3, in *History of Alexander*, trans. Yardley and introd. Heckel, p.254; *History of Alexander*, ed. and trans. Rolfe, II, p.546.

unhistorical'.[118] Such 'unhistorical' stylistic and narrative elements include many 'contrasts and ironic reversals', as well as moralistic reflections, character sketches, and lengthy speeches that outnumber 'all the other extant Alexander-historians combined'.[119] Yet many of these elements have also been seen in other works discussed in this chapter and are characteristic of ancient historiography more widely, meaning that Curtius Rufus' style and approach have parallels elsewhere.[120] For example, his focus on Alexander's character aligns him to some extent with Diodorus Siculus, Plutarch, and (as will be seen below) Arrian; like the latter, he composes a concluding summary of Alexander's character, claiming that 'his strengths were attributable to his nature and his weaknesses to Fortune or his youth' ('liquet bona naturae eius fuisse, vitia vel fortunae vel aetatis')[121] and describing both in turn. However, Curtius' Alexander degenerates morally over time in a more marked fashion than in either Plutarch or Arrian, aided by an increasing dependence on alcohol.[122] This tendency to moralize Alexander's narrative is also found in Diodorus Siculus, with whom as already mentioned Curtius may have shared a source, but there the moral focus is less personal and more explicitly focused upon general political clemency, as discussed earlier: this is a distinct difference between the two works.

Curtius' speeches add to this impression of ethical valency in the *Histories*, since their rhetoric is often morally weighted. For example, when Alexander accuses conspirators of plotting his death, a certain Hermolaus in turn accuses the king of ingratitude in words that make this seem criminal:

> How few are the Macedonians who have actually survived your ruthlessness! How few, indeed, apart from those of meanest birth! ... As far as the enemy is concerned, these are still alive today, are still standing in the battle-line, protecting you with their shields, receiving wounds for your glory and your victory. A fine thanks *you* gave them! One has spilled his blood on your table; another was not even granted a simple death; leaders of your

---

[118] *History of Alexander*, trans. Yardley and introd. Heckel, p.10; Baynham, *Unique History of Quintus Curtius Rufus*, p.5.

[119] *History of Alexander*, trans. Yardley and introd. Heckel, pp.10–11.

[120] Baynham, *Unique History of Quintus Curtius Rufus*, pp.8–10.

[121] *Historiae* x.5.26, in *History of Alexander*, trans. Yardley and introd. Heckel, p.247; *History of Alexander*, ed. and trans. Rolfe, ii, p.522.

[122] See for example the episode of Clitus' murder at viii.1.43, in which the role of alcohol in Alexander's action is strongly emphasized ('his senses had long since succumbed to the wine', 'olim mero sensibus victis', in *History of Alexander*, trans. Yardley and introd. Heckel, p.179; *History of Alexander*, ed. and trans. Rolfe, ii, p.244); although alcohol plays a part in both Plutarch and Arrian's accounts of the same episode, it is far less marked (Plutarch, *Life of Alexander*, chs 50–1, in *Age of Alexander*, and trans. Scott-Kilvert and Duff, pp.335–7; Arrian, *Anabasis* iv.8, in *Campaigns of Alexander*, trans. de Selincourt and introd. Hamilton, pp.213–6).

armies have been put on the rack to provide a spectacle for the Persians they had conquered.[123]

Here Alexander is depicted as a bloodthirsty tyrant, ungrateful for his troops' sacrifice, in terms that encourage sympathy not with the king but with the conspirators. The rhetorical and emotional appeal, even stronger in the original Latin – 'pro gloria tua, pro victoria vulnera excipiunt' – emphasizes primarily Alexander's perceived cruelty, rather than any political necessity, in executing conspirators, and entwines the personal with the political so that ethics dominates what could be seen as a historical-political perspective. Once again, this nuances the idea of the *Histories* as a political work concerned with tyranny, since it is the effects on persons, not upon kingdoms, that is emphasized first here, the individual's experience carrying more weight than that of the body politic.

This sense of Curtius' *Histories* as concerned with character, drama, and emotion as much as factual narrative has led to the text being analyzed as fiction rather than primarily as history. Harry MacLeod Currie compares it with Hellenistic Greek novels, and concludes that 'romantic description in the spirit of the novel rather than historical enquiry and analysis is his [Curtius'] standard approach'.[124] This perspective has been challenged, as Curtius himself claimed to be writing history and undertakes source analysis characteristic of that genre, but since a recurring theme in this chapter is the use of so-called romance techniques within supposed histories it seems contextually plausible that he is indeed writing a kind of history that shares features with romance discourses.[125] So Curtius is again aligned with Arrian in this, despite the latter's reception as more 'historical'. It is particularly unfortunate that both the sections that describe Alexander's birth and imminent death are missing, since these moments are likely to have demonstrated romance tendencies even more strongly.

The highly wrought, rhetorical nature of Curtius' *Histories* and their ethical reading of Alexander may well explain why the work was popular in the Middle Ages. Munk Olsen's catalogue lists eighteen manuscripts of the work.[126] Several manuscripts provide material for the missing books I and II, and it is this supplemented version that Walter of Châtillon appears to have used in the

---

[123] *Historiae* VIII.7.4–5, in *History of Alexander*, trans. Yardley and introd. Heckel, p.192; *History of Alexander*, ed. and trans. Rolfe, II, p.290, p.292.

[124] Harry MacL. Currie, 'Quintus Curtius Rufus: The Historian as Novelist?', in *Groningen Colloquia on the Novel*, III, ed. Heinz Hofmann (Groningen, 1990), pp.63–77 (p.76).

[125] Baynham highlights Curtius' own claim to be writing history (*Unique History of Quintus Curtius Rufus*, pp.6–7). See also the discussion of ancient historiography earlier in this chapter.

[126] Birger Munk Olsen, 'Quintus Curtius Rufus', in *L'étude des auteurs classiques latins aux XIe et XIIe siècles*, I: *Catalogue des manuscrits classiques latins copiés du IXe au XIIe siècles: Apicius–Juvénal* (Paris, 1982), pp.355–62.

composition of his *Alexandreis*.[127] Crucially, a twelfth-century copy shows signs of editorial work that highlights the theme of Alexander's moral decline and the role of fortune, supporting the idea of a continuing interest in an ethical and philosophical reading of the Macedonian in the medieval period. Curtius' *Histories* thus provides the first piece of firm evidence that the appeal of the so-called historical tradition of Alexander narratives in the Middle Ages was perhaps due less to its historicity than to other factors. It further confirms the idea that the antique 'historical tradition' is in fact a hybrid, multifaceted discourse, influenced by features drawn from a variety of modes of writing.

Arrian (c. AD 85/90–c.160)

Like Plutarch a generation or so earlier, Arrian was also a Greek and a Roman citizen, but unlike the former he appears to have pursued a career in imperial service, serving in various Roman provinces and becoming consul in AD 129 or 130, after which he was governor of Cappadocia.[128] His Greek *Campaigns of Alexander* (*Anabasis Alexandri*) was his self-declared masterwork, 'more precious than country and kin and public advancement', and he was influenced in particular by the ancient Greek author Xenophon's account of Cyrus' campaign in Persian territory, also called *Anabasis*, and the authors Herodotus and Thucydides.[129] It is clear from these names that he wanted to be seen as an heir to ancient Greek historiographical tradition, in line with the aspect of literary Hellenism of the era that looked back to that tradition for its style and approach; in this he resembles Plutarch, although his claim is more overt. Like Plutarch, his account was not known in the Roman West in the Middle Ages. However, Arrian is still important as he relies on the same sources as Plutarch (for example Aristobulus), and may even have been influenced by the former's thematic approach to Alexander in the *Lives*;[130] he may therefore provide important context for interpreting Plutarch.

---

[127] Edmé R. Smits, 'A Medieval Supplement to the Beginning of Curtius Rufus' *Historia Alexandri*: An Edition with Introduction', *Viator*, 18 (1987), pp.89–124 (p.94, p.96).

[128] See the overview of his career in Arrian, *Campaigns of Alexander*, trans. de Selincourt and introd. Hamilton, pp.15–17.

[129] *Anabasis* I.12, in ibid., p.68. On the influences of these three writers on the *Anabasis*, see for example Jane D. Chaplain, 'Conversations in History: Arrian and Herodotus, Parmenio and Alexander', *Greek, Roman and Byzantine Studies*, 51.4 (2011), pp.613–33.

[130] See for example B. Buszard, 'A Plutarchan Parallel to Arrian *Anabasis* 7.1', *Greek, Roman and Byzantine Studies*, 50.4 (2010), pp.565–85, who argues that Arrian read Plutarch's *Lives* of Alexander and Caesar and was influenced by some thematic elements, namely Caesar's 'unrealized plans for further conquest and his rivalry with himself', for his portrait of Alexander in the *Anabasis* (p.566). On the source of both Arrian and Plutarch, see N. G. L. Hammond, *Sources for Alexander the Great: An Analysis of Plutarch's* Life *and Arrian's* Anabasis Alexandrou (Cambridge, 1993).

The connection between the two Greek authors is a particularly interesting possibility since they are, according to their own statements, writing with somewhat different aims. Plutarch is concerned above all with ethical interpretation of character, whereas Arrian aligns himself with historians, as mentioned above. Whether directly connected or not, Plutarch and Arrian may demonstrate different potential emphases and uses of Alexander's story in this period.

It is clear from the first sentence of Arrian's *Anabasis* that he is very concerned for historical accuracy in terms that reflect to some extent the approaches of modern historians:[131]

> Wherever Ptolemy and Aristobulus in their histories of Alexander, the son of Philip, have given the same account, I have followed it on the assumption of its accuracy; where their facts differ I have chosen what I feel to be the more probable [πιστότερα] and interesting [ἀξιαφηγητότερα]. There are other accounts of Alexander's life – more of them indeed, and more mutually conflicting than of any other historical character; it seems to me, however, that Ptolemy and Aristobulus are the most trustworthy writers on this subject.[132]

Here Arrian provides an overview of his supposed historiographical method and of the multifaceted nature of the accounts of Alexander to which he had access. However, he also gives himself permission to follow the most 'probable and interesting' ('πιστότερα ... καὶ ... ἀξιαφηγητότερα') account where his two main sources contradict one another, an approach that may justify including less historically worthy material. So despite his avowed historicism, Arrian is crafting a narrative using some criteria familiar from 'fiction', such as the Greek novel. This is unsurprising, given the fluidity of Hellenistic-era literary genres as described earlier, but it is worth bearing in mind since Arrian is so frequently described as the historiographical apogee of antique Alexander texts.

Arrian's account is military in character, more so than that of Plutarch. Unlike the latter, he does not describe Alexander's conception, birth, and childhood, but begins with the young Macedonian marching towards Thrace. Throughout his narrative it is the military strategies that absorb him the most, as with the descriptions of his tactics against carts in the mountains during

---

[131] He is frequently cited as giving 'the best and most reliable account' of Alexander's conquests, to the extent that there is an 'Arriankult' from the nineteenth century onwards (Arrian, *Campaigns of Alexander*, trans. de Selincourt and introd. Hamilton, p.33; Davidson, 'Bonkers about Boys').

[132] *Anabasis* 1.1, in *Campaigns of Alexander*, trans. de Selincourt and introd. Hamilton, p.41. For the Greek text, see *Flavii Arriani Anabasis Alexandri*, ed. A. G. Roos (Leipzig, 1907), p.1.

that part of the campaign.[133] This is perhaps one reason that he frequently compresses or skirts around politically charged moments, such as the 'certain amount of trouble' involved in getting the Athenians to serve under him, a description J. R. Hamilton calls 'so brief as to be misleading'.[134] Yet Arrian's account is not simply a narrative of military tactics. He too is interested in Alexander's character, and gives him a lengthy epitaph in which he analyzes his faults and his virtues, concluding that his errors were mitigated by the king's possessing 'the nobility of heart to be sorry for his mistakes'.[135] Arrian's personal interest in the Macedonian king also results in first-person involvement in the narrative, a commentary that on occasion overcomes his supposed historical focus. We see this clearly in his account of Alexander's meeting with Darius' mother, during which she mistakes his friend Hephaestion for Alexander because of the former's greater magnificence, but the error is passed off as understandable by Alexander:

> I record this anecdote not as necessarily true, though it is credible enough. If such were indeed the facts, I cannot but admire Alexander both for treating these women with such compassion and for showing such respect and confidence towards his friend; if the story was apocryphal, it was at least inspired by Alexander's character: thus he would have acted, thus he would have spoken – and on that account I admire him no less.[136]

Arrian here admits the apocryphal nature of the incident, but says it is 'inspired' (the Greek is 'πιθανός', literally 'plausible') even if not historically true. He uses this incident to illustrate Alexander's character in terms of ethics ('compassion' ['κατοικτίσεως'], 'confidence' ['πίστεως'], and 'respect' ['τιμῆς']), thus adding a moral hermeneutic to his predominantly historical *translatio*. Like Plutarch, Arrian's work portrays Alexander's narrative using both historical and ethical approaches, although the historical one is more dominant. The approaches are of course related, even combined, features of historiography, both in this period and in ancient Greece, but Arrian's interest in ethical interpretation is an important sign that factors other than historical accuracy, 'what really happened', operate within his *Anabasis*.

Seeing Arrian not just as a historian (in the modern sense) but as an imaginative writer allows further revealing comparisons to be made with supposedly non-historical works, such as the *Alexander Romance*. Jeremy McInerney sees the Hephaestion incident in Arrian as demonstrating that 'the courtly treatment of Darius' family is as much a part of the historical tradition as the

---

[133] *Anabasis* I.1–2, in *Campaigns of Alexander*, trans. de Selincourt and introd. Hamilton, pp.42–4.

[134] *Anabasis* I.1, in ibid., p.42 and n.4.

[135] *Anabasis* VII.29, in ibid., p.396.

[136] *Anabasis* II.12, in ibid., p.123. For the Greek text, see *Anabasis Alexandri*, ed. Roos, p.76.

54

romantic [one]', and compares Arrian's 'editoralizing' of it (quoted above) as a means of illustrating character that has parallels with romance techniques ('in that sense, Arrian's work uses some of the same narrative techniques as the Romance to create his Alexander').[137] This is a vital insight into the interconnections between the 'historical tradition' and 'the romantic [sic]' one that modern critics are so keen to discern in (and impose upon) Alexander literature: it shows that where such different traditions do indeed exist, they respond to and are inspired by one another, even if that response is often in terms of repudiation of other, unreliable authors, as is frequently the case in the *Anabasis*.[138] So even in this most historical of the antique Alexander writers we see the influence of other modes of discourse, another feature that may well be inherited by the literature of the Middle Ages despite the lack of direct knowledge of Arrian in the West.

Arrian's relationship with Rome and Hellenism is more opaque than that seen in Plutarch's *Life of Alexander*, since he does not overly compare the Macedonian king with any Roman figure. However, his attitude to Greek historiography provides some insights into this political-literary context. In book I chapter 12 Arrian emphasizes the lack of any ancient 'worthy chronicler' for Alexander before claiming this role for himself in an act of self-aggrandizement:

> There has never been another man in all the world, of Greek or any other blood, who by his own hand succeeded in so many brilliant enterprises. And that is the reason why I have embarked upon the project of writing this history, in the belief that I am not unworthy to set clear before men's eyes the story of Alexander's life ... I need not declare my name – though it is by no means unheard of in the world ... [Alexander's brilliance is why] I venture to claim the first place in Greek literature, since Alexander, about whom I write, held first place in the profession of arms.[139]

Here Arrian claims that his subject elevates his writing to 'the first place in Greek literature'. This expression of cultural dominance appears to transcend ethnicity and culture ('of Greek or any other blood'), but in fact it reinforces it. Arrian the 'not unheard of' (in Greek 'οὐδὲ ἄγνωστον', a clear example of *paralipsis* or *praeteritio*) writes about the most brilliant man who ever existed, who happens to be Greek, not just in the Greek language but within

---

[137] Jeremy McInerney, 'Arrian and the Greek Alexander Romance', *The Classical World*, 100.4 (2007), pp.424–30 (p.429).

[138] See for example *Anabasis* VII.28, where in a discussion of how Alexander died Arrian mentions 'one writer [who] has even had the face to declare that when he [Alexander] knew his death was imminent he went out with the intention of throwing himself into the Euphrates' (*Campaigns of Alexander*, trans. de Selincourt and introd. Hamilton, p.395).

[139] *Anabasis* I.12, in ibid., p.68. For the Greek, see *Anabasis Alexandri*, ed. Roos, p.23–4.

the culturally prestigious tradition of 'Greek literature', in which he is 'first'. Greek military and literary achievements, the past and the first-century present, are elided here in a conscious construction of cultural supremacy. However, Arrian's apparently confident stridency is nuanced perhaps by his own situation as a Greek not just under Roman imperial rule but actively employed in promoting the latter. Simon Goldhill's observations about there being a 'tension between subordination and achievement' for 'the modern Greek politician', made with reference to Plutarch, fit Arrian's position here too.[140] Arrian proclaims Greek achievements (both past – Alexander – and present – his own 'name' and writing) from a subordinate position as a Roman citizen who was ethnically a provincial Greek from Bithynia, yet who was also in imperial service. Without emphasizing this general biographical perspective too strongly, it seems probable that Arrian's literary promotion of personal and cultural Greekness in his Alexander narrative is a reaction to the 'tension between subordination and achievement' evident in his life. For Arrian, personal and political Hellenism collide.

Arrian's status as the Alexander historian *par excellence*, therefore, is far from being his sole literary and cultural feature. He shares an interest in character and ethics with Plutarch, and his strident Greekness reveals some of the tensions of first-century AD Hellenistic culture under Roman rule. Aspects of *translatio* in his Alexander narrative therefore relate both to Plutarch's work, which may well have influenced him, and also to tendencies found in contemporary Alexander writings more widely.[141] Although Arrian's work was not read in the medieval period in the European West, the techniques shared by his text and the *Alexander Romance* highlight the fact that aspects of his compositional process were indirectly transmitted to the Middle Ages, making him an important figure in the history of Alexander literature even if he was unknown in that later era.

Justin (late second century – pre-AD 226/7: possibly fourth century)

Virtually nothing is known about Marcus Junianus Justinus. He was apparently a rhetoric teacher visiting Rome from one of its provinces when he read and epitomized Pompeius Trogus' Latin *Philippic Histories*, a forty-four-book work of universal history.[142] Trogus appears to have been roughly

---

[140] Goldhill, *Who Needs Greek?*, p.253.

[141] Diodorus Siculus' narrative shares Arrian's interest in Alexander's Greekness in terms of his blood descent from Greek heroes, and to some extent his moments of ethical *translatio*: see the section on Diodorus above. See also the comparison made with the techniques of the *Alexander Romance*.

[142] *Justin:* Epitome *of the* Philippic History *of Pompeius Trogus*, vol. 1: *Books 11–12: Alexander the Great*, trans. and introd. J. C. Yardley and Waldemar Heckel (Oxford, 1997), p.1.

contemporary with Livy (59 BC–AD 17) and Diodorus Siculus, whereas Justin was writing probably before AD 226/7, in the late second century or early part of the third.[143] Justin's epitome was read by important authors of the late fourth and early fifth century, including Jerome and Augustine, and Orosius, Cassiodorus, and Isidore all used it in their own works (early fifth, sixth, and seventh centuries respectively).[144] The epitome was popular in the Middle Ages as well as during late antiquity, as over two hundred manuscripts survive; Alcuin mentions Justin's work in his poem on York's library holdings, for example.[145] Possibly ultimately based on Cleitarchus, Justin recounts Alexander's conquests from the end of book XI and throughout book XII, providing a relatively short narrative that is 'full of fact, concise, and written in a simple style'.[146] It is of course extremely difficult to tell for which parts of the narrative Justin himself is responsible rather than Trogus since the latter's work is lost, which makes analyzing Justin's text in terms of context and motivations problematic. In what follows I rely heavily on other scholars' analyses of the idiosyncrasies of Justin's style to determine his input.

The idea that Justin's work is 'full of fact' may suggest it is a history in modern terms, an idea perhaps supported by the absence of the romance adventures of Alexander in the east. However, Justin has frequently been criticized for his historiography (chiefly because of his epitomizing technique): 'the originality and rhetorical flair of his writing … was not accompanied by good historical method (or knowledge, for that matter), and he has earned his reputation for unreliability and shoddy workmanship'. [147] Yardley suggests that criticizing Justin on this account is to miss the point, since as a teacher of rhetoric he was 'more orator than historian': 'what interests him are sudden reversals of fortune, marvels, fabulous events, scenes that evoke pity'.[148] There seems to be a contradiction, then, between Justin's prose style and his approach, as Yardley makes him sound more in tune with the *Alexander Romance* than a concise and factual historian. Certainly in comparison to the *Romance* Justin is not interested in marvels (there are no fountains of immortality), but vivid phrases such as 'curatio vulneris gravior ipso vulnere

---

[143] Ibid., p.9, p.13. Some scholars have preferred a fourth-century date; for a summary of the arguments, see pp.8–13.

[144] Ibid., p.8.

[145] *Texts and Transmission*, ed. Reynolds, p.197.

[146] *Justin*: Epitome, trans. and introd. Yardley and Heckel, p.37. The quotation is from *Texts and Transmission*, ed. Reynolds, p.197. For a detailed analysis of Justin's style, particularly the influence of Livy, see J. C. Yardley, *Justin and Pompeius Trogus: A Study of the Language of Justin's* Epitome *of Trogus* (Toronto, 2003).

[147] *Justin*: Epitome, trans. and introd. Yardley and Heckel, p.36.

[148] Ibid., p.17.

fuit' ('the treatment was riskier than the wound'[149]), referring to Alexander's killing of a man who had badly wounded him, do display a rhetorical interest in 'reversals of fortune' and 'fabulous events', albeit of a different order than those seen in the *Romance*.

Justin's purpose, as expressed in his preface, is educational:

> During a period of free time which we had in the city, I excerpted from his [Trogus'] forty-four published volumes all the most noteworthy material. I omitted what did not make pleasurable reading or serve to provide a moral, and I produced a brief anthology of sorts to refresh the memory of those who had studied history in Greek, and to provide instruction for those who had not.[150]

Justin is writing for a Latin audience that needs or wants to know more about history either for pleasure or for moral instruction, an ethical approach familiar from other writers discussed in this chapter. Given this, it is noticeable that Justin does not (unlike Curtius Rufus and Diodorus Siculus) often interject his own opinions of Alexander's actions or character. We are given a brief indication of his abilities at the start of his narrative – 'he was 20 years old, at which age he showed great promise, but he did so with such restraint that he seemed to have still more in reserve than was then apparent'[151]– but for the most part his actions are left to speak for themselves. At his death, we are told that 'he was a man endowed with superhuman greatness of spirit', which is then illustrated by the story of his mother Olympias' dream of a snake at his conception;[152] Justin (or Trogus) then gives a short eulogistic conclusion, describing him as a lover of literature in youth before mentioning his abilities as a leader of men and his military prowess, and ending with his death not by defeat but by treachery ('he was brought down not by the valour of an enemy, but by a plot hatched by his own men').[153] The tone is admiring and strikingly uncritical, without the discussion of negative traits seen even in the generally favourable accounts by Plutarch and Arrian. Any ethical interpretation of Alexander's life must be deduced from the narrative, since it is not stated explicitly. So despite Justin's avowed aim, his ethical didacticism is less marked than it is for example in Curtius Rufus' work.

Since we know so little about Justin's date, reading his Alexander narrative in terms of literary and historical context is only possible in the broadest of terms. As just mentioned, it is clear that he is writing for a Latin, potentially a

---

[149] *Epitome* XII.9.13, in *Justin*: Epitome, trans. and introd. Yardley and Heckel, p.64. For the Latin text, see *Justini Historiae Philippicae ex editione Abrahami Gronovii*, 2 vols (London, 1822), I, p.231.

[150] *Epitome* praef.4, in *Justin*: Epitome, trans. and introd. Yardley and Heckel, p.9.

[151] *Epitome* XI.1.9, in ibid., p.43.

[152] *Epitome* XII.16.1, in ibid., p.69.

[153] *Epitome* XII.16.11, in ibid., pp.69–70.

Roman, audience, since he says in his preface that he made his epitome both for those who had read history in Greek and also for those who had not done so, indicating that his work was aimed at those with little Greek in linguistic terms but with a general interest in Greek culture. His status as a rhetorician also aligns him with an important stylistic aspect of the Second Sophistic period, which ended roughly when he was active, if a date of before AD 226 is preferred for his work. These broad points perhaps relate his epitome to the interest in antiquity characteristic of that period. In terms of historical context, the late second and early third centuries were a time of unrest for the Roman Empire, resulting ultimately in the Crisis of the Third Century at the emperor Severus Alexander's assassination in 235. Given Justin's lack of commentary within his work and his matter-of-fact approach, his relationship with this (or any other) historical context is opaque, although perhaps his interest in providing his readers with morals from history rather than the present day suggests that his immediate imperial Roman context was indeed a troubled one. This is simply speculation, however.

Justin's work, as far as we can tell given the lack of Trogus' original, provides a straightforward narrative focusing on Alexander's military deeds, with little overt commentary despite his claims to an ethical purpose in writing. Crucially, his Alexander narrative is short, unlike any of the others discussed here, making him a pragmatic choice for those wanting a quick overview of events, which may be a large part of his medieval appeal. His rhetorical style, too, would have appealed to medieval readers, especially those learning and teaching the subject as part of the *trivium*. It may well be the case, then, that Justin's Alexander narrative was valued for its 'facts' and its style rather than its approach, potentially a different scenario from those posited for the other texts in this chapter.

Orosius (c. AD 385–after 418)

With the early fifth-century historian Paulus Orosius, we move into late antiquity proper, which sees the adoption of Christianity as the imperial state religion in the early fourth century. Christianity had vital implications for literary production and interpretation, since Christian theologians like Eusebius, Augustine, and Jerome had an important effect on historiography as well as upon Christian doctrine. Orosius' work, then, is composed in a context with key religious and intellectual differences from the earlier period discussed so far that may have significant consequences for his approach to Alexander.

Like Justin's epitome (and thus Trogus), who is his major source, Orosius was widely read in the Middle Ages but on a greater scale.[154] Over two

---

[154] *Orosius: Seven Books of History Against the Pagans*, trans. and introd. A. Fear (Liverpool, 2010), p.2 and pp.5–6. For the Latin text, see *Orose, Histoires (Contre Les Païens)*, ed. and trans. Marie-Pierre Arnaud-Lindet, 3 vols (Paris, 1990 and 1991).

hundred manuscripts of his *Historiarum Adversum Paganos Libri VII* (*Seven Books of History Against the Pagans*, henceforth *Histories*) survive, and the work was translated into many European vernaculars (including Old English) and into Arabic.[155] The *Histories*, which describe the events of the secular world from a Christian perspective, were used by later historians including Fulgentius, Gregory of Tours, Gildas, Bede, Ranulf Higden, and Otto of Freising, both as a source and as a historiographical model.[156] Orosius' Alexander narrative was used in one of the versions of the *Historia de preliis* (the so-called J2 redaction), which demonstrates his influence upon later Alexander writings in particular as well as historiography more widely.[157] One obvious reason for this wide diffusion is Orosius' explicitly apologetic purpose in writing his *Histories*, evident from the work's title: he wishes to convince his readers that Rome and its empire, despite its recent sacking by the Goths in AD 410, is God's instrument for earthly peace via the spread of Christianity, and that therefore paganism is a fundamental threat both to Rome and to the wider world. Writing about Roman history necessitates a wide chronological and geographical range, since Rome was seen as the last of the four empires that were to rule the world prophesied in the Bible, a conventional Christian perspective on *translatio imperii*.[158] Roman (including Greek) history for Orosius, then, was 'both universal history and Christian history', since the empire was 'the culmination of God's plans on earth'.[159] Orosius' *translatio* of Alexander's narrative is therefore bound up with the current difficult situation of Rome, a theme familiar from many of the works already considered here, but Rome as the guarantor of Christian salvation history rather than as a secular imperial power.

Orosius also benefitted from the authority of Augustine, who he claims asked him to write the *Histories* whilst the latter was still working on the *City of God*, and who had commended him to Jerome.[160] Yet Orosius' views of history rather diverge from those displayed in Augustine's work. Although he follows Augustine in the idea that past and present see the same problems

---

Lars Boje Mortensen notes that copying Justin's and Orosius' works in one manuscript 'appears to have been a speciality of scriptoria in Brittany/Normandy and southern England in the period from around the conquest up to the end of the 12th century'; see 'Orosius and Justinus in One Volume: Postconquest Books Across the Channel', *Cahiers de l'Institut du moyen âge grec et latin*, 60 (1990), pp.389–99 (p.389).

[155] *Against the Pagans*, trans. and introd. Fear, p.25. For a detailed overview of the MSS, see Lars Boje Mortensen, 'The Diffusion of Roman Histories in the Middle Ages: A List of Orosius, Eutropius, Paulus Diaconus, and Landolfus Sagax Manuscripts', *Filologia mediolatina*, 6–7 (1999–2000), pp.101–200.

[156] *Against the Pagans*, trans. and introd. Fear, p.25.

[157] Ibid., p.25, n.144.

[158] Ibid., pp.18–19. The prophecy occurs at Daniel 2.31–45.

[159] Ibid., p.17.

[160] Ibid., p.6.

(minimizing the idea of historical progress), he is keen to emphasize that current miseries in the Christian era are far less than those of past pagan times, perhaps influenced in this linear view to some extent by Eusebius' *Chronicle*, the source of his chronology.[161] The *City of God* emphasizes that it is impossible for the kingdom of heaven to be built on earth, but Orosius' view of Rome's role comes close to this position on occasion.[162] This more linear (rather than cyclical, or unchanging) historiographical hermeneutic is particularly important for Orosius' narrative of Alexander, which occupies chapters 16 to 20 of book III.

Although this narrative is based on historical events, and does not include the more fantastical eastern adventures, Alexander's story is primarily a vehicle for Orosius' desire to depict the pre-Roman past as unredeemed. Orosius portrays Alexander as a bloodthirsty, merciless tyrant who threw the world into chaos. He does this both by vivid description (Alexander's 'thirst for human blood, either of his enemies or even of his friends, was never slaked', 'humani sanguinis inexsaturabilis siue hostium, siue etiam sociorum')[163] and the alteration of inconvenient facts (Alexander's kindness to Darius' female relatives, seen for example in Plutarch and Arrian's accounts, becomes cruelty: 'he kept Darius' mother and wife and even, I should say, his little daughters in cruel captivity', 'cuius non dicam matrem uel uxorem sed etiam paruulas filias crudeli captiuitate retinebat').[164] Both in style and in factual description, his approach is a polemical one, underlining his overall historiographical purpose.

Orosius' Alexander is very different from the earlier accounts discussed in this chapter. Whilst a broadly ethical interpretation of the Macedonian might seem to align Orosius with Plutarch, Curtius Rufus, and even perhaps the Greek *Alexander Romance*, for example, Orosius' ethical focus produces a wholly negative picture. As we have just seen, Justin, Orosius' main source, is not particularly interested in ethical didacticism, good or bad, and even the narrative of moral degeneration displayed by Curtius Rufus' work allows Alexander and his adventures some positive effects. This difference is because Orosius is writing explicitly as a Christian. Despite a broad shared interest in

---

[161] For more detail on the two authors' historical perspectives, see Glenn F. Chesnut, 'Eusebius, Augustine, Orosius, and the Later Patristic and Medieval Christian Historians', in *Eusebius, Christianity and Judaism*, ed. Harold W. Attridge and Gohei Hata (Leiden, 1992), pp.687–713 and G. Zecchini, 'Latin Historiography: Jerome, Orosius and the Western Chronicles', in *Greek and Roman Historiography in Late Antiquity: Fourth to Sixth Century A.D.*, ed. Gabriele Marasco (Leiden, 2003), pp.317–45.

[162] See for example *Histories* VII.43.17, 'innumerable wars have come to an end', in *Against the Pagans*, trans. and introd. Fear, p.413.

[163] *Histories* III.18.10, in ibid., p.137. For the Latin, see *Orose, Histoires*, ed. and trans. Arnaud-Lindet, II, p.170.

[164] *Histories* III.17.7, in *Against the Pagans*, trans. and introd. Fear, p.135. For the Latin, see *Orose, Histoires*, ed. and trans. Arnaud-Lindet, II, p.167.

Alexander's conquests as a moral story in many of these Alexander texts, Orosius' ethical perspective recasts it dramatically as a tale of complete disaster in the service of his polemical Christian narrative focused on Rome, ending with a description of the king 'still thirsting for blood with a lust that was cruelly punished – for he drank poison that had been treacherously prepared by a servant'.[165] Orosius ends his Alexander section with an explicit comparison between the king's deeds and the current Roman situation:

> Now whatever name is given to these deeds [Alexander's conquests], be it courage or suffering, they are fewer in number now compared with those in times gone by. In either case we compare favourably with Alexander and the Persians, for if this is now to be called courage, then that of the enemy is less, if it is to be called suffering, then that of Rome is less.[166]

Here Alexander's history is given another dimension absent from the nuanced and/or more morally neutral accounts of earlier centuries. His narrative is not depicted as the implicit forerunner of Roman imperial dominance, in contrast to that of Plutarch in particular; rather, his actions are an indication of pagan depravity. For Orosius, the present is defined by being distinguished from, not elided with, the past. Yet despite this very different perspective on Alexander's narrative, it is important to note that the *Histories*' compositional techniques (stylistic and hermeneutic) are still shared with these Alexander earlier works, even if the overall interpretation is different; the text's confessional (and political) position is constructed by interpreting Alexander in moral terms, a common hermeneutic approach. It is in its theological interpretation, not its ethical *translatio*, that Orosius' *Histories* differ from their literary Alexander predecessors.

A historical work of this range, yet contained within a relatively modest seven books, and with an overtly Christian perspective was very well suited to the needs of the medieval period. The *Histories*' use of classical material for stylistic purposes also surely added to its authority and appeal, particularly in educational contexts.[167] As mentioned earlier, Orosius' *Histories* are influential for the J2 version of the *Historia de preliis* in the twelfth century, meaning that his ideas may also have affected other Alexander works.[168] Orosius, so widely read, bequeaths to the Middle Ages a narrative that contrasts with other late antique Alexander narratives in its interpretation of the Macedonian, complicating his already multifaceted reception yet further.

---

[165] *Histories* III.20.4, in *Against the Pagans*, trans. and introd. Fear, p.140.

[166] *Histories* III.20.13, in ibid., p.142.

[167] *Against the Pagans*, trans. and introd. Fear, p.11: Orosius 'uses the full repertoire of the rhetorical techniques available to late antique writers' and 'has had a good classical education'.

[168] See *History of Alexander's Battles*, trans. and introd. Telfryn Pritchard, p.8.

Conclusion

This chapter has covered a wide range of time periods and texts in seeking to answer the question posed at the beginning about medieval authors' inheritance of Alexander the Great. The subject of universal histories, exemplary tales, biographical comparisons, 'fiction', and Christian interpretation, his narrative is diverse from its origin. However, some key themes emerge. There is no such thing as a historical account in modern terms, since the earliest lost texts are written with a need to be favourable towards the king, especially those composed in his lifetime. The need to interpret Alexander in culturally relative terms, particularly during the period of Roman dominance in the later Hellenistic era, is consistent across the texts: even the *Alexander Romance*, whose stories are distant from contemporary historical realities, shows signs of this need in its Egyptian-inspired parts. Alexander's purported Greekness is also an important if often implicit feature in the works, especially the Greek-language ones of Plutarch and Arrian. This might suggest interpreting the texts not just in terms of empire but through the lens of an ethnic proto-nationalism related to the spread of Hellenism. From this perspective, Alexander's importance is as the leader of a dominant people conquering weaker, less civilized tribes in both east and west. Yet such an interpretative approach is mistaken, both because of the demonstrated complexities of the authors' relationships with Hellenism and empire and also due to Alexander's cultural and literary fluidity: it is very difficult to impose a single, clear meaning upon him because of the generic blurring in his narratives, particularly that between so-called 'fiction' and 'history'. Reading Alexander's antique accounts solely or mainly in terms of nationalistic imperialism fails to account for complex historical realities.[169] The fact that the most consistent hermeneutic tendency applied to his narratives is an ethical one is also a sign of the need to interpret the Macedonian using a range of strategies. It is true, however, that Alexander's narrative *translatio* is frequently ethical in the service of a historical-political interpretation. This approach is particularly characteristic of Diodorus, Plutarch, Arrian, Curtius Rufus, and Orosius. These texts, which differ from one another in language and date and do not directly influence one another (with the possible exception of Plutarch and Arrian), all use Alexander as a space in which to explore (or at least to hint at) contemporary cultural and historical situations, and all do so using ethics as a hermeneutic tool. Yet although historical approaches are certainly important, they do not revolve solely around ethnic nationalism: imperial ambivalences and theological *translatio*, to name only two possibilities, are more to the fore.

---

[169] For discussion of the same approach with reference to medieval studies, see Introduction, 'Language, Nation, Identity'.

In conclusion, the Alexander narratives considered here, both those inherited by the Middle Ages and also those that were known only by name (at least directly), highlight the generic, stylistic and hermeneutic variety of antique Alexander *translatio studii*, a variety that is often underpinned by an ethical approach. Although the medieval period's contexts and concerns potentially differ from those seen in these ancient texts, this variety sets the scene for similarly diverse Alexander poetics in the later era. In particular, ethical and historical interpretation, often combined, are key hermeneutic characteristics of antique Alexander material, so that reading Alexander in these ways may be an especially important precursor to his *translatio* during the Middle Ages.

2

Sic et Non: The *Alexandreis* and the *Ylias*

The previous chapter outlined Alexander the Great's literary history from the classical era to the early medieval period, demonstrating the varied interpretative possibilities in his *translatio* that arose from early on in his afterlife as a literary figure. This chapter and the one that follows it set two Alexander texts, one in Latin, one *en romanz*, in what is recoverable of their twelfth-century compositional contexts (as defined both by location and also by contemporary works) in order to investigate the range of meanings in which Alexander participates at this later moment in literary history. Looking at these texts in this comparative way will uncover the political and cultural narratives into which Alexander is co-opted. This in turn will help to reveal the part his literature plays in the construction of the literary identities, whether political, religious, or linguistic, which are important in the northern France of this period, where different dynasties, institutions, and languages meet and compete, and therefore enable us to see whether similarly complex relationships between texts and contexts exist in the Middle Ages as well as in antiquity.

In this chapter I shall consider the Latin epic poem the *Alexandreis* of Walter of Châtillon (published c. 1180) with another Latin epic, the *Ylias* of Joseph of Exeter (1183–90), providing some contemporary context. I shall argue that despite their shared erudite Latinity and classical subject matter they differ in their views of *translatio studii*, and that this difference indicates an ongoing debate about how and why it should be done, a debate that has so far mainly been identified between Latin and vernacular French texts.[1] I shall claim that this debate is a major concern of the *Alexandreis* in particular, and one that expands the poem's frame of reference beyond its immediate context. This interest in larger concerns is the basis for the idea that the *Alexandreis*, whilst implicated in local literary and political circumstances, is primarily a

---

[1] See Francine Mora, 'L'*Ylias* de Joseph d'Exeter: une réaction cléricale au *Roman de Troie* de Benoît de Saint-Maure', in *Progrès, réaction, décadence dans l'occident médiéval*, ed. E. Baumgartner and L. Harf-Lancner, Publications Romanes et Françaises, 231 (Geneva, 2013), pp.199–213, in which she argues that the Latin epic of Joseph of Exeter is a deliberate and hostile reaction to Benoît de Sainte-Maure's French text.

transnational text in its conception, allowing us to look beyond the confines of its local circumstances to set it and its impact in a wider perspective.

Literary Contexts: Exemplarity, History, and Fiction during the Twelfth Century

The twelfth century is one of the touchstone moments in Alexander's history, where ancient narratives, increasingly available to authors as classical studies flourished in newly important intellectual centres in northern France, became the focus for new literature. In this climate, reading Alexander from an ethical perspective, a widespread practice underlying historical and political *translatio* as demonstrated in the previous chapter, continued, so the presence of diverse and divergent interpretations of Alexander from antiquity are reflected and re-fracted in his twelfth-century appearances. Three occurrences are particularly relevant. In the prologue to his *Policraticus*, published probably in 1159, John of Salisbury aligns Alexander with Caesar as *exempla* of military skill:

> Quis enim Alexandros sciret aut Caesares, quis Stoicos aut Peripateticos miraretur, nisi eos insignirent monimenta scriptorum?[2]
>
> *For who would have knowledge of Alexanders or Caesars, who would won-der at the Stoics or the Peripatetics, if the witnessing of writers had not marked them out?*

John is emphasizing the importance of written records as preserving knowl-edge here, and hence Alexander as worthy of remembrance. The parallel with Caesar, however, makes this worthiness somewhat ambivalent. In Lucan's *Pharsalia* or *De bello civili*, ubiquitous in the twelfth century,[3] Caesar is de-picted as a bloody monster who causes the terrible Roman civil war. In this light, Alexander's alignment with him becomes uneasy, reflecting the prob-lematics of referring to a pagan military genius as an *exemplum*; in context, John seems to be approving of Alexander here, but it is a qualified approval. The Alexander of Gerald of Wales' *De instructione principum* (*On the In-struction of Princes*) (pre–1189; revised c. 1216) is less ambiguous, although in short succession he is both damned by his enthusiasm for worldly glory

---

[2] John of Salisbury, *Policraticus*, I-IV, ed. K. S. B. Keats-Rohan, CCCM, 118 (Turnhout, 1993), p.22.

[3] See for example Hilda Buttenweiser's enumeration of Lucan manuscripts in 'Popular Authors of the Middle Ages', *Speculum*, 17.1 (1942), pp.50–5 (p.52). The *Pharsalia's* opening lines were so commonly known that Walter of Châtillon uses them as a short-hand reference for the entire poem, as he does with the *Aeneid* and Statius's *Thebaid* (Poem 55, 'Tanto viro locuturi', 14.5 and 15.6, in *Walter of Châtillon: The Shorter Poems: Christmas Hymns, Love Lyrics, and Moral-Satirical Verse*, ed. and trans. David A. Traill, Oxford Medieval Texts (Oxford, 2013), pp.190–1).

and also depicted as a fine example of an educated king;[4] here his flexibility is exploited by the author for his instructional ends. Finally, in a less didactic context, Alexander appears in the *Architrenius* of John of Hauville (1184), where his meaning is harder to interpret:

> Hic puer imperii cupidus ludebat, alumnus
> Martis, Alexander, sceptrique infudit amorem
> Ambicio nutrix, totumque armavit in orbem
> Precipites animos, tenerisque induruit annis
> Bella pati, votumque duos extendit in ortus.[5]

> *Here there played a boy, greedy for dominion: Alexander, the ward of Mars. Ambition, his nurse, instilled the desire to rule, armed his impulsive spirit against all the world, steeled his tender youth to the hardships of war, and stretched his aspirations to the two horizons.*

Although the only explicitly negative phrase present in these lines is 'imperii cupidus', and the rest of Alexander's attributes could be thought of as positive and appropriate to a youthful prince or king, the lines occur during a long description of the Mountain of Ambition, and are hence easily read as negative in context. Yet the mountain itself is described as beautiful, with bitter and sweet flowers growing together (IV, chapters 2–5): it is a mixed place, where Ambition is said only to inflame the noblest hearts (chapter 7). Like the mountain itself, Alexander is a varied character, noble yet driven by ambition that stretches to encompass the entire world. This makes him not so much ambivalent as capable of a range of meanings depending on context, linking him conceptually with the explicitly exemplary depictions of John of Salisbury and Gerald of Wales. These three instances, ranging from the middle of the twelfth to the beginning of the thirteenth century, demonstrate the wide range of interpretation that Alexander encompasses. A political treatise, a didactic manual, and a generically indistinct but satirical poem, they also show the appeal of Alexander across the literary spectrum.

This provides a specific background for Alexander literature, and the *Alexandreis* in particular, but we need to consider other literary contexts to take into account additional trends that may also be important. One of these is the interest in historiography. The twelfth century is a period in which historiography flourishes across northern France and its environs. The early part of the century sees historians like Abbot Suger of St Denis and Odo of Deuil (followed by Rigord of St Denis) creating narratives focused on Capetian *gesta regum*, while during the same period William of Malmesbury, Henry of Huntingdon,

---

4 Gerald of Wales, preface, *De instructione principum*, translated as *Concerning the Instruction of Princes* by J. Stevenson (London, 1858: repr. 1991), p.7, p.9.
5 John of Hauville, *Architrenius*, trans. and introd. Winthrop Wetherbee, Cambridge Medieval Classics, 3 (Cambridge, 1994), v.111–15.

and Orderic Vitalis were engaged in 'enterprises of historical assimilation', in which previous histories were amalgamated and brought up to contemporary times.[6] These narratives often take one of their starting points from classical history, connecting the antique period with the contemporary medieval era.[7] The writing of history is therefore intimately bound up with the classical past, an unsurprising factor during the 'Renaissance of the twelfth century', but one that should be highlighted since it provides a potential model for the writing of Alexander in a different mode from the exemplary one discussed above. However, the analysis of antique Alexander texts in chapter 1 demonstrated that ethics and historiography are intimately linked, warning against the idea of easily separable 'historical' and 'exemplary' interpretations.

This medieval interest in historiography is paralleled by the rise of 'fiction', a situation also reminiscent of antique Alexander narratives. In particular, classical stories that were held to contain historical truth were adapted *en romanz*, probably initially for courts, in order to provide a myth of antique origins.[8] The resulting romances, *Thèbes*, *Eneas*, and *Troie*, blur boundaries between the writing of history, fiction, and classical narratives, questioning what it means to (re-)create all of these; once again, the complex relationship between history and fiction in the Middle Ages has to some extent been anticipated by antique Alexander narratives. The creation of twelfth-century fiction is thus also bound up with historiography, and, most obviously in the case of the *romans d'antiquité*, often with the classical past. These factors are vital for Alexander, since as a historical figure from the antique period with an already flourishing legendary he can be located at the crossing points between all three. Not simply an exemplary figure, therefore, he is an integral part of

---

[6] Henry of Huntingdon, *Historia Anglorum: The History of the English People*, ed. and trans. Diana Greenway, Oxford Medieval Texts (Oxford, 1996), p.lviii.

[7] Henry of Huntingdon discusses the Roman invasions of Britain and also includes *laudes* of Roman emperors from Paul the Deacon's work (*Historia Anglorum*, pp.lxxvii–lxxviii); Geoffrey of Monmouth, although not usually classed as a historian, claims that the Trojan Brutus settled Britain (*Historia regum Britanniae*, I.16: trans. Lewis Thorpe as *The History of the Kings of Britain* (London, 1966), p.71). Rigord of St Denis claims in his *Gesta Philippi Augusti* (chapters 37–9) that the Franks are descended from the Trojans (*Gesta Philippi Augusti*, in *Oeuvres de Rigord et de Guillaume le Breton*, ed. H. François Delaborde, 3 vols (Paris, 1882–85), I, pp.53–64).

[8] D. H. Green, *The Beginnings of Medieval Romance: Fact and Fiction, 1150–1220*, Cambridge Studies in Medieval Literature, 47 (Cambridge, 2002), pp.153–61, discusses Benoît de Sainte-Maure's *Roman de Troie* and the anonymous *Roman d'Eneas* from this perspective. *Troie* and *Eneas* are thought to have been connected with Henry II's court, although any precise patronage is unknown. On issues of Henry II's courtly patronage, see Peter Dronke, 'Peter of Blois and Poetry at the Court of Henry II', *Mediaeval Studies*, 38 (1976), pp.185–235 (pp.186–7), and the more recent and corrective view of Karen Broadhurst, 'Henry II of England and Eleanor of Aquitaine: Patrons of Literature in French?', *Viator*, 27 (1996), pp.53–84.

the debate about the relationship of both *ficta* and *facta* to *res verae* that such texts create.[9]

The examples of John of Salisbury, Gerald of Wales, and the *Architrenius*, as well as the convergence of history, fiction, and classical narratives in the person of Alexander, show that the Macedonian was an important presence in the pedagogical, didactic, and romance-focused literary landscapes of the twelfth century. This aligns him in particular with the narratives of Troy and Rome. However, in contrast to these narratives, Alexander is not the subject of a definitive epic poem or account dating from the classical or late antique period, as mentioned in the introduction; the antique works of chapter 1 describing his adventures are not prestigious verse narratives but often stylistically mundane prose accounts (in part because many of these works present themselves as history). This absence is an important point that may explain why French Alexander works start to appear early in the twelfth century, before the *romans d'antiquité*, and also why Walter of Châtillon felt able to compose his *Alexandreis*; without the potentially constricting influence of a high-status Latin epic, authors had greater freedom to adapt, rearrange, versify, and otherwise perform *translatio studii*. Alexander literature, in comparison with the Troy and Rome narratives, is a less defined and thus more creative arena in which to explore the literary debates of the day.

Social and Intellectual Networks

These literary developments – the use of Alexander in texts, newly flourishing historiography, interest in fiction – are part of a mutual intellectual landscape shared via networks of people, institutions, and texts, as described in the introduction. This landscape did not necessarily map on to the political divisions of northern France, as the known details of these networks highlight their transnational nature. Authors and readers were responsible for the spread of ideas not just between the acknowledged intellectual centres in northern France like Chartres, Orléans, and Paris,[10] or between monastic institutions, but also

---

[9] Isidore of Seville's widely known definition reads 'historiae sunt res verae quae factae sunt', cited in Green, *Beginnings of Romance*, p.135.

[10] Chartres is known for its interest in and development of neo-Platonic ideas, although the extent of this is questioned by Peter Dronke, 'New Approaches to the School of Chartres', in *Intellectuals and Poets in Medieval Europe*, Storia e letteratura: raccolta di studi e testi, 183 (Rome, 1992), pp.15–40, who disagrees with Richard Southern's assessment that the importance of Chartres as an intellectual centre has been overrated; see the latter's chapter 'The Schools of Paris and the School of Chartres', in *Renaissance and Renewal in the Twelfth Century*, ed. Robert L. Benson, Giles Constable, and Carol D. Lanham (Oxford, 1982), pp.113–37, as well as *Platonism, Scholastic Method, and the School of Chartres*, Stenton Lecture 1978 (Reading, 1979). Orléans was renowned for its commentaries on classical authors, as shown by R. H. Rouse, '*Florilegia*

between different political and geographical areas. John of Salisbury and Peter of Blois are examples of this transnationalism, moving between ecclesiastical and secular administrative posts in France, England, and areas such as Sicily.[11] John of Salisbury's career is particularly illustrative: he moved from study in Paris and possibly Chartres to working as the secretary of two archbishops of Canterbury, first Theobald and then Becket. Exiled with Becket to northern France in the 1160s, he was in Canterbury when the archbishop was killed in 1170 and ultimately became bishop of Chartres in 1176.[12] As archbishop's secretary, he went on several missions to Rome and was involved with the dispute between Becket and Henry II. Although he seems always to have worked within ecclesiastical contexts, his letters demonstrate the extent to which these overlapped with more secular regal and ducal courts.[13] His life highlights the secondary importance of national boundaries (between England and Capetian France, for example) in comparison to these ecclesiastical contexts.

As well as demonstrating the transnational nature of these networks, John of Salisbury and Peter of Blois also show how extensive they were, linking academic centres, monasteries, regal courts, the papacy, and others. They also connected languages, providing opportunities for literary interactions that often come as a surprise to modern readers. The official ecclesiastical correspondence of John of Salisbury, a Latin epic such as the *Alexandreis*, and the romances of Chrétien de Troyes seem to be divided by genre, language, and subject, but in fact all three could easily have been experienced together, since all can be connected via one such network focused on the court of

---

and Latin Classical Authors in Twelfth- and Thirteenth-Century Orléans', *Viator*, 10 (1979), pp.131–60. Paris was a major centre not just of the *trivium* and *quadrivium* but of advances in logic and dialectical process, as Peter Abelard's admittedly biased and bitter picture of the Parisian schools in the early part of the century shows (*Historia calamitatum*, ed. J. Monfrin (Paris, 1967), especially lines 31–163 (pp.63–7)).

[11] For Peter of Blois' biography, see John D. Cotts, 'Peter of Blois and the Problem of the "Court" in the Late Twelfth Century', *Anglo-Norman Studies*, 27 (2005), pp.68–84 (pp.72–3). There is an unresolved question over his identity: see Richard Southern, 'The Necessity for Two Peters of Blois', in *Intellectual Life in the Middle Ages: Essays Presented to Margaret Gibson*, ed. Lesley Smith and Benedicta Ward (London, 1991), p.103–18.

[12] On John's life, see John of Salisbury, *Policraticus*, ed. and trans. C. J. Nederman, Cambridge Texts in the History of Political Thought (Cambridge, 1990), pp.xvi–xviii.

[13] See for example the long letter John wrote to Becket in early 1164, when John was travelling around northern France soliciting support for Becket's cause against Henry II. Although it concerns ecclesiastical business, the letter gives details of John's conversation with Louis VII about his daughter Margaret and his impressions of Paris. It is edited as Letter 136 in *The Letters of John of Salisbury*, ed. W. J. Millor and H. E. Butler, rev. C. N. L. Brooke, 2 vols (Oxford, 1955 and 1979), II: *The Later Letters (1163–1180)* (1979), pp.2–15 (pp.6–7).

Champagne.[14] Linguistically and generically diverse works came into contact through these networks, widening the impact of the 'twelfth-century Renaissance' from the more rarified contexts of universities and cathedral schools towards more socially, culturally, and linguistically hybrid communities. Benoît de Sainte-Maure, author of the *Roman de Troie* (c. 1165), is a good example of this linguistic and intellectual hybridity: a Latinate clerk composing in flamboyantly descriptive French, he adds to his romance accounts of Jason and Medea, Troilus and Briseida, and Achilles and Polyxena that are probably inspired by Ovid's works, although he claims to use the Latin narrative of Dares as his source.[15] The facts provide an instructive picture of how interconnected Latin and French could be, in contrast to modern ideas about linguistic and cultural separation.[16]

Transnational, translingual, transcontinental: these networks of people, places, courts, and institutions operated across northern France and its neighbours, creating literary cultures that crossed the boundaries of nation and

---

[14] John of Salisbury probably means Walter of Châtillon when he refers to 'magistri Galteri, clerici domini Remensis' ('master Walter, cleric of the lord of Reims') in Letter 167 in *The Letters of John of Salisbury*, ed. Millor and. Butler, rev. Brooke, II: *The Later Letters (1163–1180)* (1979), pp.94–5; on this identification see *Galteri de Castellione Alexandreis*, ed. M. L. Colker (Padua, 1978), pp.xvi–xvii. Walter's connection with Champagne is claimed, perhaps too strongly, by Traill, *Shorter Poems*, p.xv, p.xvii; a more concrete link is a note in an early manuscript of Walter's short poems, Oxford, Bodleian Library, MS Bodley 603, which ascribes one work 'ad comitem henricum' (see John R. Williams, 'The Quest for the Author of the *Moralium dogma philosophorum*, 1931–1956', *Speculum*, 32.4 (1957), pp.736–47 (p.741, n.50) and John F. Benton, 'The Court of Champagne as a Literary Center', *Speculum*, 36.4 (1961), pp.551–91 (pp.571–2)). John, Walter, and the court of count Henry I 'the Liberal' of Champagne are hence connected by these literary materials.

[15] See *Troie*, Prologue, 87–144, in *Le Roman de Troie par Benoît de Sainte-Maure*, ed. Léopold Constans, 6 vols (Paris, 1904–12), I. Of the three *romans d'antiquité*, it is inevitably the *Eneas* whose Ovidianism (in newly created erotic passages between Aeneas and Lavinia) has been studied most; see for example Laura Ashe, *History and Fiction in England, 1066–1200*, Cambridge Studies in Medieval Literature, 68 (Cambridge, 2007), pp.124–44. *Troie*'s Ovidianism has received less attention, but the principle of addition of erotic scenes not in its source material to the narrative is the same as that found in *Eneas*. *Troie* may well have been dedicated to, if not commissioned by, Eleanor of Aquitaine; see Tamara O'Callaghan, 'Tempering Scandal: Eleanor of Aquitaine and Benoît de Sainte-Maure's *Roman de Troie*', in *Eleanor of Aquitaine: Lord and Lady*, ed. Bonnie Wheeler and John Carmi Parsons (Basingstoke, 2002), pp.301–17. Benoît de Sainte-Maure was also engaged to write a work about the history of Normandy by Henry II, the *Chronique de ducs de Normandie*; see Dronke, 'Peter of Blois and Poetry', p.187.

[16] Critical literature on Alexander the Great provides clear examples of this separation; see for example the studies within these modern parameters by David Maddox and Sara Sturm-Maddox, (eds), *The Medieval French Alexander* (Albany, NY, 2002), and Gerrit H. V. Bunt, *Alexander the Great in the Literature of Medieval Britain*, Mediaevalia Groningana, 14 (Groningen, 1994).

language that often define modern scholarship.[17] Twelfth-century Alexander texts are therefore part of a multilingual and multicultural literary landscape, which, although not always visible immediately within the texts themselves, can be established by examining these social and intellectual networks. The particular network on which this chapter focuses connects the *Alexandreis* with Joseph of Exeter's *Ylias*, and involves the city of Reims. Although it concerns Latin epic texts, its literary implications relate also to vernacular works, which the following chapter will consider.

The *Alexandreis* of Walter of Châtillon

The *Alexandreis* is a Latin epic in ten books of hexameters that provides a narrative of Alexander's life from his early youth until his death, covering his tutoring by Aristotle, his battles against the Persian Darius and the Indian Porus, and his intention to conquer the known world.[18] Its classicizing Latinity, drawing on Virgil, Lucan, and Statius in particular, ensured that it was a frequent presence in schools, as many of its around two hundred extant manuscripts attest;[19] but it was also important for vernacular literatures across Europe, especially in the thirteenth century, when it was used by Rudolf von Ems in his Middle High German work on Alexander (1230s and 1240s) and in the Spanish *Libro del Alexandre* (after 1180 and before 1250), as well as in French and English texts.[20] Its immediate impact at the point of dissemination in spring 1180,[21] however, has not been examined in detail, so that its primary receptions and influences remain largely mysterious. We know that it may have influenced a trend for classicizing epic in 1180s France, but this hypothesis has not been much researched, and the work's possible interactions with

---

[17] See the introduction to this book, and Elizabeth M. Tyler's lucid analysis of this situation and the problems it poses for researchers in her introduction to *Conceptualizing Multilingualism in Medieval England, c. 800–c. 1250*, ed. Tyler, Studies in the Early Middle Ages, 27 (Turnhout, 2012), pp.1–13, especially pp.3–7.

[18] See appendix 2 for a more detailed narrative synopsis.

[19] For the most complete list of MSS, see *Alexandreis*, ed. Colker, pp.xxxiii–xxxviii.

[20] *German Literature of the High Middle Ages*, ed. Will Hasty (Rochester, 2006), pp.225–31, and Charles F. Fraker, *The* Libro del Alexandre: *Medieval Epic and Silver Latin*, North Carolina Studies in the Romance Languages and Literatures, 245 (Chapel Hill, NC, 1993).

[21] The poem's dating is the subject of debate. The two options are 1178–82 (the traditional dating) or before 1176; see the useful summary of these positions given by Maura K. Lafferty in *Walter of Châtillon's* Alexandreis: *Epic and the Problem of Historical Understanding*, Publications of the Journal of Medieval Latin, 2 (Turnhout, 1998), pp.183–9. Recently the 1178–82 option has been refined to the spring of 1180 by Neil Adkin, 'The Date of Walter of Châtillon's *Alexandreis* Once Again', *Classica et mediaevalia*, 59 (2008), pp.201–11.

vernacular texts even less so.[22] The *Alexandreis*'s range of meanings hence remains to be identified, partly because of this lack of critical engagement with the poem's context, but in addition because the poem's obvious debt to the classics obscures its relationships with both its Latin and also its vernacular contemporaries, making it seem opaque and difficult to interpret from a comparative perspective.

The poem's author, Walter of Châtillon, was a cleric working as secretary for the archbishop of Reims, William of Champagne or 'the White Hands', when it was composed and published. We know very little about Walter's life, and what information there is mostly derives from *vitae* in manuscripts that postdate the twelfth century.[23] It seems likely that he experienced a similar education to John of Salisbury and Peter of Blois, potentially spending time studying at Paris and Bologna and teaching at a school in Châtillon-sur-Marne before working for William of Champagne, to whom the *Alexandreis* is dedicated. Although this dedication connects the poem to the archbishop, the passage in which it occurs forms a separate section in the text from the narrative, so could easily have been added after the main text's composition; this makes the patron–poet relationship more distant than in other texts of a similar date, such as Chrétien de Troyes' *Lancelot* or *Le Chevalier de la charrette*,[24] and indicates that other factors, not just patronage, may be relevant in contextualizing the poem. William's situation is nonetheless important for the *Alexandreis*'s frame of reference: he was the most senior ecclesiastic in France, ruler of the city of Reims, brother of the powerful duke Henry I 'the Liberal' of Champagne, and uncle of the young Capetian king Philip II 'Augustus', whom the archbishop crowned on 1 November 1179.[25]

---

[22] Jean-Yves Tilliette raises the possibility that the *Ylias* is a reaction to the *Alexandreis* in *L'Iliade: épopée du XIIᵉ siècle sur la guerre de Troie*, trad. and notes under direction of Francine Mora, introd. Jean-Yves Tilliette, Miroir du Moyen Âge (Turnhout, 2003), pp.13–18. On the interaction of the *Alexandreis* with contemporary Latin and vernacular texts, see Venetia Bridges, 'Writing the Past: The "Classical Tradition" in the Poetry of Walter of Châtillon and Contemporary Literature, 1160–1200' (unpublished PhD thesis, University of Cambridge, 2012), chapters 4 and 5.

[23] For the different *vitae*, see *Alexandreis*, ed. Colker, pp.xii–xiii, R. de Cesare, *Glosse latine e antico-francesi all'*Alexandreis *di Gautier de Châtillon*, Pubblicazioni della Università Cattolica del Sacro Cuore, n.s., 39 (Milan, 1951), Traill, *Shorter Poems*, pp.xi–xxi, and Bridges, 'Writing the Past', pp.21–9.

[24] Chrétien claims that his patron, Marie de Champagne, provided him not just with the commission for *Lancelot* but defined the material of the poem and its treatment; see Prologue, 24–5, in Chrétien de Troyes, *Oeuvres complètes*, ed. Daniel Poirion (Paris, 1994).

[25] William's life and career are described by J. Mathorez, *Guillaume aux Blanches-Mains, évêque de Chartres* (Chartres, 1911) and Ludwig Falkenstein, 'Guillaume aux Blanches Mains, archevêque de Reims et légat du siège apostolique (1176–1202)', *Revue d'histoire de l'église de France*, 91:226 (2005), pp.5–25. His literary interests are identified by John R. Williams, 'William of the White Hands and Men of Letters', in *Anniversary*

These positions and relationships place the *Alexandreis* within a context of ecclesiastical and political power that may seem to negate the comment above that the poem is difficult to interpret in contemporary terms. Certainly there has been a critical tendency, dating from the earliest book-length study of the poem by Heinrich Christensen in 1905, to read the *Alexandreis* as providing a model in its depiction of Alexander for the young Philip Augustus, the bright young hope of Capetian France who was nicknamed 'Dieu-donné' at his birth in 1165.[26] Such an identification is plausible. However, a straightforward literary use of Alexander as *exemplum* and *speculum principis* in this sense is problematic, not only because of Alexander's varied meanings in a didactic context, but also because of the literary complexities of the late twelfth century, namely the historical and fictional phenomena and re-creation of the classics surveyed earlier. The most recent study by David Townsend takes this line, highlighting the *Alexandreis*'s complexity with reference to its interpretative history in manuscript commentaries; he claims that the poem is 'marked … by a dialogic complexity', 'narrative undecidability', and is 'hermeneutically decentred',[27] leading to an early need for extended glossing. These intriguing phrases indicate that the *Alexandreis*'s complexity does not begin with the poem's receptions, but is inherent to the text itself. Exploring Townsend's idea to its logical end suggests that drawing straightforward parallels between Alexander's meanings in the *Alexandreis* and external events and characters is likely to be troubled by the poem's 'hermeneutic decentering'. The study that follows will consider the poem's poetics and also its historical contexts in order to see whether the *Alexandreis* is indeed a straightforward *speculum principis* text, or whether it has a more complex relationship with literature and history.

Essays in Medieval History by Students of Charles Homer Haskins, ed. C. H. Taylor (Boston, 1929), pp.365–87.

[26] Peter Riga's poem 'Quando fuit natus' describes the joy at Philip's birth in 1165; see William Chester Jordan, '"Quando fuit natus": Interpreting the Birth of Philip Augustus', in *The Work of Jacques le Goff and the Challenge of Medieval History*, ed. M. Rubin (Woodbridge, 1997), pp.171–88 (p.174). The identification of Philip with the Alexander of the *Alexandreis* is made by Heinrich Christensen, *Das Alexanderlied Walters von Châtillon* (Halle, 1905), p.10, and Adkin, 'The Date of Walter of Châtillon's *Alexandreis* Once Again', especially p.208. Adkin also makes this identification based on a line from the proem in 'The Proem of Walter of Châtillon's *Alexandreis*: "Si … nostros uixisset in annos"', *Medium Ævum*, 60 (1991), pp.207–15 (p.210, p.213). The most recent monograph on the *Alexandreis*, Lafferty's *Epic and the Problem of Historical Understanding*, is more subtle in its approach but still ultimately reads the work as exemplary, aimed at William of Champagne (pp.58–9).

[27] David Townsend, 'Paratext, Ambiguity, and Interpretative Foreclosure in Manuscripts of Walter of Châtillon's *Alexandreis*', *New Medieval Literatures*, 14 (2012), pp.21–61 (p.25, p.43, p.48).

The Alexandreis *as* Speculum Principis

'Magnus in exemplo est', 'the Great One is an example'.[28] The end of the *Alexandreis* appears to give a simple answer to the question of how far it is to be read as an exemplary *speculum principis* text, despite Townsend's assertions of complexity. However, the fact that the poem is a successful stylistic imitation of classical models should give modern readers pause, since it indicates a complex engagement with antique past and medieval present, an engagement that is likely to render the poem multivocal and subtle, or a work of 'dialogic complexity', to use Townsend's phrase. This would trouble the clear parallels between its main character and external events suggested by 'the Great One is an example'. The section that is usually read as a paean to Philip Augustus, and thus to William of Champagne, exemplifies this issue, since it appears to be a straightforward passage of praise, but is also one in which classical models make contemporary parallels complex.

> Numquam tam celebri iactatrix Roma tryumpho
> Victorem mirata suum tam diuite luxu
> Excepit, seu cum fuso sub Leucade Cesar
> Antonio sexti mutauit nomina mensis
> Lactandasque dedit ydris Cleopatra papillas
> Seu post Emathias acies cum sanguine Magni
> Iam satur irrupit Tarpeiam Iulius arcem,
> Et merito: nam si regum miranda recordans
> Laudibus et titulis cures attollere iustis,
> Si fide recolas quam raro milite contra
> Victores mundi tenero sub flore iuuentae
> Quanta sit aggressus Macedo, quam tempore paruo
> Totus Alexandri genibus se fuderit orbis,
> Tota ducum series, uel quos Hyspana poesis
> Grandiloquo modulata stilo uel Claudius altis
> Versibus insignit, respectu principis huius
> Plebs erit ut pigeat tanto splendore Lucanum
> Cesareum cecinisse melos Romaeque ruinam
> Et Macedum claris succumbat Honorius armis.
> Si gemitu commota pio uotisque suorum
> Flebilibus diuina daret clementia talem
> Francorum regem, toto radiaret in orbe
> Haut mora uera fides, et nostris fracta sub armis
> Parthia baptismo renouari posceret ultro,
> Queque diu iacuit effusis menibus alta
> Ad nomen Christi Kartago resurgeret, et quas
> Sub Karolo meruit Hyspania soluere penas
> Exigerent uexilla crucis, gens omnis et omnis

---

[28] *Alexandreis*, ed. Colker, x.448.

Lingua Ihesum caneret et non inuita subiret
Sacrum sub sacro Remorum presule fontem.[29]

Never did boastful Rome receive her victor
with adulation of so great a triumph,
not when at Leucas Caesar struck down Antony,
and Cleopatra's breasts gave suck to asps –
thereby he changed the sixth month's name – nor when
the blood of mighty Pompey sated Julius,
who went forth from Emathia's battlefield
to break Tarpeius' citadel. And rightly:
for if you recollect the wondrous deeds
of kings, and praise them justly by their titles;
if you recall with what a meagre host
the Macedonian approached such deeds,
in flower of tender youth, against world conquerors,
and in how brief a time the whole world lay
before the knees of Alexander – then
that whole array of dukes will seem mere rabble,
whether the men the Spanish poet sings
with high-flown melody, or those whom Claudian
distinguishes by his lofty verses' strains.
Lucan would blush to sing his victory-song
for Caesar and the fall of Rome; Honorius
would yield to Macedonia's bright arms.
If pious prayers and tearful lamentation
moved mercy from on high to grant the Franks
a king like this, the True Faith would shine forth
unhindered through the earth, and Parthia,
broken by our arms, would beg unbidden
for baptism's renewal, while high Carthage,
which long lay ruined, soon would rise again
at mention of Christ's name. The penalties
that Spain deserved to pay under great Charles
would be exacted by the cross's banners,
and every race and tongue would sing of Jesus,
and freely would approach the holy font
under Reims' holy bishop's tutelage.[30]

This passage occurs at the end of book v, the midpoint of the *Alexandre-is*. Alexander enters Babylon in triumph, supposedly more impressive than

---

[29] *Alexandreis*, ed. Colker, v.491–520. All subsequent textual references are to this edition.
[30] The translation is by David Townsend, *The* Alexandreis *of Walter of Châtillon: A Twelfth-Century Epic* (Philadelphia, PA, 1996), pp.94–5 (570–604). Townsend's translation uses different line numbers from Colker's edition; the former are given in brackets, with page numbers.

any other ancient conqueror, after his defeat of the mighty Persian emperor Darius. Yet in order to read this as triumphalist we have to ignore the way in which the poet deploys his classical comparisons. What seems like a paean to Alexander in the first few lines ('Numquam tam celebri iactatrix Roma tryumpho/Victorem ... excepit', 'Never did boastful Rome receive her victor with ... so great a triumph') is made problematic by the examples used to illustrate his successes, which are Julius Caesar's triumphs over Antony and Pompey. These of course were victories over other Romans in civil wars,[31] hardly events of which 'boastful Rome' should be proud. Alexander's success here is being tainted by association with Caesar, the anti-hero of Lucan's poem, meaning that his achievement becomes subject to implicit criticism. A similar criticism is found later at 504–9, when it is claimed that other poets will fall silent at Alexander's deeds in comparison with their heroes' actions. Setting aside Walter's poetic self-aggrandizement, it seems that Alexander's triumph is so spectacular that it silences the authoritative voices of the classics; but if Lucan, Statius, Claudian, and Virgil are absent, then the entire point of the comparison with them collapses. The idea of such giants of the mental landscape of the twelfth century losing their authoritative status at the hands of the notorious Alexander is almost comic in its hyperbole. Yet with the silencing of these figures, a darker picture emerges. Alexander overcomes all epic precedent to surpass the triumphs of Caesar, the figure of Lucan's exaggerated loathing as responsible for a bloody civil war. The implications of Alexander's triumph over not just Persia but the *auctores* themselves are not encouraging for an exemplary *speculum principis* reading.

Given this context, the wish for 'talem/Francorum regem', 'such a king of the Franks', is problematic rather than encomiastic. Alexander, having defeated all classical precedents with his military might in a manner that the passage suggests is ominous, is now supposedly an example for a Christian king.[32] This appears to be supported by the poet's claim that if Alexander's equal existed today, the Christian faith would rule the world (510ff). However, these

---

[31] The presence of Cleopatra at v.495 is not a shift in focus away from the Roman civil wars, but serves to emphasize the degeneracy of Caesar and Anthony, both of whom had had sexual relationships with her, as well as to remind the reader of her involvement in the conflicts.

[32] Claudia Wiener, *Proles vaesana Philippi totius malleus orbis: Die Alexandreis des Walter von Châtillon und ihre Neudeutung von Lucans Pharsalia im Sinne des typologischen Geschichtsverständnisses* (Munich, 2001), reads Alexander as a 'sub lege' *exemplum* for Philip Augustus, pp.91–109. See also Maura K. Lafferty, 'Walter of Châtillon's *Alexandreis*', in *A Companion to Alexander Literature in the Middle Ages*, ed. Z. David Zuwiyya, Brill's Companions to the Christian Tradition, 29 (Leiden, 2011), pp.177–99 (p.199). See also Christensen, *Alexanderlied*, p.10, and Adkin, 'The Date of Walter of Châtillon's *Alexandreis* Once Again', especially p.208; both view the king described in this passage as Philip Augustus.

lines are an elaborate wish, governed grammatically by an emphatic 'si' and verbs in the subjunctive mood, suggesting that this hyperbole ('gens omnis et omnis/Lingua Ihesum caneret', 'every race and tongue would sing of Jesus') is more a wistful longing than an achieved or achievable desire.[33] The failure of the Second Crusade (1145–49) looms in the background here, in which there had certainly been no 'second Alexander' taking part, despite it being led by kings, in particular Louis VII, Philip's father.[34] The passage's wistful longing rather suggests that there is no extant king to achieve such a goal. The supposed referee of these lines, Philip Augustus, was young (fifteen in 1180) and untried, and these lines underline that fact with their subjunctive mood.

Interpreting this complex passage as subtle doubt disguised as praise is supported by the poem's date. In the spring of 1180, the probable date when the work began to circulate, Philip quarrelled with his uncle William and his other Blois relatives to the extent that they were excluded from his betrothal and marriage to Isabella of Hainault, an extremely public rebuff.[35] Oblique doubt, even criticism, of Philip, presented as praise, would have been highly appropriate at this time of tension. Walter's elusiveness and subtlety here has a whiff of practical diplomacy about it, since for less quick minds this passage would seem to be one of straightforward praise, whereas the highly educated clerics of the archbishop's *familia* would perceive its *sic et non* nature and grasp its implied criticism.[36] Poetry here provides a space for both interpretations, making the *Alexandreis* at this point a political work that seems to celebrate the king of France while suggesting the internal quarrels that were occurring.

In combination with the problematics of the classical parallels adduced here, this desire for 'such a king' makes the passage difficult to read in terms of kingly Christian exemplarity. Yet the passage also deliberately appears to construct such a reading using the grandiose classical *exempla* and desire for Christian expansionism; it is only through close attention to detail that we perceive its true *sic et non* character. Townsend's phrase 'dialogic complexity'

---

[33] Adkin suggests in 'The Date of Walter of Châtillon's *Alexandreis* Again' (*Bollettino di studi latini*, 23:2 (1993), pp.359–64) that the use of the subjunctive in encomiastic poetry is a convention, expressing 'in hypothetical terms what was already acknowledged to be the case', and cites Horace, *Odes*, II, in support of this (p.362). Yet the desires in this passage are manifestly not accomplished by 1180, so the poet is surely expressing hope, not concrete achievement.

[34] On the Second Crusade, see Jonathan Phillips, *The Second Crusade: Extending the Frontiers of Christendom* (New Haven, NJ, 2007); particularly revealing is the chapter on the Crusade's aftermath, pp.269–79.

[35] Adkin, 'The Date of Walter of Châtillon's *Alexandreis* Once Again', p.209.

[36] Peter Dronke uses this phrase to describe Walter of Châtillon's work in 'Peter of Blois and Poetry', claiming that his work is marked by 'ambivalence' and 'a continual embodiment of that *sic et non* which characterizes not only Abelard's contradictions and inner tensions but also the outlook of many of his most sensitive successors', concluding that '*sic et non* seems to have pervaded all his thought' (p.189, p.190).

sums up its poetics accurately. If we place a significant emphasis upon this passage, which its location at the midpoint of the poem encourages, then what this analysis highlights is a difficult and subtle exploitation of the different perspectives available regarding Alexander, an exploitation paradoxically using the poetics of exemplarity to undermine that very practice.

This *sic et non* discussion of Alexander can be identified elsewhere in the poem. At the start of book VI, Alexander is described as 'luxu Babilonis et auro/Corruptum', 'corrupted by Babylon's luxury and gold' (capitula, 1–2) and in the passage immediately following the poet hints that he would have ruled the whole earth if he had continued as he had begun.[37] Yet this criticism is juxtaposed with a description of Alexander's achievements as a wise ruler, and the corrupting luxury of Babylon later appears to have more effect upon his troops than upon Alexander himself.[38] The reader is here faced with two overlapping descriptions of Alexander: the wise ruler who dispenses justice and the man appreciative of Oriental licentiousness. Whilst the poet has made Alexander more praiseworthy than his material source, Quintus Curtius Rufus,[39] claiming at the start that his fame should be greater than that of Roman deeds, by the end of the poem he is 'demens' and insatiable.[40] This is not simply a rake's progress, as these conflicting, or at least overlapping, descriptions are a feature of the poetics throughout.[41] The seemingly clear-cut phrase 'Magnus in exemplo est', rather than simply being a 'cautionary exemplum',[42] actually gives rise to further questions: does it refer to the immediate context, in which Alexander is supposedly an example of the futility of worldly glory,

[37] *Alexandreis*, ed. Colker, VI.8–10, 'Rex erit ille tuus a quo se posceret omnis/Rege regi tellus si perduraret in illa/Indole uirtutum qua ceperat ire potestas.'

[38] *Alexandreis*, ed. Colker, VI.20–32.

[39] Quintus Curtius Rufus, *Historiae Alexandri Magni*, ed. Carlo M. Lucarini, Bibliotheca Scriptorum Graecorum et Romanorum Teubneriana (Berlin, 2009). See for example the telling phrase 'Fortuna quos uni sibi credere coegit magna ex parte avidos gloriae magis quam capaces facit' when Alexander consults the oracle of Jupiter Ammon in Egypt at IV.7.29–32. See also the analysis of Walter's presentation of Alexander as more positive than Curtius Rufus's depiction in R. Telfryn Pritchard, 'Gautier de Châtillon's *Alexandreis* as an Historical Epic', *Bien Dire et Bien Aprandre*, 7 (1989), pp.35–49 (p.40).

[40] *Alexandreis*, ed. Colker, I.5–11 and X.191–5.

[41] See also I.284–348, in which Alexander is asked to spare Thebes but instead razes it to the ground and kills every citizen. Whilst depicting the terror of the city's fall and Alexander's wrath, as well as the plea from Cleades, the poet also claims that Alexander is right to be angry because the city resisted him, thus making it difficult to read him as an example of vice.

[42] This is Dennis M. Kratz's phrase, who considers that here 'Walter stresses the limitations of Alexander's greatness' in his reading of the *Alexandreis* as 'mocking' epic, but his assumption that this can therefore be extended as an interpretative tool throughout the poem is flawed because of Alexander's multiple frames of reference; see Kratz, *Mocking Epic: Waltharius, Alexandreis, and the Problem of Christian Heroism*, Studia Humanitatis (Milan, 1980), pp.78–9.

or is it a broader hermeneutic? As we have seen, the *sic et non* poetics regarding the figure of Alexander suggests that this uncertainty is deliberate.

The idea of Alexander as a kingly *exemplum*, in terms of simplistic positive or negative readings, is not tenable as an interpretative key for the entirety of the *Alexandreis*, particularly with reference to the idea that he is supposed to be read throughout as instructive for Philip Augustus. If exemplarity in this straightforward sense is problematic, then questions arise concerning the poem's interpretation: within what framework/s can we read it? How does it relate to contemporary literary and political contexts? What follows is an attempt to examine some of these contexts, and to see whether they are instructive for understanding the poem's range of meanings. I shall focus particularly on the poem's historiography, since its relationships with contemporary literature and politics, both important intellectual and social contexts, are refracted through a variety of historical perspectives. In addition, the intimate relationship between twelfth-century historiography and fiction, and Alexander's position between both discourses, suggests contemporary literary interests in the writing of history that may be important for the *Alexandreis*.

Christian Epic?

One important historiographical narrative much used by twelfth-century authors is naturally that of Christian salvation, which would have been particularly suitable for the *familia* of an archbishop such as William of Champagne. This narrative was often found at the top of a hierarchy of different kinds of historical narrative, since it was the most prestigious.[43] Lafferty perceives this kind of historiographical pluralism in the *Alexandreis*: 'Walter repeatedly forces his readers to recognize that they must choose between historiographies.'[44] In her analysis, it is the Christian perspective that Walter is forcing his readers to choose, since it offers 'a unified understanding of time'.[45] The *Alexandreis* thus appears to be consonant with historiography of the time. However, given that its poetics of *sic et non* have so far exploited literary conventions in order to problematize, if not wholly contradict, them, it is likely that here too Christian history is not a clear-cut interpretative possibility.

It is important to distinguish between Old and New Testament narratives within Christian history, as Walter also inserts extended accounts of Old

---

[43] Geoffrey of Monmouth aligns Christian, Trojan, and British history in his *Historia regum Britanniae* (c.1136); see for example chapter 25, which collocates the lives of the prophet Samuel, Silvius Aeneas, and Homer (*The* Historia regum Britannie *of Geoffrey of Monmouth*, ed. Neil Wright and Julia Crick, 5 vols (Cambridge, 1985–91), I, ed. Wright). Universal chronicles, operating on a synoptic principle, are also a common feature of historiography (see for example that of Orderic Vitalis, *The Ecclesiastical History of Orderic Vitalis*, ed. and trans. Marjorie Chibnall, 4 vols (Oxford, 1969–80)).

[44] Lafferty, *Epic and the Problem of Historical Understanding*, p.63.

[45] Ibid.

Testament histories as ecphrases, which will be discussed in detail later. His use of explicitly Christian narrative (i.e. the New Testament) is the only anachronistic narrative (to Alexander) that is mentioned, which ascribes it even more importance. This importance is confirmed when we see that the references to post-Incarnation events are deliberate and limited. Several of them refer to the future history (from Alexander's narrative's perspective) of cities, so that Jerusalem is described as the place 'ubi uirginis edita partu/Vita obiit' ('where, sprung from virgin womb, Life died').[46] Tarsus is similarly depicted with reference to Paul:

> Hic, ut scripta ferunt, illustri claruit ortu,
> Per quem precipue caecis errore subacto
> Gentibus emersit radius fideique lucerna.

> *Tarsus that was adorned, as Scripture tells,*
> *by his illustrious birth through whom faith's lamp*
> *shone on nations long blinded by their error.*[47]

There is also a reference to the massacre of Christians by the emperor Maximian, which is part of a simile.[48] Since the rest of the text is not characterized by anachronistic content in this way, such references are marked, operating rather as geographical asides for the medieval audience than as parts of the narrative. This idea is confirmed by the vocabulary. Neither Paul nor Christ, the subjects of these excursus, is explicitly named, making the reference to them oblique even if strongly marked. Maximian is named, but, as part of a simile, he is also separated from the main narrative. These three references operate as colour for the medieval audience and do not have a significant impact on the tale.

There is, however, a more extensive and explicit reference to Christianity at the end of book v, the passage already discussed with reference to Alexander as a kingly *exemplum* for Philip Augustus. It appears to be a much more thorough intervention of Christianity, with its mentions of Charlemagne, Walter's patron William of Champagne, and Christ himself, using what David Townsend has called 'the rhetoric of the Crusades'.[49] Yet, as already discussed, this extract is wholly wishful thinking; ironically, despite its overt referencing, the implication is in fact that such conditions for Christianity's renewal are absent. This irony is reinforced by the passage's position away from the main narrative, which has already ended with a sumptuous description of Alexander's progress through the city. The Christianity of this passage

---

[46] *Alexandreis*, ed. Colker, I.422–3; *Alexandreis*, trans. Townsend, p.18 (495).
[47] *Alexandreis*, ed. Colker, II.145–7; *Alexandreis*, trans. Townsend, p.27 (164–6).
[48] *Alexandreis*, ed. Colker, II.318b–18f and v.314–18.
[49] *Alexandreis*, trans. Townsend, p.126, n.4. Heinrich Christensen also reads this moment in the light of the Third Crusade in particular (*Alexanderlied*, p.10).

does not engage with the main story in any way, operating like the other references discussed above as an aside, although here a more dramatic and descriptive one. This is not to say that it is irrelevant, given the comparison with Alexander it seems to draw; but, as we have already seen, the question of Alexander as a model for a Christian king is a vexed one.

There is one more important episode in which Christianity seems to play a vital part. In an addition to the tale as found in his main source Quintus Curtius Rufus, Walter adds a katabasis in his final book, in which Nature travels to a classical hell to complain of Alexander's domination of the world. Hell's ruler, named here as Leviathan, is concerned that Alexander may be the fulfillment of a prophecy that states Hell will be ravaged by a 'New Man':

> Est tamen in fatis, quod abhominor, affore tempus
> Quo nouus in terris quadam partus nouitate
> Nescio quis nascetur homo qui carceris huius
> Ferrea subuersis confringet claustra columpnis,
> Vasaque diripiens et fortia fortior arma,
> Nostra triumphali populabitur atria ligno.

> *Still is that fated which I loathe to tell:*
> *a time shall come when some New Man, brought forth*
> *by some great novelty upon the earth,*
> *will overturn the pillars, and will break*
> *the iron cloisters [of this prison (my addition)]: seizing stronger arms,*
> *he'll ravage with triumphal wood our halls.*[50]

This is of course a prophecy of Christ's harrowing of Hell, nothing to do with Alexander at all. It is, unlike the other episodes that refer to Christianity, a turning point in the narrative, since it is Leviathan's fear of this coming true that leads directly to Alexander's death. It has been pointed out that Leviathan spectacularly misreads the prophecy as he has no knowledge of Christianity, in contrast to the medieval audience, which is of course accurate;[51] yet there is more to this passage than simple misreading. Leviathan's hermeneutic process is allegorical: he reads Alexander as Christ in a misplaced typological parallel. The fact that Alexander is mentioned in the Old Testament reinforces this as a typological mistake.[52] Leviathan here is shown to be inaccurate not just in terms of subject matter (Alexander is not Christ), but in terms of the interpretation of this subject matter (typology). This is an important point, since typology, and allegorical processes more generally, are common strategies not

---

[50] *Alexandreis*, ed. Colker, x.134–9; *Alexandreis*, trans. Townsend, p.173 (154–9).
[51] Lafferty, *Epic and the Problem of Historical Understanding*, p.60.
[52] Daniel 11.2–4 is a prophecy of Alexander's conquests and their scattering after his death.

just for contemporary theology but also in literature.[53] This sets the *Alexandreis* apart, momentarily at least, from its broad literary context.

Why is it important that Leviathan's typological hermeneutic is seen as a mistake? One possible answer is that Walter thought the application of this mode of interpretation to a non-Christian narrative was inappropriate, chronologically and/or spiritually. The problem of chronology is also suggested by the lexis of the passage, which is deliberately opaque as it strives to conceal its anachronistic subject. Although phrases such as 'triumphali … ligno' were common in describing the Cross in the twelfth century,[54] there are no explicitly Christian words here; the passage, in terms of vocabulary, uses words common in classical poetry.[55] This lexical obscuring of Christianity means that the prophecy of Christ is not used to interpret the main story in terms of a post-Incarnation narrative of salvation. Both lexis and hermeneutics deny the Christian salvific narrative interpretative power, despite the fact of its introduction in veiled terms. Once again there is a sense of simultaneous suggestion and denial, of *sic et non*, present here.

In the *Alexandreis*, Christian history, starting with the birth of Christ, is a narrative that, whilst seeming strongly present on several occasions via emphatic references, in fact emerges as conspicuous through its absence, or at least through the occluding nature of the text. It is of course the interpretative framework that surrounds the poem and one context through which the audience would have interpreted its meaning, but this is only inferred, not stated. This is intriguing, since it contrasts with much contemporary historiography: for example, reading the poem as an epic with Christianity as a dominant hermeneutic, like the early thirteenth-century *Philippis* of William the Breton, is not possible. The deliberate and limited use of Christianity also differentiates the poem from the kind of collated histories of William of Malmesbury and Geoffrey of Monmouth. This suggests that a different kind of historical

---

[53] Hugh of St Victor's *De sacramentis* creates a textual hierarchy moving upwards from reading 'ad littera' to allegory and then to moral interpretation, all in aid of spiritual progress. Alan of Lille's *Anticlaudianus*, for example, uses the allegory of Prudence's journey to heaven to gain a soul for the perfect 'New Man' to describe the struggles of the Christian life.

[54] See for example Venantius Fortunatus' seventh-century hymn to the Cross, 'Vexilla regis prodeunt', which addresses it as 'Arbor decora et fulgida,/ornata regis purpura' ('Hymn to the Holy Cross (2)', no.55 in *The Oxford Book of Medieval Latin Verse*, ed. and trans. F. J. E. Raby, 2nd end (Oxford, 1974), verse 5, line 1, p.75).

[55] Colker's edition cites Ovid, *Metamorphoses* i.256 as a stylistic comparison here (*Alexandreis*, ed. Colker, p.259). Juvencus, composing his *Evangeliorum libri quattuor*, similarly portrays Christian concepts in epic lexis although in a very different narrative context. He invokes the Holy Spirit instead of the Muses, for example: 'ergo age, sanctificus adsit mihi carminis auctor/Spiritus' (Preface, lines 33–4, *Evangeliorum libri quattuor*, ed. John Hümer, CSEL, 24 (Vienna, 1891): trans. in *Juvencus' Four Books of the Gospels*: Evangeliorum Libri Quattuor, trans. Scott McGill (London, 2016)).

hermeneutic may be more important in understanding the *Alexandreis* in literary and political terms.

Pre-Christian Histories

If Christian interpretation in the *Alexandreis* is mainly silent, then the question of historiography focuses upon other historical narratives. The most evident of these is naturally Alexander's life story or *vita*, part of Greek history that is cast as epic, but other historical narratives are also important; in book I Alexander visits the site of Troy and sees the grave of Achilles, which inserts Trojan and Greek mythological history into his story as an overt comparison.[56] The most complex historiographical moments, however, occur when Walter inserts extended accounts of Persian, Greek, and Old Testament histories as ecphrases, three lengthy descriptive passages depicting Darius' shield, his wife Stateira's tomb (although she herself is not named), and Darius' own grave.[57] These moments too are separate from the primary narrative of Alexander's *vita*, and they act as periods of reflection before or after momentous events. In both modern and medieval writing they are the best-known and most commented on passages of the poem, with glosses on them circulating separately from the main text.[58] Usually they are read from the perspective of classical texts and traditions, relating to questions of ethics and to genre within that paradigm; Christine Ratkowitsch, for example, sees them as warnings against pride and *cupiditas*, and David Townsend reads them as moments at

---

[56] Trojan history was of vital importance as a myth of origins for several dynasties in the twelfth century; see for example Geoffrey of Monmouth's claim of British descent from Brutus in the *Historia regum Britannie* and also Christopher Baswell's argument about the Angevins' portrayal in the mid-century *Roman d'Eneas* ('Men in the *Roman d'Eneas*: The Construction of Empire', in *Medieval Masculinities: Regarding Men in the Middle Ages*, ed. Clare A. Lees (Minneapolis, MN, 1994), pp.149–68).

[57] For detailed discussion of the ecphrases, see Maura K. Lafferty, 'Mapping Human Limitations: The Tomb Ecphrases in Walter of Châtillon's *Alexandreis*', *Journal of Medieval Latin*, 4 (1994), pp.64–81, and *Epic and the Problem of Historical Understanding*, pp.103–40 (which share material); David Townsend, '"Michi barbaries incognita linguae": Other Voices and Other Visions in Walter of Châtillon's *Alexandreis*,' *Allegorica*, 13 (1992), pp.21–37; Christine Ratkowitsch, 'Walter von Châtillon, *Alexandreis*', in *Descriptio picturae: Die literarische Funktion der Beschreibung von Kunstwerken in der lateinischen Grossdichtung des 12. Jahrhunderts* (Vienna, 1991), pp.129–211; Neil Adkin, 'Walter of Châtillon: "Alexandreis" IV 206–207', *MJ*, 32:1 (1997), pp.29–36; and Venetia Bridges, 'L'estoire d'Alixandre vos veul par vers traitier [...]': Passions and Polemics in Latin and Vernacular Alexander Literature of the Later Twelfth Century', *Nottingham Medieval Studies*, 58 (2014), pp.87–113.

[58] For medieval commentaries, see *An Epitome of Biblical History: Glosses on Walter of Châtillon's Alexandreis 4.176–274*, ed. David Townsend, Toronto Medieval Latin Texts, 30 (Toronto, 2008) and id., 'Paratext, Ambiguity, and Interpretative Foreclosure'. Glosses on the first two passages mentioned here are found in London, British Library, MS Additional 20009, fols.235–49, without the full text of the poem.

which the text interrogates its generic status as 'epic'.[59] Lafferty, however, sees them as relating to the different concepts of history she discussed earlier in her book: 'the ekphraseis … present a variety of histories, each drawn from a different tradition, and demonstrate the limitations inherent in each.'[60] Lafferty's idea about the 'limitations' of concepts of history places Christianity in a dominant position, which we have seen is not tenable elsewhere in the poem. This presents the question as to how these different concepts of history in the ecphrases should be read: what do they contribute to the poem's narrative and interpretations?

An important factor in discussing the ecphrases is their style, which separates them yet further from the rest of the poem. Townsend sums up this style as containing 'an absolute minimum of descriptive detail or other literary ornamentation',[61] as can be seen in this example from Stateira's tomb.

> Hic patriarcharum seriem specialius aurum
> Exprimit. emeritos uideas ridere parentes,
> Venantemque Esau, turmisque redire duabus
> Luctarique Iacob. sequitur distractio Ioseph
> Et dolus et carcer et transmigratio prima.

> *Rarer gold*
> *decks out the sequence of the patriarchs:*
> *Here you may see the aged parents laugh*
> *and Esau hunting. Jacob comes again*
> *returning with two companies. He wrestles.*
> *Joseph's abduction follows next. The trick.*
> *The prison. And at last the first migration.* [62]

The lines are terse and allusive, contracting rather than expanding linguistically ('et dolus et carcer et transmigratio prima'). This style is an unusual departure from Walter of Châtillon's poetic technique in the rest of his poem and a break from classical tradition, as Townsend realizes.[63] Such difference highlights the ecphrases' separation from the main narrative even further, which may be one reason for this strange style's deployment.

I shall discuss only the first ecphrasis, a description of Darius' shield, in detail here, which narrates Persian history (some aspects via the Old Testament).[64]

---

[59] Ratkowitsch, 'Walter von Châtillon, *Alexandreis*'.

[60] Lafferty, *Epic and the Problem of Historical Understanding*, p.140.

[61] Townsend, '"Michi barbaries incognita linguae"', p.31.

[62] *Alexandreis*, ed. Colker, IV.203–7; *Alexandreis*, trans. Townsend, p.66 (253–9).

[63] Townsend, '"Michi barbaries incognita linguae"', pp.31–2.

[64] For my argument as developed in the other two ecphrases, see Bridges, 'Passions and Polemics in Latin and Vernacular Alexander Literature'.

It draws particularly on the shield of Aeneas in the *Aeneid*.[65] In about fifty lines, the passage depicts the past history of the Persian empire, from the early history of Babylon via the Biblical conquest of the Hebrews to the imperial rule of Belshazzar and Cyrus. Just as Aeneas' shield depicts Rome's future history, so Darius' shield contains his 'origo patrum', 'the origins of [his] fathers' (II.498). Yet it is a selective history. Walter uses the device of *praeteritio* to include the unsuitable behaviour of Persia's kings, such as Nebuchadnezzar's madness, but the omissions from his *descriptio* are more interesting than his inclusions. Walter ignores the role of Cyrus in the rebuilding of the Hebrew Temple, surely a praiseworthy deed; instead, his description of the king focuses on the fact that despite being 'qui totus et unus/Malleus orbis erat' ('the one and only hammer of the world', II.538–9) he was destroyed by a woman. Combined with the *praeteritio*, these omissions suggest that Walter is creating a discreditable history of the Persian realm, a suggestion confirmed by his reference to Belshazzar. Seemingly neutral – 'in sacro libantem Balthasar auro' ('Belshazzar drinking from the sacred gold', II.523) – this Biblical episode would have been well-known to listeners and readers, along with the disastrous result of the king's act, the loss of his kingdom and his death.[66] The idea of a negative regnal history is made explicit by the lines 'proch gloria fallax/Imperii, proch quanta patent ludibria sortis/Humanae!' ('Imperial glory, lo! How you deceive! How many snares engross the human lot!', II.533–5). Walter's criticism of 'gloria fallax' is here clearly linked to the desire for domination found in the following lines, where Cyrus is described as ruler of land and sea and the hammer of the world. In contrast to the shield's description in the *Aeneid*, which ends in triumph and rejoicing despite Aeneas' ignorance of its meaning, here the poet has created a history of imperial domination that ends in disaster by selective use of his Biblical sources.

The phrase 'gloria fallax imperii' therefore seems to sum up this negative portrayal of Persian history, which is depicted here via the Old Testament. This might be seen as a straightforwardly Christian interpretation, in which temporal human power is inferior to the eternal *imperium* of God. Lafferty suggest such a Christian reading, claiming that the narrator, whom she sees as distinct from the artist, perceives Persian history 'from a Judeo-Christian perspective'.[67] However, given the critique of typology with regard to Leviathan, it is potentially important to consider the Jewish Old Testament separately from the Christian New Testament.[68] Despite the presence of Biblical

---

[65] Virgil, *Aeneid* VIII.626–731, in *Opera*, ed. R. A. B. Mynors, Scriptorum Classicorum Bibliotheca Oxoniensis (Oxford, 1969; repr. 1972).

[66] See Daniel 6.1–31 for the story of Belshazzar.

[67] See Lafferty, *Epic and the Problem of Historical Understanding*, p.113.

[68] This division is supported by Walter's polemical *Tractatus contra Judaeos* in which he criticizes Jewish scriptural interpretation.

material, the moral drawn here about deceitful empire is not an explicitly Christian one because the content is from the Old, not the New, Testament, and, crucially, Christian hermeneutics are unrevealed in the primary narrative in chronological terms; this warning against human *imperium* could be read if anything more easily in a Jewish Old Testament context. It seems that the reader remains within pre-Christian history hermeneutically as well as in terms of subject matter here.

However, this *moralitas* concerning imperial power that ends the ecphrasis proper is followed by a second, separate interpretation connecting such worldly glory explicitly with spiritual failure.

> Parcite, mortales, animos extollere fastu
> Collatis opibus aspernarique minores.
> Parcite, uictores, ingrati uiuere summo
> Victori. uires sceptrum diadema tryumphos
> Diuicias dare qui potuit, auferre ualebit.

> *You mortals, curb the pride by which you raise*
> *your spirits and with heaped-up wealth despise*
> *your lessers. Cease, you conquerors, to live*
> *ungrateful to the highest conqueror.*
> *He who was able to bestow the crown*
> *and sceptre, strength, and wealth, and victory*
> *retains the power to remove them all.*[69]

Once again, the language here is both appropriate to a pagan historical narrative and also to a spiritual reading, which could by implication be Christian, but is not explicitly cast as such.[70] This second interpretation changes the ecphrasis' focus, ensuring the book ends on a different and spiritual note. The reader is presented with two interpretations, the worldly followed by the spiritual, the latter being consonant with Christianity but not explicitly cast as such. It is the separation of the two *moralitates* that is crucial here: despite their similarity of interpretation (worldly power will not last), the poet conceives of them as different entities, occupying individual hermeneutic and textual space. This seems to support Lafferty's idea about different histories and their limitations, but there is a further point to be made about the relationships between these histories. In this ecphrasis, the careful separation of hermeneutic modes (worldly and spiritual) suggests an interest in matching a particular historical account with an appropriate mode of reading. Here a literal-historical reading is followed by a separate allegorical one, in which a broad analogy is intimated between classical, pagan events and their implicitly Christian interpretation.

---

[69] *Alexandreis*, ed. Colker, II.540–4; *Alexandreis*, trans. Townsend, pp.39–40 (631–7).

[70] For example, the idea of the 'summo/Victori' could also be applicable to Jupiter as well as the Jewish or Christian God.

Yet the deliberate textual separation of the two readings indicates that, their similar conclusions notwithstanding, they cannot operate simultaneously. The second *moralitas*, like the end of book v, is not part of the ecphrastic text, but is a direct address to 'mortales', with whom it is tempting to identify the medieval audience, not the characters of the poem (despite the inclusive nature of the language). We are made aware of 'hermeneutic decentering', as two historical narratives that seem to overlap to produce similar readings are shown to be separate: pagan historical narrative, even when it involves the Old Testament, cannot be interpreted via a process of Christian allegorization within the text. This in fact troubles Lafferty's idea that the ecphrasis' 'use of history' is as 'a source of illustrative *exempla*'[71]: by definition, an *exemplum* is a historical event that may be interpreted through the prism of a different narrative. Here Walter once again calls into question the exemplary process by not allowing a straightforward Christian reading, in a different context from the supposed paean to Philip Augustus at the end of book v.

The other two ecphrases, the tombs of Darius and his wife Stateira, also demonstrate similar historical deconstruction. All three ecphrases, which appear to proffer a view of different historical narratives as unified, in fact problematize such a view via this complex practice of presenting an interpretation only to question it using a second one, which is often separated from the narrative text. This *sic et non* technique, albeit in a more direct fashion, has also been located in the explicitly Christian (meaning New Testament) references within the poem. Why does the poet do this, and in such a difficult and elusive fashion? Part of the answer no doubt is intellectual one-upmanship, which is evident in Walter's short poems,[72] but this is not the only reason. A more complete answer lies in contemporary ideas about literary inheritance and *translatio studii*.

The question of how to rewrite and adapt history in the twelfth century was being answered in a variety of ways, many of which involved texts that were in the process of becoming fictional.[73] Walter's insistence on the problems of allegorical interpretation for historical narrative is in direct contrast to this process, which necessitates the elision of historical difference in order to operate effectively. In the three ecphrases, the passages in which this insistence

---

[71] Lafferty, *Epic and the Problem of Historical Understanding*, p.114.

[72] It is especially marked in his quotation or *auctoritas* poems, which use famous lines from classical authors as the culmination of each verse. On these, see Venetia Bridges, '"Goliardic" Poetry and the Problem of Historical Perspective: Medieval Adaptations of Walter of Châtillon's Quotation Poems', *Medium Ævum*, 81.2 (2012), pp. 249–70, and on the form more generally, Paul Gerhard Schmidt, 'The Quotation in Goliardic Poetry', in *Latin Poetry and the Classical Tradition*, ed. P. Godman and O. Murray (Oxford, 1990), pp.39–55.

[73] See Green, *Beginnings of Medieval Romance*, pp.153–61, and discussion in 'Literary Contexts', above.

is given centre stage, the allusive style becomes part of his technique: disrupting any easy construction, it highlights the conflict by making reading itself difficult, forcing the audience to confront their interpretative assumptions and thus creating space for new, complex meanings. An easy (lazy?) and single typological interpretation, temptingly suggested, is ultimately denied, and the difficult style of these passages is a clue to the audience that correct interpretation is meant to be hard work. For Walter, pagan history should not be read and interpreted using the same hermeneutic tools (i.e. allegorical ones) as Christian salvific narrative. Yet, of course, this is not an absolute position, since the composition of a classicizing epic about a pagan hero at this point in the Middle Ages naturally indicates this kind of interpretation (seen more explicitly in romance texts) in order to make it acceptable to a Christian audience.[74] Rather than being a literary fundamentalist or an Italian fourteenth-century humanist untimely born, it seems that the poet is using specific passages in his *Alexandreis* to highlight a prevalent form of interpretation that he viewed as problematic in its application of a spiritual and Christian hermeneutic technique to a pagan historical narrative. This sets what we might call his 'historicism' within a recognizable literary context, although it is a context with which the poet is clearly at odds.

This analysis has demonstrated the complex and often paradoxical *sic et non* poetics of the *Alexandreis* across its narratives of Christian and pre-Christian history, and has suggested that reasons for such poetics can be found in the contemporary fashion for rewriting classical material using broadly allegorical methods. This has located the *Alexandreis* within broad literary and intellectual currents dominant during the twelfth century. It remains to consider whether the poem's political relationships are also presented using these poetics, and, if so, what the implications are for the *Alexandreis* as a political text.

'Gloria fallax imperii': The Politics of the Alexandreis

If the process of allegory, particularly typology, is problematic in the poem, then the drawing of parallels, even opaque ones, with current or recent events is likely to be equally difficult. Reading the *Alexandreis* as a political text will also involve deciphering its complex poetics of *sic et non*, meaning its allegiances may be opaque and contradictory. However, as we have seen, the description of Darius's shield contains an explicit warning against secular *imperium*, which may have contemporary resonances: simply because the political stance/s of the *Alexandreis* are probably obscure does not make them non-existent.

---

[74] Thus Alexander can be described as a proto-Christian at points in the *Roman d'Alexandre*: see chapter 3 for discussion of this work.

Unsurprisingly for a classicizing and deliberately elusive work, contemporary events are noticeable by their absence in most of the poem. Leaving aside Walter's dedication to William of Champagne, there are only three major moments that can be seen as politically charged in this way. They occur at the end of book v, already discussed; in book vii, after the description of Darius' tomb; and at the end of the poem. All three engage with the phrase 'gloria fallax imperii' that describes Darius' Persian history on his shield.[75]

Following the *sic et non* approach to Philip Augustus seen at the end of book v, the longest passage with overt references to contemporary events occurs immediately after Darius' death in book vii, just before his tomb ecphrasis. It is around forty lines listing a catalogue of contemporary sins such as avarice, gluttony, drunkenness, simony, schism, and murder, intended as an incitement to moral behaviour. Like the second *moralitas* of Darius' shield, it begins with a direct address, this time to 'felices animae' (306), which serves to separate the passage from its surrounding text and potentially to suggest a different audience for its messages than the characters in the poem. That this audience was a clerical and political one is indicated by the text's movement from general sins such as greed to explicitly ecclesiastical ones like simony, culminating in unequivocal references to contemporary clerical figures and events.

> Non aspiraret, licet indole clarus, auiti
> Sanguinis inpubes ad pontificale cacumen
> Donec eum mores, studiorum fructus, et etas
> Eligerent, merito non suffragante parentum;
> Non geminos patres ducti liuore crearent
> Preficerentque orbi sortiti a cardine nomen ...
> Non caderent hodie nullo discrimine sacri
> Pontifices, quales nuper cecidisse queruntur
> Vicinae modico distantes equore terrae.

> *No beardless boy, however bright his ancestry,*
> *would set his sights upon a bishop's greatness,*
> *until his age and character and learning*
> *had gained him an election – and no matter*
> *what excellence of lineage spoke for him.*
> *The fathers who derive their name 'a cardine'*
> *would not be led by malice to create*
> *two lords over the world...*
> *Neither would two lands*
> *at equal distance over narrow straits*

---

[75] I am grateful to Peter Godman for suggesting the importance of this phrase to me.

> *mourn for their bishops, slain without respect*
> *for holy office.*[76]

The first reference to the 'beardless boy' is a daring comment on William of Champagne himself, who was refused consecration as bishop of Chartres upon election in 1164/5 by Alexander III on the grounds that he had not attained the canonical age of thirty and neither was he in diaconal or priestly orders.[77] This bold reference implies a close and complicit relationship between him and the poet. Again, these lines appear to praise whilst external knowledge indicates the reverse. The second reference is clearly to the papal schism of 1159–77, which had only recently ended; Walter here suggests, with characteristic word-play, that this was due to the cardinals' financial corruption. The third reference is to the murders of the ecclesiastics Robert of Cambrai in 1174 and Thomas Becket in 1170.

All these figures and events seem to be ecclesiastical, which moves this passage far away from its immediate textual context, the murder of Darius by his own men. Yet a closer look, combined with knowledge of what is *not* said, suggests a more relevant reading. All these references are to ecclesiastical events in which temporal power was abused. William of Champagne's election to Chartres so young was because of his family's power, which is twice emphasized in these lines. The papal schism rapidly developed into a situation in which the papacy's main opponent was the imperial ruler Frederick Barbarossa, who supported a succession of antipopes.[78] Finally, the murders of Robert of Cambrai and Thomas Becket are instances of the dominance of temporal over spiritual power, the latter death being of particular note since it was thought to be caused by Henry II.[79] The poetic context of this passage

---

[76] *Alexandreis*, ed. Colker, VII.320–5, 328–30; *Alexandreis*, trans. Townsend, p.124 (351–8, 360–3).

[77] Falkenstein, 'Guillaume aux Blanches Mains', p.7. The connection was noted by medieval glossators: the thirteenth-century Vienna, Österreichische Nationalbibliothek, MS 568, printed in *Alexandreis*, ed. Colker, p.452, reads 'non aspiraret: hoc ideo dicit auctor quia in tempore suo quidam iuuenis electus est in episcopum Carnotensem eo quod erat de nobili prosapia, licet esset infra triginta annos.' An earlier, if less explicit, gloss is found in the twelfth-century Geneva, Bibliothèque publique et universitaire, MS Latin 98 (*Alexandreis*, ed. Colker, p.291). Christensen, however, claims that the reference is not to William but to the contested election of Rainald of Angers in 1102 (*Alexanderlied*, p.7), which seems unlikely considering the above evidence from the Vienna MS.

[78] For an overview of the schism, see C. Morris, *The Papal Monarchy: The Western Church from 1050 to 1250*, Oxford History of the Christian Church (Oxford, 1989; repr. 1991), pp.182–204.

[79] Robert of Cambrai was murdered after he was denounced to the pope as having been elected bishop through imperial power; see Patrick Demouy, *Genèse d'une cathédrale: les archevêques de Reims et leur Église aux XIe et XIIe siècles* (Langres, 2005), p.420. Thomas Becket's accidental murder was because of his opposition to regal dominance

suggests that it is this issue of abuse of power that is key. Bessus, one of Darius' men, murders him when 'regni flammatus amore' ('enflamed with love of power').[80] This regicide inverts the hierarchical order of things by treachery. Walter's list of crimes is framed by this regicide, and it is this un-natural event that is used to contextualize a parallel inversion of hierarchy, in which ecclesiastical power is made subordinate to temporal jurisdiction. This would be a familiar context for a late twelfth-century audience who had lived through these political events and the aftermath of the Investiture Controversy. In medieval political theory at this point, temporal and spiritual *imperium* were intended to complement each other, with the latter ultimately greater but reliant upon the support of secular power.[81] This passage's clerical crimes are not simply abuses, but abuses that have occurred due to the dominance of secular over spiritual authority. Yet the absence of secular authority from this passage is notable; there is no explicit mention of any regal involvement in the schism nor in the episcopal murders. It is the context of regicide that provides a clue as to the reason for these abuses. What appears to be a simple passage of ethical complaint about clerical crimes becomes, via its framing text, an implicit criticism of the temporal (i.e. regal and imperial) power that is, from the narrator's perspective, the root cause of such sins. This alters the passage from a satirical wail against current evils into a pointed observation on a charged point of political theory. Once again, this extract functions in a double fashion, criticizing ecclesiastical abuses but also implying that these are caused by misuse of temporal power. Within the archbishop's *familia*, with its mixture of spiritual and temporal functions and responsibilities, as well as William of Champagne's own similarly double position as regally connected archbishop, this passage would have been a clever negotiation of loyalties.

The third and final passage acts as the *moralitas* of the poem, although as we have seen the idea of a single interpretation for such a complex work is unlikely. It begins in similar fashion to the previous section, 'O felix mortale genus si semper haberet/Eternum pre mente bonum' ('O happy race of mortals, if at all times we might consider/the eternal Good') (x.433–4). However, the passage continues with a more specific example of human folly:

---

of church affairs: for an overview of the conflict and its intellectual context, see Beryl Smalley, *The Becket Conflict and the Schools: A Study of Intellectuals in Politics* (Oxford, 1973).

[80] *Alexandreis*, ed. Colker, vii.341.

[81] A clear statement of the relationship of church and empire is found in clause six of the 1177 Treaty of Venice, which expresses the relationship of the church and state as that of a father and son. See *Select Historical Documents of the Middle Ages*, ed. and trans. Ernest F. Henderson (London, 1896; repr. 1921), p.426. John of Salisbury's 1159 work also demonstrates this belief in book iv.1, which deals with the relationship of the prince to his people and the clergy under the divine will of God (*Policraticus*, ed. Keats-Rohan, pp.231ff).

Cumque per Alpinas hiemes turbamque latronum
Romuleas arces et auare menia Rome
Cernere solliciti, si cursu forte beato
Ad natale solum patriumque reuertimur orbem,
Ecce repentinae modicaeque occasio febris
Dissoluit toto quecumque parauimus euo.

Perhaps through Alpine winters and a horde of thieves
we strive to reach the walls of greedy Rome
and Romulus' citadels: if by some chance
we come again to our ancestral land
and native soil, the onset of a slight
and sudden fever scatters all we've gathered
in all our years.[82]

This description of a journey to Rome would have been relevant to the poet's medieval ecclesiastical peers, especially as Townsend rightly points out that condemnation of the Roman curia was standard in twelfth-century satire.[83] It is particularly appropriate to Reims since the Alps lie on the direct route between that city and Rome.[84] It seems that this reference, therefore, can be interpreted as a warning to Walter's audience to beware of ecclesiastical ambition or 'auare ... Rome'. Yet there is potentially another more subtle meaning. The 'repentinae ... febris' is not a vague illness, but a specific fever,[85] one contracted after a journey to Rome. In July 1167, Frederick Barbarossa had led troops into Italy and besieged Rome itself in an attempt to capture Alexander III, only for many of his army and advisers, including his chancellor Rainald of Dassel, to die of malaria.[86] Although the illness occurs back at home in the text, in combination with the desire to conquer Rome and the reference to the Alps (also a feature of Barbarossa's journey) expressed here it is tempting to read it as an oblique reference to the imperial expedition, which had nearly ended in disaster for the papacy. This temptation is increased by the mention of Alexander in the next line, 'Magnus in exemplo est',[87] as an explicit regal *exemplum* of such imperial futility. It is admittedly a subtle reference if it

[82] *Alexandreis*, ed. Colker, x.442–7; *Alexandreis*, trans. Townsend, p.183 (529–36).
[83] *Alexandreis*, trans. Townsend, p.211, n.1.
[84] Many routes to Rome from northern Europe would cross the Alps, however.
[85] This specificity differs from Walter's other, better-known poem referring to illness, which begins 'Dum Galterus egrotaret' (printed as no.18 in *Moralisch-satirische Gedichte Walters von Châtillon*, ed. Karl Strecker (Heidelberg, 1929), and as no.67 by Traill, *Shorter Poems*), in which the all-compassing verb 'egrotare' is all the explanation provided.
[86] For an overview of this incident, see Peter Munz, *Frederick Barbarossa: A Study in Medieval Politics* (London, 1969), pp.252–3. For a papal perspective, see Morris, *Papal Monarchy*, p.195.
[87] *Alexandreis*, ed. Colker, x.448.

is indeed to Barbarossa, but, as we have seen, such subtlety is part of the poet's technique. If this is the case, then once again Walter has used an overt criticism of clerical corruption and ambition ('auare ... Rome') to conceal an implicit condemnation of contemporary regal abuse of power.

This pattern of misdirection, of *sic et non*, is a familiar one. In these last two passages, it is from ecclesiastical towards regal criticism – 'gloria fallax imperii' – whereas in the one at the end of book v it concerned a shift from positive to negative views of the young Philip Augustus. It is also familiar from the use of historical narratives at key moments, where one narrative that seems to interpret the text is unexpectedly questioned, if not contradicted, by another. Both in a political and an intellectual sense, this misdirection is the cause of the *Alexandreis*'s 'dialogic complexity', 'narrative undecidability', and 'hermeneutically decentred' nature.[88]

Sic et Non

The *Alexandreis*, in this reading, is far from being a nostalgic classicizing poem that is detached from contemporary literary and political circumstances, since its interest in historical narrative locates it among other twelfth-century texts. However, Walter of Châtillon's conception of *translatio studii* is unusual. Far from following the routes of historical collocation or allegorical treatment, the poem questions, if not repudiates, both via its difficult *sic et non* poetics. This intriguing rejection supports the idea that *translatio studii* at this point in time is not a single or uncontested practice but plural, a practice under discussion; the intellectual framework of this discussion needs further investigation to see if the debate is played out locally and/or more widely across geographical and political boundaries. Reading the *Alexandreis* as a politically engaged poem has shown that its discussion of secular and sacred authority is deeply relevant to its local circumstances, namely William of Champagne and his regal connections, but these transnational issues also indicate a political framework that encompasses the local as part of gesturing towards a larger, transnational stage; politically, too, the poem is pluralist. In the next section, I shall argue that the *Alexandreis*'s *sic et non* character, which enables this literary and political pluralism, is inspired by the city of Reims, where the work was most probably composed and published.

Reims

Reims, located in north-eastern France, was an important city in both political and geographical terms, since it was a focal point upon which different interests and networks converged. By the end of the twelfth century it was home

---

[88] Townsend, 'Paratext, Ambiguity, and Interpretative Foreclosure', p.25, p.43, p.48.

to around ten thousand people. William of Champagne was responsible in particular for planning the development of the suburbs to the south-west of the city, which demonstrates clearly the archbishop's role as Reims' ruling lord.[89] Unsurprisingly, as the site of France's major archiepiscopal see, the city was heavily dominated by clerical institutions; as well as the cathedral and its canons, there were many religious institutions within the walls, and just outside these was the powerful (although then in decline) abbey dedicated to Saint Remi. During the eleventh and twelfth centuries, four church councils were held at Reims, demonstrating its wider importance within the western Church and also underlining the status of its archbishop.[90] The city was of course the administrative centre of the eponymous diocese, which covered much of Flanders as well as what is now France, so that its position as the heart of the see involved broader regional relationships.

These regional relationships position Reims as a meeting place not just for ecclesiastical politics, but secular ones too. It was here that the first king of West Francia, Clovis, was baptized by the then archbishop in the fifth century, and the city was also close geographically to the Capetian demesne. The importance of Reims both ecclesiastically and to the monarchy is clearly demonstrated by the elections of William of Champagne and his predecessor Henry of France to the see; both were blood relatives of the Capetian kings as well as ecclesiastics.[91] Yet Reims's secular political connections were not just with the Capetians. The city is positioned on the most direct route between southeast England and Rome, and was used as a stop on that journey.[92] It was also close to Angevin (Anglo-Norman) territories and to those of German princes as well as to Flanders.[93] The city's position made it an ideal meeting place for people moving between all these areas, which may be one reason that it was the site of so many church councils. Finally, on a more local yet still important scale, Reims was within the territory of the counts of Champagne and Blois, another reason why William of Champagne's appointment as archbishop was an intelligent decision from a political perspective.

All these factors demonstrate that Reims was an important entity within multiple political networks. Political issues could be both local and transnational. For example, the city had a turbulent relationship with its archbishop during the years of Henry of France's tenure from 1162 to 1175; the issues raised (concerning its inhabitants' rights of government) were only resolved through

---

[89] See Pierre Desportes, *Reims et les Rémois aux XIIIᵉ et XIVᵉ siècles* (Paris, 1979), pp.56–92.

[90] See Demouy, *Genèse d'une cathédrale*.

[91] Henry of France was Louis VII's brother, and William was Philip Augustus' maternal uncle (and thus Louis's brother-in-law).

[92] Demouy, *Genèse d'une cathédrale*, p.395.

[93] Ibid., pp.395–6.

William of Champagne's diplomacy some years later.[94] Reims' involvement in transnational affairs, however, is where the city becomes most crucial for the *Alexandreis*. Firstly, the poem's reference to Thomas Becket's murder, and hence implicitly to Henry II, involves it in a political-ecclesiastical situation that saw Reims play host to Becket at the church council of 1164, and in which archbishop William acted as a strong partisan of the exiled churchman.[95] Secondly, the potential reference to Frederick Barbarossa at the end of the *Alexandreis* can be explained by situating it alongside the poem's mention of the papal schism, another situation in which Reims, as a pro-Alexander III city, directly played a part by hosting the pope during the schism, and indirectly by its support of Becket.[96] Both these deliberate and unusual (in the context of the poem) references to contemporary politics are underpinned by Reims' multifaceted position as an ecclesiastical stronghold surrounded by secular territories.

It is this position that provides a further insight into their meaning. Walter has chosen to highlight two issues that illustrate conflict with these imperial powers (Henry II and Frederick Barbarossa), powers that he criticizes for the same reasons in his short poems, where he castigates Henry as the 'wicked ruler of Britain' and Barbarossa as the savage cause of papal schism.[97] His subtle pro-ecclesiastical stance and oblique criticisms of kings in the *Alexandreis* set 'gloria fallax imperii' in a contemporary setting that is particularly appropriate to Reims's and its archbishop's situation: a city dominated by ecclesiastical rule but with an important geographical position tying it politically to territories controlled by secular princes, in particular the powerful rulers of whom he so strongly disapproved in his other works. The tensions between secular and spiritual power in Reims, embodied by William of Champagne himself (blood relative of the king yet senior churchman), are surely a major part of the reason for Walter's *sic et non* poetics in the *Alexandreis*. The poet, aware of Alexander's varying interpretations, was able to take advantage of the hermeneutic space that these provided to explore the problems of secular

---

[94] William granted the city the Wilhelmine Charter, which enshrined some of its traditional rights in statute; see Desportes, *Reims et les Rémois*, p.73.

[95] Becket spent much of his years of exile during the 1160s in the vicinity of the city.

[96] The Becket affair became aligned with the schism since it involved the same issue of temporal vs spiritual authority: see Smalley, *Becket Conflict*, pp.119–35.

[97] Walter's poem 'Dum contemplor animo', edited as no.58 in Traill, *Shorter Poems*, pp.206–17, describes both kings as precursors of Antichrist; in addition, Henry II is the 'Britannie reprobum rectorem,/qui … inpudenter messuit sacerdotum florem', and Barbarossa is 'per quem scismatis semina sevisti' (16.2–4 and 24.2), which are references to Becket's death and Barbarossa's perceived role in the 1159–77 schism respectively. The imperial nature of Angevin rule at this point was shifting, given the rebellions of Henry's sons in 1173 and 1174, but Henry II still had control of a large number of disparate territories. See Ashe, *History and Fiction in England*, p.127 on the idea of Angevin rule as fragmented.

and/or sacred rule, *imperium*, so relevant to late twelfth-century Reims. He did so, however, in a way that acknowledged the overlap between them and diplomatically avoided outright criticism.

The political nature of the *Alexandreis*, then, places the poem in a complex relationship with local and more transnational affairs. The work's interest in the Becket controversy and the papal schism is transnational, involving Angevin, Capetian, Imperial, and ecclesiastical territories, but its particular frame of reference is a local one, since both concerns coalesce in Reims's situation during the 1170s, in which its archbishop negotiated between potent secular rulers whilst maintaining ecclesiastical rule in a restive city. For the *Alexandreis*, Reims is the immediate local context for the poem's exploration of broader transnational concerns.

Intellectual Reims

Politically, then, the *sic et non* poetics of the *Alexandreis* relate to Reims' and its archbishop's position. It remains to be seen if the poem's poetics can also be illumined by its composition and publication in that city in a literary sense. Whilst far from being an intellectual centre like Paris or Chartres in the later twelfth century, Reims had a history of academic pursuits. Although its cathedral school is, according to John R. Williams, 'a very elusive entity' whose fortunes seem to have fluctuated, leaving virtually no documentary trace,[98] it produced or housed several notable literary figures during the tenth and eleventh centuries. Gerbert of Aurillac, the future pope Sylvester II, was the schoolmaster before becoming archbishop in 989, and under him the school became 'the most flourishing school of Northern Europe'.[99] He may have taught the historian Richer of St Remi, who wrote a four-volume history of West Frankish kings between 991 and 998 dedicated to Gerbert. Gerbert was enthusiastic about classical literature, but the school declined during the early eleventh century until the rule of Guy of Châtillon, archbishop from 1033 to 1055.[100] Under archbishop Manasses I (r. 1069–80), the schoolmaster was the poet Godfrey of Reims, who was part of a literary community in northern France that included Baudri of Bourgeuil and Marbod of Rennes.[101] The poet Fulcoius of Beauvais was in archbishop Manasses' entourage at the same

---

[98] John R. Williams, 'The Cathedral School of Reims in the Eleventh Century', *Speculum*, 29 (1954), pp.661–77 (p.672, p.677).

[99] See the overview of Gerbert's career given in Richer of Saint-Rémi, *Historiae*, ed. and trans. Justin Lake, Dumbarton Oaks Medieval Library, 2 vols (Cambridge, MA, 2011), I, pp.xi–xv; Williams, 'The Cathedral School of Reims', p.661.

[100] Williams, 'The Cathedral School of Reims', p.663.

[101] Thomas C. Moser Jr, *A Cosmos of Desire: The Medieval Latin Erotic Lyric in English Manuscripts* (Ann Arbor, MI, 2004), p.18.

time, and was also part of the literary circle of Baudri and Marbod.[102] In addition to these tenth- and eleventh-century figures connected to the cathedral school, the ninth-century archbishop Hincmar of Reims was a prolific author, whose most relevant work in terms of secular literature is his continuation of the *Annales Bertinani*;[103] an earlier Reims historian is the tenth-century Flodoard (894–966).[104]

This list is selective from lack of evidence, but these figures show that Reims had produced or housed notable historians and poets in the two centuries before the *Alexandreis*'s composition. This might suggest that Walter of Châtillon was continuing, or seeking to revive, a tradition that had fallen into abeyance in the early twelfth century.[105] All the authors mentioned engaged to some extent with classical materials, whether historiography or poetry, but the most significant authors for Walter of Châtillon in the later twelfth century are the poets Fulcoius and Godfrey. This is because they interact most overtly with poetic classical material, and also since their relationships with Marbod and Baudri place them within a wider literary context towards the end of the eleventh century. This context has been characterized as an 'Ovidian subculture', 'a literary community reading Ovid' based in the cathedral schools and lower ranks of monastics.[106] The work of Baudri in particular is seen as the precursor to the *aetas Ovidiana* that begins in the twelfth century.[107] Suggesting that Reims poets were part of such a context implies that Ovidianism could be important for Walter as reviver of a literary tradition. Yet there are two issues that trouble this idea. Firstly, the examples of Godfrey and Fulcoius highlight that of course there was more than one way of reading and reacting to Ovid's works. Thomas C. Moser Jr's analysis of the two poets concludes that Fulcoius's poetry is more 'heroic and Virgilian', although still influenced by Ovid, whereas in Godfrey's works the 'Virgilian warrior and poet is replaced by something much more Ovidian'.[108] The individualism of poetic responses to Ovid indicates that an 'Ovidian subculture' was a broad church, making specific influences difficult to trace. Secondly, Walter's own relationship with

---

[102] Williams, 'The Cathedral School of Reims', p.671 and p.676; Moser, *Cosmos of Desire*, p.18 and p.22.

[103] See Richer, *Historiae*, ed. and trans. Lake, p.xvii.

[104] Ibid., p.xvii.

[105] Williams, 'The Cathedral School of Reims', describes this period as 'the sterile years', p.677.

[106] Gerald A. Bond, *The Loving Subject: Desire, Eloquence and Power in Romanesque France* (Philadelphia, PA, 1995), pp.66–7.

[107] The phrase was coined by Ludwig Traube in *Vorlesungen und Abhandlungen*, ed. Franz Boll, Paul Lehmann, and Samuel Brandt, 3 vols (Munich, 1909–20; repr. 1965), II: *Einleitung in die lateinische Philologie des Mittelalters*, ed. Paul Lehmann, p.113. On Baudri, see Bond, *The Loving Subject*, pp.42–69; his importance for the *aetas Ovidiana* is discussed at p.43.

[108] Moser, *Cosmos of Desire*, pp.22–34 (at p.23 and p.29).

Ovid is not as explicit as his interest in epic poets like Virgil, Statius, and particularly Lucan, probably because he is writing an epic poem that is modelled stylistically on such classical authors.[109] There is very little obvious Ovidianism in the *Alexandreis*, certainly in the style of Baudri, the most Ovidian of the eleventh-century poets in the literary circle, whom Bond characterizes as fundamentally interested in Ovid's potential as a mode of developing ideas about identity, personal and poetic, in erotic works.[110] In the *Alexandreis*, issues of identity are not cast in Ovidian terms; Alexander's self-reflections, clearest in his speeches, are concerned with heroic values such as martial glory and honour, in a mode more reminiscent of Lucan and/or Virgil.[111] In addition, the episode in which the queen of the Amazons comes to Alexander to request a child from him is limited to only a few lines and feels truncated, perhaps deliberately; an obvious moment for Ovidian content, as well as style, is passed over.[112] The *Alexandreis* is not part of any Ovidian tradition traceable to Reims or any other cathedral school. It might be possible to perceive a tenuous link between Fulcoius' more Virgilian use of Ovid and Walter's interest in Virgil, which he states in the *Alexandreis*'s prologue,[113] but it is much more likely that Walter's Virgilianism comes directly from that poet.

However, there is an important caveat. Although Walter does not appear to draw on Ovid in a way that can be associated with earlier Reims poets, he is nevertheless deeply influenced by the Roman author. Ovid's poetics are notoriously shifting and complex, suggesting and denying meanings simultaneously, making any definition of Ovidianism difficult.[114] His poetics are perhaps best described as Protean, recalling the eponymous sea-god who appears in Walter's short poems.[115] As we have seen, Walter's poetic style can also be described as *sic et non*, aligning it in this aspect with Ovid's poems in terms of Hardie's 'equivocation between absence and presence'.[116] Ovid is therefore

---

[109] For a penetrating analysis of Walter's style, particularly his 'Lucanism', in the *Alexandreis*, see Fraker, *Medieval Epic and Silver Latin*, pp.145–65.

[110] Bond, *The Loving Subject*, sees Ovidian subculture as important to poets 'attracted to the problem of constructing a new identity', and describes Baudri's preoccupations in this context as, among others, 'the practice of voice ... his idea of the self, his decriminalization of desire, his treatment of friendship' (pp.42–3).

[111] See for example Alexander's frustration at his youth and desire for glory expressed in *Alexandreis* I.33–47.

[112] *Alexandreis*, ed. Colker, VIII.36–48.

[113] *Alexandreis*, ed. Colker, Prologue, 19–23.

[114] See Philip R. Hardie, *Ovid's Poetics of Illusion* (Cambridge, 2002), who, using the idea of duplicity to analyze the poet's works, states that 'the equivocation between absence and presence haunts the Ovidian *corpus* to a degree that makes of it a recognizably Ovidian response to language and literature' (p.3).

[115] He appears in the prosimetrum edited as Poem 62, verse 23, lines 5–6, in Traill, *Shorter Poems*, pp.246–7.

[116] Hardie, *Poetics of Illusion*, p.3.

a hugely influential poet for Walter of Châtillon, despite the naturally more obvious influences of epic Roman poets in the *Alexandreis*.[117] Even if direct influence between earlier Reims poets with Ovidian tendencies and Walter is not likely, a local literary culture that placed a heavy emphasis on Ovid and Ovidian poetics could well have been an important factor for the twelfth-century poet. In this broader sense, then, Reims's tradition of poetic interest in Ovid provides some of the literary background for the *Alexandreis*'s poetic style. Fraker's observation that there is a 'strong case' 'for a mixed media Ovidian-Lucanesque narrative mode in the years around 1200' is highly appropriate to the *Alexandreis*.[118]

Reims clarifies the *Alexandreis*'s *sic et non* poetics in political and to some extent in literary terms. However, the issues that are local to Reims – ecclesiastical, political, and literary concerns – are also regional and transnational. To understand the poem's gestures towards this larger sphere of influence, in particular the idea that *translatio studii* is a debated and plural phenomenon, we need to look beyond Reims and to investigate the *Alexandreis*'s broader literary contexts and influences via its social and textual networks. One such network connects the *Alexandreis* with Joseph of Exeter's *Ylias*, textually and geographically. Both poems were composed at Reims, and the *Ylias* is thought to be a response to the *Alexandreis* since it contains verbal reminiscences and imitations of that poem. In addition, both poems are engaged in the *translatio studii* of antique narratives in Latin epic poetry, making the *Ylias* an important comparison for the *Alexandreis*. In the next section, I shall consider the *Ylias*'s poetics to see whether it too engages in literary and political *sic et non*.

The *Ylias* of Joseph of Exeter

Although the *Ylias* is an important comparison for the *Alexandreis*, their relationship has yet to be studied in detail, a surprising fact given that the former, an epic Troy narrative in six books based on Dares and Dictys describing the Trojan War and its aftermath, is said to use the *Alexandreis* as a model and was probably also composed at Reims in the 1180s.[119] These connections

---

[117] Walter's many verbal reminiscences of Ovid show his acquaintance with the standard medieval range of the latter's works. The apparatus of Colker's edition of the *Alexandreis* gives a useful overall impression of Walter's use of Ovid in these terms.

[118] Fraker, *Medieval Epic and Silver Latin*, p.126.

[119] There is a reference to Champagne at *Ylias* I.522. See Francine Mora-Lebrun, 'D'une esthétique à l'autre: la parole féminine dans l'*Iliade* de Joseph d'Exeter et le *Roman de Troie* de Benoît de Sainte-Maure', in *Conter de Troie et d'Alexandre: pour Emmanuèle Baumgartner*, ed. Laurence Harf-Lancner, Laurence Mathey-Maille, and Michelle Szkilnik (Paris, 2006), pp.31–50, at p.32; *L'Iliade: épopée du XIIe siècle*, p.13; and *Ylias*, in *Joseph Iscanus: Werke und Briefe*, ed. Ludwig Gompf (Leiden, 1970), p.21. For a more detailed synopsis of the poem, see appendix 2.

indicate that the two poems might share literary attitudes towards *translatio studii*; politically, however, they may diverge, since the *Ylias*'s author, Joseph of Exeter, was connected to the Angevin circles of Henry II via his relationship with the archbishop of Canterbury Baldwin of Forde (r. 1185–90), the poem's dedicatee.[120] This fact reminds us of the complex interactions of political-ecclesiastical relationships already demonstrated in the *Alexandreis*, since the *Ylias* also, although from a different angle, seems to inhabit a range of political and geographical contexts. The analysis that follows will consider aspects of the *Ylias*'s *translatio studii* as well as the poem's political stances. This will contextualize the same aspects of the *Alexandreis*.

The poem's relationship with the *Alexandreis* currently rests upon identification of possible quotations and imitations, as well as the likelihood of composition at Reims.[121] Whether or not the *Ylias* is textually indebted to the *Alexandreis*, it resembles that poem in terms of its antique subject matter; it remains to be seen whether it also resembles it in its approach to that same *materia*. The poem, composed like the *Alexandreis* in epic hexameters but in more florid Latin, has provoked a wide range of critical responses. In stylistic terms, Fraker's valuable comparison of the two poems concludes that both are more interested in Lucan than Virgil in narrative terms, although the extent of this preference differs.[122] In hermeneutic terms, Mora claims that the *Ylias* displays a harsh Augustinianism towards its pagan subjects who are not able to benefit from the illumination of Christianity, which may demonstrate a historical separatism similar to that identified in the *Alexandreis*.[123] The poem has also been seen as epic masquerading as satire, as a critical, clerical response to the *Roman de Troie* of Benoît de Sainte-Maure, and as a Boethian critique of false philosophy.[124] A broad unifying factor between these different interpretations is that they all see Joseph as writing from an overtly Christian

---

[120] Gerald of Wales claims Joseph was Baldwin's nephew in *De rebus a se gestis*, 2.20, cited by Geoffrey Blundell Riddehough, 'The Text of Joseph of Exeter's *Bellum Troianum*' (unpublished doctoral dissertation, Harvard University, 1951), p.4.

[121] A survey of the editions by Gompf and Riddehough indicates that the identification of quotations and allusions is problematic, however (see *Joseph Iscanus: Werke und Briefe*, ed. Ludwig Gompf (Leiden, 1970), and Riddehough, 'Joseph of Exeter's *Bellum Troianum*'). Gompf's edition gives three such references, whereas Riddehough's edition gives thirteen, of which only one corresponds to any of Gompf's three.

[122] Fraker, *Medieval Epic and Silver Latin*, passim, but especially p.129, p.138, p.145, p.165.

[123] Francine Mora, 'Y a-t-il des circonstances atténuantes dans l'*Iliade* de Joseph d'Exeter et dans le *Waltharius*?', in *La Faute dans l'épopée médiévale: Ambiguïté de jugement*, ed. Bernard Ribémont (Rennes, 2012), pp.205–18 (p.215, p.217).

[124] J. Roger Dunkle, 'Satirical Themes in Joseph of Exeter *De bello troiano*', *Classica et mediaevalia*, 38 (1987), pp.203–13 (p.213); Mora, 'L'*Ylias* de Joseph d'Exeter'; Douglas Kelly, 'Troy in Latin and French: Joseph of Exeter's *Ylias* and Benoît de Sainte-Maure's *Roman de Troie*', in *The Conspiracy of Allusion: Description, Rewriting, and*

perspective, a perspective that, if a dominant hermeneutic strategy with regard to the *materia*, would differentiate the poem significantly from the *Alexandreis*. Unlike that poem, the *Ylias*'s prologue explicitly addresses the problem of historical veracity, and does so from a Christian perspective.

> Meoniumne senem mirer Latiumne Maronem
> An vatem Frigium, Martem cui certior index
> Explicuit presens oculus, quem fabula nescit?
> Hunc ubi combiberit avide spes ardua mentis,
> Quos superos in vota vocem? Mens conscia veri
> Proscripsit longe ludentem ficta poetam.
> Quin te Cicropii mentita licentia pagi
> Et ledant figmenta, pater.

> *Should I admire old Homer, Latin Virgil, or*
> *The Bard of Troy (unknown to tale), whose present eye,*
> *A surer witness of the truth, disclosed the war?*
> *And now my mind's high hope has grasped this trusty source,*
> *What gods should I invoke? My mind, aware of truth,*
> *Has banished far the teasing poet and his tales,*
> *Lest Athens' licensed fabrications and its lies*
> *Offend you, father.*[125]

Joseph here claims that his source, Dares Phrygius, is more reliable than Homer or Virgil, a stance that is also found in the *Roman de Troie* (c.1165),[126] and goes on to decry the 'ludentem ficta poetam', 'the teasing poet's tales' (Virgil) explicitly in the context of the archbishop of Canterbury ('pater'), i.e. not just the poem's dedicatee but Christianity's representative. This seems to indicate that the poet's historical perspective will be an overtly post-Incarnation one, despite the antiquity of his subject matter, which would differentiate its *translatio studii* from that of the *Alexandreis*. Yet there is a hint in these lines that its historicity will be more complex. The question 'Quos superos in vota vocem?', 'What gods should I invoke?', indicates awareness of an interpretative problem: if the pagan gods are removed, then the story's pre-Christian status becomes less obvious, and historical differentiation, which Joseph has just explicitly set up, is troubled. Paradoxically, the pagan gods are needed to underline a Christian approach to the *materia*.

Authorship from Macrobius to Medieval Romance, Studies in the History of Christian Thought, 47 (Leiden, 1999), pp.121–70 (p.142).

[125] *Ylias,* ed. Gompf, I.24–31. The translation is by A. G. Rigg, *Joseph of Exeter: Iliad* (Toronto, 2005), <http://medieval.utoronto.ca/ylias/> [accessed 14 August 2017]. All subsequent translations and quotations are from these editions.

[126] On the possible relationship between the texts, see Mora, 'L'*Ylias* de Joseph d'Exeter', passim.

This paradox may well have caused Joseph to add the gods into his version, since they are notably absent from Dares' text. Their addition has been discussed by several critics, who broadly agree that they have been included as part of the 'epic machinery' of the poem and as such are not very active participants.[127] By adding them, Joseph indicates that his classical model is not just that of Dares' 'eyewitness' history, but poets such as Virgil, whose fables he decries in favour of Dares.[128] This inclusive approach undermines Joseph's stated usage of his sources and troubles his repudiation of 'mentita licentia pagi/Et … figmenta' (I.30–1). Dissembling could simply be part of Joseph's poetic technique, a witty and paradoxical acknowledgement of those poets he claims to dismiss, but there is another dimension involved. One of Joseph's methods of dealing with pagan gods, according to A. G. Rigg,[129] is to use them to highlight the false nature of antique religious belief. A passage at the end of book III (454–6), for example, criticizes in vivid terms the idea that the twins Castor and Pollux became divine.

> Desine, Cicropii funesta licentia pagi,
> Incestos generare deos! Non fabula celum,
> Sed virtus non ficta dabit.

> *Cease, deadly licence of antiquity! Invent*
> *No more immoral gods, for heaven's won by real*
> *Good life, not lying tales.*

The use of interpolated pagan deities to criticize their own classical pantheon's existence is ironic, but, more importantly, this deploying of pagan machinery in the service of Christian reflection troubles that very reflection. As Rigg points out, sometimes the existence of pagan gods seems to be accepted, leading to inconsistency in the dichotomy of pagan past and Christian present that is necessary in order for the poem to be consistently hostile to the former.[130] This is particularly clear in the expanded Judgement of Paris scene in book II, which is very brief in Dares. All three goddesses, Juno, Minerva, and Venus, make lengthy speeches decrying their rivals and supporting their own claims; apart from displaying the author's rhetorical skills, the speeches are also a way of condemning the goddesses out of their own mouths. Despite her elevated rank, each goddess speaks not with divine wisdom but resorts to

---

[127] H. C. Parker, 'The Pagan Gods in Joseph of Exeter *De bello Troiano*', *Medium Ævum*, 64.2 (1995), pp.273–8. This is qualified by A. G. Rigg, 'Joseph of Exeter: Pagan Gods Again', *Medium Ævum*, 70.1 (2001), pp.19–28.

[128] *Ylias* I.24–9.

[129] Rigg, 'Pagan Gods Again', pp.20–1.

[130] Ibid., p.21; Mora, 'Circonstances atténuantes?', p.215, cites Jean-Yves Tilliette's idea that the *Ylias* and its now-fragmentary successor the *Antiocheis* were meant to form a pagan–Christian diptych.

slandering her rivals and thus exposing herself to the ridicule of the poem's audience. Juno effectively bribes Paris by offering him any sceptre and lands he may want; Minerva, despite laying claim to modesty, exposes her breasts and manages to mention Venus' immodest birth; and Venus questions Minerva's virginity, a spectacular triumph of malice over intelligence.[131] They are depicted ultimately as poor speakers, and thus entirely lacking in the sacred inspiration that might seem proper to genuine divinities; hence the implication is that they too are part of the lying fictions of pagan poets. The pagan divinities exemplify both the crimes of antique history and the sin of spurious rhetoric, one of the medieval seven liberal arts that were supposed to lead to contemplation of the divine.[132] Yet the false nature of their divinity can only be noted via their presence; the intermingling of classical material and implied Christian hermeneutic here means that this important scene cannot easily be read as either a straightforward classical borrowing or as a condemnation of such borrowing.

The multifaceted nature of the divinities in the *Ylias* troubles a clear reading of the poem as a Christian disapproval of the pagan past (such as Mora's), and thus also problematizes the consistent deployment of a Christian hermeneutic with regard to its *materia*. Joseph's use of classical material is, despite his claims, not a straightforward use of the most sober (and non-poetic) account, but a more complex process of selection. However, the seeming repudiation of 'lying' classical poets and an explicit disapproval of the 'credulus error' of the Britons' belief in Arthur's resurrection at the end of book III does suggest a methodological emphasis upon Christianity, even if not a consistent one, that is absent from the *Alexandreis*. The end of the poem in particular demonstrates this:

> Hactenus Yliace questus lamenta ruine
> Confusa explicui veteris compendia veri,
> Etsi quando auctor, rarus tamen. Altera sacre
> Tendo fila lire. Plectro maiore canenda
> Antiochi nunc bella vocant, nunc dicere votum
> Christicolas acies et nostre signa Sibille,
> Que virtus, que dona Crucis. Nec fundit hanela
> Hos michi Cirra pedes, animi fidentis hiatum
> Celsior e celo venit impleturus Apollo.

> *Till now I've mourned the tragic fall of Ilium,*
> *Unfolding brief and tangled webs of ancient truth,*
> *And adding only here and there. But now I pull*

---

[131] II.309–12, 347–8, 391–2, 430, 510–11.

[132] See Alan of Lille's conception of the Liberal Arts as forming Prudence's chariot on her journey to heaven (*Anticlaudianus*, ed. R. Bossuat (Paris, 1955), II.325–IV.82).

> *The string of sacred lyre: the wars of Antioch*
> *Now call, requiring greater tunes, for now I wish*
> *To speak of Christ's crusade, the standards of the Church,*
> *The Cross's mighty gifts. No panting Muse pours feet*
> *Of verse for me: a greater Phoebus, heaven-sent,*
> *Comes down to fill the chasm of my faithful mind.*[133]

This passage seeks to place Joseph's poem about Troy lower in a textual hierarchy than his epic about crusading, the *Antiocheis*, of which only a few lines remain.[134] Although such epilogues do not always characterize a poem in its entirety, as we have seen in similar moments in the *Alexandreis*, here this explicit hierarchy can be related to the use of the pagan gods, since both the epilogue and the use of the gods indicate a Christian perspective. Whilst the poem cannot be read as a simple Christian updating of the Troy narrative, a consciously Christian hermeneutic is much more visible than in the *Alexandreis*, in partial agreement with Mora's view of the poem. This hermeneutic also suggests that the issue of anachronism, consciously avoided in the Alexander poem's concern for historical veracity, is not a similar concern for the *Ylias*; this too differentiates the two texts' *translatio studii*.

This significant difference in hermeneutics suggests that an implicit debate about the practice of *translatio studii* does indeed exist, and is one that in this instance takes place between Latin texts. Similarly, the *Ylias*' political engagement differs from the *sic et non* situation located in the *Alexandreis*. Joseph's connection with Baldwin (with whom he undertook the Third Crusade) and also his probable location at Exeter indicate his links to Angevin concerns,[135] as mentioned earlier, and these links are brief but explicit in his text. The poet refers to Henry the Young King (d. 1183) as the equal of Hector, an explicit exemplary parallel without any of the subterfuge visible in the *Alexandreis*.[136]

---

[133] *Ylias*, ed. Gompf, vi.959–67.

[134] It is printed in *Ylias*, ed. Gompf, p.12. The poem is thought to have been a description of the Third Crusade focusing on Baldwin and Richard I of England's deeds, but Riddehough believes it is more likely to have dealt with the capture of Antioch in the First Crusade; see Riddehough, 'Joseph of Exeter's *Bellum Troianum*', p.9, and *Joseph of Exeter, The* Iliad *of Dares Phrygius*, trans. and introd. Gildas Roberts (Cape Town, 1970), p.x and p.89, n.11.

[135] Several letters between Joseph and his friend Guibert, abbot of Florennes (1188–94) and then of Gembloux (1194–1206), are extant, in one of which Joseph states his plan to go with Baldwin on the Third Crusade (he is thought to have gone in 1190 and have been back in Britain after 1194). The correspondence is edited in *Ylias*, ed. Gompf, pp.220–8. Joseph has been tentatively identified as a witness to an Exeter charter dating from before 1160 by Dom Adrian Morey, *Bartholomew of Exeter, Bishop and Canonist: A Study in the Twelfth Century* (Cambridge, 1937), p.107, who identifies him with the 'magister Joseph' in the charter. Cited by Riddehough, 'Joseph of Exeter's *Bellum Troianum*', p.3.

[136] *Ylias*, ed. Gompf, v.533–7.

Apart from this reference to the Young King, there is only one other passage
that refers to contemporary events, which is the poem's dedication to Baldwin.

> In numerum iam crescit honos, te tercia poscit
> Infula: iam meminit Wigornia, Cantia discit,
> Romanus meditatur apex et naufraga Petri
> Ductorem in mediis expectat cimba procellis.
> Tu tamen occiduo degis contentus ovili
> Tercius a Thoma Thomasque secundus et alter
> Sol oriens, rebus successor, moribus heres.
> Felices, quos non trahit ambitus! Ardua nactus
> Non in se descendit honos; non ceca potestas,
> Quid possit Fortuna, videt; non perfida sentit
> Prosperitas flevisse humilem, qui ridet in altis.
> Parcite sacrilega superos incessere preda,
> Parcite! Venales quisquis venatur honores,
> Unde ruat, tabulata struit.

> *Your honours grow apace: the third great office calls,*
> *For Worcester first knew you, now Canterbury knows*
> *You, Rome itself eyes you, for Peter's sinking ship*
> *Requires a leader, one to guide it through the storms.*
> *Yet with your western flock of sheep you live content,*
> *From Becket third, a second Thomas, second sun*
> *Arising, heir in worldly wealth and moral worth.*
> *Happy are those that no ambition drives, for*
> *Honour won won't come down from the heights. Blind power*
> *Sees not the force of Fortune: false prosperity*
> *Knows not that he who laughs is soon reduced to tears.*
> *Don't tempt the gods with sacrilegious plundering!*
> *Whoever seeks for honours up for sale, erects*
> *A scaffold he may fall from.*[137]

Here Joseph gives an overview of Baldwin's episcopal career and aligns him
with Becket – 'a second Thomas' – who was his predecessor bar one at Canterbury, before appearing to move on to familiar moral commentary.[138] The
overt citation of Baldwin as in direct descent from Becket as archbishop of
Canterbury, as well as the mention of Worcester and his 'western flock', seems
to place Baldwin firmly within an Angevin and insular context. Yet it is Becket
as moral *exemplum* rather than as a politician that is important here; there is no

---

[137] *Ylias*, ed. Gompf, I.33–46.
[138] Rigg sees this commentary as a pointed reference to the ambition of Richard of Dover,
Baldwin's immediate predecessor as archbishop of Canterbury, although this is debata-
ble; see Rigg, *Iliad*, p.2.

suggestion of occluded criticism of the kind demonstrated in the *Alexandreis*.[139] This view of the reference to Becket as fundamentally an ethical, rather than primarily a political, one can be paralleled by moments of ethical emphasis elsewhere in the poem, such as the re-casting of Jason's voyage in the *Argo* as the result of human avarice ('aurique cupido', 'with desire for gold', I.61), giving the initial cause of Greek–Trojan strife a moral background absent from Dares' version.[140] This framing moves the poem away from its Angevin context, despite the indication of 'the western flock', towards the transnational and sacred ethical realm. The moral focus is also a reminder that Becket was an example of the transnational question of the relationship between sacred and secular *imperium* that just happened to be localized in England. In this sense, the poem resembles the *Alexandreis* in its deployment of local references to discuss transnational concerns. However, these local references are made without the *sic et non* gestures of seeming explanation followed by denial that make the Alexander poem's politics so opaque.

It seems that Walter of Châtillon's concern for concealed politics, as well as for appropriate historically focused hermeneutics, is not found to the same extent in the *Ylias*, despite their mutual interest in classicizing epic poetry. The idea that there is a 'school of Reims' that focuses on such poetry is seductive, but as we have seen this does not suggest that epic poetry will share intellectual perspectives on its *materia*. Although Joseph of Exeter is likely to have taken the *Alexandreis* as a model in a broad sense, his work does not display the hermeneutic subtleties and the occluded political references that are a major feature of that poem, and thus does not share in its *sic et non* poetics. The *Ylias*' more straightforward and Christian historicity, as well as its less political nature and its moments of ethical emphasis, make it a much less 'hermeneutically decentered' and difficult poem than the *Alexandreis*. As the vernacular texts of the next chapter will highlight, it is a more conventional example of *translatio studii*, and can be much more easily categorized as 'ethice supponitur'.

Yet there is an important similarity between the poems. The *Ylias*'s geographical framework places it with an Angevin context, with references to

---

[139] Although it could be thought that the very mention of Becket is in itself a concealed criticism of Henry II, this is unlikely given that Baldwin was a trusted counsellor of that king as well as a supporter of Becket before the latter's death, which was over ten years before the most likely date of the *Ylias*' composition. This incidentally is a reminder that to be pro-Becket as a churchman was not necessarily to be anti-Henry, at least by the 1180s.

[140] The idea of the arrogance of sailing could have been taken from Ovid's description of the Age of Bronze in *Metamorphoses* I.125–50, during which mankind creates ships for the first time out of the desire for gain, 'amor sceleratus habendi./vela dabant ventis' (*Metamorphoses*, ed. William S. Anderson, Bibliotheca Scriptorum Graecorum et Romanorum Teubneriana (Leipzig, 1991), I.131–2).

Becket, Baldwin, Henry the Young King, and the Britons. However, such a context does not make it insular in its concerns. The archbishops of Canterbury and the Young King were players on a transnational stage as well as in Angevin domains (both insular and in France); the 'credulus error' of the Britons about Arthur's resurrection also does not necessarily refer to an insular/Angevin tradition, since Chrétien de Troyes had composed his Arthurian works within continental contexts during the 1170s. Its composition at Reims, as we have seen, also places the *Ylias* within a context in which local concerns are intimately entwined with broader transnational ones. So we should not rush to characterize the *Ylias* as different in poetics from the *Alexandreis* on the basis of its seeming allegiance to Angevin and/or insular issues; it is not a question of the former poem having an insular/Angevin identity in contrast to the *Alexandreis*'s Capetian/continental one. That simplistic analysis would overlook the fact that both poems are concerned with poetic and political issues that transcend national boundaries. The poetic issues relate to the ways in which *translatio studii* could and should be performed, specifically to appropriate methods of adapting and recreating pagan classical material in a post-Incarnation world; as we have seen, Walter and Joseph come up with varying answers. The political issues treated in both poems turn out to be the same, namely the relationship between secular and sacred powers, although the *Alexandreis* is a much more political poem in this sense than is the *Ylias*. Both works refuse to be confined by the geographical and political circumstances of their composition, relevant though these are.

The *Alexandreis* and the *Ylias* suggest the existence of a broader literary and cultural debate about the performance of *translatio studii* and *translatio imperii* (the latter here can be said to define the problems of devolved church and state authority, derived ultimately from God). I shall go on to examine this debate from a vernacular perspective in the next chapter, but what is particularly interesting about it here is the different stances of the two Latin poems. Despite their mutual interest in classicizing epic, their reworking of classical *materia* and their poetics differentiate them from each other.[141] Since Latin is often thought of as a static language, certainly in comparison to the evolving and novel literary vernaculars, this difference is a timely reminder of the variety within Latin poetry in this period.[142] This difference also locates both poems explicitly within the broader context of the debate about *translatio*, since the texts take individual approaches to the question of historiography,

[141] See Fraker, *Medieval Epic and Silver Latin*, for a detailed discussion of the two poets' stylistic differences.
[142] Janet Martin's discussion of variety in terms of style is illuminating, touching on both Walter's and Joseph's work and pointing out that classicizing composition is only one aspect of this variety: see 'Classicism and Style in Latin Literature', in *Renaissance and Renewal in the Twelfth Century*, ed. Benson and Constable with Lanham, pp.537–68.

and hence to the relationship between history and fiction; in the *Ylias*, the two are more closely related as aspects of historiography than in the *Alexandreis*.

Another question posed by this analysis is the extent to which the two poetic approaches to *translatio* relate to the different *materia*. The Troy narrative also contains elements with contrasting interpretations,[143] but they are far less prominent than the 'noire et rose' ('negative and positive') history of Alexander.[144] How far can the *Alexandreis*'s complex poetics and 'hermeneutic decentering' be related to its eponymous character's multifaceted history? We have located this phenomenon at Reims, but it may also be extant, for different reasons, in Alexander works composed and circulating elsewhere. If this turns out to be the case, Walter's suggestion in his prologue that no ancient poet had composed poetry on Alexander because he was too difficult may have some truth to it after all.[145] The following chapters will take up this question of poetics in more detail, but we have established here that the *Alexandreis*, for all its seeming nostalgia for a lost classical past, is deeply involved in contemporary debates about literary and political cultures, debates that transcend boundaries of genre, geography, and polity. The Alexander of the *Alexandreis* is truly transnational in his range of meanings.

---

[143] The accounts of Dares and Dictys are told from a Greek and a Trojan viewpoint respectively, and hence their depiction of Antenor's behaviour (for example) varies in emphasis.

[144] On Alexander's history, see Laurence Harf-Lancner, 'Alexandre le Grand dans les romans français du moyen âge: un héros de la démesure', *Mélanges de l'école française de Rome: Moyen Âge*, 112.1 (2000), pp.51–63 (p.52).

[145] *Alexandreis*, ed. Colker, Prologue, 34–6.

3

Anxious Romance: The *Roman d'Alexandre*, the *Roman de Troie*, and *Cligès*

The previous chapter highlighted some of the literary and political contexts in which the Latin *Alexandreis* participates in the later twelfth century, and the characteristic issues with which that text is preoccupied. The transnational nature of the *Alexandreis'* concerns poses the question as to whether its poetics of *translatio* are found in that work alone, or whether they are a wider feature of Alexander's multifaceted textual history; in other words, can similar issues, and poetics, be found in other Alexander texts of this date, texts that may have distinctively different origins and may be composed in other languages? To answer this, I shall consider the literary and political identities of a contemporary French-language romance Alexander work, the *Roman d'Alexandre*, which was compiled c. 1180 or shortly thereafter by Alexandre de Paris, and therefore offers a particularly important comparison for the *Alexandreis* since its *translatio studii* is performed in parallel with that text.[1] I shall go on to compare other contemporary romances with the *Roman d'Alexandre* in order to contexualize its poetics. Focusing on the *Roman de Troie* of Benoît de Sainte-Maure, one of the three *romans d'antiquité* – with *Thèbes* and *Eneas* – dating from the middle of the twelfth century (c. 1150–65) that share stylistic and antique themes with the *Alexandre*, and Chrétien de Troyes' *Cligès*, a text that is explicitly concerned with *translatio studii*, I shall argue that, just as Latin *translatio studii* is not monolithic, neither is that of texts *en*

---

[1] Representative views regarding dating are Catherine Gaullier-Bougassas, *Les Romans d'Alexandre: aux frontières de l'épique et du romanesque* (Paris, 1998), who dates the text to c. 1185 (p.29); *The Medieval French* Roman d'Alexandre, ii: *Version of Alexandre de Paris*, ed. E. C. Armstrong et al., which suggests 'after 1180' (p.x); Martin Gosman, 'Le Roman d'Alexandre et ses versions du XIIe siècle: une réécriture permanente', *Bien Dire et Bien Aprandre*, 13 (1996), pp.7–23, who is more precise, suggesting 1184/5 (p.9); Laurence Harf-Lancner, 'De la biographie au roman d'Alexandre: Alexandre de Paris et l'art de la conjointure', in *The Medieval Opus: Imitation, Rewriting and Transmission in the French Tradition*, ed. Douglas Kelly (Amsterdam, 1996), pp.59–74, who is more circumspect, suggesting 'dans les années 1180' (p.59), although elsewhere she gives the date as 'peu après 1180' (*Le Roman d'Alexandre*, trans. and introd. L. Harf-Lancner, Lettres Gothiques (Paris, 1994), p.21).

romanz. From this perspective, the *Roman d'Alexandre*, and in particular the debate about *translatio studii* in which it participates, extends Alexander's impact beyond the immediate literary, political, and geographical contexts of the French text in a similar fashion to, but with a different viewpoint from, the *Alexandreis*. This comparative analysis will aid our understanding of Alexander as a local and/or a wider literary phenomenon in these contexts.

Courtly Contexts and Textual Connections

In the course of the previous chapter, I briefly outlined the multilingual and multicultural context of the *Alexandreis* before focusing on that context from a Latin perspective. Here, I want to consider the vernacular aspects of the literary landscape of the 1170s and 1180s in northern France and Angevin territories, bringing into play the other side of the linguistic coin, in order to understand what the relationships might be between the Latin *Alexandreis* and other Alexander texts. I shall move on to discuss the potentially direct interaction of the *Alexandreis* and the *Alexandre* texts shortly, but first I want to outline the shared contexts that would have enabled any such interaction.

As mentioned in the last chapter, during the 1170s the author of the *Alexandreis*, Walter of Châtillon, was in the household of William, archbishop of Reims, the younger brother of Henry I 'the Liberal', count of Troyes and Champagne. Recently David A. Traill has suggested that before his work for William, Walter was a member of Henry's household 'from c. 1161 (or earlier) to early 1164'.[2] Traill's suggestion, made on the basis of Walter's poetic attitudes towards the papal schism that seem to reflect count Henry's ambivalent stance, is supported to some extent by an early manuscript of Walter's short poems that notes one of them is inscribed 'ad comitem Henricum'.[3] If Walter was at some point connected to Henry's household, whether in the early 1160s, as Traill posits, or later by virtue of working for William, as I have suggested elsewhere,[4] then he would have experienced at first hand the vibrant

[2] Walter of Châtillon, *The Shorter Poems: Christmas Hymns, Love Lyrics, and Moral-Satirical Verse*, ed. and trans. David A. Traill, Oxford Medieval Texts (Oxford, 2013), p.xv.

[3] The manuscript is Oxford, Bodleian Library, MS Bodley 603: see discussion in chapter 2, '*Sic et Non*'. See John R. Williams, 'The Quest for the Author of the *Moralium dogma philosophorum*, 1931–1956', *Speculum*, 32.4 (1957), pp.736–47 (p.741, n.50), and also John F. Benton, 'The Court of Champagne as a Literary Center', *Speculum*, 36.4 (1961), pp.551–91 (pp.571–2). Traill's biography of Walter in *Shorter Poems* is intriguing but almost entirely drawn from later manuscript *vitae* and the poems themselves, which are notoriously difficult to interpret; it should therefore be viewed as plausible rather than definitive.

[4] See Venetia Bridges, 'Writing the Past: The "Classical Tradition" in the Works of Walter of Châtillon and Contemporary Literature, 1160–1200' (unpublished PhD thesis, University of Cambridge, 2012), p.41, and id., '"L'estoire d'Alixandre vos veul par

literary culture of the court of Champagne. This culture was a linguistically and textually multifaceted one, since although John F. Benton characterizes count Henry's tastes as 'conservative', revolving around religious and classical literature in Latin, a version of the *Iliad* story and the vernacular *Venjance Alixandre* of Jehan de Nevelon were perhaps also written for him.[5] His wife Marie, the daughter of Louis VII and Eleanor of Aquitaine, is well known for her probable patronage of Chrétien de Troyes' romances.[6] So Walter's presence at this court in the 1160s and the 1170s would have exposed him to the innovations of French romances as well as to more traditional Latinate literary culture.[7] The intriguing idea of the *Alexandreis* gestating not only in the refined air of the cloisters and cathedral schools but also in the hybrid linguistic and literary context of the court of Troyes/Champagne places Latin epic and French romance in dialogue: the *Alexandreis* could well have been composed with knowledge of Chrétien de Troyes' *Cligès*, for example (1176). This links the set of networks that coalesce around the Troyes/Champagne court with those in which the *Alexandreis* is implicated, creating a diverse set of overlapping literary cultures connecting Angevin territories, Capetian lands, and the duchies of Troyes/Champagne. These networks in turn encompass the *Alexandre*, *Troie*, and *Cligès*, which can all be located in one or more of these areas. Such contextual connections reinforce the three romances' mutual interest in the retelling of prestigious narratives, both ancient and contemporary, which in turn aligns them further with Latin texts like the *Alexandreis* and the *Ylias*. These connections underline the importance of vernacular texts, not just Latin works, for a wider understanding of *translatio studii* in northern France.

Specific interactions between Latin and French texts through these overlapping literary networks and cultures can be seen in the case of the *Alexandreis* and the *Roman d'Alexandre* in terms of shared knowledge of textual interactions, sources, and also potentially a direct intertextual relationship. Although in contrast to the direct Latinity of the *Alexandreis* the French text relies on vernacular sources (now mostly lost) composed in the 1170s, the *Roman d'Alexandre*'s textual relationships are not restricted to French material since

---

vers traitier [...]": Passions and Polemics in Latin and Vernacular Alexander Literature of the Later Twelfth Century', *Nottingham Medieval Studies*, 58 (2014), pp.87–113 (p.108).

5 Benton, 'The Court of Champagne', p.586.

6 On Marie's patronage activities, see June Hall McCash, 'The Cultural Patronage of Medieval Women: An Overview', in *The Cultural Patronage of Medieval Women*, ed. June Hall McCash (Athens, GA, 1996), pp.1–49 (p.19).

7 Ad Putter discusses the interaction between knights and clerics, and hence the hybrid nature of the court, in 'Knights and Clerics at the Court of Champagne: Chrétien de Troyes' Romances in Context', in *Medieval Knighthood V: Papers from the Sixth Strawberry Hill Conference, 1994*, ed. Stephen Church and Ruth Harvey (Woodbridge, 1995), pp.243–66.

behind this lie Latin works like Julius Valerius' *Epitome* and the *Historia de preliis*, sources that may also be present in the *Alexandre* directly as some of its episodes suggest a first-hand acquaintance with them.[8] The two texts are therefore indirectly connected via Latin material. This demonstrates that the *Roman d'Alexandre* is part of a network of directly and indirectly connected French and Latin texts,[9] implicating the *Roman d'Alexandre* not only in the developing medieval French history of literary Alexander material but also in the antique Latin (and Greek) textual traditions that preceded it. As well as positioning the poem within the Latinate world of the *Alexandreis*, this locates it at several textual crossing-points and makes it a truly multivocal work.

Dialogue between the two Alexander works is supported by direct sources as well as by textual traditions. Although the *Alexandreis* is likely to have been published before the *Alexandre*, earlier attempts at creating a complete cycle of Alexander material were already in existence.[10] These attempts draw on the same French-language texts from the 1170s as Alexandre de Paris' version, so it is possible that these earlier cycle versions or indeed the 1170s texts themselves influenced the composition of the Latin text, an intriguing inversion of the expected linguistic movement of *translatio studii*. In addition, both the *Alexandreis* and the *Alexandre* share a direct awareness of the same Latin sources. Whilst the *Alexandreis* is based in narrative terms on the history of Quintus Curtius Rufus, its oblique reference to Nectanebus as Alexander's father shows that Walter was aware of some elements of the 'romance

---

8   The 1170s vernacular works from which the *Alexandre* was drawn are inspired by the Greek *Alexander Romance* and its descendants the *Epitome* of Julius Valerius (originally composed in the fourth century AD and abridged in the ninth century) and the *Historia de preliis*, as well as the *Epistola Alexandri ad Aristotelem*: see chapter 1. On the 1170s French texts, see Penny Simons, 'Theme and Variations: The Education of the Hero in the *Roman d'Alexandre*', *Neophilologus*, 78 (1994), pp.195–208 (pp.196–7), Harf-Lancner, *Le Roman d'Alexandre*, pp.15–21, and id., 'Medieval French Alexander Romance I', in *A Companion to Alexander Literature*, ed. Z. David Zuwiyya, Brill's Companions to the Christian Tradition, 29 (Leiden, 2011), pp.201–30 (pp.202–6). Harf-Lancner considers that the *Historia de preliis* is the immediate source for the *Roman d'Alexandre* episodes concerning Alexander's submarine and aerial adventures owing to precise correspondence of details between the two versions; see her 'Alexandre de Paris et l'art de la conjointure,' in *The Medieval Opus*, ed. Kelly, pp.65–9.

9   It became the most popular of them all, judging by the admittedly problematic method of counting the extant medieval manuscripts. See Paul Meyer, 'Étude sur les manuscrits du *Roman d'Alexandre*', *Romania*, 11 (1892), pp.213–332 (pp.247–325), who lists twenty-one MSS with complete texts (as opposed to fragments or excerpts), seventeen of which contain a whole version of the *Roman d'Alexandre*.

10   For discussion of the relationship between these MSS (Paris, Bibliothèque de l'Arsenal, MS 3472 and Venice, Museo Civico Correr, MS VI.665) and Alexandre de Paris' text, see Gosman, 'Le Roman d'Alexandre et ses versions du XIIᵉ siècle', pp.16–17, and Simons, 'Theme and Variations', p.197.

tradition' of Alexander found in other Latin sources, sources upon which the *Alexandre* draws directly.[11]

Finally, and most interestingly, there is a possible intertext between the *Alexandreis* and the *Alexandre*. The Latin text describes Darius' tomb as shaped like a pyramid, as is Alexander's tomb in the French work. It has been suggested that the tomb descriptions in both texts are inspired by the elaborate tomb ecphrases in the earlier *romans d'antiquité*,[12] but none of these texts contains tombs shaped like pyramids. This shared detail may indicate an intertextual relationship here, despite the poems' linguistic differences.

These are all admittedly small indications. However, taken together they suggest that the *Alexandreis* and the *Alexandre* are not just connected by their similar dating, but also by mutual knowledge of contemporary, as well as antique, Alexander material. If this is the case, then it may result in similar *translatio studii*. I have already highlighted the *Alexandreis'* concern for historicity and appropriate interpretation; it remains to be seen whether this concern is shared by the *Alexandre*, or whether the French text takes a different approach.

The *Roman d'Alexandre*

The *Roman d'Alexandre* is a complex phenomenon, a vast compendium proffering a version of Alexander the Great's life from birth to death in over sixteen thousand lines.[13] It is composed using a twelve-syllable line with end-rhyme (the 'Alexandrine' line) in *laisses* that vary in length, and is commonly referred to as a 'cycle', as it is not the work of a single author but an accumulation of various different texts and literary techniques. The version that is commonly known as the '*Roman d'Alexandre*' was created by Alexandre de Paris (or Bernay) and as mentioned above is a re-versification of French texts mainly composed in the 1170s, texts that are mostly no longer extant. Alexandre de Paris' text is usually described, following Paul Meyer, in terms of 'branches'.[14] The first branch describes Alexander's birth, youth, and early military encounters, and is based on the earlier twelfth-century text of Alberic of Besançon and the *Decasyllabic Alexander* (1160–70); the second branch covers Alexander's conquest of Darius and the Persian empire, and is based on the *Decasyllabic Alexander* and the *Fuerre de Gadres* of Eustache; the third branch describes

---

[11] The reference occurs at I.46–7.

[12] Maura K. Lafferty, *Walter of Châtillon's* Alexandreis: *Epic and the Problem of Historical Understanding*, Publications of the Journal of Medieval Latin, 2 (Turnhout, 1998), p.115.

[13] This total is that in the standard modern edition of the text, *The Medieval French* Roman d'Alexandre, II: *Version of Alexandre de Paris*, ed. E. C. Armstrong et al. (Princeton, 1937). All quotations are taken from this edition.

[14] Meyer, 'Étude sur les manuscrits du *Roman d'Alexandre*', pp.214–19.

Alexander's defeat of the Indian king Porus and travels in the East (including encounters with strange men and beasts, the Fountain of Youth, and prophetic trees), based on the *Decasyllabic Alexander* and the *Alexandre en Orient* of Lambert le Tort; and the fourth and final branch tells of Alexander's coronation at Babylon and death, based on a now lost *Mort d'Alexandre*.[15] It is difficult to establish for which aspects of the text Alexandre de Paris is responsible, given the complex textual situation of the *Alexandre*, but the term 'architect'[16] rather than 'author' gives a sense of his role in shaping the cycle.

Ethics and Exemplarity

Despite this complication regarding authorship, Alexandre's narratorial presence is prominent in the text:

> Alixandres nos dist, qui de Bernai fu nes
> Et de Paris refu ses sornons apelés
> Que ci a les siens vers o les Lambert jostés.[17]

> *Alexander tells you this, who was born at Bernay*
> *and who takes his surname from Paris,*
> *who here has joined his verses to those of Lambert.*

His enthusiasm for naming himself here is paralleled at the work's start by an explanation of his purpose in creating his version:

> L'estoire d'Alixandre vos voeil par vers tretier
> En romans qu'a gent laie doie auques profitier ...
> A lui prengne regart qui se veut affetier
> Et de bonnes coustumes estruire et enseignier.[18]

> *I wish to recount the history of Alexander to you in verse*
> *and in French, so that the lay people may benefit ...*
> *Anyone should take Alexander as a model*
> *who wants to learn and teach good habits.*

---

[15] For a more detailed synopsis of the narrative, see Appendix 2. Most of these component texts are now lost. For the sources, see Simons, 'Theme and Variations', pp.196–7; Harf-Lancner, *Le Roman d'Alexandre*, pp.20–5; *The Medieval French* Roman d'Alexandre, II: *Version of Alexandre de Paris*, ed. Armstrong et al., p.x. For a timeline of their dates, see *The Medieval French Alexander*, ed. David Maddox and Sara Sturm-Maddox (Albany, NY, 2002), pp.17–19. The extant portions are edited in the various volumes (seven in total) of *The Medieval French* Roman d'Alexandre.

[16] This term is used in the discussion of the impact of Alexandre de Paris on the structure of the *Roman d'Alexandre* by Harf-Lancner, 'Alexandre de Paris et l'art de la conjointure', p.74.

[17] *Alexandre*, ed. Armstrong, II.3098–9. All translations are my own.

[18] *Alexandre*, ed. Armstrong, I.30–3, 59–60. The whole passage is I.30–61.

Here Alexander's poetic persona, emphatic in its use of the first person singular ('voeil'), claims that his purpose is an ethical one, to educate 'gent laie' in 'bonnes coustumes'. The strength of his ethical feeling spills over into a criticism of other poets' poetics in similarly morally valent terms, as he describes them as 'trouveour bastart' who 'ne conoissent bons mos', or 'bastard poets' who 'are not aware of appropriate words'. The presence of Alexandre de Paris' poetic persona here is difficult to separate from this ethical emphasis; it is suggestive that it comes to the fore at the moment in which he seeks to define his approach to the material, since it indicates that this may be ethical and exemplary. The desire of the narratorial persona to emphasize this, combined with the criticism of other 'trouveour bastart', may also suggest anxiety about interpretation: will the audience actually benefit from this story of Alexander's 'good habits', as stated? This concern is not made explicit here, but the repeated emphasis on ethical understanding in these lines introduces it subtly.

The suggestion of anxiety regarding ethical hermeneutics located in this narratorial intervention can be paralleled much more explicitly elsewhere in the text. One of the episodes that Alexandre de Paris is thought to have composed himself, drawing on the *Historia de preliis*, which highlights this anxiety, is the descent of Alexander under the sea in a glass submarine, where he observes marine life:

> Alixandres li rois o les deus chevaliers
> Est el fons de la mer, dont clers est li graviers,
> Ens el vaissel de voirre qui bons est et entiers.
> Ardent les lampes cler, car ce lor est mestiers;
> Onques poisson n'i ot, tant fust ne gros ne fiers,
> Qui osast aproismier, car n'en iert coustumiers.
> Alixandres resgarde les grans et les pleniers
> Qui les petis trangloutent, itels est lor mestiers.[19]

> *Alexander the king and the two knights*
> *are at the bottom of the sea, on the shining sand,*
> *in a vessel of glass that is well-made and whole.*
> *The lamps burn brightly, which is their role;*
> *no fish present, no matter how large or fierce,*
> *dares to approach this unaccustomed object.*
> *Alexander watches the large and the powerful [fish]*
> *swallow the small ones, as is their appropriate function.*

Alexander does not fail to draw a parallel between humans and sea creatures, interpreting the life of the fish as a sign that:

> Covoitise nos a tous sorpris et vaincus,

---

[19] *Alexandre*, ed. Armstrong, III.465–72.

Certes par avarisse est li mons confondus.
Je vi as grans poissons devorer les menus,
Ainsi as povres homes est li avoirs tolus.[20]

Greed has surprised and conquered us all,
and certainly the world is drawn to its end by avarice.
I have seen how the large fish eat the smaller ones,
just as poor men are robbed of their goods.

This ethical interpretation of natural phenomena is consistent with the grandiose statement of story-telling for moral improvement made by the narratorial persona at the start of the *Alexandre*, implicating the marvels experienced by Alexander in this hermeneutic. However, the extrapolation of such a hermeneutic from Alexander's marvels is not always straightforward. Why should the larger fish devouring the small ones, which is described as natural, be emblematic of greed in humans? Drawing this parallel between fish and humans in fact indicates that greed is a natural state for humanity, the opposite message from the one that Alexander emphasizes here. In this light, the desire for an ethical reading of this passage to some extent contradicts the narrative facts, which once again indicates the strength of the authorial need for (and hence anxiety concerning) such a reading.

The passage that immediately follows Alexander's submarine adventure sees his subordinates criticize him for his selfish temerity, enabling Alexander to hold forth about what he has learnt from the experience once more:

'Tholomé,' dist li roi, 'se Dieus me beneïe,
Ce sachiés por tout l'or qui est tresq'a Pavie
Remés ne vausisse estre, ne vos celerai mie,
Car molt i ai apris sens de chevalerie,
Comment guerre doit estre en bataille establie
Aucune fois par force et autre par voisdie,
Car force vaut molt peu s'engiens ne li aïe.'[21]

'Tholomé,' said the king, 'may God protect me,
Know well that I would not have renounced this [experience]
for all the gold from here to Pavia,
since I have learnt much about the art of chivalry,
how war ought to be joined in fighting
sometimes using force and at other times finesse,
since force is worth little without the help of guile.'

Here Alexander reflects upon chivalry in warfare, underlining the interpretation of his experience at some length (for almost as long as the initial

---

[20] *Alexandre*, ed. Armstrong, III.508–11.
[21] *Alexandre*, ed. Armstrong, III.526–32.

description of his undersea adventure). Again, the insistence upon an application for the marvellous experience seems over-emphasized, displaying a
strong desire for hermeneutic certainty; like the earlier passage, the effect of
the lengthy analysis is almost to counteract its explanation, which is here that
marine life has taught Alexander about military skill.

In short, these two examples show that the interpretation of the submarine
episode, in ethical terms, is not as obvious as the redactor-poet would like
it to be. Visible here is both the desire for an ethical and exemplary mode
of reading Alexander's exploits and also the literary effort required to create
such an interpretation. This concern for ethical exemplarity is a clear contrast
with the *Alexandreis*, which as already demonstrated is much more interested
in appropriate historicism and is opposed to the kind of allegorically derived
hermeneutic that ethical reading requires. The *sic et non* approach of the Latin
text, in which a reading is proffered only to be subtly contradicted, is not
present in the *Alexandre*: in the examples examined so far, the whole focus
is on the promotion of an ethical *translatio* of the antique *materia*. To some
extent, as discussed in chapter 1, this is a feature shared with the Greek *Alexander Romance*, the French work's ultimate source, yet the kind of anxious
interpretation seen in the *Alexandre* is not paralleled there.

This anxious *translatio* is found in Alexander himself. In the text, he is
often described as noble, a brave king, a good knight, generous, and wise,[22]
an implicit *exemplum* for the 'bonnes coustumes' Alexandre de Paris highlighted for his audience at the text's beginning. However, this reimagining of
Alexander as a contemporary knight, 'un avatar d'un héros français',[23] also
demonstrates poetic concern for his interpretation. Alexander's tomb, for example, a bejewelled pyramid balanced upon four ivory pillars with windows
of snakeskin, emphasizes the unique and wonderful character of Alexander,
but to make the point explicit a statue is included that enables the author to be
more specific.

> C'est l'ymage le roi qui iluec desous gist,
> Ice nos devisa cil qui l'estoire fist;
> Tholomés la dita a celui qui l'escrist.
> La pome fu reonde que ens el poing li mist,
> Si est li mons reons q'Alixandres conquist.
> Maint prince en afola et maint roi en malmist.[24]

---

[22] All these attributes can be found together at ı.645–60, but are scattered individually
throughout the text.
[23] Martin Gosman, 'Alexandre le Grand: les avatars d'un héros français', in *Polyphonia Byzantina: Studies in Honour of Willem J. Aerts*, ed. Hero Hokwerda, Edmé R.
Smits, and Marinus M. Woesthuis, Mediaevalia Groningana, 13 (Groningen, 1993),
pp.179–88.
[24] *Alexandre*, ed. Armstrong, ıv.1543–8.

> *That statue represented the king who lay under the stone,*
> *as the author of the tale explains to you.*
> *Ptolemy dictated that story and caused it to be carved on the marble.*
> *The round apple that it held in its fist*
> *represented the earth that Alexander had conquered;*
> *he ruined princes and kings utterly.*

This physical epitaph acts as Alexander's and the tomb's interpretation, despite the fact that Tholomé has caused Alexander's history to be written on the tomb anyway. This commentary on a commentary displays the author's concern that the audience should understand Alexander's *significatio* correctly, as master of the world and lord of many kings. However, the meta-commentary does not end there, but continues to make an ethical point in phrasing reminiscent of *chansons de geste*: 'Se il fust crestïens, ainc tels rois ne fu nes,/Si cortois ne si larges, si sages, si menbrés' ('if he had been Christian, such a king would never have existed who was so courteous and so generous, so wise, so renowned').[25] Here a Christian reading is imposed on Alexander's narrative that explicitly places the king within what is for him an anachronistic frame of reference, probably as part of the ongoing attempt to set the tale in a recognizable contemporary medieval context.[26] This is a moment of culmination, as the hero is read as supreme both in terms of ethical exemplarity and also by the powerful Christian typological mode of interpretation. However, the two have an uneasy relationship, as the interpretation of Alexander as superlative – 'si cortois … si larges' – is conditioned by his lack of Christianity; he would have been the best king ever seen 'se il fust crestïens', suggesting that despite this extravagant praise he is not so because of his paganism. In other words, the Christian hermeneutic here problematizes the ethical reading of Alexander; thus the text's anxiety for the ecphrasis' (Alexander's) 'correct' interpretation as concerning extraordinary prowess and virtue leads paradoxically to hermeneutic ambiguity. Such ambiguity regarding the figure of Alexander is not unusual,[27] but the point here is that this particular manifestation of his ambiguity is ironically created by efforts to 'fix' his meaning.

This might seem, despite the text's interest in ethics and typology, to align this moment in the *Roman d'Alexandre* with the *sic et non* poetics of the *Alexandreis*. However, there is a crucial difference. Alexander's exemplarity as a Christian king here is not consciously undermined by the deliberate

---

[25] *Alexandre*, ed. Armstrong, IV.1556–7. The phrasing 'Se…' followed by a corresponding phrase is common in the *Chanson de Roland*, for example at 258 (*La Chanson de Roland*, ed. Louis Cortés and trans. Paulette Gabaudan (Paris, 1994)).

[26] This technique is found throughout the poem: see for example the description of Alexander's initiation as a knight (I.503–73).

[27] See Laurence Harf-Lancner, 'Alexandre le Grand dans les romans français du moyen âge: un héros de la démesure', *Mélanges de l'école française de Rome: Moyen Âge*, 112.1 (2000), pp.51–63 (p.52).

introduction of a different hermeneutic; rather, the Christian typology is intended to *reinforce*, not to question, Alexander's already emphasized ethical exemplarity (far less a feature of the *Alexandreis*). Here the *Roman d'Alexandre* and the *Alexandreis* perform *translatio studii* that is almost oppositional, so strongly marked is the difference between them. Moments that appear to be similar in terms of poetic *sic et non* in fact confirm this difference.

Oriental Marvels

The *Roman d'Alexandre* demonstrates a marked concern for an ethical interpretation of Alexander's narrative and his person, underlining this by rewriting the antique material in recognizable, contemporary terms so that the Macedonian thinks, acts, and fights like a twelfth-century duke or king. This very different approach to the same basic narrative from that seen in the *Alexandreis* confirms the existence of an ongoing debate over *translatio studii* between Latin and vernacular texts. However, a significant aspect of the *Roman d'Alexandre*'s narrative, the marvels of the East, relates more closely to other romance texts and is not paralleled in the *Alexandreis*. Looking at these marvels and comparing their treatment with similar occurrences in *Troie* and *Cligès* will enable the *Alexandre*'s poetics to be understood in a vernacular as well as a Latin context.

Much of Branch III of the *Alexandre* is concerned with the description of marvels.[28] As mentioned above, Alexander encounters talking trees, the Fountain of Youth, innumerable wild beasts, a forest of women who turn into flowers, and a perilous valley, from which he escapes by tricking a demon. Contemporary fascination with marvels is found elsewhere,[29] but in the *Alexandre* this is increased by the fact that they take place mainly in the Orient. Interest in the East during the medieval period is demonstrated by the enduring appeal of texts such as the *Letter of Alexander to Aristotle*, and indeed the Greek *Alexander Romance*, but the First and Second Crusades made such an interest a reality for crusaders from the West and hence literary audiences during the twelfth century.[30] Whereas the *Letter of Alexander to Aristotle* describes many

---

[28] Much of this part of the work is based on an earlier twelfth-century text *Alexandre en Orient*, which is lost in the original, and also (possibly independently) on the *Letter of Alexander to Aristotle*.

[29] Bestiaries are a clear indication of this fascination: see for example Gervaise's thirteenth-century French verse *Bestiaire*, edited by Paul Meyer as 'Le *Bestiaire* de Gervase', *Romania*, 1 (1872), pp.420–43, which includes the unicorn, phoenix, and siren alongside the rather more mundane badger and hedgehog.

[30] This interest is a key factor in the composition of *chansons de geste* concerning crusade narratives at the end of the twelfth and beginning of the thirteenth century; works like the *Crusade Cycle*, which includes the *Chanson d'Antioche* and the *Chanson de Jerusalem*, draw upon recent historical events. See E. Mickel, 'Writing the Record: The Old French Crusade Cycle', in *Epic and Crusade: Proceedings of the Colloquium of*

encounters with animals, the *Alexandre* (and its component texts) expands such encounters to include more exotic marvels, such as the forest of flower-girls and the Perilous Valley. These strange mythical happenings are used to underline Alexander's courage as a chivalric hero, but they also have a second, related function, as is shown in the Perilous Valley episode:

> Ainc Dieus ne fist mervelle dont li puist sovenir,
> Fiere, laide et hideuse, que on doie cremir,
> Dont ne voie entor soi grans batailles tenir:
> Les dragons fu getans qui font l'erbe bruïr
> Et grans serpans volans qui font l'air escroissir
> Et maufés rechingnans quil veulent assaillir
> Et font as cros de fer samblant de lui saisir.[31]

> *God has not made a marvel that he could recall,*
> *Fierce, ugly, and hideous, which one should fear,*
> *That did not see him [Alexander] and surround him to attack:*
> *Dragons whose breath sets the grass on fire,*
> *And huge flying snakes that make the air hiss,*
> *And grimacing demons that wish to attack him*
> *And seek to seize him in their iron claws.*

The dragons and serpents that Alexander encounters here are clear manifestations of the 'other', both wondrous and terrifying, which the East represents for contemporary authors.[32] They are implicitly contrasted with the hero Alexander, who defeats them despite his own fear: 'li rois ot paour ne fait a mentevoir' ('the king was afraid, to tell the truth').[33] Similarly, marvels that are not terrifying or dangerous, but simply spectacles, like the flower-girls, demonstrate Alexander's role as explorer and discoverer 'par cel dieu qui forma trestoute creature' ('in the name of God who formed every creature').[34] One of the functions of both kinds of marvels is thus to increase the sense that Alexander, despite being a pagan Greek culturally and temporally far removed from medieval Christians, is representative of the latter, a statement already implied by his presentation as a contemporary chivalric king throughout the text. This analysis helps to explain why the marvels form such a large part of

---

the *Société Rencesvals British Branch*, ed. P. Bennett, A. Cobby, and J. Everson, British Rencesvals Publications, 4 (Edinburgh, 2006), pp.39–64, especially pp.44–6.

[31] *Alexandre*, ed. Armstrong, III.2748–54.

[32] The exotic animals mentioned in Gervaise's *Bestiaire* are again relevant here. The classic description (and criticism) of traditional Western ideas about the 'otherness' of the East in modern times is Edward Said's *Orientalism* (London, 1978); for a more recent survey of Said's impact and current views on the subject, see A. L. Macfie, *Orientalism* (London, 2002).

[33] *Alexandre*, ed. Armstrong, III.2722.

[34] *Alexandre*, ed. Armstrong, III.3522.

the *Alexandre*: paradoxically, they help to create a sense of familiarity with regard to Alexander himself. In their lengthy presence and Alexander's reaction to them we may perceive another indication of hermeneutic anxiety about the interpretation of the narrative as exemplary; presenting the Macedonian as culturally familiar is evidently essential to his role as an *exemplum*, as we have already seen.

The dominance of exotic marvels and the relentless rewriting of the narrative in culturally contemporary terms suggests that the *Alexandre*'s response to its *materia* is moving away from historical accounts towards a greater fictionality, a claim that is to some extent supported by the presence of exotic marvels. The *Alexandre*'s interest in the antique historicity of Alexander appears to be minimal. However, to see the text as invested in its fictionality alone is misleading: its concern for Alexander to be presented in contemporary terms as a Christian prince instead makes the *Alexandre* 're-historicized', a work whose historicity is reformatted to ensure its cultural relevance to a twelfth-century audience.[35] Lines such as 'Se il fust crestïens, ainc tels rois ne fu nes,/Si cortois ne si larges, si sages, si menbrés' ('if he had been Christian, such a king would never have existed who was/So courteous nor so generous, so wise, so renowned') show the mechanics of this reformatting in action, as Alexander is positioned between his antique historicity and his medieval re-creation. Despite the *Alexandre*'s evident fictional tendencies, its consistent concern for Alexander's contemporary relevance as an *exemplum* in fact displaces his historicity towards a different period. This displacement of history is exactly what the *Alexandreis* opposes, meaning that it is not only with regard to exemplarity and its poetics that the *Roman d'Alexandre* differs radically from the Latin text; their interpretations of history are likewise poles apart. However, the two texts' very different approaches to these hermeneutic questions are a sign of their mutual fascination with the Alexander narrative's *translatio*, and hence an indication of the broader debate over this in which, despite their contrasting versions, they both participate.

Politics

The *Alexandre*'s interest in contemporary cultural and ethical interpretation leads us to the question of its relationship with its literary and political contexts: does it, like the *Alexandreis*, relate to issues that are local in specifics but transnational in import? The *Alexandre*'s political leanings are mostly a matter of speculation, since unlike the *Alexandreis* it does not refer to contemporary figures or events, except for Alexandre de Paris; no patron is named. The brief information that Alexandre de Paris provides about himself, that he was born

---

[35] Gosman, 'Alexandre le Grand: les avatars d'un héros français', interprets the *Alexandre*'s narrative on grounds of what is truly 'historical' (p.184) as well as in terms of a *speculum principis* text.

at Bernay and chose to take the surname 'de Paris', is the only suggestion of the text's geographical and political locations.[36] Bernay is in Normandy, south of Le Havre and Rouen, meaning that Alexandre was born within Angevin-ruled territory, but the aspirational surname 'de Paris' indicates that Alexandre looked towards that vibrant intellectual centre for inspiration in *belles lettres*. Focusing on Paris does not make the whole complex *Alexandre* Capetian, however, since that city was not a single political or literary entity despite its position within the royal demesne, but a place of multiple political and literary identities reflecting the internationalism of its scholarly inhabitants. Similarly, reading Alexander as a model for the king Philip Augustus, a plausible contextual interpretation given Philip's traditional identification in the contemporary *Alexandreis*,[37] also does not make the work Capetian, especially given the lack of any overt reference to Philip; the text was read in other places and at other times as a *speculum principis* work relevant to subsequent rulers.[38] What is more helpful than defining this vast and complex poem as 'Angevin' or 'Capetian' is the movement, physical and/or metaphorical, that the references to Bernay and Paris indicate between these different territories, suggesting that, like the *Alexandreis*, the *Alexandre*'s literary concerns do not correlate to political divisions. Although its continental French linguistic character seems to give the *Alexandre* a more obvious geographical context than the Latin *Alexandreis*, this is deceptive given the wide use of French beyond Capetian territorial confines, as discussed in the introduction.[39] The *Alexandre* too is transnational in the remit of its intellectual positions, even if as a political text it is opaque.

This discussion of the *Alexandre* as a political text may seem to focus on what the text is not rather than what it is, but this is important in the context of the other *romans d'antiquité*, which are often claimed as Angevin productions.[40] The refusal of political hermeneutics in the *Alexandre* may itself turn out to be a positive claim. In this politically neutral analysis, the *Alexandre* in Alexandre de Paris' version demonstrates a concern for ethically valent interpretation

---

[36] *Alexandre*, ed. Armstrong, II.3098–9.

[37] See Heinrich Christensen, *Das Alexanderlied Walters von Châtillon* (Halle, 1905), p.10.

[38] Mark Cruse's work on the *Roman d'Alexandre* as found in Oxford, Bodleian Library, MS Bodley 264 shows that the text was of interest in the fifteenth century in England and Burgundy: see Cruse, *Illuminating the* Roman d'Alexandre *(Oxford, Bodleian Library, MS Bodley 264): The Manuscript as Monument*, Gallica, 22 (Cambridge, 2011), pp.181–98.

[39] See the 'Terminology' section in this book's introduction. The use of French in Italy in particular is noteworthy: see the useful overview of this in Alison Cornish, *Vernacular Translation in Dante's Italy: Illiterate Literature*, Cambridge Studies in Medieval Literature, 83 (Cambridge, 2011), pp.70–4.

[40] See for example Aimé Petit, *Naissances du roman: les techniques littéraires dans les romans antiques du XIIe siècle*, 2 vols (Paris, 1985), I, p.11.

for a contemporary audience. However, the complex phenomenon that is the *Alexandre* is not reducible to a single meaning, despite scholarly claims of its overriding ethical intention, claims which are to some extent supported here.[41] It is possible to identify particular tendencies and concerns, but ultimately the text's immense imaginative world and its historical revisionism makes any single dominant interpretation problematic. Once again the Alexander narrative exploits the creative space between history and fiction to construct itself as transnational, relevant to all in terms of broad exemplarity.

The *Roman de Troie*

As mentioned earlier, this is the final one of the works traditionally grouped as the *romans d'antiquité* that date from the mid-twelfth century (c. 1150–65).[42] Known as the *Roman de Thèbes*, the *Roman d'Eneas*, and the *Roman de Troie*, they are based on the legends of Thebes, Aeneas (as found in the *Aeneid*), and the Trojan War respectively. *Troie* proffers an extremely long version of the Trojan War tale, beginning with the story of the Golden Fleece and the first destruction of Troy before describing the rape of Helen and its military aftermath in twenty-three battles. Amidst the fighting, the narrative includes descriptions of marvels and several love episodes between Jason and Medea, between Troilus, Briseida, and Diomedes, and Achilles and Polyxena. The work ends with the handing over of the city by Antenor and Aeneas to the Greeks, and the latters' often disastrous homecomings.[43] In terms of subject matter, the *Roman d'Alexandre* fits well amongst these romances despite its later date, as observed by Aimé Petit in 1985,[44] and this connection is made

---

[41] Martin Gosman is particularly insistent on this in 'Le Roman d'Alexandre et ses versions du XIIᵉ siècle', p.7, and 'Alexandre le Grand: les avatars d'un héros français'. See also Emmanuèle Baumgartner, 'L'Image royale dans le roman antique: le *Roman d'Alexandre* et le *Roman de Troie*', in *Cours princières et châteaux: Pouvoir et culture du IXᵉ au XIIIᵉ siècle en France du Nord, en Angleterre et en Allemagne. Actes du Colloque de Soissons (28–30 septembre 1987)*, ed. Danielle Buschinger (Greifswald, 1993), pp.25–44.

[42] This is the generally accepted dating, although it is based rather on probability than hard evidence. See Aimé Petit, *L'Anachronisme dans les romans antiques*, Nouvelle bibliothèque du Moyen Âge (Villeneuve d'Ascq, 1985; repr. Paris, 2002), p.9, and *Eneas, roman du XIIe siècle*, ed. J.-J. Salverda de Grave, 2 vols, Classiques français du moyen âge, 44 and 62 (Paris, 1925 and 1929), I, pp.xix–xx. The order of *Eneas* and *Troie* was analyzed by Edmond Faral, *Recherches sur les sources latines des contes et romans courtois du moyen âge* (Paris, 1913), pp.169–87, who concluded that *Troie* was composed after *Eneas*.

[43] For a more detailed synopsis, see appendix 2.

[44] Petit, *L'Anachronisme*, pp.9–10.

stronger by perceived stylistic resemblances between them and the *Alexandre*.[45] *Troie*, as the final one of these texts (c. 1165), is the closest temporally to the *Alexandre*, and its lengthy descriptions of various marvels in addition to its antique subject matter position it as the closest stylistically to the later romance as well. Considering *Troie*'s *translatio* of its subject matter and its poetics will therefore contextualize the *Alexandre* from a vernacular perspective.

What is recoverable of *Troie*'s socio-political context appears to differentiate it from the *Alexandre*, however. As already discussed, the *Alexandre* is difficult to locate from this perspective. By contrast, the three *romans d'antiquité* are usually thought of collectively as definitively Angevin productions, based on several facts: *Troie* contains a probable reference to Eleanor of Aquitaine as a 'riche dame de riche rei' ('wealthy wife of a rich king');[46] at least two (sometimes three) of the romances are found together in later medieval manuscripts;[47] perceived stylistic imitation between the romances;[48] and the fact that the author of *Troie*, Benoît de Sainte-Maure, also composed the *Chronique des ducs de Normandie* in 1170 at Henry II's request.[49] Although it is difficult to link the romances definitively to the person of Henry or his wife Eleanor of Aquitaine, taken together these factors seem to connect the *romans*

---

[45] The *Alexandre*'s editors consider that the description of Alexander's tomb relates to those of the *Roman d'Eneas*, for example: see *The Medieval French* Roman d'Alexandre, VII: *Version of Alexandre de Paris: Variants and Notes to Branch IV*, introd. Bateman Edwards and Alfred Foulet (Princeton, NJ, 1955), p.122. The relationship between the tombs of *Eneas* and *Troie* is discussed by Emmanuèle Baumgartner, 'Tombeaux pour guerriers et amazones: sur un motif descriptif de l'*Eneas* et du *Roman de Troie*', in *Contemporary Readings of Medieval Literature*, ed. G. Mermier, Michigan Romance Studies, 9 (Ann Arbor, MI, 1989), pp.37–50, who concludes that Benoît de Sainte-Maure develops tomb descriptions in *Troie* to surpass those of *Eneas*, possibly under Byzantine influence (p.45). Thus all three texts' tomb descriptions are interconnected.

[46] *Troie*, 13468–70. All quotations are taken from *Le Roman de Troie par Benoît de Sainte-Maure*, ed. Léopold Constans, 6 vols (Paris, 1904–12); the lines here are printed in volume II. See Tamara F. O'Callaghan, 'Tempering Scandal: Eleanor of Aquitaine and Benoît de Sainte-Maure's *Roman de Troie*', in *Eleanor of Aquitaine: Lord and Lady*, ed. Bonnie Wheeler and John Carmi Parsons (Basingstoke, 2002), pp.301–17 (p.303). O'Callaghan dates the poem 1165–70.

[47] They are found together in six manuscripts: *Eneas* and *Thèbes* in London, British Library, MS Additional 34114 (end of the fourteenth century) and Paris, BnF, MS français 784 (late thirteenth/early fourteenth century), *Thèbes* and *Troie* in Paris, BnF, MS français 375 (1280–88), and all three in Montpellier, Bibliothèque de l'École de médecine, MS 251 (mid-thirteenth century), Paris, BnF, MS français 60 (end of the fourteenth century), and Paris, BnF, MS français 1450 (thirteenth century). See *Le Roman d'Eneas*, introd. and trans. Aimé Petit, Lettres gothiques (Paris, 1997), pp.22–3.

[48] See Baumgartner, 'Tombeaux pour guerriers et amazones'.

[49] See Jean Batany, 'Benoît, auteur anticlerical? De Troïlus à Guillaume Longue-Épée', in *Le Roman Antique au Moyen Âge*, ed. Danielle Buschinger (Göppingen, 1992), pp.7–22 (p.18–19).

d'antiquité with the wider Angevin court.[50] Yet *Troie* is the only one of the three that has both textual and external connections to that court. Although Henry II's circle has been described in literary terms as a school of classical imitation,[51] this differentiation of *Troie* from *Thèbes* and *Eneas* is a reminder that the three romances do not form a political or literary monolith but are in origin individual works.[52] This reminder is also important for the perceived connections of *Troie* and the *Alexandre*, since, despite their temporal, material, and stylistic proximity, their *translatio* may differentiate the two texts.

This broad Angevin context seems to be very different from the vague aspirational mention of Paris that suggests a transnational remit in political and geographical terms for the *Alexandre*, but Alexandre de Paris' additional reference to Bernay in Normandy indicates possible physical proximity between the two romances; at the least, it indicates that any borders between Angevin and Capetian or other continental territories were porous. The two texts could have circulated in similar areas, as is indicated by the *Alexandre*'s perceived stylistic resemblance to *Troie*. Even if the two are not connected by the kind of verifiable external links and networks that juxtapose the *Alexandreis* and the *Ylias*, these resemblances of style and subject matter, combined with geographical proximity, collocate the romances in terms of their context, and make them intriguing companions in the discussion of *translatio studii*.

Intellectualism: Ethics and History

Troie is the only one of the traditional three *romans d'antiquité* in which the author names himself, like the *Alexandre*; like Alexandre de Paris, the narratorial voice of the author Benoît de Sainte-Maure suggests in the Prologue that his intention is an ethical one:[53]

> Qui vueut saveir e qui entent,

---

[50] The problem of specific patronage of literature within the court was redefined by Karen Broadhurst, 'Henry II of England and Eleanor of Aquitaine: Patrons of Literature in French?', *Viator*, 27 (1996), pp.53–84, who concludes that without evidence of patronage 'texts that contain references or possible allusions to historical personages constitute instances of inspiration only' (p.84).

[51] Francine Mora, 'De l' *Énéide* à l' *Énéas*: le traducteur médiéval à la recherche d'une nouvelle stylistique', *Bien Dire et Bien Aprandre*, 13–14 (1996), pp.21–40 (p.21), citing Emmanuèle Baumgartner, *Histoire de la litterature française*, vol. ı: *Moyen Âge* (Paris, 1987), pp.97–8.

[52] Baumgartner's idea about the tomb descriptions of *Troie* as competing with those of *Eneas*, and thus as invoking and repelling the latter text simultaneously (my extrapolation), is relevant here ('Tombeaux pour guerriers et amazones').

[53] Barbara Nolan, *Chaucer and the Tradition of the Roman Antique* (Cambridge, 1992), concludes that Benoît's aim in *Troie* is 'to instruct aristocrats in the secular art of responsible moral conduct' (p.47). For her useful discussion of the Prologue, see pp.15–17.

Sacheiz de mieuz l'en est sovent.[54]

Know that he who wishes to have knowledge and who understands
will often become a better person.

However, where the *Alexandre* is concerned explicitly for the 'bonnes coustumes' of its audience, the Prologue of *Troie* sets this ethical ideal within an
intellectual context, analyzing the historical status of its source material as
part of a conscious discussion of its *translatio studii*. Benoît gives a detailed
description of his view of his sources and his role as romance creator, insisting
that he will follow his Latin sources accurately, 'le latin sivrai e la letre' ('I
follow the Latin and the text'), although he allows himself some 'bon dit'.[55]
His analysis of Homer, 'clerc merveillos' (99), criticizes that poet's account
because it is not that of an eyewitness, indicating a preference for Dares' more
historically accurate account that was supposedly written during the siege:

Chascun jor ensi l'escriveit
Come il o ses ieuz le veeit.[56]

Each day he thus wrote down
what he saw before his eyes.

Benoît's Prologue explicitly engages with different models of historiography
as part of this learned approach to his sources and his text. Such an intellectual approach differs from that of the *Alexandre*; although the stated goal of
Benoît's discussion of his *translatio studii* is to induce virtuous actions, its
focus on the value of different sources suggests an interest in historiography
that extends the discussion beyond ethics. For Benoît, *translatio studii* in the
form of *romanz* retelling is first and foremost an intellectual good, in order to
preserve 'scïence' or knowledge;[57] at this point at least, the ethical application
of such knowledge is left implicit.

This distinction between the two texts' authorial interventions may appear
to be a nice one, but it is significant. Benoît's acknowledgement of the techni-
calities of the *translatio studii* that lie behind his work shows his awareness of
Latin traditions of interpreting his famous *materia*; he places himself among
Homer and Dares as their vernacular heir. Alexandre de Paris makes no such
acknowledgement. This may be because his material does not have the same
weighty interpretative traditions behind it as the Trojan legends,[58] but the

---

[54] *Troie*, ed. Constans, I, 25–6. All translations are my own.
[55] *Troie*, ed. Constans, I, 139 and 142.
[56] *Troie*, ed. Constans, I, 105–6.
[57] *Troie*, ed. Constans, I, 19, 23.
[58] The commentary tradition on the *Aeneid* alone is vast: Servius' commentary of the late
      fourth/early fifth century, *In tria Virgilii Opera Expositio*, was influential during the

analysis of the *Alexandre* demonstrated that its narrator is less interested in the antique historical contexts of his work, so that in this *Troie* differs from the later text. Although both authorial interventions focus upon ethical interpretations, Benoît de Sainte-Maure's persona indicates a historical perspective, at least in the Prologue, that the *Alexandre* lacks.

This difference between the two texts is the more intriguing since in many ways their poetics are similar. Both present their characters as contemporary twelfth-century knights, so that in *Troie*, Hector's portrait (based on the much shorter one of Dares) depicts him in glowing terms as a near-perfect noble,[59] in other words as an *exemplum* for medieval audiences.[60] This *speculum principis* idea sets Hector alongside Alexander. Yet here too in this exemplary poetics, which is so often mutual, there is a difference between *Troie* and *Alexandre*. In *Troie*, in contrast to the *Alexandre*, major characters are not presented in Christian terms, even fleetingly; there are no wistful 'if he were a Christian' comments, only the occasional temporal reference to Christian feasts that appears to function more as a seasonal indication.[61] The absence of Christian lexis in *Troie*, taken together with the Prologue's concern for an intellectual approach to history, suggests the text avoids explicit anachronism as part of its re-historicization for exemplary purposes. In this subtle sense, then, *Troie*'s exemplary *translatio* differs from that of the *Alexandre*, meaning further that it is not characterized by the anxious interpretation observed in the later text. This increased interest in historical accuracy to some extent aligns *Troie* with the *Alexandreis*, despite its far more straightforward poetics.

Marvels of Descriptio

It is important, however, not to read the whole poem as a historicist and Latinate tract upon *translatio studii*, as it is such a long and complex work, with the narratorial voice shifting in prominence throughout. The poem also alternates between narrative and description, containing long interludes of the latter that are inspired by the earlier *romans d'antiquité*.[62] These descriptive interludes are important since they are authorial embellishments of the traditional story and can act as moments of interpretation, as we saw in the *Alexandre* (and the

---

later medieval period, as was Fulgentius' sixth-century work, and helped to inspire new works on the poem like that attributed to Bernard Silvestris in the twelfth century.

59   *Troie*, ed. Constans, I, 5313–80.
60   Nolan, *Chaucer and the Tradition of the Roman Antique*, p.47.
61   An example is the mention of Easter at *Troie* 4807 (ed. Constans, I) which is present to herald the arrival of spring and Helen and Paris' marriage.
62   See Baumgartner, 'Tombeaux pour guerriers et amazones'. For examples of the importance of *descriptio* as a twelfth-century literary fashion, see Matthew of Vendôme, *Ars versificatoria*, Part I, sections 38–58 (in *Opera*, ed. Franco Munari, 3 vols, Storia e letteratura, 144, 152, and 171 (Roma, 1977–88), III). Matthew's text was composed c. 1175.

Alexandreis in chapter 2). Like the later text, much of the description focuses around marvellous objects, such as tombs, cities, and the famous Chamber of Beauties,[63] although sadly there are no wild beasts or submarine episodes. Although *Troie* does not engage with Oriental marvels like the *Alexandre*, it is nevertheless an exotic text for its early northern French or insular audiences, since Troy and Greece were themselves distant, strange places to the east. Its marvels, although different in terms of subject matter, are therefore parallel to those of the *Alexandre*.

Like the *Alexandre*, description of a marvel in *Troie* is often followed by commentary, as is the case with Hector's tomb. After the depiction of its miraculous architecture (a tabernacle with four golden statues representing youth and age, carrying columns made of precious stones), we are told that Hector is represented by a statue brandishing a sword, 'mostrot/Qu'ancor sereit vengiez un jor' ('showing that still he will be avenged one day').[64] It also has an epitaph in Greek telling of Hector's extraordinary knightly prowess and Achilles' responsibility for his death; the author supplements this with an epitaph of his own, listing Hector's noble conquests.

> Puis que li mondes comença,
> Ne ja mes tant cum il durra
> Ne nasqui nus de sa valor,
> Ne ne fera ja mais nul jor.[65]

> *Since the world began,*
> *And never as long as it lasts,*
> *Was ever born [a knight] of his worth,*
> *And never in the days to come.*

The poet then explains that Hector's death occurred because of Fortune's opposition: 'Mais Aventure nel sofri/Ne Envie ne Destinee' ('but Fortune nor Envy nor Destiny would not allow it [his victory]').[66] This is an intriguing passage, since it combines several ways of interpreting Hector. He is evidently an ethical figure, in terms of being a chivalric *exemplum* and an indication of the power of Fortune, but the avenging statue with its ominous threat for the future complicates this reading. Hector's vengeance foreshadows the bloody returns of the Greeks to their homes, where many (such as Ulysses)

---

63 *Troie*, II, ed. Constans, 14631–958.
64 *Troie*, III, ed. Constans, 16794–5. The statue is reminiscent of that on Alexander's tomb at the end of the *Alexandre*, suggesting that *Troie* was influencing the later text specifically at this point.
65 *Troie*, II, ed. Constans, 16823–6.
66 *Troie*, III, ed. Constans, 16842–3.

are killed.[67] This foreshadowing adds a more historical perspective to Hector's meaning, as the indication of the future expands the time frame of the narrative. Historical and ethical hermeneutics operate here in the same textual space, demonstrating the work's multiple frames of reference. This is not a unique moment: the sense of historical perspective is even more strongly marked at Paris' tomb description, where the regalia laid upon it becomes a symbol of the doom of Troy and its ruling family.[68] Such moments underline the sense of historical perspective combined with ethical interpretation found in the Prologue, situating *Troie* as a text that conceives of historicity and ethics as reinforcing one another.

This idea of reinforcement, rather than tension, again subtly differentiates *Troie* from the *Alexandre* despite their often shared poetics of exemplarity and description. In addition, this emphasis on historicity within marvellous description connects *Troie* with the *Alexandreis*, although the idea of historical separatism so prominent in that text is actively contradicted in *Troie*. *Translatio studii* is evidently not just debated between Latin poems, or between Latin and vernacular texts, but also, as here, between two French works. Even more interesting is the discovery that it is the later French text, the *Alexandre*, which appears to display more anxiety concerning ethical hermeneutics. This could be a reaction to *Troie*'s greater intellectualism and historical focus, aspects that in the very broadest sense are shared by the *Alexandreis*. This means that the *Alexandre*'s increased interest in ethical *translatio* could be a reaction to both these earlier texts.

Politics: Troie *and the 'Galaxy of Celebrities'*

The geographical and political context of the *Alexandre*, although indistinct, suggested it was a text whose *speculum principis* possibilities were not confined to a particular monarch but which moved across political boundaries. Unlike that text, *Troie* can be placed within the purview of the Angevin court, which may mean that its increased interest in intellectual and historical traditions (in comparison with the *Alexandre*) can be ascribed to this context. In other words, does this famously literary and intellectual network define *Troie*'s *translatio studii*?

Henry II's court has been studied in detail, since it contained (in Ian Short's words) a 'galaxy of celebrities': the 'austere' John of Salisbury, the 'suave' Peter of Blois, 'creepy' Gervase of Tilbury, 'unpredictable' Gerald of Wales, and 'indescribable' Walter Map, as well as Wace, Benoît de Sainte-Maure,

---

[67] *Troie*, IV, ed. Constans, 29815–30300 (the episode in which Ulysses is killed by his son Telegonus).

[68] For elaboration of this episode, see Bridges, 'Writing the Past', pp.96–7.

and troubadours.[69] This roll-call of literary figures suggests what Short calls 'productive pluralism', created by 'hitherto unheard oral traditions … in particular narrative ones' now finding their way into Latin literature.[70] The idea of pluralism is key here, since it reinforces the impression, already indicated by these different characters, that the court of Henry II was not a single entity in literary terms, but a place in which different narratives, traditions, and texts coalesced and potentially competed. Short also uses the phrase 'cultural permeability' to describe 'the age of vernacularisation of culture, of multilingualism, of multiculturalism' that he perceives within Anglo-Norman circles in the middle of the century.[71] *Troie*'s plural *translatio*, exemplary, marvellous, and historical, drawing on both Latin and French predecessors, is an appropriate product of this similarly plural set of contexts.

There may be a more specifically political context for *Troie* as part of this court, however. Chris Baswell's reading of the *Eneas* as 'a carefully controlled social and political work that articulates and then limits new feminine powers, and leaves them … at the margins of a far more central construction of emergent Angevin manhood and patriarchal imperialism' makes sense of one aspect of that text against the background of the early years of Henry II's reign.[72] This kind of imperial interpretation might also be appropriate for *Troie*, itself the prequel to the *Aeneid* narrative on which *Eneas* is based. The *Eneas*' interest in Ovidian-inspired eroticism, which is a key factor in its *translatio*, is evident too in *Troie* in scenes such as the amours of Jason and Medea and of Troilus, Briseida, and Diomedes, all episodes that Benoît de Sainte-Maure has expanded and/or created for his version.[73] Similarly, the figures of Paris and Helen might also be read as Henry and Eleanor, an interpretation made possible by their generally positive presentation in the text.[74]

---

[69] Ian Short, 'Literary Culture at the Court of Henry II', in *Henry II: New Interpretations*, ed. Christopher Harper-Bill and Nicholas Vincent (Woodbridge, 2007), pp.335–61 (p.341).

[70] Ibid.

[71] Ibid., p.340.

[72] Christopher Baswell, 'Men in the *Roman d'Eneas*: The Construction of Empire', in *Medieval Masculinities: Regarding Men in the Middle Ages*, ed. Clare A. Lees (Minneapolis, MN, 1994), pp.149–68 (p.165).

[73] *Troie*, ed. Constans, I, 1167–2044; II,13261–866; III, 15001–186, 20202–340. On Benoît de Sainte-Maure's creation of the Briseida scenes, see Douglas Kelly, 'The Invention of Briseida's Story in Benoît de Sainte-Maure's *Troie*', *Romance Philology*, 48 (1995), pp.221–41. The *Eneas* poet creates new scenes in which Lavinia falls in love with Eneas.

[74] On this positive presentation and its contrast with the hostility displayed in the *Ylias*, see Francine Mora, 'L'*Ylias* de Joseph d'Exeter: une réaction cléricale au *Roman de Troie* de Benoît de Saint-Maure', in *Progrès, réaction,décadence dans l'occident médiéval*, ed. E. Baumgartner and L. Harf-Lancner, Publications Romanes et Françaises, 231 (Geneva, 2003), pp.199–213 (pp.206–11).

However, as discussed earlier, the *romans d'antiquité* do not have a single identity, meaning that political imperialism in one does not necessarily recur in another. In addition, the later date of *Troie* (c. 1165) locates it in a less positive political context than the early and hopeful days soon after Henry's accession, as by this point his conflict with the Church (and Becket in particular) was well under way; this makes the 'emergent Angevin manhood and patriarchal imperialism' perceived by Baswell in *Eneas* less appropriate for *Troie*. The lack of a single central figure also makes *Troie*'s narrative more problematic in terms of a specific *speculum principis* interpretation, as does the lack of any explicit reference to any contemporary figure save for the 'riche dame de riche rei'. Paris and Helen, although generally presented as positive, would be problematic role models for Henry and Eleanor given the adulterous nature of the literary relationship.[75] The idea that an Angevin reading of *Troie* in this specifically *speculum principis* way is forced is supported by interest in the Trojan legend outside Anglo-Norman contexts; despite the well-known phenomenon of Anglo-Norman fascination with the Trojan legend (demonstrated in mid-century by Wace's *Roman de Brut* based on Geoffrey of Monmouth's *Historia regum Britanniae*), other dynasties in Europe were also claiming Trojan descent in literature as a legitimization strategy.[76] The simple fact of *Troie*'s composition within this context does not mean its *translatio* is politically Angevin without further evidence of specific imperial leanings, and the text's multivalent poetics, as well as its lack of references, mean that these are absent.

All these seemingly negative points, adding up to the conclusion that *Troie* is not an imperial Angevin narrative, should in fact be seen in a positive transnational light. *Troie*'s *translatio studii*, rather than being ascribed to an insular imperialist context, relates to broader intellectual interests concerning the rewriting of classical narratives, such as the fascination with historiography that is also observable in the *Alexandreis*, interests which we have already seen are not confined by political or geographical boundaries.[77] In this, *Troie* resembles both the *Alexandre* and the *Alexandreis*, despite their different contexts.

---

[75] Eleanor's annulment from Louis VII in 1152 and her swift marriage to Henry II the same year had increased her notoriety, along with rumours that she had had an affair with her uncle Raymond of Poitiers; for an overview of these events, see J. Bradbury, *The Capetians: Kings of France, 987–1328* (London, 2007), pp.155–8.

[76] See for example the *Philippis*, an epic about Philip Augustus composed by William the Breton in the early thirteenth century, at the start of which the king's descent is traced from 'Francio', supposedly a son of Hector. The text is edited in *Oeuvres de Rigord et de Guillaume le Breton*, ed. H.-F. Delaborde, 3 vols (Paris, 1885), II: *Philippide de Guillaume le Breton*.

[77] This transnational perspective on the literature of Henry II's court is supported by Rosalind Field's analysis in 'Children of Anarchy: Anglo-Norman Romance in the Twelfth Century', in *Writers of the Reign of Henry II: Twelve Essays*, ed. Simon Meecham-Jones

Cligès

Chrétien de Troyes' *Cligès* is, at first glance, a very different text from the *Alexandre*, despite its similar date of c. 1176.[78] A tale of the trials of love when one partner is unhappily married (sometimes thought of as an answer to the Tristan and Isolde story), as well as about kingship and inheritance, *Cligès* has an erotic narrative as a major aspect of its plot, unlike the *Alexandre*.[79] It is also less interested in exotic marvels, and is not an explicit rewriting of an antique narrative. Despite this and other contrasts, the two texts are connected, firstly by *Cligès'* naming of a Byzantine character as 'Alexander' and more importantly by potential intertexts in the scene of Alexander's dubbing, in which *Cligès*, drawing on the *Alexandre décasyllabique* (a component text of the *Alexandre*) and other Alexander texts, may in turn have influenced the later poem.[80] Catherine Gaullier-Bougassas, in an article comparing the Alexander characters of the *Alexandre* and *Cligès*, claims that Chrétien's Alexander, Cligès' father, can be read 'en contrepoint à l'Alexandre historique et à celui des *Romans d'Alexandre* écrits en laisses épiques'.[81] Beyond this Alexander feature, the *Alexandre* and *Cligès* have a shared interest in the Orient, both in terms of narrative and, explicitly in *Cligès'* Prologue, as the origin of the 'ancïens savons' ('ancient learning') that has passed from the East to the West and is now resident in France.[82] *Cligès* is an important yet unexamined parallel text for understanding the *Alexandre* in terms of subject matter and its *translatio studii*.[83] It is particularly important since it brings the Arthurian material made popular by twelfth-century authors like Geoffrey of Monmouth and Wace into play, material which does not initially seem as clearly relevant to the issue of *translatio studii* as the antique subject matter of *Alexandre* and *Troie*, but which in *Cligès* is also the object of such *translatio*.

---

and Ruth Kennedy (Basingstoke, 2006), pp.249–62, which distinguishes the 'international' productions of court circles from most other Anglo-Norman romances (p.249). For further discussion of this, see chapter 4, 'Insular Exceptionalism' section.

[78] Suggested by A. Fourrier, *Le Courant réaliste dans le roman courtois en France au moyen âge* (Paris, 1960), pp.160–74, and cited by Lucie Polak, *Chrétien de Troyes* Cligès, Critical Guides to French Texts, 23 (London, 1982), p.13 and Ruth Harwood Cline, *Cligès* (Athens, GA, 2000), p.ix. In the standard edition (*Cligès*, ed. Claude Luttrell and Stewart Gregory, Arthurian Studies, 28 (Cambridge, 1993)), however, the editors suggest 1185–87. The first option is more favoured by specialists, and is followed here.

[79] For a full narrative synopsis, see appendix 2.

[80] For the possible common texts for both poems, see Polak, *Cligès*, p.23, and Catherine Gaullier-Bougassas, 'L'altérité de l'Alexandre du *Roman d'Alexandre*, et en contrepoint, l'intégration à l'univers arthurien de l'Alexandre de *Cligès*', *Cahiers de recherches médiévales et humanistes*, 4 (1997), pp.1–7 (p.4).

[81] Gaullier-Bougassas, 'L'altérité de l'Alexandre', p.4.

[82] *Cligès*, ed. Luttrell and Gregory, 33–6.

[83] Gaullier-Bougassas, 'L'altérité de l'Alexandre', is the only contribution I have seen that focuses closely on a comparison of the two works.

Beyond these intriguing intellectual and narrative possibilities, the *Alexandre* and *Cligès* are connected by geographical and social networks. Chrétien de Troyes probably composed *Cligès* within the literary culture of the court of Champagne, placing it within the area controlled by the count Henry I 'the Liberal', which included the centres of Troyes and Blois. This area skirts around Paris at its centre, the possible and certainly the aspirational location for the *Alexandre*; the two texts are hence not only in temporal but also in physical proximity. In addition, *Cligès'* probable knowledge of the *romans d'antiquité* connects it to these texts too, which as we have seen are influential for the *Alexandre*, so that *Cligès* is in intellectual, if not necessarily physical, proximity to *Troie* as well as to the *Alexandre*.[84] Finally, *Cligès'* location within Champagnois literary culture of course connects it to the *Alexandreis* via William of the White Hands' fraternal interactions with Henry 'the Liberal', even if David A. Traill's claim that Walter of Châtillon was part of the Champagne court during the 1160s is not definitive.[85] All these interactions, direct and indirect, demonstrate *Cligès'* importance to Alexander material, both Latin and vernacular, and its participation in the ongoing debate over *translatio studii* already described in this part of northern France.

The *translatio studii* performed in *Cligès*, and its explicit statement in the Prologue in particular (lines 1–44), which describes the process in detail, has been the focus of much scholarly study.[86] It is often cited as a classic example of the poetics of this process, demonstrating the movement of culture westwards from the East to its natural home in France. Douglas Kelly discusses *translatio studii* in the text in terms of honour, and Sharon Kinoshita argues for the importance of the historical relationships between East and West that are reflected in the poem.[87] Both of these scholars conclude that the movement of *studium* (honour, chivalry, learning) does indeed follow this trajectory, although Kinoshita in particular emphasizes some of the contradictions in this

---

84 See Karl D. Uitti, 'Chrétien de Troyes' *Cligès*: Romance *Translatio* and History', in *Conjunctures: Medieval Studies in Honor of Douglas Kelly*, ed. Keith Busby and Norris J. Lacy (Amsterdam, 1994), pp.545–57 (p.546). Michelle A. Freeman, *The Poetics of* Translatio Studii *and* Conjointure: *Chretien de Troyes'* Cligés (Lexington, KY, 1979), makes the claim that *Cligès* is a direct reaction to historical romances including *Troie* and *Alexandre en Orient*, the latter being the source material for Branch III of the *Alexandre* (p.37).

85 See Traill, *Shorter Poems*, p.xv (and also nn.2 and 3 at the start of this chapter).

86 See for example Freeman, *The Poetics of* Translatio Studii, pp.21–42.

87 Douglas Kelly, 'Honor, Debate, and *Translatio imperii* in *Cligés*', *Arthuriana*, 18.3 (2008), pp.33–47, claims that 'honor has begun to move out and away from Greece toward the West' (p.47); Sharon Kinoshita, 'The Poetics of Translatio: French-Byzantine Relations in Chrétien de Troyes' *Cligès*', *Exemplaria*, 8.2 (1996), pp.315–54, decides that 'the result is the vindication of the moral and cultural supremacy of the Arthurian West' (p.354).

that *Cligès* incorporates.[88] However, given that one of the major features of *Cligès* is artifice,[89] and that the poem is difficult to locate in terms of a single interpretation, the question is raised as to whether the *translatio* from East to West is as straightforward as is generally claimed. If it is more complex than the Prologue and the text appear to state, then what impact does this have upon *Cligès'* poetics, and hence its relationship with the other texts that also ostensibly uphold this narrative, *Troie* and *Alexandre*? What can this tell us about the *translatio studii* that these texts foreground as a reaction to inherited prestigious material? Considering *Cligès* from this perspective enables us to see whether similar *translatio* to that found in the *Alexandre* is also a feature of an Arthurian text that does not focus on an antique narrative (like *Troie*) but which shares with the former a fascination with the Orient. In turn, this allows us to highlight the local and/or transnational character of *translatio* in these different works *en romanz*.

Cligès: *Geographical and Intellectual Parallels*

The concept of *translatio imperii et studii* in *Cligès* is geographically defined by migration from East to West in the Prologue:

> Puis vint chevalerie a Rome
> Et de la clergie la some,
> Qui or est an France venue.[90]

> *Then chivalry went to Rome* [from Greece],
> *and the height of learning,*
> *and has reappeared, now, in France.*

Unlike *Troie* and *Alexandre*, its *translatio* of its Arthurian *materia* appears to be literal, involving physical movement. However, Arthurian material itself does not derive from the East, but from the West;[91] this may seem to be an obvious point, but is one still worth making in consideration of *Cligès'* movements between Orient and Occident, which are often read as supporting an

---

[88] Sharon Kinoshita, 'Chrétien de Troyes' *Cligès* in the Medieval Mediterranean', *Arthuriana*, 18.3 (2008), pp.48–61, notes that the Byzantine harem for future empresses is caused by the behaviour of the western empress Fenice, i.e. 'reverse' *translatio* (p.57).

[89] For this emphasis, see Peggy McCracken, 'Love and War in *Cligés*', *Arthuriana*, 18.3 (2008), pp.6–18 (pp.6–7), and Uitti, 'Romance *Translatio* and History', p.546 (and throughout).

[90] *Cligès*, ed. Luttrell and Gregory, 33–5. All quotations are taken from this edition.

[91] Geoffrey of Monmouth, often seen as the *fons et origo* of much Arthurian material, of course composed his material in and about Britain, probably drawing on Welsh material: for a brief overview of this, see the introduction in *The History of the Kings of Britain*, trans. Lewis Thorpe (London, 1966), pp.14–15.

East–West trajectory, as shown by Kelly and Kinoshita. The text's *translatio* of its material may not in fact embody such a trajectory.

The idea that *Cligès'* literary *translatio* is more complex than a simple East–West movement is supported by the fact that in the text physical journeys are not all made in one direction. Alexander, son of the Greek emperor, indeed travels from Greece to Britain in quest of chivalry, but returns to Constantinople to reclaim his inheritance, thus performing a circular journey. Cligès similarly travels from Greece to Britain with the same aim, but with a difference: he goes via Germany, in order to help his uncle Alis obtain the emperor's daughter Fenice as bride, before heading to Britain on the same quest as his father Alexander, then returning to Constantinople. Even this very brief survey indicates some of the complexities of East–West movements that a simple dichotomy and unidirectional trajectory between the two does not take into account, and which are likely to complicate the question of poetic, as well as physical, *translatio* in the text.

These complexities are illustrated in a central passage in which Cligès, after his triumphant chivalric sojourn in Britain, tries to persuade Fenice that they should leave Constantinople:

> 'Dame', fet il, 'je croi et cuit
> Que mialz feire ne porrïens
> Que s'an Bretaingne en alïens;
> La ai pansé que vos an maingne.
> Or gardez qu'an vos ne remaingne,
> C'onques ne fu a si grant joie
> Eleinne receüe a Troie,
> Qant Paris l'i ot amenee,
> Qu'ancor ne soit graindre menee
> Par tote la terre le roi,
> Mon oncle, de vos et de moi.'

> *'My lady,' he said, 'I can't*
> *Believe there's a better solution*
> *Than exile in Britain, the place*
> *Where I can best bring you:*
> *Don't say you won't go: please!*
> *When Paris brought beautiful*
> *Helen to Troy, her welcome*
> *Was joyous, but not so splendid*
> *As yours and mine will be,*
> *All through the lands ruled*
> *By King Arthur, my uncle.'*[92]

---

[92] *Cligès*, ed. Luttrell and Gregory, 5274–84. The English translation is *Cligès: Chrétien de Troyes*, trans. Burton Raffel (New Haven, NJ, 1997), 5277–87; all subsequent

Here Cligès suggests that love should perform the same journey that chivalry already is said to have done, moving from Constantinople to the far west in Britain, and underlines the theme of *translatio studii* (or *amoris* here) by citing the example of Helen of Troy. Fenice's reply, however, illuminates some of the intellectual, as well as practical, complications of this simple-seeming solution:

> 'Et je dirai
> Ja avoec vos ensi n'irai,
> Car lors seroit par tot le monde
> Ausi come d'Ysolt la blonde
> Et de Tristant de nos parlé ...
> Et ci et la totes et tuit
> Blasmeroient nostre deduit.'

> *'I can't*
> *Run away like that:*
> *They'd talk about us, all*
> *Across the world, as if*
> *We were Tristan and Iseult ...*
> *Everyone here*
> *And there would accuse us of wild*
> *Passion.'*[93]

A literary narrative is used here to reject physical *translatio* from East to West. The use of the Tristan legend is logical at this point, since it is associated not only with its narrative locations of Ireland and Cornwall, both Celtic lands, but also with its literary incarnations by Thomas of Britain and Béroul in the mid-twelfth century;[94] it therefore is doubly representative of the West that Fenice and the poet are rejecting. Fenice refuses both the origins of *translatio imperii et studii*, represented by Helen of Troy, as a model, and also *studium*'s supposed new western home. Neither the ancient learning of Greece nor the

---

quotations are from this edition.

[93] *Cligès*, ed. Luttrell and Gregory, 5289–93, 95–96; trans. Raffel, 5292–96, 98–300.

[94] Both poems probably date from the second half of the twelfth century. Thomas of Britain's *Tristan* now exists in eight fragments, edited as *Les Fragments du Roman de Tristan, poème du XIIe siècle*, by Bertina H. Wind, 2nd edn (Paris, 1960). Béroul's text is also fragmentary: see *The Romance of Tristan by Béroul*, ed. Stewart Gregory (Amsterdam, 1992). *Cligès* has been read as an 'anti-*Tristan*' text, since it creates a different model of erotic love: see for example Kelly, 'Honor, Debate, and *Translatio imperii*', pp.42–4, who discusses love in ethical terms, and Uitti, 'Romance *Translatio* and History', p.551, p.553, p.557, who argues that *Cligès*, in contrast to *Tristan*, is grounded in reality rather than story. A useful overview of the debate over *Tristan*'s and *Cligès*' relationship is given by Joan Tasker Grimbert, '*Cligés* and the Chansons: A Slave to Love', in *A Companion to Chrétien de Troyes*, ed. Norris J. Lacy and Joan Tasker Grimbert, Arthurian Studies, 63 (Cambridge, 2005), pp.120–36 (pp.123–5).

newly fashionable Arthurian tales of the West is to be her intellectual or practical model.[95] Instead, her decision is to remain in Constantinople, and to use Greek magic (via Thessala) to accomplish her desires.[96]

Constantinople is crucial in this analysis of the complexities of *translatio*. Kinoshita has described the awe of twelfth-century crusaders at the sight of Constantinople's splendour, which was swiftly followed by resentment at perceived Greek treachery and ultimately the sacking of the city by the 'Franks' in 1204.[97] The Byzantine capital, interestingly barely described in *Cligès*,[98] is not easily dismissed as purely the Oriental 'other', since it is the focal point of eastern Christendom; the conflation of the exotic Orient with Byzantium risks overlooking the crucial fact that in religious terms Constantinople would be relatively familiar to a northern French audience.[99] Rather than being simply 'other', the city is a meeting place for the 'pagan' cultures of the Middle East and those of the West, an important staging-post for *translatio*. As a place of cultural exchange, it provides a complex setting for Cligès' and Fenice's negotiations and decisions concerning love and honour, negotiations which conclude the narrative with the ambivalent statement that because of their behaviour Greek empresses are kept locked away.[100] Constantinople, part of Christendom but in many ways closer to the Eastern world increasingly dominated by Islam, matches the genealogically mixed Cligès (partly Arthurian, partly Greek). As such, in Constantinople, *translatio*, supposedly defined by movement between East and West and already complicated by the characters' numerous journeys, becomes unidentifiable, with East and West indistinguishable from each other. This leads to situations of inversion and ambivalence: life imitates death, as Fenice's faked demise shows, and illusions, such as the extraordinary tower, where 'par tel engin et par tel art/est fez li hui de pierre dure/que ja n'i troveroiz jointure' ('the door is carved out of rock/and so cleverly made that no-one/can see more than mere stone'), turn out to be reality.[101]

---

[95] The point about Helen of Troy as a model for Fenice is made, although not in these terms, by Kelly, 'Honor, Debate, and *Translatio imperii*', p.44.

[96] On Thessala and her use of 'esoteric arts of the east', which are 'another alternative to the routes of *translatio*', see Kinoshita, '*Cligès* in the Medieval Mediterranean', pp.53–4.

[97] Kinoshita, 'Poetics of Translatio', pp.315–27.

[98] Kinoshita, '*Cligès* in the Medieval Mediterranean', observes its lack of conventional decorative motifs (p.51).

[99] Catherine Gaullier-Bougassas, in 'L'altérité de l'Alexandre', implicitly includes Byzantium in her idea of 'l'altérité orientale', although she is mostly referring to the exotic and distant lands beyond Persia and India where Alexander the Great encounters marvels, p.5.

[100] *Cligès*, ed. Luttrell and Gregory, 6755–60. See also Kinoshita, '*Cligès* in the Medieval Mediterranean', p.57.

[101] *Cligès*, ed. Luttrell and Gregory, 5570–2; trans. Raffel, 5573–5.

Such ambivalence is crucial in understanding the text's *translatio* of its material. As demonstrated earlier, both *Troie* and *Alexandre* engage with their antique material from an ethical perspective, although in different ways. Although characters like Alexander and Cligès himself are in the broadest sense exemplary knights,[102] *Cligès* does not explicitly claim that its aim in performing literary *translatio* is ethical, in contrast to the other texts. Whilst *Cligès* has been read as an 'anti-*Tristan*' romance answer to the ethical question of what kind of erotic love is honourable,[103] the ambivalence identified in Constantinople makes ethical interpretation complex. Codes of chivalric conduct, Chrétien's 'chevalerie' brought to France by *translatio studii*, become opaque: Cligès and Fenice are true lovers, ending up as husband and wife, but they deceive their liege lord the emperor, to whom they owe allegiance, and their behaviour raises questions about the unity of love and marriage. Constantinople halts the movement of *translatio* in any direction, resulting in uncertainty and ambivalence: what is East or West? What is 'chevalerie' and what is dishonour? In this light, Chrétien's romance moves from exemplifying a clear East–West trajectory to reflecting uneasy cultural relativities, both literary and ethical.

The portrayal of Germany underlines this shift. Left undescribed like the Byzantine city, it is also a meeting place for East (the Greeks) and West (the Germans), despite its geographical location in the west. Here, in Regensburg and Cologne, promises are broken by representatives of both peoples: the emperor Alis marries Fenice against his promise to Alexander not to do so, and the emperor of Germany goes back on his word to the duke of Saxony that Fenice will be his bride. These broken promises demonstrate that Germany is also, despite its implied position as a recipient of *translatio*, a place of cultural and ethical relativism, in which the love between Fenice and Cligès begins despite her marriage to Alis. The German cities depict, in an unobtrusive fashion, the preoccupations and complexities of *translatio* that come to fruition in Constantinople; they are in many ways that city's mirror image in the West, although without its implications of exoticism and mystique. Perhaps this mirroring is one reason that neither place is described in detail, despite the fashion for elaborate *descriptio* found in contemporary texts: the greater possibilities for this with regard to Constantinople would undo the necessary parallel between East and West.

The character of Alexander, an intertextual avatar of Alexander from the *Roman d'Alexandre* as noted by Gaullier-Bougassas,[104] also demonstrates this ethical and cultural relativism. The Alexandrian part of *Cligès* can seem strange to modern readers, an unnecessary prequel to the main narrative of

---

[102] See for example the depiction of Alexander's generosity at 402–21, a virtue unsurprisingly emphasized for emulation by contemporary authors.

[103] See n.94 for scholarship addressing this issue.

[104] Gaullier-Bougassas, 'L'altérité de l'Alexandre', p.4.

the eponymous hero.[105] In contrast, Gaullier-Bougassas reads Alexander's presence as crucial to *Cligès*, seeing him as an attempt to integrate Alexander the Great within an Arthurian universe involving chivalric values not present in the *Alexandre* (such as love), in contrast to Alexandre de Paris' text, which tries to reduce the alterity of the Orient by making its hero more akin to these values but which ultimately cannot do so owing to his irreducible singularity.[106] Alexander's narrative is indeed vital for the romance, since it allows the text to engage with its complex *translatio*, but his presence in *Cligès* as a hybrid character (Arthurian, Oriental, and Byzantine) is not primarily an attempt to over-write Oriental alterity by means of ethical exemplarity. Rather, he is a sign of the slippage between East, West, and the intermediate places that problematizes traditional *translatio studii* for the narrator. Reading *Cligès* as a text promoting ethical-chivalric values such as romance within marriage, however, is problematic due to this very *translatio*, as already discussed; it is not Alexander's 'irreducible singularity' that is the barrier to the Alexander narrative's ethical integration within this Arthurian world, but the text's depiction of ethical problems themselves as relative. In this light, even the exemplary knight Alexander cannot become a straightforward personification of chivalric virtues, demonstrating the issues involved in ethical interpretation in a different context.

This analysis has demonstrated the complicated fashion in which physical movement is linked to intellectual and literary *translatio* in *Cligès*, and the implications of this for its interpretation as a paean to romantic marriage and the ethics of 'chevalerie' in general. Its Arthurian material, which of course forms only a part of the narrative but which inspires the themes of the rest, is exploited to highlight the complexities of various kinds of *translatio studii*. The presentation of a clear East–West trajectory and its subsequent querying is broadly reminiscent of the *Alexandreis*, an intriguing connection between these very different texts that strengthens the possibility of their mutual gestation within the purview of the court of Champagne. The text's lack of concern for history, possibly related to the more contemporary temporality of its Arthurian *materia*, differentiates *Cligès* from the *Alexandreis*, however, and also to some extent from the *Alexandre* and certainly from *Troie*.

Minimal Marvels

Marvels and their often-exotic *descriptio*, an important feature in the *Alexandre* and *Troie*'s poetics, seem at first glance not to form a key part of *Cligès*' narrative. As just noted, *Cligès* does not engage with this trend in depicting

---

[105] Kinoshita, 'The Poetics of Translatio', p.319.

[106] Gaullier-Bougassas, 'L'altérité de l'Alexandre', p.5. However, she also thinks that Alexandre in the eponymous text is resisting 'un processus d'assimilation aux valeurs occidentales'.

Constantinople, a clear moment for such a *topos* (as occurs during the narrative of Carthage in *Eneas*). Nor, intriguingly, is Fenice's tomb elaborately described; we are simply told that it was 'riche et noble' ('splendid and fine').[107] The only moment in which any such description does occur is during Cligès' visit to the tower in which he later hides Fenice, and even here it is tantalizing in its brevity. The tower is 'estoient point a ymages/Beles e bien anluminees' ('full of shining paintings,/vividly coloured') (5538–9), containing 'beles chanbres et vostes paintes' ('beautiful rooms with painted ceilings') (5617) and even pipes for hot water (5608–9). These quick glimpses are far from the lengthy, minutely detailed depictions of *Troie* and *Alexandre*. Yet, despite this brevity, there is a different kind of *descriptio* in operation in the text. It is seen most clearly in the builder John's teasing challenge to Cligès:

> 'Mes cuidiez vos avoir veüe
> Tote ma tor et mes deduiz?
> Encor i a de tex reduiz
> Que nus hom ne porroit trover,
> Et se vos i loist esprover
> Au mialz que vos savroiz cerchier,
> Ja n'i savroiz tant reverchier,
> Ne nus tant soit soutix et sages
> Que plus trovast ici estages.'

> *'You're sure you've seen*
> *It all, my tower and its charms?*
> *Ah, but there's more, much more,*
> *That no one could find for himself.*
> *Would you like to try? Search*
> *As hard as you can, you'll never*
> *Uncover its secret places,*
> *And neither will anyone else,*
> *No matter how subtle or wise.'*[108]

The numerous negatives here form a kind of anti-*descriptio* to emphasize the tower's secrecy; it is so secret that words are not allowed to depict its beauties. Glee at the failure of human intelligence in *descriptio* – 'tant soit soutix et sages' ('no matter how subtle or wise') – is paradoxically depicted here in negative terms, in that all the items described are unable to be seen. This is different from the frequent *topos* of a person or object being too beautiful or difficult to picture;[109] the point is that no-one can even *access* the tower's

---

[107] *Cligès*, ed. Luttrell and Gregory, 6105; trans. Raffel, 6107.
[108] *Cligès*, ed. Luttrell and Gregory, 5552–60; trans. Raffel, 5555–63.
[109] See for example *Troie*, ed. Constans, II, 13830–5, in which Benoît de Sainte-Maure claims that Calchas' tent is too spectacular for any author, however learned, to describe in either Latin or French.

marvels for descriptive purposes. We see this anti-*descriptio* still more clearly in the lack of elaboration regarding Fenice's tomb; again we are told briefly that it smelled sweet and contained soft cushioning (6090–4), but the actual structure is conspicuous by its descriptive absence.

These passages are significant reactions to contemporary habits of *descriptio*, but why is this the case in a text that engages so strongly with the Orient, usually a favourite location for elaborately depicted marvels? The answer, leaving aside the undeniable consideration of Chrétien's poetic individualism, surely lies in the complexities of *translatio studii* already discussed. In order for the idea that *translatio* is not a clear-cut dichotomy of East and West to be emphasized, the narrator has deliberately disappointed literary expectations that equate the Orient with particularly fabulous description; to make the point clear, he has created a teasing anti-*descriptio* composed of negatives with brief, frustrating details. This refusal of *descriptio* undercuts any anticipated sense of a distinctively Oriental location, and therefore of the East as culturally different. Such a marked refusal is a strong contrast with both *Alexandre* and *Troie* and paradoxically demonstrates Chrétien's awareness of the literary tradition of marvels and their description; his creation of anti-*descriptio* is similar in this to the hostile reaction seen in the *Alexandreis'* depiction of Darius' shield, another intriguing suggestion that the two texts were potentially aware of one another as well as of this pervasive literary fashion.[110]

In terms of *translatio studii*, then, *Cligès* critiques the straightforward statement of the Prologue that 'puis vint chevalerie a Rome/et de la clergie la some,/qui or est an France venue' ('then chivalry went to Rome, and the height of learning, and has reappeared, now, in France').[111] Rather, the poem demonstrates that uncertainty, not certainty, of identity defines its poetics. The question that follows is whether it also displays a similarly complex political identity or identities, and how this relates to those identified in the other texts.

Politics

As mentioned above, *Cligès* is usually associated with the court of Champagne, although the knowledge of England displayed in the text (Wallingford, Oxford, Windsor) has led to the suggestion that it might have been intended for a Plantagenet milieu;[112] of course, the two are not mutually exclusive. The Champagne connection becomes more plausible, however, in light of the text's interest in those places of cultural and ethical relativism, Constantinople, Regensburg, and Cologne. One of the factors in dating the poem to c. 1176 is the failed attempt by the duke of Saxony, Henry the Lion, to secure the daughter of the emperor of Constantinople as a bride for the German emperor

---

[110] See chapter 2.
[111] *Cligès*, ed. Luttrell and Gregory, 33–5.
[112] See Joseph D. Duggan, 'Afterword', in *Cligès*, trans. Raffel, pp.215–26.

Frederick Barbarossa's son in 1171, which is important for Chrétien's text because the duke of Saxony, who in the romance is a coward betrayed by the emperor of Germany, was married to Marie of Champagne's half-sister Mathilda.[113] This complex situation involving Constantinople and Germany was thus of particular relevance to the Champagne duke and duchess, who had family ties to the duke of Saxony but also held fiefs from Barbarossa; in addition, Henry 'the Liberal' had been knighted by the emperor of Constantinople, Manuel Comnenus.[114] Such a web of conflicting loyalties is a highly appropriate background for *Cligès'* exploration of cultural and ethical relativism; the idea that particular ethical questions like love in marriage and the relationships between East and West are not fixed by a single narrative of *translatio* but are shifting and relative is a reflection of these contemporary situations.

However, such a reading, important as it is in understanding *Cligès'* immediate environment, is not the only possible mode of interpretation. The use of the Tristan legend shows *Cligès'* interest in and engagement with more transnational literary culture, and the possibility of a Plantagenet patron for the romance likewise suggests its importance in a larger landscape. As demonstrated by the *Alexandreis*, discussion of issues appropriate to local contexts can be a way of addressing a wider audience; in this, *Cligès* again resembles the Latin text. So *Cligès'* engagement with *translatio studii* is both local and on a broader scale, confirming the idea that debates about the performance of *translatio* are played out across a transnational context.

Conclusion

This chapter has demonstrated that, like Latin, romance *translatio* is far from monolithic, but is addressed from various perspectives. What I have termed the 'anxious ethics' of the *Alexandre* is not found in *Troie* or in *Cligès*, both of which engage with ethical concerns amongst their other preoccupations but in far less obtrusive ways. This ethical concern in the *Alexandre* sets it apart too from the *Alexandreis*, which broadly rejects exemplarity on historical grounds. *Troie* shares an interest in historical perspective with both the *Alexandreis* and the *Ylias*, although again with significant differences, and the *Alexandre*'s consciousness of historical difference as seen in its use of Christianity to some extent relates it to the *Ylias*. In addition, *Cligès'* playful refusal of *descriptio* aligns it too with the *Alexandreis*, although from a much more parodic perspective. All of these texts' interactions (and this is only a brief and selective list) coalesce around issues of historicity and exemplarity

---

[113] For a summary of these events, see Duggan, 'Afterword', pp.221–2, and also Uitti, 'Romance *Translatio* and History', pp.554–6.

[114] Duggan, 'Afterword', p.221.

in *translatio*, providing some insight into the parameters of what (following Mora) I have called the debate that is ongoing concerning this.

Crucially, this debate is not primarily related to language or to local political needs, although these are both factors, but transcends both to focus on transnational cultural and literary practices of *translatio studii* across a range of works. Although my focus has been on classical narratives, with a brief look at Arthurian material in *Cligès*, the pervasive nature of the debate these analyses have highlighted strongly suggests other subject matter will also be involved, as well as other languages. To extend the investigation into other *materia* and languages (or dialects), to see whether this debate about *translatio* is only found in the twelfth century, and to discover if *translatio* remains a transnational phenomenon in other places, I shall now turn to Britain in the thirteenth century and two other Alexander texts, the Anglo-Norman *Roman de toute chevalerie* and the Middle English *Kyng Alisaunder*.

4

Insular Alexander? The *Roman de toute chevalerie* and the *Roman de Horn*

Insular Exceptionalism: Anglo-Norman Romance, Alexander, and the *Roman de toute chevalerie*

In this chapter, my focus moves from Alexander texts composed in northern France (the Angevin, Capetian, and Champagne contexts of previous chapters) to those probably created in the British Isles or Angevin territories on the continent, often called 'Anglo-Norman' romances. This raises important questions of definition, geographical, political, and linguistic.

As discussed in the introduction, 'Anglo-Norman', 'the French of England', and 'Anglo-French' are all terms describing the French used in England after the Norman Conquest, in which many twelfth- and thirteenth-century romances were composed.[1] My decision to opt for Anglo-Norman on linguistic grounds does not lay the issue of terminology to rest, however, but raises further questions highly relevant to any definition of insular literary culture in these centuries. Firstly, in addition to the problems inherent in the terminology, using language to define Anglo-Norman texts can be simplistic, since the manuscripts, often of later date than the works' identified origins, sometimes alter linguistic features, recopying Anglo-Norman works into different French dialects and complicating the linguistic clarity implied by the label.[2] Secondly, lost or fragmentary Anglo-Norman works sometimes have an afterlife via continental adaptations and reworkings, and thus may be included in surveys of Anglo-Norman literature although they no longer exist as complete works

---

[1] 'The French of England' is used for example in *Language and Culture in Medieval Britain: The French of England, c.1100–c.1500*, ed. by Jocelyn Wogan-Browne et al. (York, 2009), and in the French of England Translation Series (FRETS) edited by Wogan-Browne and Thelma Fenster (Tempe, AZ). Ardis Butterfield proposes 'Anglo-French', in *The Familiar Enemy: Chaucer, Language, and Nation in the Hundred Years War* (Oxford, 2009).

[2] This phenomenon occurs in the Paris manuscript of the *Roman de toute chevalerie* (BnF, MS fonds français, 24364) discussed later in this chapter, for example.

in that linguistic register.[3] Thirdly, works like the *romans d'antiquité* are often excluded from analyses of insular literature, despite their potential connection to the Henrician court and their Anglo-Norman linguistic nature, being habitually discussed as continental productions relating rather more to the history of French national literature than to that of the British Isles.[4] Describing a work as 'Anglo-Norman', then, leads to consideration of what makes a text 'Anglo-Norman' (or 'insular') beyond language and/or geographical location or circulation, facts that may well be redundant or assumed. Are there in fact distinctive identifying features enabling us to define Anglo-Norman texts as such and then to analyze them as a corpus?

Recent scholarship on twelfth- and thirteenth-century Anglo-Norman romances (here referring to texts' linguistic status) answers yes to these questions. Rosalind Field, for example, considers these works to have a distinctive narrative identity:

> The majority of the Anglo-Norman romances seem to owe little to the international and peripatetic court of Henry and Eleanor ... [they are] baronial, local, and insular ... ambitious in scope and inter-textual with a marked preference for English settings and 'history'.[5]

These 'local' and 'insular' works, distinguished here from the Henrician context considered in the previous chapter for *Troie*, are characterized by 'concern for good rule and evident anxiety about disorder, tyranny, and the mundane realities of warfare', as well as by insular locations.[6] Field traces these concerns back to the years of 'the Anarchy' when the English crown was disputed between Stephen and Matilda, arguing that there is a pattern of 'ancestral romances' containing 'narratives of disruption', in which deprivation of inheritance and its restoration are recurrent themes.[7] Narratives like *Haveloc*, *Horn*, *Boeve de Haumtone*, and *Gui de Warewic* are all included in this definition of Anglo-Norman romance. One factor in seeing them as

---

3 Judith Weiss discusses two such works, *Fergus* and *Amadas et Ydoine*, in her survey chapter 'Insular Beginnings: Anglo-Norman Romance', in *A Companion to Romance: From Classical to Contemporary*, ed. Corinne Saunders, Blackwell Companions to Literature and Culture, 27 (Oxford, 2004), pp.26–44 (pp.39–40).

4 Weiss makes this point in 'Insular Beginnings', p.28, as does Laura Ashe for the *Roman d'Eneas* in *History and Fiction in England, 1066–1200*, Cambridge Studies in Medieval Literature, 68 (Cambridge, 2007), pp.121–58. Christopher Baswell's work on *Eneas* as a Henrician text is a notable exception to this habit: see 'Men in the *Roman d'Eneas*: The Construction of Empire', in *Medieval Masculinities: Regarding Men in the Middle Ages*, ed. Clare A. Lees (Minneapolis, MN, 1994), pp.149–68.

5 Rosalind Field, 'Children of Anarchy: Anglo-Norman Romance in the Twelfth Century', in *Writers of the Reign of Henry II: Twelve Essays*, ed. Simon Meecham-Jones and Ruth Kennedy (Basingstoke, 2006), pp.249–62 (p.249).

6 Ibid., p.249.

7 Ibid., p.256.

'insular romance'[8] is probably also that they all give rise to English texts in the thirteenth century; boosted by our modern understanding of English as a strong signifier of identity, the shared basis of, and connections between, the Anglo-Norman and English versions may make the former seem more insular in their nature.[9] We therefore seem to have a coherent corpus of romances with distinct themes, going beyond linguistic affiliations, in answer to my questions above.

The narrative facts of these texts are not in dispute: they are indeed stories characterized by themes of injustice and restitution, inheritance and its loss, and with roots in insular locations.[10] The related intellectual step is to argue that this identity, as it manifests itself in these features, is specific to insular romance. Laura Ashe states this claim succinctly:

> It is now well accepted that the French language romances of the late twelfth and early thirteenth centuries may be divided into two distinct traditions: the insular, written in these islands, characterized by a historical and geographical specificity, mainly drawing their material from the history and pseudo-history of pre-Conquest England; and the continental, including most importantly the Arthurian romance, written in continental Francophone territory, and characterized by a free fictionality, and extensive development of courtly psychology.[11]

Here 'two distinct traditions' are identified, insular and continental, with contrasting material ('the history and pseudo-history of pre-Conquest England' as opposed to 'Arthurian romance') and treatment ('historical and geographical specificity' against 'free fictionality' and 'development of courtly psychology'). Ashe implicitly defines insular and continental romances in opposition to one another; their differences, not any potential similarities, are the crucial point in her analysis of the conceptualization of the hero, which she sees as following these divergent traditions. Yet, as Judith Weiss has pointed out, French-language romances from both sides of the Channel share important contexts and networks:

---

[8] This phrase is the title of Susan Crane's definitive study of Anglo-Norman and English romances, *Insular Romance: Politics, Faith, and Culture in Anglo-Norman and Middle English Literature* (Berkeley, CA, 1986).

[9] See discussion in the 'Language, Nation, Identity' section of the introduction.

[10] See Field, 'Children of Anarchy', on Gaimar's potential role in this 'more localized movement' (p.251).

[11] Laura Ashe, 'The Hero and His Realm', in *Boundaries in Medieval Romance*, ed. Neil Cartlidge (Cambridge, 2008), pp.129–47 (p.135). Ashe is developing the argument made by Crane, *Insular Romance*, that 'during the later twelfth century … French literature in England can be divided into continental (including Norman) works that flourished in the royal courts, and works in Anglo-Norman dialect that were more deeply rooted in insular history and society' (p.3).

[They are] often written for patrons, and directed to audiences, who would have had lands and kin on both sides of the Channel, and who would have had similar interests and tastes; they are written by authors with similar education, influenced by the same classical school-texts.[12]

Weiss also reminds us that distinguishing Anglo-Norman from continental French is difficult until about 1150, nearly a century after the Conquest, although from that date the two kinds of French begin to diverge.[13] We appear to have a situation, then, in which contexts similar in terms of the class of patron and audience, education and interests have produced distinctly different kinds of romances. Many reasons for the 'precocity' of French romances produced in the British Isles have been adduced, a subject that I shall not add to here.[14] The point I want to make is that what appears to divide these French-language romances is narrative material, not context, and, crucially, not stylistic treatment. Although Ashe briefly refers to thematic and stylistic features (like 'free fictionality' or 'geographical specificity'), most definitions of insular romance focus more strongly on narrative aspects, like Field's idea about 'narratives of disruption' discussed above. Narrative and stylistic features are of course intertwined issues, so it is especially interesting to discover that the latter often seem to be left to one side in defining insular romance. This poses a broader question about French romances: does the proposed separation between insular and continental French romance in the twelfth and thirteenth centuries, observed primarily via narrative, hold true if we adopt a more thematically and stylistically focused perspective? Moving beyond consideration of subject matter *per se*, do authors educated in potentially the same places (Paris, for example) display different *translatio* in their compositions, *translatio* that can be explained by their locations?

This question is especially important for the *Roman de toute chevalerie* (*RTC*), the main textual focus of this chapter. Although this Anglo-Norman Alexander romance is dutifully discussed by scholars like Crane, Field, and Weiss in their important analyses of the insular corpus, the work is not a major pillar of their studies, perhaps because it does not fit easily into the category of insular romance as it is collectively defined. The *RTC* is not a romance focusing on insular locations, nor does it have dispossession of the protagonist as a major theme, nor is its source pre-Conquest insular history. To

---

[12] Weiss, 'Insular Beginnings', p.26.

[13] Ibid., p.26.

[14] This word has often been used to characterize Anglo-Norman romances, as in M. Dominica Legge, 'La Précocité de la littérature anglo-normande', *Cahiers de civilisation médiévale*, 8 (1965), pp.327–49; also in Rosalind Field, 'Patterns of Availability and Demand in Middle English Translations *de romanz*', in *The Exploitations of Medieval Romance*, ed. Laura Ashe, Ivana Djordjević, and Judith Weiss (Cambridge, 2010), pp.73–89 (p.75).

complicate matters further, the romance is also distinct from Ashe's definition of continental romance in many ways, not having a 'courtly psychology' (in the Ovidian erotic sense at least) and not drawing on Arthurian material. It is, under these narratively focused definitions, an anomaly, fitting neither pattern, a fact that may explain its relative neglect by scholars interested primarily in romances locatable within specific political and geographical areas (such as Angevin territories or Capetian France). However, if we focus on the *RTC*'s *translatio*, its literary-stylistic habits with regard to its inherited materials, then fruitful comparison with other romance works from any location becomes possible. This will naturally involve consideration of narrative, since as mentioned above this is intertwined with style and form; however, the primary focus will be not on narrative *per se*, but rather on the stylistic features of its individual *translatio*. Considering the *RTC* and other insular texts from this perspective allows us to look beyond the issue of narratives' sources to make true comparisons.

The question of a distinct insular identity is also important for the *RTC*'s *translatio* in terms of the Alexander background on which it draws. Interest in Alexander in the British Isles, and hence availability of sources, can be traced back centuries before the Norman Conquest: Alcuin is said to have sent Alexander material to Charlemagne around 781, and the translation of Orosius' *Histories* and the *Letter of Alexander to Aristotle* into Old English both demonstrate earlier fascination with Alexander's narratives.[15] Charles Russell Stone's studies of Alexander material circulating in the British Isles have highlighted the keen interest displayed in the Macedonian during the High Middle Ages.[16] Stone has recently argued for a specifically insular engagement with Alexander that casts the Macedonian and his empire as 'a collective example of political discord', contrasting this insular, broadly negative Alexander with his more positive exemplary presentation on the continent.[17] Such British interest in Alexander poses a major question that this chapter seeks to address: whether the idea of an insular Alexander tradition is traceable in the *RTC* in terms of its *translatio*, its poetic approach, or approaches to its material.

Stone claims that the *RTC* shares the more negative approach to Alexander that he sees as characteristic of insular texts in its *translatio* as well as its

[15] See G. L. Hamilton, 'Quelques notes sur l'histoire de la légende d'Alexandre le Grand en Angleterre au moyen âge', in *Mélanges de philologie et d'histoire offerts à M. Antoine Thomas par ses élèves et ses amis* (Paris, 1927), pp.195–202 (pp.197–8).
[16] Charles Russell Stone, 'Investigating Macedon in Medieval England: The *St Albans Compilation*, the *Philippic Histories*, and the Reception of Alexander the Great', *Viator*, 42.1 (2011), pp.75–111, and id., *From Tyrant to Philosopher King: A Literary History of Alexander the Great in Medieval and Early Modern England* (Turnhout, 2013).
[17] Charles Russell Stone, '"Many man he shal do woo": Portents and the End of an Empire in *Kyng Alisaunder*', *Medium Ævum*, 81.1 (2012), pp.18–40 (p.18). Stone's argument is presented most fully in *From Tyrant to Philosopher King*.

materia: he reads the *RTC* as a critical approach to Alexander derived from Roman sources, focusing upon the predictions of the break-up of Alexander's empire after his death that he perceives as current throughout the romance.[18] In this more negative and historically focused approach, he sees the *RTC* as 'atypical of medieval romance yet emblematic of his [Alexander's] insular reception in the twelfth to fourteenth centuries'.[19] In this reading, the *RTC* is a distinctively insular production, an idea implicitly shared with Foster and Short, Gaullier-Bougassas and Harf-Lancner. Yet the relative paucity of scholarship on the *RTC*, due no doubt to the lack of a modern edition until the late 1970s, means that this idea, and indeed the general poetics of the *RTC*, has not been interrogated in detail, a gap my analysis seeks to address.[20]

In a related point, Stone goes on to state that history and romance have broadly different interpretations of Alexander: 'while the former stressed both his personal degradation and the civil wars that destroyed his empire after his death, the latter praised his exploits, lamented his death, and ignored the fate of Macedon'.[21] As we have already seen with reference to twelfth-century material, Alexander narratives within what we now think of as 'the romance genre' are more nuanced and ambivalent than this admittedly brief description of a positive Alexander indicates: in fact, Stone himself considers that the *RTC* is an exception to his general rule of generic difference, since to some extent it combines (in his terms) historical and romance presentations of Alexander.[22]

---

[18] Stone, 'Portents and the End of an Empire', p.18, p.22, p.23.

[19] Ibid., p.18.

[20] The most comprehensive overview of the romance is the introduction to *Le roman d'Alexandre ou le roman de toute chevalerie*, trans. and introd. by Catherine Gaullier-Bougassas and Laurence Harf-Lancner (Paris, 2003), pp.vii–lxviii; see also Catherine Gaullier-Bougassas, *Les Romans d'Alexandre: aux frontières de l'épique et du romanesque* (Paris, 1998). Discussions have mainly revolved around issues of dating and provenance, for example Brian Foster, 'The *Roman de toute chevalerie*: Its Date and Author', *French Studies*, 9 (1955), pp.154–8, Alfred Foulet, 'La date du *Roman de toute chevalerie*', in *Mélanges offerts à Rita Lejeune*, ed. F. Dethier, 2 vols (Gembloux, 1969), II, pp.1205–10, and M. Dominica Legge and D. J. A. Ross, 'Discussions: Thomas of Kent', *French Studies*, 9.4 (1955), pp.348–51. Scholars have also been interested in the question of boundaries and their significance, as seen in Suzanne Conklin Akbari, 'Alexander in the Orient: Boundaries and Bodies in the *Roman de toute chevalerie*', in *Postcolonial Approaches to the European Middle Ages*, ed. Ananya Jahanara Kabir and Deanne Williams (Cambridge, 2005), pp.105–26. The illustrations in some of the MSS have also received attention from D. J. A. Ross, 'A Thirteenth-Century Anglo-Norman Workshop Illustrating Secular Literary Manuscripts?', in *Mélanges offerts à Rita Lejeune*, I, pp.689–94, and Laurence Harf-Lancner, 'From Alexander to Marco Polo, from Text to Image: The Marvels of India', in *The Medieval French Alexander*, ed. David Maddox and Sara Sturm-Maddox (Albany, NY, 2002), pp.235–57.

[21] Stone, 'Portents and the End of an Empire', p.19.

[22] The epic *Alexandreis*, too, although not 'history' in the sense that Stone means here, is likewise complex in its relationship to Alexander, as is antique 'historical' material: see

Stone's analyses therefore position the *RTC* firmly within insular intellectual territory in both Alexandrian and generic terms. This aligns his readings with Ashe's point that insular and continental French-language texts are two different traditions; for Stone, albeit in an Alexander context, there is likewise a separation between insular works and their continental counterparts. My analysis of the *RTC*'s poetics and potential insularity will therefore be framed around this wider question of reception and adaptation as defined by genre as well as by location.

The questions I ask of the *RTC*'s poetics of *translatio* in this chapter are all posed against the backdrop of this narrative of insular exceptionalism. To bring this narrative into a comparative focus from a romance perspective, I shall set the *RTC* alongside the *Roman de Horn*, a work in Anglo-Norman French composed at around the same time as the *RTC* that is very much part of the insular romance canon. Since *Horn* also retells a supposedly ancient narrative, considering the two texts' poetics together may reveal whether they share *translatio* that can be ascribed to their insular locations. Following this, in order to analyze the *RTC* from an Alexander perspective (as well as to provide the work with a possible location and provenance), I shall consider it in the context of St Albans, the context of several of the important insular Alexander works discussed by Stone. Thinking about St Albans also highlights the literary culture that might have produced or been relevant to the *RTC*, which may provide insight into Stone's idea that perspectives on Alexander vary depending on genre. So considering the *RTC* in the contexts of *Horn* and St Albans allows me to set the Alexander text in a variety of informative insular locations.

The *Roman de toute chevalerie*

Text(s) and Context

The *RTC* is perhaps best described not as an individual text but as a series of literary events ranging from the later twelfth to the mid-fourteenth century. Whilst the poem is usually given a composition date of around 1175, since it uses material from Peter Comestor's *Historia scholastica* (1169–73), its modern editors suggest a range of between 1174 and 1200.[23] This fluidity is important when we consider the Alexander texts discussed in the previous two chapters. If the *RTC* was composed a few years after 1175, then the possibility of influence by the *Roman d'Alexandre* or the *Alexandreis* is raised. This possibility exists in any case for the *Roman d'Alexandre*'s constituent texts

---

discussions in chapters 1 and 2.
[23] On this dating, see Thomas of Kent, *The Anglo-Norman Alexander* (Le Roman de Toute Chevalerie), ed. Brian Foster and Ian Short, 2 vols, ANTS, 29–33 (London, 1976 and 1977), II, pp.73–6. All textual references are to this edition.

given the conventional date of 1175 for the *RTC*, since these Alexander works were extant in the 1170s or potentially earlier.[24] It is all the more interesting, then, that the *RTC* is considered to be a work independent of continental Alexander versions, even though its author may have been aware of these earlier texts and the poem itself uses many of the same sources.[25] This independence sets the scene once more for the text to be an insular phenomenon, an Anglo-Norman Alexander in character as well as in language, as Stone has suggested. Indeed, Brian Foster's and Ian Short's title for their modern edition, *The Anglo-Norman Alexander*, suggests just this kind of literary as well as linguistic independence from continental Alexander material. The likelihood of the *RTC*'s presence at, if not composition in, the abbey of St Albans, which I shall analyse below, also lends weight to this idea of insular exceptionalism discussed in detail above.

The *RTC* follows Alexander's narrative from his conception and birth to his death, describing his battles against and victory over the Persian Darius, his defeat of the Indian Porus and his travels in the East, where he encounters strange men and beasts, and his death in Babylon by poison.[26] The romance's narrative material, like that of *Alexandre*, is taken from works ultimately derived from the Greek *Alexander Romance*'s texts, the *Epitome* of Julius Valerius, the *Letter of Alexander to Aristotle*, and (with less emphasis) the *Historia de preliis*.[27] In addition to these narrative sources, the *RTC* also draws on other texts including Bede and Isidore of Seville, a fact that David Ross rightly interprets as a sign that its author had access to a good library, probably monastic.[28] The author, who names himself in the text as Thomas of Kent, is therefore drawing on 'a long-standing English interest',[29] one that appears to

---

[24] See chapter 3, '*Roman d'Alexandre*' section.

[25] See *Anglo-Norman Alexander*, ed. Foster and Short, II, p.1, and the analysis in Gaullier-Bougassas and Harf-Lancner, *Le roman d'Alexandre*, pp.xvi–xx, where the translators conclude that the *RTC* does not engage with the texts of the *Roman d'Alexandre*, although he may have known of them (p.xx). They see the *RTC* as 'parallèlement' (p.xvii) to the continental versions of the *Roman d'Alexandre*. For a detailed comparison of the two works, and a useful overview of the *RTC*, see Gaullier-Bougassas, *Les Romans d'Alexandre*.

[26] For a more detailed narrative synopsis, see appendix 2.

[27] For overviews of the sources, see *Anglo-Norman Alexander*, ed. Foster and Short, II, pp.1–2; Gaullier-Bougassas and Harf-Lancner, *Le roman d'Alexandre*, pp.xvii–xx. The most detailed analysis is Johanna Weynand, *Der Roman de toute Chevalerie des Thomas von Kent in seinem Verhältnis zu seinen Quellen* (Bonn, 1911).

[28] D. J. A. Ross, *Alexander historiatus: A Guide to Medieval Illustrated Alexander Literature*, 2nd edn (Frankfurt am Main, 1988), p.25. Dominica Legge agrees, stating that 'the library must have been rich in Alexandrine material' (*Anglo-Norman in the Cloisters: The Influence of the Orders on Anglo-Norman Literature* (Edinburgh, 1950), p.38).

[29] *Anglo-Norman Alexander*, ed. Foster and Short, II, p.64.

have been especially strong at St Albans, although there is no evidence that he was a monk there.[30]

However, the beguiling idea of a distinctively insular Alexander romance, whether at St Albans or elsewhere, is made problematic by the *RTC*'s textual and manuscript situation. As is the case for so many vernacular romances, we have no extant manuscripts that date from the probable era of the *RTC*'s composition, making the question of its origins difficult. There are five extant manuscripts, two of which are single leaves. Of the three so-called 'complete' manuscripts, the Cambridge manuscript has lost at least five gatherings from its originally around ninety-six folios and the Paris manuscript has been revised by a Continental redactor, which in the modern editors' eyes 'makes it unsuitable for use as the basis of an edition'.[31] All three more complete witnesses also contain material added to the Anglo-Norman work from Alexandre de Paris' *Roman d'Alexandre*.[32] The modern edition is based on the Durham manuscript, which has the largest amount of text, with reference to the Paris and Cambridge witnesses used to complete some gaps where necessary, but does not contain this added material from the *Alexandre*.[33] In removing these sections, which relate to the Fuerre de Gadres and death of Alexander, the editors attempt to separate what they see as 'the original work' from 'the borrowings from *RAlex*': in telling lexis, the modern edition is 'shorn' of its continental interpolations 'in order to recover a poem that may well approximate to the original work of Thomas of Kent'.[34] Although they do not explicitly say so, Foster and Short are trying to (re)create this 'original work' by Thomas as a specifically insular narrative. Yet simply removing continental material alone surely does not make a text insular in character. As

---

[30] On Thomas, see *Anglo-Norman Alexander*, ed. Foster and Short, II, pp.68–73, and Legge and Ross, 'Discussions'. Dominica Legge thought it likely that Thomas was a St Albans monk (*Anglo-Norman in the Cloisters*, pp.36–8), but Foster and Short, whilst agreeing, point out that there is no mention of a monk with this name in the unbroken series of St Albans records from the Conquest to the reign of Henry VIII (*Anglo-Norman Alexander*, II, pp.70–1).

[31] Durham Cathedral Library, MS C. IV. 27 B, Paris, BnF, MS fonds français 24364, and Cambridge, Trinity College, MS O.9.34 (1446). The manuscripts are described in detail in *Anglo-Norman Alexander*, ed. Foster and Short, II, pp.3–14 (quotation p.10): see also the useful overview in Keith Busby, '"Codices manuscriptos nudos tenemus": Alexander and the New Codicology', in *The Medieval French* Alexander, ed. Donald Maddox and Sara Sturm-Maddox (Albany, NY, 2002), pp.259–73 (pp.265–8), and the survey of witnesses and Foster and Short's editorial practice given by Gaullier-Bougassas and Harf-Lancner, *Le roman d'Alexandre*, pp.lxvi–lxviii. The Durham manuscript contains five passages found only in this manuscript, but since it dates from the middle of the fourteenth century I shall not analyze them here.

[32] *Anglo-Norman Alexander*, ed. Foster and Short, II, pp.1–2.

[33] Ibid, p.10.

[34] Ibid., p.2.

we have already seen, ascribing French romances of this period to Anglo-Norman/Angevin or continental French/Capetian origins is a dubious pastime, partly because of the manuscripts' later dates, partly because so often a work's political and cultural affiliations are vague and/or irrecoverable.[35] In addition, putative places of origin, even where they are known, do not necessarily define later audiences and receptions: texts travel across territorial and linguistic boundaries. The *Alexandre* is very likely to have circulated widely and early in Angevin territories and the British Isles despite its supposedly continental nature, as its textual presence in the *RTC* confirms: its circulation in the thirteenth century makes it too an insular text in a broad sense, although it is surely more appropriate to think of it as a transnational one given its European travels.[36] Further, the *RTC*'s revision in the Paris manuscript by a continental redactor in 'a conscious effort to adapt the whole style and vocabulary of the text to Continental standards', and the Durham witness's alteration of the Anglo-Norman spellings to continental ones, complicates any separation between Anglo-Norman and continental French, both linguistically and also in terms of potential circulation.[37] Given these factors, ideas about possible origins and language are not enough to define the *RTC* as insular or continental in the absence of the original text. The *RTC* that we have is therefore a hybrid of insular and continental material dating from the mid-thirteenth (the date of the earliest manuscript witness), not the twelfth, century and is a product of several different literary moments. Stone sums up this situation succinctly from a temporal perspective:

[35] See chapter 3, '*Roman d'Alexandre*' section, on Alexandre de Paris' naming of himself as both 'de Bernai' and 'de Paris', areas in Angevin and Capetian territories respectively.

[36] A recent (as yet incomplete) study of the manuscripts of the *Alexandre* is provided by the Medieval Francophone Literary Culture Outside France project at <www.medievalfrancophone.ac.uk/textual-traditions-and-segments/alexandre/manuscripts-and-periods-of-production/> [accessed 28 July 2015]: see also Busby, '"Codices manuscriptos nudos tenemus"'. Its manuscripts are certainly present in the British Isles at the end of the Middle Ages. Oxford, Bodleian Library, MS Bodley 264 was bought by the Woodville family in 1466 and was probably in England earlier, since the *Alexandre* was bound with extracts from Middle English Alexander material in the early 1400s (i.e. the reverse situation of the *RTC*): see Mark Cruse, *Illuminating the* Roman d'Alexandre *(Oxford, Bodleian Library, MS Bodley 264): The Manuscript as Monument*, Gallica, 22 (Cambridge, 2011), p.182. Manuscripts of a comparable and equally popular French romance, the supposedly Anglo-Norman and Angevin *Roman de Troie*, circulate widely across Europe from an early date, indicating that separation between insular and continental circles is a false dichotomy: see Marc-René Jung, *La Légende de Troie en France au moyen âge: analyse des versions françaises et bibliographie raisonée des manuscrits* (Basle, 1996) and <www.medievalfrancophone.ac.uk/textual-traditions-and-segments/troie/manuscripts-and-periods-of-production/> [accessed 28 July 2015].

[37] See *Anglo-Norman Alexander*, ed. Foster and Short, ii, p.18. The editors do not go into detail about their definition of 'Continental French' here.

[The *RTC*] does not, properly speaking, survive as a text of the Middle Ages
… modern readers of the RTC encounter a work quite distinct from that met
by readers in the twelfth century (when the romance is thought to have been
composed) or the fourteenth century (from which the last manuscript dates)
or any point in between.[38]

Literary scholars with a historicist focus (and who decide not to despair) must
in essence choose a moment during this period at which they want to locate
the textual phenomenon that has become known as the *RTC*. In this analysis,
I shall focus on the *RTC* in the middle of the thirteenth century, a moment
when it is at its most defined textually and geographically. From a textual perspective, this means including the episodes taken from the *Alexandre* where
necessary (although they are not a major feature of my analysis), and from a
geographical standpoint it locates the romance very probably at St Albans,
where it appears the Durham and Cambridge manuscripts were illustrated and
may have been produced.[39]

Historical Narrative: Profit and Pleasure

As we have already seen in the previous chapters, an enduring question that
Alexander texts of all genres and languages raise is the conception of historical narrative and its relationship to Alexander's legend: it is a key aspect of
texts' poetics of *translatio*. In addition, it is an important part of the modern
definitions of insular romance adduced by Field and Ashe and of the insular
Alexander tradition perceived by Stone. The *RTC* and its presentation of history, then, is a good starting point for considering its potentially insular poetics.

The modern French translators of the *RTC* consider that Thomas of Kent's
concept of history is 'la vision morale de l'histoire comme source d'exem-
ples'.[40] At the introduction of the part of the narrative of Alexander's conflicts
with Darius, Thomas of Kent provides a thoughtful discourse on how to write
history, which I quote here in full:

> Geste qui voet conter ou estorie traiter,
> A quel fin doit trere voie il al comencer,
> E die tel chose qui puisse profiter
> Ou tel fet ou la gent se deive deliter,
> Autrement son travail put malement enplaer.
> E quant ot estorie tuit a l'atucher,

---

[38] Stone, 'Portents and the End of an Empire', p.20.
[39] See Ross, *Alexander historiatus*, pp.25–7, and M. Dominica Legge, *Anglo-Norman in
the Cloisters*, pp.36–43, especially pp.36–9. Ross's earlier suggestion that the Cambridge MS might have been copied in a secular workshop ('Anglo-Norman Workshop')
is supported by Stone in his forthcoming book (Toronto) on the *RTC*: see 'Chapter Four:
The Two Deaths of Alexander in Cambridge, Trinity College MS O. 9. 34', p.1 n.2.
[40] Gaullier-Bougassas and Harf-Lancner, *Le roman d'Alexandre*, pp.xviii–xix.

Bien doit par reson dire e versifier.
Verité doit dire e mensonge lesser,
E rien ne die for ceo qe ly soit mester.
L'en fet sovente foiz beauté pur envoiser,
Car a qui matir faut si covient purchacer.
Nel dy pas pur la moie, assez ay dont diter,
Car l'estorie en est grant e ly fet sunt plener;
E ceo poent ly clerk tresbien tesmoigner
Qui se volent a Cesar e Pompe acointer
E lire Aristotle e Solin versiler,
Orosie e Ysidre e Jerome li bier
E les autres autors mestres de translater
Qe les fez Alisandre descristrent [al] primer.[41]

*He who wants to narrate deeds or tell histories must have in mind his aim
from the start and report the things that are able to benefit people or those
deeds that give them pleasure, otherwise his labour will be misplaced.
When he mentions historical events, he must narrate well and make verses correctly. He must tell the truth and omit false things, and say nothing
beyond that which is relevant. Authors frequently create beautiful features
for pleasure, because someone who is lacking in material must strive for
[something]. I do not speak on my own behalf, since I have enough to tell,
as the history is great and the events are copious; clerks are very well able
to confirm this, those [scholars] who wish to get to know Caesar and Pompeius Trogus, and to read Aristotle and discuss Solin, Orosius, and Isidore,
and noble Jerome, and the other authors, those masters of translation who
first described Alexander's deeds.*

Rigour, truth, no lies or superfluity, but beauty to inspire pleasure, especially
when 'matir' or material is lacking: much of this is familiar from Benoît de
Sainte-Maure's prologue to *Troie*.[42] In addition, we are presented here with
a list of Thomas' sources, including Orosius, one of the historians mentioned
above as particularly important in the development of an insular tradition of
Alexander writing.[43] This emphasis on accuracy and referencing supports
Gaullier-Bougassas' and Harf-Lancner's idea that this aspect of Thomas' historical perspective is more akin to that of modern historians.[44] Yet Thomas' interest in source citation and accuracy is only one part of this description. What

---

[41] *Anglo-Norman Alexander*, ed. Foster and Short, I, 1324–42. All translations are my
own.

[42] See chapter 3, 'Anxious Romance'.

[43] See Stone, 'Investigating Macedon', pp.77–8. The late eleventh-century insular Alexander collection in London, British Library, MS Royal 13. A. I discussed there is, according to Stone, 'the first genuine, Anglo-Latin investigation into the history of Macedon'
(p.78) and is 'informed' by Orosius. On Orosius, see chapter 1, 'Orosius' section.

[44] Gaullier-Bougassas and Harf-Lancner, *Le roman d'Alexandre*, pp.xviii–xix.

is particularly interesting here in comparison with Benoît's prologue, and indeed with the *Alexandre*, is Thomas' engagement with ethical hermeneutics in interpreting and adapting Alexander's 'estorie'. Instead of the dominant concern for personal improvement ('Qui vueut saveir e qui entent,/Sacheiz de mieuz l'en est sovent') seen in *Troie* and even more so in Alexandre de Paris' anxiety for 'bonnes coustumes', there is a single mention of 'tel chose qui puisse profiter' ('those things that enable [one] to benefit/profit', 1326). The idea of 'profit' here playfully encompasses both personal/moral and material gain,[45] but its collocation with pleasure ('tel fet ou la gent se deive deliter', 'those deeds that give people pleasure', 1327) suggests that profit in either sense is in implicit opposition to pleasure here. So alongside Thomas' worthy academic approach we are presented with an apparent dichotomy between profit and pleasure, 'tel chose ... ou tel fet', an 'either ... or' that takes two hermeneutics and explicitly places them in opposition to one another. This opposition becomes even stronger later in the passage, where the idea that beautiful features create delight when 'matir' is lacking describes this dichotomy in terms of presence and absence (1333–4).

This may seem a minor point, but its impact is substantial. It raises the question of how and why 'estorie' should be read, composed, and interpreted, and suggests that two of the conventional answers can be mutually exclusive; it indicates that there may be a choice to be made between them, and that therefore interpretation is not single or straightforward. The 'vision morale' of history as a source of examples observed by Gaullier-Bougassas and Harf-Lancner in the *RTC* in fact emphasizes hermeneutic plurality rather than a single, over-arching ethical narrative. Thomas' intellectual and literary analysis of historiography, then, contains an additional vital element, this sense of questioning and of choice, with specific reference to hermeneutic strategies.

A similar theme, but more strongly marked, can be found at the very beginning of the *RTC* in its prologue, a key point where authors (for example Benoît de Sainte-Maure and Alexandre de Paris) often discuss their narrative technique. Gaullier-Bougassas and Harf-Lancner rightly note the prologue's 'originalité' whilst also mentioning that it draws on both *chanson de geste* and *romanz* predecessors.[46] Despite these models, like the *RTC*'s discussion of historical composition just mentioned, the prologue does not reproduce the approaches of Benoît de Sainte-Maure or Alexandre de Paris, nor does it invoke the theme of *translatio studii* like *Cligès*. Neither explicitly didactic in an intellectual or ethical sense, nor concerned for the justification of *translatio*, it is constructed around a dichotomy between pain and pleasure that queries widely held definitions of both:

---

45 Both meanings are given in the *AND* for the verb: see <www.anglo-norman.net/cgi-bin/form-s1> [accessed 29 July 2015].

46 Gaullier-Bougassas and Harf-Lancner, *Le roman d'Alexandre*, p.xxi.

Cist siecles est culvert e perillus,
Fors a ceus ky servent le haut roy glorius
Qui pur sa gent dona le seon sanc precius.
Si cum mester nous est, il ait mercy de nous,
Car vie d'ome est breve e le mond lab[o]rus,
Deceivables a toz e a multz ennuius.
Nequedent n'ad el siecle nul si bosoignus
Qe alcun delit n'ait, si trop n'est meseurous.
Mult put estre dolent al jugement irus,
Au jour ou tanz serront e tristes e pourous,
Qui pur sa char norir est en ceo mond penus
A ceo k'om entent est son quer desirus.
Un deduit ay cho[i]si qe mult est delitus;
As tristes est confort e joie as dolerus,
E assuagement al mal as amerus.
Deliter se put bien home chevalerus
E tuit cil qui sunt de romanz coveitus.
A enviouse gent sunt ly bon fet costus,
Car joie e envoisure est doel as envius.
Le mal le tient al quer, dont vient le dit quitus,
Autrement crevereit, car tut est venimus.
Si envius me reprent, seignors, ceo dy a vous,
L'em mesprent bien sovent en overe meins grevous.[47]

This world and the age is base and dangerous, except for the servants of the high king of glory who gave his own precious blood for his people. He took pity on us in our need, because the life of man is short and the world is arduous, deceitful for everyone and troublesome for many. Nevertheless, there is no-one in the world so busy that they do not have some pleasure, if they are not too unfortunate. Many will suffer and lament at the harsh Judgement Day, that day where so many, who were [only] eager to feed themselves in this world, will be sad and fearful, those who have eagerly awaited their heart's desires. I have chosen a pleasure that is full of delight; it is a comfort in sorrow, a joy in suffering, and a relief for those lovers who are heartsick. It is well able to give pleasure to knights and all those who are eager for tales in French. The tale of good deeds is painful for envious people, because joy and gladness are pain for those who are jealous. It pierces evil people to the heart, from where angry words come; otherwise they burst, because they are consumed with poison. If envious people criticize me, lords, I tell you, they frequently make mistakes in undertakings less weighty.

The misery of life in this world and the uncertainty of one's future in the afterlife after the Day of Judgement is depicted graphically here before the author abruptly shifts to his active choosing of 'un deduit … mult est delitus',

---

[47] *Anglo-Norman Alexander*, ed. Foster and Short, i, 1–23.

'a pleasure ... full of delight', which comforts the unhappy and the suffering and aids lovers' pains. 'Deduit''s range of possible meanings includes sexual pleasure and an enjoyable tale,[48] so Thomas' choice of lexis here matches his subsequent description of the groups to whom this will be particularly applicable; it is evidently meant to be an all-embracing 'deduit', matching in its over-arching nature the equally widely spread pains of 'le mond lab[o]rus'. This juxtaposition of pain (in which Christianity itself is implicated) with the benefits of worldly pleasures is provocative, since despite emphasizing the pains of earthly life it also highlights its joys, whilst in addition describing the suffering brought on by the Day of Judgement without mentioning the bliss of heaven. *Contemptus mundi* as a *topos* is here given an intriguing twist. This is perplexing: why would Thomas choose to construct such a provocative dichotomy in the vital opening lines of his work instead of justifying his opus on intellectual or ethical grounds, like his predecessors mentioned above? A possible answer is hinted at in the outwardly conventional final lines of the prologue, where Thomas castigates 'enviouse gent' 'car joie e envoisure est doel as envius' ('for joy and gladness are pain for those who are jealous', 19). This explicit and paradoxical reversal of pleasure and pain, in which one becomes the other, crowns the prologue's witty inversion of the traditional *contemptus mundi* trope and poses the question highlighted by the dichotomy created between pain and pleasure earlier in the prologue, namely what is pleasure and what is pain, and how they can be identified and/or separated from one another. This approach – two seemingly opposed concepts that are interrogated and ultimately shown to share characteristics, ending with a paradox and a question – is a highly intellectual one, a scholastic and pedagogical investigation using dialectics playfully translated into a romance narrative. Thomas' *translatio* and poetics, as demonstrated in this crucial opening section, create dichotomies and oppositions in a similar but even more marked manner to the excursus on historical composition analyzed above. The effect of such dialectical poetics here is again to question received interpretations, in this instance the accepted locations of pleasure and pain, suggesting that how to read and interpret material in a variety of contexts will be a major theme of the poem.

This intellectual questioning, characterized by the collocation or juxtaposition of opposites, is also seen at the start of the poem during the narrative of Alexander's conception and birth. This part is read by Stone as a key aspect of 'the anxieties over the conqueror's career' that he perceives in *RTC*, since Philip's foreboding over Alexander as evil after his birth results in 'a disastrous royal lineage, anticipates the political troubles that follow his death, and thus

---

[48] The *AND*, <www.anglo-norman.net/cgi-bin/form-sl> [accessed 30 July 2015]. It occurs again in an erotic sense at 1652, describing the love-pangs of Darius' knights.

has a more ominous effect on Macedon and Philip'.[49] However, the sense of doom is not as inevitable nor as straightforwardly presented as this suggests. Philip's foreboding is only one aspect of a multivalent narrative that sets up a series of questions, questions that coalesce around how to interpret narratives of different kinds. One such is the story of Nectanebus. He is presented as 'le plus sage de toz' of all the 'plusur baron' who study the universe (47, 46), but this is dependent on 'artimage' or magic (52) that is evoked using 'charmes en estrange sermon' (72). Whether such hidden art is indeed representative of 'le plus sage' is questionable given this emphasis on its unknowability, especially in conjunction with Nectanebus' presentation as an 'home desvé' (146) or madman to Olympias, and his later death at Alexander's hands despite his knowledge of a prophecy predicting this.[50] This is not simply ambivalence, or uncertainty about Nectanebus' character and nature, since he is depicted first as wise and then as foolish (or at least as not necessarily wise). Rather, this is another example of the dialectical process, in this instance moving between wisdom and folly, which highlights the problem inherent in applying herme- neutics to inherited narratives: what is the meaning of this tale or character, and how is it to be read?

This interpretative issue is not confined to Nectanebus' wisdom or folly, but is extended throughout the narrative of Alexander's origins. Nectanebus tells Olympias that he has come to tell her a true thing – 'venuz vous sui dire une verité' (150) – but his revelations to her veer between truth and lies, or at least creative fabrications. He explains astronomy to her, and uses it to confirm her prophecy that Philip will repudiate her, which does indeed happen, but then lies that Alexander will be conceived by Amon, the god of Libya.[51] He goes to great lengths to disguise himself as Amon in order to pres- ent this fiction as truth, but it is of course clear to the reader that this aspect is simply fabrication. Yet Alexander will indeed become a 'riche empereur' (313), as the dream that Nectanebus creates for Philip foretells. Such dialecti- cal switching between truth and fabrication highlights the narrative's various truth claims and the need to interrogate them, especially with reference to the interpretation of the portents, dreams, and visions that are so numerous in this part of the tale. Thomas of Kent emphasizes this issue of interpretation explicitly via Olympias, who asks Nectanebus if the god Amon will return to her in terms that imply a certain doubt or at least the desire to test the truth of her supposedly divine experience: 'Il n'est pas dieu de Libye s'il me fet danger,/Car iceo est resons qe dieu seit dreiturer' ('He is not the god of Libya if he rejects me, since it is right that a god is just', 284–5). The possibility that her nocturnal visitant is not Amon is subtly yet significantly raised here

---

[49] Stone, 'Portents and the End of an Empire', p.20, p.21.
[50] *Anglo-Norman Alexander*, ed. Foster and Short, I, 476–509.
[51] *Anglo-Norman Alexander*, ed. Foster and Short, I, 191–214.

by Thomas in another dialectical movement between truth and fabrication, once again highlighting the need to distinguish between them. Whether to believe dreams or not, whether to trust in astronomy and magic, or indeed the evidence of one's own eyes, and thus the broader question of how to discern truth: these are the larger questions that Thomas' *translatio* engages with in this crucial part of the tale.

This has interesting ramifications for the *RTC*'s engagement with history in 'romanz'. The need to discern what is accurate emphasized in this dialectical process relates to the need for authors to compose 'par reson' (1330) that Thomas discusses in his excursus on historical composition analyzed above. Yet highlighting the need for discernment in reading and interpreting narratives does not preclude the presentation of 'beauté pur envoiser', 'beautiful things to create delight' (1333), which in this context can mean fictional narratives of wondrous and strange happenings such as Alexander's conception and birth. In fact, Thomas uses such narratives to highlight the issue of truth here. 'Estorie' (1329) does not have to be true to lead to a true understanding.

This is a more expansive view of history than that perceived by Stone in his reading of the *RTC*, which is not to deny that his ideas about its criticism about the break-up of the Macedonian empire are wrong; rather, this analysis shows that alongside a critical interest in sober political and historical fact sits a more nuanced dialogue about how to read and interpret historical narratives. This dialogue has not been characteristic of the romances studied so far, which have broadly been less concerned for the truth claims of their historical narratives than for the ethical hermeneutics by which such narratives may be interpreted. In fact, the *RTC*'s interest in different kinds of historical narratives aligns it rather with the *Alexandreis*, although it does not share that epic's concern for correct historicity, but rather rejoices in posing open-ended questions about history and interpretation. Another intriguing connection between the two texts is the concept of *sic et non*, which although differently expressed in the *RTC* is related to the more sophisticated dialectic of the *Alexandreis*. The Latin poem's highly intellectual practice of presenting an interpretation only to question it using a second one is not reproduced in the *RTC*, but the Anglo-Norman romance's interest in discerning what is true and what is false allows room for different perspectives, as does the *Alexandreis*. Perhaps what both texts share, despite their great contrast of language and approach, is composition in and for consciously intellectual milieux, in which the pedagogy of the schools was never far away. Such milieux were surely very different – the highly educated archiepiscopal *familia* in Reims must have differed from any potential courtly or monastic point of origin for the *RTC* – but the basic fact of these contexts' interest in the life of the mind connects them despite this.

In conclusion, the *RTC*'s *translatio* of parts of its historical narrative relates clearly to that of the *Alexandreis* in terms of highlighting hermeneutic processes. It also relates to romances' stronger emphasis on ethical interpretation, but this appears to be a lesser priority despite the poet's introduction of 'profit and pleasure': it is the dialectical process, rather than the ethics this produces, that seems to be of greatest interest, perhaps because of its pedagogical importance. Returning to the definitions of romance described above, both insular and continental, it is evident that the *RTC*'s poetics of historical *translatio* do not align it easily with either category. Its concern for history (although it is of course not insular history) may broadly equate to the historical fascination seen in Anglo-Norman romances (such as *Haveloc* and *Horn*) and other twelfth- and thirteenth-century works, but this over-arching interest alone does not make it an insular text: as we have seen, this is also a feature of the *Alexandreis*, a text of non-insular origin even if it circulated widely in Britain and Angevin France.[52] The *RTC*'s *translatio* of historical narrative, then, does not seem to be geographically inflected in any clear sense. Interestingly, if we consider this finding in generic terms, it appears that the *RTC* has more in common hermeneutically with so-called historical works (which is how the *Alexandreis* perceives itself) than with the romances studied so far, problematizing generic differences based on treatment of narratives and therefore nuancing Stone's idea about the distinction between history and romance Alexanders.

Sources

The question of historical narrative is related to that of sources: does the *RTC* adopt a similar approach to its source material more generally, not just in relation to its narrative technique? The modern French translators of the *RTC* consider that Thomas of Kent's narrative is 'fondée sur une exploitation plus scrupuleuse des sources'.[53] Thomas' enthusiasm for naming his sources indicates that this description may well be correct. If so, then this raises an important question, namely how far what appear to be characteristic aspects of his *translatio* identified here – interest in dialogue between opposites, and questioning of narrative claims – are not in fact original to him, but taken over from his sources. If either or both of these aspects are indeed present to a large extent in his material sources, then the idea of the *RTC* as an individually crafted response to Alexander narratives with localizable features needs to be nuanced.

As mentioned above, the main material resources Thomas used for his work are the *Epitome* of Julius Valerius and the *Letter of Alexander to Aristotle*.[54] I

---

[52] On some of these MSS, see David Townsend, 'Paratext, Ambiguity, and Interpretative Foreclosure in Manuscripts of Walter of Châtillon's *Alexandreis*', *New Medieval Literatures*, 14 (2012), pp.21–61, and Venetia Bridges, 'Reading Walter of Châtillon's *Alexandreis* in Medieval Anthologies', *Mediaeval Studies*, 77 (2015), pp.81–101.

[53] Gaullier-Bougassas and Harf-Lancner, *Le roman d'Alexandre*, pp.xviii–xix.

[54] The *Epitome* is edited by Julius Zacher as *Julii Valerii Epitome* (Halle, 1867), and is therefore often known as the 'Zacher Epitome' to distinguish it from other works with

shall only consider the relationships briefly here, since the issue is so vast and has been treated elsewhere, but hopefully this will nevertheless be instructive. Thomas' use of the Nectanebus narrative does indeed remain close to that of the *Epitome*, in line with the idea of 'une exploitation … scrupuleuse des sources', but there are some interesting and significant changes. A major addition, the section describing Olympias (96–153), is surely inspired by the blazoning of women in other romance narratives,[55] not a surprising finding, although it perhaps also supports the idea of inclusive poetics, but other alterations in the *RTC* indicate a desire to amplify or diminish themes in the *Epitome*. For example, the important and subtle moment in which Olympias implicitly queries whether Amon is a god if he fails to return to her is not present in the *Epitome*. Instead, in a wondering tone and using vocabulary suggesting simple belief in his divinity, she simply says she would like him to return because she enjoyed the experience: 'ergone ultra adesse dignabitur? nam est mihi ad tales nuptias amor!' ('will he therefore deign to be present again? for I have a love for such marital experiences!')[56] This is a significant, if small, difference that shows Thomas' characteristic concern for poetics highlighting both the implicit need to question truth claims and also his interest in opposites. Interestingly, however, Thomas is not wedded to the principle of amplification, despite the encyclopaedic interest displayed in the Eastern marvels part of the narrative discussed below. Comparison of the Nectanebus episode in the *Epitome* and the *RTC* shows that the Thomas streamlines his narrative, often by omitting details or making them more general, in order to preserve its momentum: examples are the omission of a list of the kings who attack Nectanebus, described more fully in the *Epitome* ('Indos, Arabes Phoenicesque … et quaecumque sunt Orientis barbarae gentes', 'the Indians, Arabs and Phoenicians … and whatever strange peoples there are in the East') than in the *RTC*, where they are simply 'tresze roys', and the reduction of an explanation about precious stones in the magical process.[57] This narratively informed treatment of the *Epitome* in the *RTC* makes the encyclopaedic inclusivity of the Oriental marvels section in the latter all the more noticeable.

---

a similar name. The *Letter* is translated into English on pp.140–56 of Lloyd L. Gunderson, *Alexander's Letter to Aristotle about India* (Meisenheim am Glan, 1980). Thomas also used the *Iter ad Paradisum* and the *Disciplina Clericalis* by Petrus Alfonsi: see D. R. Howlett, *The English Origins of Old French Literature* (Dublin, 1996), p.127.

55 See for example the description of Camille in the *Roman d'Eneas*, 3959–4084 (*Eneas: roman du XIIᵉ siècle*, ed. J.-J. Salverda de Grave, 2 vols, Classiques français du moyen âge, 44 and 62 (Paris, 1925 and 1929), ɪ).

56 Zacher, *Epitome*, ɪ.7, 15–16 (p.9). The verb 'dignor' in its deponent form means 'to deem worthy, honour, deign, condescend' <www.perseus.tufts.edu/hopper/morph?l=dignabitur&la=la> [accessed 3 August 2015].

57 The passages in the *Epitome* are ɪ.2, 3–6 and ɪ.4, 24–8 and in the *RTC* 64 and 193–97 (*Anglo-Norman Alexander*, ed. Foster and Short, ɪ).

about Horn's pride (expressed for example by Rigmel), over whose positive or negative impact critics have argued? One possibility is that the author is attempting to raise awareness of the understandable temptation, given his outstanding abilities, for Horn to be proud, and then to demonstrate his refusal to give in to this particular failing. Rigmel's fear of Horn's pride is thus born from her awe at his outstanding abilities: how could anyone as talented as Horn *not* be proud?[97] Representing Horn as resisting the temptation to be proud thus adds to his chivalric exemplarity. Yet the concern expressed and the emphasis on humility do create a slight question about Horn's character and his status as an *exemplum*, the same kind of question that we have seen the author of the *Alexandre* try hard to edit out of his narrative (by almost excessive interpretation). Here Thomas uses two opposed elements, pride and humility, to create his effects, setting up an implicit dialectic between pride and its opposite.

This point about dialectic and pedagogy naturally relates to the idea of chivalric didacticism discussed in terms of poetic elaboration above, but importantly it also highlights a new feature of *Horn*'s *translatio*, an interest in Latinate pedagogical procedures. This is something shared by the *RTC*, although it does not occur with relation to the major protagonist in that poem. In this instance at least there is some similarity between the poetics of the two works, a similarity born of mutual acquaintance with pedagogical procedures experienced in the schools. So even though the poetics of exemplarity have a different thematic focus in *Horn* from the *RTC*, they still display similarities in this aspect of their *translatio*. It is important to note, however, that the two works' mutual interest in dialectic does not make them equally learned: the *RTC*'s intellectual nature is demonstrated in a variety of contexts, as already discussed, whereas *Horn* appears so far to be more concerned with chivalric exemplarity.

Horn *and History*

The explicit Christianity of *Horn*'s narrative, another difference from the *RTC* despite the latter's occasional (anachronistic) reference to that faith, is particularly important since it provides us with insight into the romance's poetics of history. The narrative is set in a past Christian era, so there is no religious anachronism similar to that seen in the *Alexandre* and the *RTC*.[98] References to the power of the Christian God to ordain events, however, are used to create moments of narrative prolepsis, such as during Horn's abandonment at sea:

> E il sunt senz cunseil; as undes vunt walcrant.
> Deus lur est cunseilliers ki salveres est puissant.

---

[97] See *Horn*, ed. Pope, I, 1231–42.
[98] For discussion of this in the *Alexandre*, see chapter 3, 'Anxious Romance'; for the *RTC*, see the analysis of the Prologue above.

Si iert il, si li plest, cum l'orrez en avaunt ...
Kar Deu lor aovri un'aventure grant,
Ki un vent lor dona – del norwest [est] ventant –
K(i) en Bretaigne les mist u Hunlaf fu manant ...
Icist norrira Horn, cum Deu fu purvëant,
Ki es undes de mer li fud bon esturmant,
Taunt qu'i[l] l'ot delivré, qu'il ne fud[t] perillant
E qu'a port le mena, si cum fu son comant.

*They were helpless, tossing on the waves. God was their helper, our pow-
erful Saviour. And it will turn out as He wishes, as you will hear presently
... For God granted them good fortune, sending then a wind that blew from
the northwest and landed them in Brittany, home of Hunlaf ... He was to
nurture Horn, as ordained by God, who was a good pilot to him on the
waves of the sea until He had saved him from danger and brought him to
port at His behest.*[99]

At this moment Horn and his companions are adrift at sea, entirely powerless:
not until the next *laisse* do they reach the shore, and for several further *laisses*
they are afraid as they are unsure if they are in Christian or pagan lands. This
moment of prolepsis, created by the introduction of the Christian God, has
the effect of removing the narrative briefly from its linear, historical context
and placing it within a more remote temporal realm in which historicity, the
relationship between linear time and events, is unimportant: all history is
preordained by God. If human history is ordered in this way, then cause and
effect – a major feature of any narrative – is redundant, as is time: everything
is essentially in the past because the outcome is already decreed. This and
similar moments, such as lines 3586–8, in which the poet reminds the audience that nothing happens without God's permission,[100] have the effect of di-
minishing the historicity of *Horn*'s narrative, making it seem timeless despite
the specifics of its surroundings.[101]

Alongside this Christian prolepsis, *Horn* is set in a Christian past at some
distance from the poet's time. The poetic use of linguistic archaisms and
neologisms, a noted feature of Thomas' language, may be fortuitous, but it
adds to the sense of a poem interested in the relatively recent past as well as
the developing literary fashions of its time of composition.[102] The continual
concern for genealogy, seen for example in Wikele's family treachery and

---

[99] *Horn*, ed. Pope, I, 95–7, 104–6, 109–12; trans. Weiss, *Birth of Romance*, p.47.

[100] 'Seignurs, mal le creëz, ke ja avienge neent/A nul home del mund de sun purposement,/
Si Deus n'en ad aunceis fait sun ordenement', *Horn*, ed. Pope, I.

[101] On the importance of Christianity for *Horn*, specifically in terms of parallels between
signification in faith and language, see Ashe, *History and Fiction in England*, pp.146–50.

[102] Legge describes *Horn*'s language as a 'mixture of archaisms and neologisms' (*Anglo-Norman Literature and its Background*, p.97). See M. K. Pope, 'Notes on the

Thomas' insertion of Horn's narrative into a family trilogy, also highlights interest not only in the past but in its connections with more recent times. Authorial intervention mentions the playing of the harp 'in those days', as quoted earlier, with perhaps a sense of *sic transit gloria mundi*. This idea is extended in the same passage with the intriguing imagining of Rigmel (and potentially Horn) as subjects of *lai*: 'Rigmel est mut loéé,/Bele soer, de beauté en meinte cuntréé/E de Horn ai oï meinte feiz renoméé', 'Rigmel is admired for her beauty in many a land and I've often heard of Horn's renown'.[103] The pair are inserted into literary history as hero and heroine, emphasizing their extraordinary qualities and their relationship, but also implicitly moving them out of the historic present into a more timeless realm for a brief moment in the narrative. This movement, and the casting of the pair as timeless literary characters, creates a sense almost of nostalgia: the flower of chivalry has shifted, however briefly, out of the narrative present into the literary, and more distant, world of the *lai*. This complex interplay between texts also relates to the point made earlier about prolepsis, since it too suggests that the narrative is already finished, with fixed parts for its protagonists, despite being ongoing: Horn's knowledge and performance of the *lai* in its entirety (unlike Lenburc's half-knowledge) thus becomes significant as another indication of the proleptically completed tale.

History in *Horn*, then, is a moveable feast. Whilst there is deliberate authorial demarcation of different historical moments, this is often paradoxically to remove the narrative from its present, in other words the opposite result of the same habit as seen in the *Alexandreis*, but a similar effect, although using a different method, to that seen in the *Alexandre*. This differentiates *Horn* from the *RTC*, as the latter text is interested most in historical accuracy (seen in the careful attention paid to its sources) and history's hermeneutic possibilities; there is no sense of prolepsis in the *RTC* in order to create a sense of interpretative stability, as here in *Horn*.[104] The two insular romances differ greatly from one another in their attitudes towards history, but interestingly *Horn* and the *Alexandre* resemble one another somewhat in this context. This small observation is nevertheless important, since it shows that *Horn*'s relationship to history is not primarily driven by poetics derived from its insular location, but is a relationship found in romances originating in different places.

Vocabulary of the Romance of Horn and Rimel', in *Mélanges de philologie romane et de littérature médiévale offerts à Ernest Hoepffner* (Paris, 1949), pp.63–70.

[103] *Horn*, ed. Pope, I, 2799–801; trans. Weiss, *Birth of Romance*, p.95.

[104] Where the *RTC* does refer to God, for example, it is most often in gnomic terms to decry the general folly of the world, as at 740–4, which begins 'Hay! Dieus sovereins, Piere esperitables,/Tant est cist siecle faus, cheitis e deceivables' (*Anglo-Norman Alexander*, ed. Foster and Short, I).

Marvels

Unlike the *RTC*, *Horn*'s narrative does not contain any places or beasts depicted in exotic terms. Yet this absence does not mean that marvels of a different but related kind are not important in the poem. The marvels of *Horn*, in line with my analysis of the poem's dominant preoccupations, are human craft and skill in courtly pursuits. I have already discussed some aspects of the music-making episode, but I shall return to it from this perspective, as its description of Horn's harping demonstrates a 'poetics of the marvellous' clearly.

> Lors prent la harpe a sei, qu'il la veut atemprer.
> Deus! ki dunc l'esgardast cum la sout manïer,
> Cum ces cordes tuchout, cum les feseit trembler,
> Asquantes feiz chanter asquantes organer,
> De l'armonie del ciel li poüst remembrer!
> Sur tuz homes k'i sunt fet cist a merveiller.
> Quant ses notes ot fait si la prent a munter
> E tut par autres tuns les cordes fait soner:
> Mut se merveillent tuit qu'il la sout si bailler.
> E quant il out (is)si fait, si cummence a noter
> Le lai dunt or ains dis, de Baltof, haut e cler,
> Si cum sunt cil bretun d'itiel fait costumier.
> Apres en l'estrument fet les cordes suner,
> Tut issi cum en voiz l'aveit dit tut premier:
> Tut le lai lur ad fait, n'i vout rien retailler.
> E deus! cum li oianz le porent dunc amer!

> *Then he [Horn] took the harp, for he wanted to tune it. Lord, whoever then watched his knowledgeable handling of it, how he touched the strings and made them vibrate, sometimes causing them to sing and at other times join in harmonies, would have been reminded of the harmony of heaven! Of all the men there, this one caused most wonder. When he had played his notes, he began to raise the pitch and to make the strings give out completely different notes. Everyone was astonished at his skilful handling of it. And when he had done this, he began to sing the lay of Balthof, which I mentioned just now, loudly and clearly, just like the Bretons, who are versed in such performances. Next he made the harp strings play exactly the same melody as he had just sung. He performed the whole lay for them and did not want to omit any of it. And Lord, how his audience then had occasion to love him!*[105]

Here we see detailed description of the art of harp-playing and singing, which is explicitly compared to 'the harmony of heaven' in an authorial comment to underline the point that the performance is miraculous. This kind of *descriptio* is familiar from *Alexandre* and *Troie* in particular, but here it relates to the noble (in every sense) art of music. Especially interesting are the authorial

---

[105] *Horn*, ed. Pope, I, 2830–45; trans. Weiss, *Birth of Romance*, pp.95–6.

comments in this passage: a frequent feature of Thomas' poetic style, as is clear here and in the other passages quoted above, they seek to emphasize the marvellous nature of Horn's performance. Whilst the overall tenor of this passage once again casts Horn as a chivalric *exemplum*, as discussed earlier, the authorial comment about his harmonies refines this and makes him akin to the heavenly angels.[106] So the marvellous *descriptio* here is interpreted as a sign of godliness, a poetics that we have not seen in the other works considered so far. This is of course partly due to the ultimate historicity of the narrative, but the explicit emphasis on Horn's musicality as similar to the divine differentiates these poetics hermeneutically from those seen in *Cligès*, for example, a tale also set in Christian times.

There are other moments of authorial awe, such as during feasts: again, it is human noble customs, like the serving of drinks by noble girls out of elaborate cups, that are the focus of narrative wonder.[107] However, the musical scene is the most explicitly marvellous episode in *Horn*, whose narrative is not dominated by them in the same way as those of *Alexandre*, *Troie*, or even the *Alexandreis*. This does not make such moments unimportant, however, since as we have seen they are explicitly interpreted by the narrator as worthy of potentially divine status. They also serve to emphasize the interest in past times, 'costume iert a idonc en icele cuntréé', 'the custom in that land' (4137), which are part of the poetics of history as already discussed. So the presence and description of marvels reinforce the poem's concern for chivalric achievements and exemplarity seen in Horn himself, and the divine nature of Horn's music-making speaks to the Christian poetics of the narrative.

Insular Politics?

Weiss's plausible connection of *Horn*'s composition and performance with Richard FitzGilbert, earl of Clare, and Henry II at Dublin in 1171–72 gives us an unusually precise context for the poem's genesis. It comes at a high moment for Henry II, when he had managed to gain control over both the Irish and the Anglo-Norman lords holding land in the country. This success contextualizes *Horn*'s 'positive portrayal of decisive kingship', rare in Anglo-Norman romance.[108] Prince Horn's chivalric exemplarity and strong rule are textual aspirations that seem to be, for once, reflective of reality. Thomas' emphasis on Horn's loyalty as a vassal first of Hunlaf and then of Gudreche also appears to compliment Richard FitzGilbert and his obedience to Henry II. However, the insistence on Horn's exemplarity, in particular his humility

---

[106] Horn is explicitly compared to an angel several times in the text, for example in appearance at the start (15) and when Rigmel meets him (1054 and 1056) (*Horn*, ed. Pope, i).

[107] See for example lines 4137–63, in which this Germanic custom is described (*Horn*, ed. Pope, i).

[108] Field, 'Children of Anarchy', p.253.

and loyalty, which as we have seen is queried and ultimately reinforced by a broadly dialectical poetics, is telling. Richard FitzGilbert's loyalty to Henry II was questionable: he had supported Stephen rather than Henry's mother Matilda during the Anarchy and was consequently deprived of his title as earl of Pembroke by Henry at the latter's accession. His Irish adventures, initially in support of the deposed king of Leinster, were attempts to reverse his fortunes, and one of the reasons Henry himself came to Ireland in 1171 was to control de Clare's growing power and influence in that land.[109] Richard, in this context, is not primarily a loyal vassal, but a potentially dangerous threat to Henry's overlordship. From this perspective, *Horn*'s emphasis on loyalty to one's lord, seen in its eponymous hero's humility, as a defining feature of chivalry is not only a paean to the king and the earl, nor simply broadly culturally aspirational, but a reminder of contemporary political anxieties about the loyalties of barons to the king. We might go further and say that the question of Horn's pride, which is solved poetically by his humility, is raised subtly by the poet to emphasize these anxieties. Concealed to some extent by the poem's historical (and sometimes ahistorical or timeless) setting and its Christian hermeneutics, therefore, are perhaps messages of concern about contemporary politics.

Horn seems therefore to reflect a particular moment in insular and Irish political history. Does this, however, make it primarily an insular text from a political perspective? As we have seen, it shares aspects of its poetics with the *RTC*, another insular romance, but these poetics themselves are not confined to the British Isles. Likewise, *Horn*'s political concerns about loyalty of lords and strength of kings, although naturally they are strongly related to the Irish context in which the poem was composed and first performed, are a feature of other non-insular works, such as *Cligès* and the *Alexandreis*. The poem's general interest in the past as a source of marvels (including extraordinary chivalry) and the occasional timelessness and prolepsis of its narrative also balance its contemporary political references, again aligning it in a broad sense with poems from other geographical and political contexts that we have considered. So even though a political reading of *Horn* as an insular (possibly colonial?) text is illuminating, the themes of loyalty and strength that enable its political interpretation relate it beyond its immediate context of Ireland in the 1170s to other times and regions. For example, the poem would have resonated in the British Isles in the early thirteenth century under John's rule, when similar concerns were prevalent, and also in other contexts at that date, like the minority of the Capetian Louis IX (r. 1226–70).[110] Given that the three

---

[109] On FitzGilbert, see Weiss, 'Thomas and the Earl', pp.3–4.

[110] For a recent assessment of John's reign, see Stephen D. Church, *King John: England, Magna Carta and the Making of a Tyrant* (London, 2015); for Louis, see Jacques Le Goff, *Saint Louis* (Paris, 1996).

most complete (out of five) manuscripts of *Horn* all date from the thirteenth century, it is plausible that the poem's political themes were still relevant in that period. This of course means that the poem was current to some extent at the same time as the *RTC* was probably being edited and added to; the fact that *Horn* is found with Alexander material in London, British Library, MS Harley 527 is an intriguing hint that both narratives were being read together during the thirteenth century.[111]

Horn *and the* RTC

These two insular poems appear generally to differ in terms of their *translatio*, despite their similar dates, form, and manuscript situations. The *RTC*'s enthusiasm for learning is only shared by *Horn* in terms of a much less explicit dialectic between pride and humility, and the romances' poetics of exemplarity, history, and marvels diverge. Even their political contexts seem to differ, although of course that of the *RTC* is essentially lost. Yet both works have a conscious and complex interaction with their inherited narratives, although their engagement with these is driven by different aesthetic and interpretative priorities. What this comparison has shown, however, is that there does not seem to be an insular poetics of *translatio* shared between them. Both poems are doubtless responding to local factors (patrons, locations such as courts or monasteries, literary sources, and the availability of books or narratives), but these local factors are far from being specific to insular circles alone, as Weiss's point about shared contexts cited at the start of the chapter highlights.[112] Given this, I shall now analyze one possible local factor relevant to the *RTC* in more detail to see if it confirms this lack of specificity, or whether conversely it enables us to provide the Alexander romance with an insular location that does affect its *translatio*. The context in question is the monastery of St Albans.

St Albans and the *RTC*

If the *RTC* was at St Albans in the thirteenth century we are able to identify in some sort a local habitation and a home for this otherwise rather free-floating work at this period in its elusive history. M. R. James thought that the mid-thirteenth-century Trinity Cambridge manuscript was written at St Albans, an idea supported by Legge and Stone, although D. J. A. Ross initially disagreed.[113] It is possible that the mid-fourteenth-century Durham manuscript was also

---

[111] Weiss, *Birth of Romance*, p.10.

[112] Weiss, 'Insular Beginnings', p.26.

[113] M. R. James, *The Western Manuscripts in the Library of Trinity College, Cambridge: A Descriptive Catalogue*, 4 vols (Cambridge, 1904), III, p.482; Legge, *Anglo-Norman in the Cloisters*, pp.36–43 (p.36, p.38); Stone, 'Investigating Macedon', p.103; Ross, 'Anglo-Norman Workshop'; id., *Alexander historiatus*, p.25.

copied at St Albans for Richard of Bury, bishop of Durham between 1334 and 1345, and that at the sale of his books on his death the work was bought by the monks of the cathedral for their library.[114] This opens up the possibility that the *RTC*, even if it was not originally copied at St Albans, was present in the house on at least two occasions (c. 1250 and c. 1350), and may well have remained there for the intervening century. Taking this reasonable assumption as a starting point enables us to ask what happens if we read the *RTC* against this particular background.

St Albans, as is well known, was an important centre for book production during the twelfth and thirteenth centuries, the period of the *RTC*'s initial composition and copying. It was essentially a contemporary library, 'largely of Anglo-Norman origins', having few pre-Conquest books or charters (although like its fellow Benedictine foundation, Westminster Abbey, it is known to have forged some such records).[115] By the end of the later twelfth century, St Albans possessed a well-stocked monastic library, 'strong in patristics, monastic theology, and scriptural exegesis', with 'few rarities', although it did have some unusual Arabic material and some early complete copies of classical authors.[116] In addition, the twelfth century saw the creation of the St Albans Psalter book (also known as the Hildesheim manuscript), potentially produced and/or illustrated at the abbey and possibly connected with Christina of Markyate; it may have been adapted there specifically to commemorate her.[117] Setting aside this potential Christina connection, the St Albans Psalter book is an exception among monastic productions for its many illustrations and the presence of a vernacular saint's life, the *Chanson d'Alexis*, among more expected contents (a liturgical calendar and the psalter itself).[118] Yet

---

[114] *Anglo-Norman Alexander*, ed. Foster and Short, II, pp.71–2; Stone, 'Investigating Macedon', agrees (p.104).

[115] James Clark, *A Monastic Renaissance at St Albans: Thomas Walsingham and his Circle, c.1350–1440* (Oxford, 2004), p.79. On forgery at St Albans in comparison with Westminster, see Julia Crick, 'St Albans, Westminster, and Some Twelfth-Century Views of the Anglo-Saxon Past', *Anglo-Norman Studies*, 25 (2003), pp.65–83.

[116] Clark, *Monastic Renaissance*, p.79. For a useful survey of the abbey's book history, see R. M. Thomson, *Manuscripts from St Albans Abbey 1066–1235*, 2 vols (Cambridge, 1982), I. See also Richard W. Hunt, 'The Library of the Abbey of St. Albans', in *Medieval Scribes, Manuscripts and Libraries: Essays Presented to N. R. Ker*, ed. M. B. Parkes and Andrew G. Watson (London, 1978), pp.251–77.

[117] On the complexities of this book and the various possible relationships it may have had with St Albans, see Donald Matthew, 'The Incongruities of the St Albans Psalter', *Journal of Medieval History*, 34.4 (2008), pp.396–416. Matthew summarizes the critical debates and concludes that parts of the manuscript were held at Markyate under Roger, Christina's protector, before being altered and bound with the *Chanson d'Alexis* at St Albans in the mid-twelfth century.

[118] The manuscript is available online at <www.abdn.ac.uk/stalbanspsalter/english/essays/introduction.shtml>, with a useful survey of its possible dates and production contexts [accessed 10 August 2015].

despite its exceptional nature it is instructive for contextualizing the *RTC*, since these two features, imagery and vernacularity, are also key aspects of the romance in the extant witnesses. The manuscript is not the only St Albans book to contain vernacular literature, the feature relevant to this study, since a local monk called Beneit composed an Anglo-Norman *Vie de Thomas Becket* at the end of the twelfth century.[119] These two hagiographical works demonstrate an interest in the possibilities of vernacular literature at St Albans at much the same time as the *RTC* was probably initially composed; although there is no evidence for the composition of the Alexander romance at St Albans (or anywhere else), written use of the Anglo-Norman vernacular as well as Latin in the abbey during this era suggests a wider enthusiasm for the possibilities of the contemporary literary landscape. These possibilities become realities at St Albans in the thirteenth century, exemplified in particular in the work of Matthew Paris (1200–59). Historian, illustrator, hagiographer, companion of royalty, supplier of books to aristocratic women, Matthew's output is prolific and important in defining St Albans as a literary centre.[120] I shall focus here on his literary activities in order to see whether they enable us to contextualize the *RTC* as it stands in the earliest witness, the Trinity manuscript, which was probably produced during Matthew's later life.

Matthew Paris and the RTC

Matthew's literary production is dominated by his historiographical writings. His *Chronica majora*, begun around 1240, starts with the world's creation and runs until 1259; he made an epitome of this focusing on English affairs named the *Historia Anglorum*, and also composed two other shorter chronicles, the *Abbreviatio chronicarum* and *Flores historiarum*.[121] In addition, he wrote a history of St Albans, the *Gesta abbatum monasterii Sancti Albani*, whose first part was finished by 1250. Antonia Gransden sees Matthew's historical works as important because of their 'comprehensiveness' and because they 'developed historical method'.[122] In the *Chronica majora*, for example, Matthew used his literary sources closely but not 'slavishly'; in the later parts he used his own observations and gathered material using St Albans' monastic connections; he also realized the importance of documents, and copied many into

---

[119] Thomson, *Manuscripts from St Albans Abbey*, p.68.

[120] The definitive work on Matthew remains Richard Vaughan, *Matthew Paris* (Cambridge, 1958). There is a large bibliography on Matthew's work, much of which focuses on his historical writing (as 'history' in modern terms) and artistic output. Less appears to have been produced on his works as 'literature' rather than as historical documents, with some few exceptions (noted below).

[121] For an overview of Matthew's historiography, see Antonia Gransden, 'Matthew Paris and the St Albans School of Historiography', in *Historical Writing in England*, 2 vols (London, 1974), I: *c.550–c.1307*, pp.356–79.

[122] Ibid., p.356.

the *Chronica* (including a unique text confirming the Magna Carta) as well as creating a separate book of these, the *Liber additamentorum*, as a supplement.[123] Matthew had 'an encyclopaedic quality', adding details of art, heraldry, and natural history to his narrative, which led to 'an almost uncontrollable amount of data' in the *Chronica*; he attempted to rationalize this by creating epitomes, and also by composing summaries at the end of individual annals within the *Chronica* itself.[124] An unusual feature of his writing is a strong interest in European history, not simply as it reflected on English matters, but as 'a subject in its own right'; he is the only contemporary historian in Europe to give a full account of the Council of Lyons in 1245, for example.[125] Broadly, then, Matthew's historiography can be defined (in Gransden's terms) as 'comprehensive' and 'encyclopaedic', including documents as well as artistic and zoological material in its narratives, European as well as English history, but with a distinct methodology behind these features that attempted to balance inclusion with narrative coherence. His inclusivity and breadth makes him more than simply 'the great nationalist historian', as claimed by Geraldine Heng: his perspective is far wider.[126]

We have seen a similar interest in an encyclopaedic approach in the analysis of the *RTC*, with reference to Alexander's journeys in the East. This is not a surprise in a time when Isidore of Seville's *Etymologiae* was ubiquitous, but it is interesting to find this shared feature between two works, differing in subject and language, that may have occupied the same physical and intellectual space. It is especially intriguing, however, to find Matthew's considered and learned approach to historical writing paralleled in the Alexander romance in a way that is not the case for the *Alexandre*, for example. The combination of these two features in both Matthew's work and the *RTC* indicates why, at the very least, the romance would have been of interest from a methodological and intellectual perspective at St Albans. This claim does not, however, mean that we should consider the romance to have a distinctively local identity that overrides its interaction with broader intellectual and literary trends. What we see at St Albans with reference to these works is a local example of literary phenomena that are found in different incarnations in learned centres across Europe, as the study in chapter 2 of Reims' late twelfth-century interest in historical 'fiction' demonstrated.

Matthew's hagiography may provide further insights into the *RTC*'s context at St Albans. Hagiography as a mode of literary discourse has several

---

123 Ibid., pp.360–1, p.357.
124 Ibid., pp.362–3.
125 Ibid., p.361.
126 Geraldine Heng, 'The Romance of England: *Richard Coeur de Lyon*, Saracens, Jews and the Politics of Race and Nation', in *The Postcolonial Middle Ages*, ed. Jeffrey Jerome Cohen (Basingstoke, 2000), pp.135–71 (p.151).

parallels with Alexander narratives, since both share an overall focus on the protagonist's *vita* and its hermeneutic possibilities, as well as specific narrative elements such as miraculous *enfances*, remarkable achievements, miracles, and the nature of their death.[127] Four surviving vernacular saints' lives are ascribed to Matthew: Alban, Edmund of Canterbury, Thomas Becket, and Edward the Confessor.[128] Of these, the *Vie de seint Auban* is a particularly useful companion for the *RTC*, since this life also features a protagonist with historical-fictional roots inherited from the classical or late-antique past.[129] Alban, of Roman descent, was held to be the English protomartyr, and the twelfth and thirteenth centuries saw increased emphasis upon his cult and the development of that of his supposed teacher, Amphibalus, whose relics were discovered in 1178.[130] Matthew's *Vie de seint Auban* survives in an autograph manuscript, Dublin, Trinity College, MS 177, with several other Latin lives of the saint and liturgical material for his feast, as well as descriptions of the miracles and invention of Amphibalus.[131] One of these Latin lives, the twelfth-century prose *Passio sancti Albani* by William of St Albans, is Matthew's material source.[132] Interestingly, *Auban* is the only one of Matthew's saints' lives composed using Alexandrine *laisses*, the same metrical form as the *RTC*.[133] Admittedly it is especially noted as a *chanson de geste* metre, but its mutual use in the *RTC* and *Auban* suggests a specifically St Albans parallel between the two works, a

---

[127] This is of course true not just of Alexander material but of romances more widely, as the concept of 'hagiographic romance' demonstrates: see for example Muriel Cadilhac-Rouchon, 'Revealing Otherness: A Comparative Examination of French and English Medieval Hagiographical Romance' (unpublished PhD thesis, University of Cambridge, 2009).

[128] *Thomas Becket* is extant in several folios only. Paris also composed a Latin life of Stephen Langton, archbishop of Canterbury, which is also mostly lost.

[129] On St Alban's cult, see P. A. Haywood, 'The Cult of St. Alban, *Anglorum Protomartyr*, in Anglo-Saxon and Anglo-Norman England', in *More than a Memory: The Discourse of Martyrdom and the Construction of Christian Identity in the History of Christianity*, ed. Johan Leemans (Leuven, 2005), pp.169–200.

[130] For an overview of this development, see *The Life of Saint Alban by Matthew Paris*, trans. and introd. Jocelyn Wogan-Browne and Thelma S. Fenster, FRETS, 2 (Tempe, AZ, 2010), pp.13–15.

[131] For the MS contents, see ibid., pp.14–17, and for a recent study, Christopher Baswell, 'The Manuscript Context', in ibid., pp.169–94. On the Latin lives, see W. McLeod, 'Alban and Amphibal: Some Extant Lives and a Lost Life', *Mediaeval Studies*, 42 (1980), pp.407–30, and Florence McCulloch, 'Saints Alban and Amphibalus in the Works of Matthew Paris: Dublin, Trinity College, MS 177', *Speculum*, 56.4 (1981), pp.761–85.

[132] On William's *Passio*, see Monika Otter, '"New Werke": St. Erkenwald, St. Albans, and the Medieval Sense of the Past', *Journal of Medieval and Renaissance* [Early Modern] *Studies*, 24.3 (1994), pp.387–414.

[133] *Auban*'s verse form is described in detail in *Life of Saint Alban*, trans. Wogan-Browne and Fenster, pp.42–8, and that of the *RTC* by Foster and Short in *Anglo-Norman Alexander*, ii, pp.24–46.

parallel indicated more broadly in the general resemblance between hagiography and Alexander narratives noted above.

A full comparative study of the two texts will have to wait for another occasion, but I want to note here some features of *Auban* that are significant in relation to the *RTC*. Firstly, Matthew frequently uses verbal forms familiar from romance and/or *chanson de geste*, so that Alban addresses God as 'Beu Sire Deus' at his martyrdom, for example.[134] He also makes an important change to his source, the *Passio*, in giving the soldier who becomes a Christian after seeing Alban's martyrdom a name, Aracle (Heraclius), and in presenting him as a 'noble knight'.[135] He is 'a *gentil chevaler*' whose conversion is depicted in the accompanying illustration 'after an image of a knight's initiation'.[136] This new focus on Aracle as an individual knight upholding chivalric virtues, familiar to contemporary audiences of romance and *chanson de geste*, demonstrates Matthew recasting his narrative along recognizable generic lines. Finally, Matthew makes the Romans of the *Passio*, who persecute Alban, into Saracens, who worship 'Mahom' and 'Tervagant'.[137] Wogan-Browne and Fenster cite the contemporary importance of the Crusades here, and Hahn similarly sees this as another way of making the story relevant to a thirteenth-century audience, but the crucial point is surely that like the other aspects of Matthew's *translatio* the effect also creates more parallels with romance and *chanson de geste* modes of discourse.[138]

This form of *translatio*, in which a narrative set in a distant mainly pre-Christian past is recast in a contemporary romance form, is also seen in the *RTC*. This is of course a broad and fundamental parallel: there are many ways in which the two works differ vastly from one another, in particular the Christian nature of *Auban*'s narrative. Yet Matthew's attempts to locate *Auban* as a text that shares features of romance and *chanson de geste* demonstrate the currency these discourses had at St Albans in the mid-thirteenth century. Stephen Jaeger's idea that chivalry as a code originated from saintly clerics rather than from kings and 'received full narrative development in Latin and finally romance literature, a literature written by clerics to correct and edify the behavior of kings and knights' further connects hagiography and romance in terms of function:[139] both are to edify and instruct their readers on related

---

[134] *Auban*, 779. The text is edited by A. R. Harden as *La Vie de seint Auban*, ANTS, 19 (Oxford, 1968).

[135] Cynthia Hahn, 'Proper Behavior for Knights and Kings: The Hagiography of Matthew Paris, Monk of St. Albans', *Haskins Society Journal*, 2 (1990), pp.237–48 (p.240).

[136] Ibid., p.240, p.241.

[137] *Auban*, 821.

[138] *Life of Saint Alban*, trans. Wogan-Browne and Fenster, pp.27–8; Hahn, 'Proper Behavior', p.242. McCulloch also makes this point with reference to 'epic' ('Saints Alban and Amphibalus', p.777).

[139] Summed up in Hahn, 'Proper Behavior', pp.238–9.

issues, Christian and chivalric ethics. Although the *RTC* is less ethically than intellectually didactic, the broad comparison still holds, demonstrating why in a vibrant and creative vernacular hagiographical context like St Albans the *RTC* would have been a suitable occupant of the library.

Once again, this St Albans context should not be seen as excluding the *RTC* from participating in wider insular and transnational trends, such as the presentation of past heroes in contemporary chivalric terms so characteristic of Anglo-Norman and continental romance; rather, it exemplifies the wide currency of these trends. However, the combination of features shared between two kinds of Matthew Paris' output (historiography and hagiography) and the *RTC* does demonstrate intriguing literary and methodological connections between thirteenth-century St Albans and the Alexander romance. Of course, Matthew Paris' writings are not the only feature of literary life at the monastery, but as its major historian at this time he is explicitly its defining figure, meaning that the *RTC* is aligned with St Albans' dominant literary characteristics at a high point in the latter's intellectual history.

Alexander at St Albans

Another factor especially relevant to the *RTC* is the study of Alexander material in twelfth- and thirteenth-century St Albans, since it seems that the monastery contained a lot of Alexander texts and may well have created its own works based on these. Charles Russell Stone's studies of insular Alexander texts have demonstrated that St Albans is the probable origin of a redaction of the *Philippic Histories* made in the twelfth century, the as yet unedited *St Albans Compilation* (*SAC*).[140] This work is apparently distinguished by 'its intellectual agenda' as a product of skilful editing, resulting in 'a thematically pointed, five-book narrative, the work of both a well-read, thoughtful compiler and one with considerable information on Alexander and Macedon at his disposal'.[141] The *SAC* is a key element in Stone's argument that St Albans is the spearhead of an insular movement to rewrite Alexander's story from a historical, rather than a legendary, perspective:

> [The *SAC* is] the most intensive Insular investigation into the account of Alexander as found in Justin's epitome of the *Philippic Histories* ... [it shows] an unparalleled, dogged adherence to Justin's history of Macedon and the utter exclusion of legendary accounts.[142]

---

[140] See Stone, 'Investigating Macedon', and the similar account in *From Tyrant to Philosopher-King*, pp.77–110. The *St Albans Compilation* is extant in two manuscripts, Cambridge, Corpus Christi College, MS 219 and Gonville and Caius, MS 154/204; there is also a fragment in Cambridge, University Library, Dd. 10. 24.

[141] Stone, 'Investigating Macedon', p.83.

[142] Ibid., p.80.

The *SAC* reads Alexander's life as emblematic of 'the corruptive influence of success and unmitigated power', a historical warning in the *speculum princip-is* mould.[143] As discussed above, Stone implicates the *RTC* in this movement to rewrite Alexander, seeing its narrative as a critical approach in which 'the conqueror and his empire [is] a collective example of political discord'.[144] In his analysis, the *RTC* is a work very much in tune with the negative view of Alexander promulgated in the *SAC* and that he sees as characteristic of St Albans. As is I hope clear from this chapter, my analysis of the *RTC* has highlighted a rather different perspective (or series of perspectives): the romance is strongly characterized by intellectually themed *translatio* in several different textual locations and from a variety of perspectives, and thus appears to me to be primarily learned rather than ethically valent as Stone suggests. So, whilst Stone's reading of parts of the *RTC* is informative, especially as it connects the romance firmly with St Albans, the *RTC* does not seem to me to aid in the construction of a St Albans or an insular Alexander tradition, especially given its divergence from the *SAC* in terms of hermeneutics. In fact, the *SAC* and the *RTC* demonstrate the pluralism of possible responses to Alexander, a pluralism that fits well with the varied literary culture at St Albans in the late twelfth and early thirteenth centuries.

This point about texts and institutions as plural also applies to genre, another key part of Stone's idea of an insular Alexander tradition in evidence at St Albans. We have seen in broad terms how hagiography and some romance (or *chanson de geste*) texts imitate one another at St Albans, a salutary reminder that genre does not necessarily define style or vice versa. To agree with Stone that there are distinctive and separable history and romance views of Alexander is to oversimplify extremely complex phenomena even before considering how such views are reflected and refracted in literary texts based on inherited sources. Whilst there may certainly be historical or romance tendencies (for example the habit of re-creating antique heroes as contemporary knights), the relationship between history and romance Alexanders is best viewed as occupying a broad spectrum of possibilities in which any perceived genre boundaries are habitually elided or ignored. For example, the *RTC* is extremely interested in historical accuracy as well as invoking the more common romance poetics of anachronism, making it a far more hybrid and complex work than the label 'romance' often allows. Similarly, but in a different context, the *Alexandreis'* attempt to outdo romance *descriptio* also paradoxically gives it some features previously unusual in epic but more often seen *en romanz*. Identity politics in all these contexts, literary and geographical, are frequently a pluralistic phenomenon, and the Alexander works at St Albans discussed here are no exception to this rule. St Albans' Alexander material is certainly

---

[143] Ibid., p.79.
[144] Stone, 'Portents and the End of an Empire', p.18.

important for the *RTC*, but its importance does not alone make that text's *translatio* a St Albans, an insular, or even a romance, production.

St Albans: Multiple Identities

The multifaceted literary nature of both the *RTC* and St Albans discussed here suggests that text and monastery need to be considered not just as local or even insular phenomena but more widely as part of transnational culture.[145] This raises the question of whether St Albans' literary variety, exemplified so strongly in the *RTC*, is matched by its political influence and importance: can the monastery, and thus its literature, be shown to play a definitive role in a wider European arena? Potentially supporting a positive answer to this question is the fact that St Albans was both a famous individual house and also one link in the Benedictine network encompassing foundations throughout Europe. St Albans' textual productions, whilst characteristic of an individual intellectual atmosphere, were often specifically designed to promote the abbey and its cults in a wider context, as Matthew Paris' notes about which aristocratic women he wished his works to be sent to (admittedly within the British Isles) make amply clear.[146] Paris' unusual interest in European history as a subject in its own right, mentioned above, also highlights the possibility that this wider context was not just British but European.

The British and European possibilities of St Albans, and its texts, become evident if we set the house in its wider Benedictine context. The monastery is often found in modern scholarly works in company with other prominent, mainly southern, houses like Abingdon, Bury St Edmunds, Christ Church (Canterbury), Durham, and Westminster, and has been described as 'the premier Benedictine monastery of all England' from the mid-twelfth century.[147] Wealthy, large, dedicated to England's protomartyr, and with significant literary interests as described above, it was a prestigious foundation both within the British Isles and in its relationships with continental houses. Within an insular context, St Albans benefited from royal support, especially in the twelfth century, receiving many gifts and favours that increased its power and influence

---

[145] The *RTC*'s interest in intellectually engaged *translatio* connects it strongly to the kind of 'transnational' perspectives we have seen in the *Alexandreis*, for example, speaking to literary fashions not bound by political or geographical boundaries.

[146] Dublin 177 names Isabel, countess of Arundel and the countess of Cornwall as borrowers, and mentions illustrations intended for a book of the countess of Winchester; Paris dedicated his life of Edmund of Canterbury to Isabel. See *Life of Saint Alban*, ed. Wogan-Browne and Fenster, pp.32–5.

[147] See for example Julie Kerr, *Monastic Hospitality: The Benedictines in England, c. 1070–c. 1250* (Woodbridge, 2007), p.3, and Michelle Still, *The Abbot and the Rule: Religious Life at St Albans, 1290–1349* (Aldershot, 2002), p.3. The quotation is from Still, *Abbot and the Rule*, p.2.

throughout the country.[148] It also competed for these things with other important Benedictine foundations: it was in conflict with the house at Durham during the twelfth century over the rights to Tynemouth Priory, for example, which was ultimately a battle for influence in the north.[149] These factors clearly demonstrate St Albans' ability, and desire, to extend its influence beyond its local geographical area and to play a role on a wider stage. That this stage was not confined to the British Isles is demonstrated by St Albans' connection with Pope Adrian IV (1154–59). Pope Adrian's father had become a St Albans monk in 1151, and the abbot of the day, Robert de Goron (1151–66), exploited this to the house's full advantage. Abbot Robert visited the pope himself, gave him valuable gifts, and gained many privileges from Adrian. Crucially, some of these confirmed the monastery's 'exemption from diocesan authority and its direct dependence on the pope'.[150] Whilst not new privileges, they strengthened St Albans' direct relationship with the papacy, and therefore its transnational status as a house at once free from local diocesan control and having a strong connection to the centre of ecclesiastical power.

St Albans, therefore, was a monastery with multiple links in different spheres of influence. At once local, national, and transnational, it was important in each of these contexts. This is of course hardly unusual, but St Albans appears to have been particularly dominant in each area, at least in the later twelfth century and into the thirteenth, the time of the *RTC*'s composition and editing. St Albans' literary character matches this political importance: whether by using tropes derived from French romance or *chanson de geste* in its Latin hagiographies, or in the lending of its books to aristocratic secular women, its often innovative texts speak to insular and transnational concerns and interests. This desire to reach beyond physical, linguistic, and generic textual boundaries is paralleled by the *RTC*'s intellectual curiosity and its vernacularity, paradoxically giving it a St Albans identity whether it was composed there or not.

Conclusion

This chapter's investigation of Anglo-Norman and Latin texts has shown that when narrative features are removed from the equation, it is not possible to identify a poetics of *translatio* specifically produced by insular circumstances. This is partly because the *RTC* and *Horn* are much harder to contextualize

---

[148] Paul A. Haywood, 'Sanctity and Lordship in Twelfth-Century England: Saint Albans, Durham, and the Cult of Saint Oswine, King and Martyr', *Viator*, 30 (1999), pp.105–44 (p.117).

[149] Ibid., p.118.

[150] Antonia Gransden, *A History of the Abbey of Bury St Edmunds*, 2 vols (Woodbridge, 2007 and 2015), I: *1182–1256, Samson of Tottington to Edmund of Walpole*, p.22.

geographically and politically than the *Alexandreis*, the *Ylias*, *Cligès*, or even the *Alexandre*: both are difficult to date, are textually problematic, and are now anomalies, lonely texts that seem to have spawned small narrative traditions in comparison with the ubiquity of Arthur and more importantly the large body of continental French Alexander material.[151] Paradoxically, our scanty information about these texts' origins and circumstances can lead to assumptions of their insularity in terms of exceptionalism: they must display relevant local characteristics because they do not have obvious connections to other, broader textual traditions. Their Anglo-Norman language, itself of course often problematic in manuscripts, can feel like a relief, a seemingly definite landmark in the otherwise impenetrable mist of unknown contexts. However, as we have seen, the romances' singularity, especially in the case of the *RTC*, is most apparent if we only think of them as 'Anglo-Norman romances'. If we consider them as works engaged in *translatio* far less restricted by linguistic, geographical, political, and generic boundaries than modern scholars often like to think, then we are much freer to read them against a broader literary background that may be more productive. For the *RTC*, this has highlighted the intellectualism that aligns it not just with its fellow Alexander text the *Alexandreis*, but with transnational learned culture in both a local sense at St Albans and also more widely in the new universities like Bologna and Paris as well as in the cathedral schools. This context also means we see the *RTC* from a less romance-inflected standpoint despite its comparison here with *Horn*, a valuable counterbalance to analyses that to my mind focus too much on genre as a defining feature.

The *RTC* is not, however, an intellectual Alexandrian anomaly that reinforces Alexander literature as a phenomenon somehow separate from other contemporary texts, whether romance or not. It is interesting that *Horn*, despite scholarly deductions about its Dublin provenance, displays poetics of *translatio* that focus on elaboration and amplification. These features, which are similar to the *descriptio* analyzed in the previous chapters, are found not just in French romances but in Latin epics, and not only in (possibly) Angevin texts like *Troie* but also in less politically aligned works such as the *Ylias*. Admittedly this is a broad observation, but it is a vital reminder that an insular romance work whose narrative is taken from 'the pseudo-history of pre-Conquest England'[152] may have relationships beyond these boundaries, just as the *RTC* does. Similarly, the local Alexandrian tradition of St Albans

---

[151] The later history of the *Roman d'Alexandre* is a case in point, since it was influential for the *Roman d'Alexandre en prose*, a text that was frequently found in high-value and prestigious illustrated manuscripts, such as London, British Library, MS Royal 20 B. xx (fifteenth century). On the prose text, see D. J. A. Ross, *Studies in the Alexander Romance* (London, 1985).

[152] Ashe, 'Hero and his Realm', p.135.

turns out to be a pluralistic phenomenon in line with the monastery's other literary productions and with Matthew Paris, no doubt with many connections to insular and continental institutions that are as yet untraced.

In conclusion, if there is one single feature of insular literature (particularly romance) that this chapter has repeatedly highlighted, it is its variety, which should be a familiar theme by now. The idea of an explicit debate about *translatio* occurring between texts, highlighted in earlier chapters, is more difficult to trace, however, although the pluralism of Alexander material potentially from or at St Albans in the twelfth and thirteenth centuries certainly allows for the possibility. Like chapter 3's study of continental romance and chapter 2's analysis of Latin epic, we have seen here that romance *translatio* is still far from monolithic in an insular context in the twelfth and thirteenth centuries. The next chapter will investigate whether this pluralism is also found in the following century, in which the use of English as a language of literature increases so markedly.

5

English and International? *Kyng Alisaunder, Of Arthour and of Merlin*, and *The Seege or Batayle of Troye*

The title of this chapter is a conscious invocation of Elizabeth Salter's work *English and International: Studies in the Literature, Art and Patronage of Medieval England*.[1] In that work, Salter provocatively calls Chaucer's decision to write in English 'the triumph of internationalism', suggesting that his writing is an indication of a context that is 'essentially European, not narrowly insular'.[2] After the analysis of the *RTC* in chapter 4, this attitude should not be a surprise, nor especially provocative. However, in terms of critical context Salter's observation remains unusual. The increasing dominance of English in the insular literature of the later Middle Ages has naturally led to a scholarly focus on the local resonances of texts because of the limited geographical range of the language, and therefore the related idea that English-language material is interested in issues of identity that are local and/or peculiar to the English has been particularly to the fore in scholarship. Thorlac Turville-Petre's 1996 book *England the Nation*, which analyzes the period 1290–1340, is often cited as a key moment in crystallizing this approach.[3] Although the final chapter, 'Three Languages', argues against 'nationalist polemics' regarding English, French, and Latin and for 'a tradition of languages existing in harmonious and complementary relationship', the book's main emphasis is firmly upon the construction of a single culture based upon national identity, 'one culture in three voices'.[4] This perspective incorporates Latin and French with English into a unified cultural and political narrative, but crucially in doing so it elides the possibility of difference, whether linguistic or in terms

---

[1] Edited by Derek Pearsall and Nicolette Zeeman (Cambridge, 1988).
[2] Salter, *English and International*, p.244 and p.239.
[3] See for example Thomas H. Crofts and Robert Rouse, 'Middle English Popular Romance and National Identity', in *A Companion to Medieval Popular Romance*, ed. Raluca Radulescu and Cory Rushton (Cambridge, 2009), pp.79–95 (p.79).
[4] Thorlac Turville-Petre, *England the Nation: Language, Literature, and National Identity, 1290–1340* (Oxford, 1996), p.181.

of function: all three languages have effectively become, or have been sub-sumed into, English, culturally and politically. Geraldine Heng sums up the prevailing critical view of the coterminous relationship between the English language (or languages) and insular culture succinctly:

> The choice of English was a choice in favor of exclusivity, since English ensured that the romances addressed only an insular audience, eschewing the outside, and all possibility of international reception.[5]

This 'exclusivity' makes English romance actively insular, 'eschewing ... international reception'. From this perspective, Salter's observation about Chaucer's internationalism seems remote, applicable perhaps only to a poet composing in multilingual and cosmopolitan court circles for elite patrons rather than to the more widely consumed popular romances that the same author parodies in *The Canterbury Tales*.[6] However, as the analysis of the *Roman de toute chevalerie (RTC)* in chapter 4 highlighted, linguistically local texts do not necessarily display a distinct form of *translatio* closely related to their location. Salter's point about Chaucer's English as 'a triumph of in-ternationalism' is an important reminder that even within English-language material we see the formative influences of other texts and traditions. In this chapter, I shall attempt to build upon this perspective by firstly considering the *translatio* of *Kyng Alisaunder* and then by comparing the romance with other Middle English texts in order to provide a literary context for its linguistic and cultural identities. In doing so, I hope to query assumptions about the re-lationship between language and culture that underpin scholarship on Middle English romance.

Alexander in Later Medieval England

The previous chapters have demonstrated the variety inherent in Alexander works' *translatio* during the twelfth and thirteenth centuries, a pluralism that is not defined by language or polity but that is transnational in several dif-ferent contexts. Whether these transnational perspectives continue into the later Middle Ages in northern Europe, when political developments such as the Hundred Years' War do undoubtedly create incipient nationalist attitudes,

---

[5] Geraldine Heng, 'The Romance of England: *Richard Coeur de Lyon*, Saracens, Jews and the Politics of Race and Nation', in *The Postcolonial Middle Ages*, ed. Jeffrey Jerome Cohen (Basingstoke, 2000), pp.135–71 (p.155). Heng is referring specifically to late thirteenth-century popular romances, but her conclusion is applicable to Eng-lish-language material of a similar date more widely.

[6] 'The Tale of Sir Thopas' in *The Canterbury Tales* is a parody of romance conven-tions (*The Riverside Chaucer*, gen. ed. Larry D. Benson, 3rd edn (Boston, MA, 1987), pp.213–16).

remains to be seen.[7] However, it is suggestive that both the originally continental Alexander texts I have discussed so far, the *Alexandreis* and the *Roman d'Alexandre*, exist in many later medieval manuscripts, indicating that their potential for spreading such varied *translatio* beyond their immediate compositional context (chronologically, territorially, and politically) is substantial. For example, many of the *Alexandreis'* over two hundred extant manuscripts are known to have been copied and/or circulated in the British Isles, both soon after the poem's composition and later; although fewer in number, several of the *Roman d'Alexandre*'s manuscripts parallel this textual history, especially the beautifully illustrated Oxford, Bodleian Library, MS Bodley 264, in England by the fifteenth century, in which the French Alexander text is found alongside extracts from the Middle English poem *Alexander and Dindimus*.[8]

From the late thirteenth or early fourteenth century, however, the renewed composition of English-language material may start to alter this transnational literary-cultural situation. The Middle English romance *Kyng Alisaunder* was probably composed at this moment, and during the second half of the fourteenth century it is joined by several other Alexander texts (*Alexander A*, *Alexander B*, and *Alexander C*). The fifteenth century sees the advent of a prose text (the *Prose Life of Alexander*) and Scots versions.[9] The production of English-language Alexander texts, combined with the idea of English as

---

[7] On this, see Ardis Butterfield, *The Familiar Enemy: Chaucer, Language, and Nation in the Hundred Years War* (Oxford, 2009), and also Joanna Bellis, *The Hundred Years War in Literature, 1337–1600* (Cambridge, 2016).

[8] On the histories of some thirteenth-century English *Alexandreis* manuscripts, see Venetia Bridges, 'Reading Walter of Chatillon's *Alexandreis* in Medieval Anthologies', *Mediaeval Studies*, 77 (2015), pp.81–101, and David Townsend, 'Paratext, Ambiguity, and Interpretive Foreclosure in Manuscripts of Walter of Châtillon's *Alexandreis*', *New Medieval Literatures*, 14 (2012), pp.21–61; for a list of the known MSS, see *Galteri de Castellione* Alexandreis, ed. M. L. Colker (Padua, 1978), pp.xxxiii–xxxviii. The *Roman d'Alexandre*'s extant known MSS (twenty-one complete versions) are listed in vols III, VI, and VII of *The Medieval French* Roman d'Alexandre, ed. Armstrong et al. (Princeton, NJ, 1937–55), and P. Meyer, 'Étude sur les manuscrits du *Roman d'Alexandre*', *Romania*, 11 (1892), pp.213–332. On Bodley 264, see Mark Cruse, *Illuminating the* Roman d'Alexandre *(Oxford, Bodleian Library, MS Bodley 264): The Manuscript as Monument*, Gallica, 22 (Cambridge, 2011); Cruse suggests that the manuscript circulated in an 'elite milieu' in later medieval England, since it was bought in 1466 by Richard Woodville, Lord Rivers, father of Edward IV's wife Elizabeth (p.182).

[9] These texts are edited as follows: *Alexander A = The Romance of Alisaunder*, ed. W.W. Skeat, EETS, e.s., 1 (London, 1867); *Alexander B = Alexander and Dindimus*, ed. W. W. Skeat, EETS, e.s., 31 (London, 1878); *Alexander C = The Wars of Alexander*, ed. Hoyt N. Duggan and Thorlac Turville-Petre, EETS, s.s., 10 (Oxford, 1989); *The Prose Life of Alexander*, ed. J. S. Westlake, EETS, o.s., 143 (London, 1913 for 1911). The Scots versions are *The Buik of Alexander*, ed. R. L. Graeme Ritchie, 4 vols, STS, n.s., 12, 17, 21, and 25 (Edinburgh, 1921–29), and *The Buik of King Alexander the Conquerour*, ed. John Cartwright, 3 vols (2 published to date), STS, n.s., 16, 18 (Edinburgh, 1986 and 1990).

an insular and exclusive language, suggests that the question as to whether *Kyng Alisaunder* constructs the Macedonian king primarily for a local English audience thematically as well as linguistically may be answered in the affirmative. This certainly appears to be true of comparable early Middle English narratives similar to Alexander works in terms of their historicity-fictionality: the opening lines of Layamon's *Brut*, for example, set his *translatio* of 'æðela boc' or 'noble books' firmly not just in an English but in a specifically West Midlands setting, 'at Ernleȝe … vppen Seuarne staþe … on-fest Radestone'.[10] It is plausible that these and other texts demonstrate not the internationally focused *translatio* seen in the earlier chapters, but a more local approach, suitable for a language with a limited range and local audience.

In Britain during the later Middle Ages, then, we appear to have an intellectual and literary culture in which the localism of English and the backdrop of inter- or transnational literature are both important. These two potentially contradictory facts are especially crucial for English-language Alexander texts, which not only draw on this backdrop in terms of sources but which may also participate in the debate about *translatio* inherited from other circulating Alexander material.

Shared Literary Cultures: Texts and Manuscripts

In order to investigate Middle English Alexander literature's *translatio* at the turn of the fourteenth century, I shall consider three romance texts: *Kyng Alisaunder*, *Of Arthour and of Merlin* (*AM*), and *The Seege or Batayle of Troye* (*SBT*). An important feature that connects these works is the fact that all three narratives have a long history. Although the Arthurian material that inspires *AM* is of course not inherited from the classical era, it still has a prestigious textual pedigree both in France and Britain, just like the Trojan and Alexander narratives.[11] The connection is even stronger between *Kyng Alisaunder* and *SBT*, both of which retell classical narratives in Middle English. In terms of date, both *AM* and *SBT* were composed like *Kyng Alisaunder* at the end of the thirteenth or the start of the fourteenth century, meaning that all three texts are contemporaries.[12] Given that all perform poetic and linguistic *translatio* upon

---

[10] Layamon, *Brut*, lines 15 and 3–5 in London, British Library, MS Cotton Caligula A. ix, in Layamon, *Brut*, ed. by G. L. Brook and R. F. Leslie, 2 vols, EETS, n.s., 209 and 277 (Oxford, 1963 and 1978), I, p.2.

[11] Geoffrey of Monmouth's *Historia regum Britannie* is a clear example of this, as are the Arthurian works of Chrétien de Troyes.

[12] Macrae-Gibson claims that *AM* was composed at 'the end of the thirteenth century' (*Of Arthour and of Merlin*, ed. O. D. Macrae-Gibson, 2 vols, EETS, o.s., 268 and 279 (Oxford, 1973 and 1979), II, p.62). Mary Elizabeth Barnicle suggests 'the first quarter of the fourteenth century' for *SBT*, although she also points out that the armour described in the text places the work 'somewhere between the end of the thirteenth and the first

inherited prestigious material, both classical and early medieval, their shared date suggests that perhaps they also have similar approaches to this material.

Like the texts discussed in the earlier chapters, all three works are also connected via several networks, although in contrast to these previous texts such networks are formed primarily via manuscripts, authorship, and dating rather than via known careers of authors, patrons, or literary centres. As with most English romance works, all three poems are anonymous and not precisely datable from internal evidence, making the question of their circulation and readership an open one that has to be deduced (as far as this is possible) from extant manuscripts, which I shall now briefly discuss.

Edinburgh, National Library of Scotland, MS Advocates 19.2.1 ('The Auchinleck Manuscript')

Both *Kyng Alisaunder* and *AM* are found in the well-known Auchinleck manuscript (Edinburgh, NLS, MS Advocates' 19.2.1), which gives their composition a *terminus ad quem* of c. 1331–40, the probable compilation date of Auchinleck.[13] Although its texts are not all of London origin, the London provenance of the manuscript has been established for a long time, leading to suggestions that Chaucer may have read it.[14] G. V. Smithers, who edited *Kyng Alisaunder*, apparently considered that the romance was by a London author, although he never published details of his argument.[15] The presence of both *Kyng Alisaunder* and *AM* in Auchinleck, a London witness, suggests that they were intended for a London audience, probably a broad one.[16] The compendious nature of the manuscript (of its forty-four extant items, eighteen

---

quarter of the fourteenth century' (*The Seege or Batayle of Troye*, ed. id., EETS, o.s., 172 (London, 1927), p.xxx). Derek Pearsall places its composition later, after around 1320 ('The Development of Middle English Romance', *Mediaeval Studies*, 27 (1965), pp.91–116 (p.104).

[13] On Auchinleck's date range, see Helen Cooper, 'Lancelot, Roger Mortimer and the Date of the Auchinleck Manuscript', in *Studies in Late Medieval and Early Renaissance Texts in Honour of John Scattergood*, ed. Anne Marie d'Arcy and Alan J. Fletcher (Dublin, 2005), pp.91–9. For current perspectives on Auchinleck, see the essays in *The Auchinleck Manuscript: New Perspectives*, ed. Susanna Fein (York, 2016).

[14] The suggestion of Chaucer as one of Auchinleck's readers was made by Laura Hibbard Loomis, 'The Auchinleck Manuscript and a Possible London Bookshop of 1330–1340', *PMLA*, 57.3 (1942), pp.595–627. Ralph Hanna III comments on the non-London origins of some of Auchinleck's texts in 'Reconsidering the Auchinleck Manuscript', in *New Directions in Later Medieval Manuscript Studies*, ed. Derek Pearsall (York, 2000), pp.91–102 (pp.100–1).

[15] Hanna, 'Reconsidering the Auchinleck Manuscript', p.101, and id., *London Literature, 1300–1380*, Cambridge Studies in Medieval Literature, 57 (Cambridge, 2005), p.105.

[16] Hanna, *London Literature*, p.107.

are romances[17]) is unusual, and should warn us not to assume an over-arching compilatory narrative, but it seems plausible that the audience for *Kyng Alisaunder* and *AM* was mostly different from those posited for the French and Latin Alexander texts in the previous chapters. Instead of the clerics and courts of the *Alexandreis*, the *Roman d'Alexandre*, and the *Roman de toute chevalerie*, Auchinleck's audience was probably more mercantile and less learned, although not homogenous. Auchinleck therefore places *Kyng Alisaunder* in a different intellectual and cultural reception context from these earlier Alexander texts, but, importantly, this context is itself one in which a variety of perspectives is explicit, given the voluminous nature of the anthology.

Kyng Alisaunder and *AM* are connected by more than their mutual appearance in Auchinleck, however, since several critics have suggested that they were composed by the same author, based on stylistic and linguistic resemblances between the two poems.[18] I shall address this question in more detail below, but for now it is enough to note that even if the romances are not by the same author, they may well derive from a shared literary culture, 'a group of authors writing in the same area at the same time, using naturally therefore the same sort of language'.[19] Such a shared literary culture draws the two romances into a closer dialogue than does their mutual presence in Auchinleck, making *AM* an important comparative context for *Kyng Alisaunder*'s poetics of *translatio*.

London, Lincoln's Inn, MS 150

This example of a shared literary culture is potentially supported by all three romances' presence in another manuscript, London, Lincoln's Inn, MS 150. The manuscript, probably dating from the first quarter of the fifteenth century and copied by a single scribe, is in a Shropshire dialect, but possibly used exemplars exported from London, thus linking it with the London provenance of Auchinleck.[20] Horobin and Wiggins' study locates the manuscript in a 'provincial household and for reading aloud within a household context'.[21] What is particularly interesting about Lincoln 150's texts of *AM* and *Kyng Alisaunder* is that they seem to have been edited to make them both more performative and also more akin generically to other romances; Horobin and

---

17 An online edition of Auchinleck by David Burnley and Alison Wiggins is at <http://auchinleck.nls.uk/editorial/importance.html> [accessed 6 March 2017].

18 Eugen Kölbing, G. V. Smithers, and O. D. Macrae-Gibson; see *AM*, ed. Macrae-Gibson, II, pp.65–75, for an in-depth analysis of the authorship question.

19 *AM*, ed. Macrae-Gibson, II, p.73, p.67.

20 Simon Horobin and Alison Wiggins, 'Reconsidering Lincoln's Inn MS 150', *Medium Ævum*, 77.1 (2008), pp.30–53 (p.31). The Shropshire connection is examined in more detail by Barnicle in *SBT*, pp.xi–xiv. The date of the MS is given by Macrae-Gibson, *AM*, II, p.40 as 1450.

21 Horobin and Wiggins, 'Reconsidering Lincoln's Inn MS 150', p.32.

Wiggins note that many of their 'literary forms, epic styling, and ... linguistic innovations' are 'removed or replaced' and 'their language [has been] brought within the traditional range and compass of a ME romance'.[22] In particular, the unusual seasonal headpieces are reduced in number, and in *Kyng Alisaunder* a 1,300-line section describing Oriental marvels is omitted. Likewise *AM*, in its longest version over ten thousand lines, is here just 1,981 lines long, as the second part of the narrative that focuses on Arthur is not present; the tale in Lincoln 150 only describes Merlin's birth, youth, and early deeds. *SBT* does not seem to have experienced the same treatment in Lincoln 150, but this may be owing to its shorter nature.[23] In other words, the literary culture shared by the Lincoln 150 versions of the three romances is distinguished by a desire for simplification, both regarding language and texts. This means that all three romances experience not just one shared literary culture, but two: firstly that of the early fourteenth century, as represented by *AM* and *Kyng Alisaunder* in Auchinleck and *SBT*'s date of composition, and secondly that of the early fifteenth century, when all three texts are found in Lincoln 150 (*AM* and *Kyng Alisaunder* in significantly different versions from their incarnations in Auchinleck). Although the main focus of my argument will be upon the first of these, the existence and character of the second may shed some light upon the former, so it is important to bear Lincoln 150's texts in mind in order better to understand the earlier performance of *translatio*.

Anthologies and 'Englishness'

The existence of these three romances in anthologies of almost entirely English material feeds strongly into the idea of English's localism or exclusivity, since as we have seen the manuscripts were probably used in contexts where knowledge of Latin and/or French was less common, meaning in turn that literary culture was less consciously international than for the earlier Alexander texts. However, this localism need not exclude a wider outlook, for two reasons. Firstly, assuming that all manuscript anthologies, with their multiple contents, display a 'continuing thematic meta-narrative' (to use Derek Pearsall's term) is unwise, since often such a meta-narrative is imposed by the reader's preoccupations rather than generated by the material;[24] homogeneity is not inevitable. Secondly, French and Latin material usually lies behind

---

22 Ibid., p.43.

23 Barnicle notes that the Lincoln 150 version of *SBT* is in fact the longest of its four texts (*SBT*, ed. Barnicle, p.xxxix).

24 Derek Pearsall, 'The Whole Book: Late Medieval English Manuscript Miscellanies and Their Modern Interpreters', in *Imagining the Book*, ed. S. Kelly and J. J. Thompson (Turnhout, 2005), pp.17–29 (p.18). The debate over anthologies and miscellanies and how to distinguish them is a perennial one, but has become increasingly important in recent years: on this, see Julia Boffey's observations in 'Short Texts in Manuscript Anthologies: The Minor Poems of John Lydgate in Two Fifteenth-Century Collections', in

English texts of this period, both in terms of sources and also more widely in terms of inspiration: *AM, Kyng Alisaunder*, and *SBT* are all indebted to French and Latin material, as will become more evident below. Whilst of course not all French and Latin texts necessarily display a consciously transnational outlook, they are likely to engage with broader literary contexts than does English by virtue of those two languages' wider spread. What both these facts mean for the three romances in question is that we need to focus primarily not upon the undoubtedly English-language audiences of their manuscripts, but rather upon their textual strategies and their presence in complex witnesses with many potential narratives. This takes the idea of reception back a stage, away from the audience and towards the material contexts of the romances.

Kyng Alisaunder

The fact that *Kyng Alisaunder* has been ignored by scholars interested in locating insular identity politics within romance texts exposes the inadequacies of this critical model: what can one do with a text that does not appear either to deal with an English hero or to reclothe its foreign hero in recognizably English cultural dress? In contrast to Arthurian material (for example *AM*, discussed below) or even Charlemagne romances (*Roland and Vernagru* and *Otuel a Knight*), *Kyng Alisaunder* has been left well alone from this perspective.[25] Given the thematic (as well as linguistic) localism perceived within other early Middle English texts, this omission seems strange. It gives rise to several questions. Firstly, what are the issues of identity at work in *Kyng Alisaunder*? Secondly, are these issues local ones of primarily insular importance, or are they ones that resonate beyond insular boundaries despite the romance's English-language nature? The analysis that follows seeks to highlight the complex nature of the romance's *translatio* and hence its cultural identity/ies.

One of the reasons that the poem has been neglected by critics interested in Englishness is perhaps that, at a basic level, *Kyng Alisaunder* is not as linguistically English as other contemporary romances. Its richly French-derived diction has been intriguingly related to larger issues of the romance's identity by Chris Baswell:

The Whole Book: Cultural Perspectives on the Medieval Miscellany, ed. S. G. Nichols and S. Wenzel (Ann Arbor, MI, 1996), pp.69–82 (p.73).

[25] *Of Arthour and Merlin, Roland and Vernagru* and *Otuel a Knight* are all in Auchinleck, which may explain this interest in them to some extent, but so is *Kyng Alisaunder*. Representative scholarship includes Elizabeth S. Sklar, '*Arthour and Merlin*: The Englishing of Arthur', *Michigan Academician*, 8.1 (1975), pp.49–57, in which she sees the major theme as 'the need for and the achievement of national unity' (p.54), and the more nuanced study of Crofts and Rouse, 'Middle English Popular Romance and National Identity', where the authors conclude that these Middle English Charlemagne romances are concerned with chivalry rather than nationalism (p.95).

> Is [*Kyng Alisaunder*] fundamentally French but largely coded in a more accessible tongue that is nonetheless easily penetrated, at intense moments, by its genuine voice? Is the narrative universe of this Middle English poem still, in fact, French?[26]

With these provocative questions, Baswell loosens the ties between language and politico-cultural identity by suggesting that the romance could have more in common with French romance literary culture than with the English equivalent, despite its linguistic Englishness. The Frenchness of *Kyng Alisaunder* may be another reason for its relative critical neglect, as, if the answers to Baswell's questions are in the affirmative, the romance does not appear to uphold the implicit and important connection between language and cultural identity that is the fundamental basis of any nationalist reading. In this instance, to compose in English is not necessarily to create a culturally English work. We need to bear this intriguing observation in mind when considering the text's *translatio*.

Kyng Alisaunder's material source is the Anglo-Norman romance the *Roman de toute chevalerie* discussed in the previous chapter. It follows the same narrative structure as the French work, beginning with Alexander's conception by Nectanebus, youth, victories against Darius and the Indians, travels in the East, and death by poison.[27] Smithers describes the English poem as 'a fairly free adaptation', whose author engages in 'abbreviation or expansion, omission or addition, and the use of stylistic devices intended as ornament', especially 'the apparatus of epic style'.[28] Interestingly, the author also appears to use the *Alexandreis*, although Smithers claims its influence is limited as it is a 'subsidiary source ... a check on RTC or as material for decoration'.[29] The poem's relationship with the *Alexandreis* will be considered in more detail below, but for now it is enough to note that the English poem's poetics with reference to the *Roman de toute chevalerie* appear to be open, allowing us to identify many different instances of his *translatio*.

Kyng Alisaunder *in Auchinleck: Textual Troubles*

Reading *Kyng Alisaunder* necessitates engaging with large issues of language and identity. These issues become even more important when we consider the romance's context in Auchinleck, its earliest witness. As mentioned above, this manuscript has been the basis for investigation into Englishness, and

---

[26] Christopher Baswell, 'Multilingualism on the Page', in *Middle English*, ed. Paul Strohm (Oxford, 2007), pp.38–50 (pp.43–4).

[27] For a detailed synopsis, see appendix 2.

[28] *Kyng Alisaunder*, ed. G. V. Smithers, 2 vols, EETS, o.s., 227 and 237 (London, 1952 and 1957), ii, p.15. For an analysis of the romance's relationship with the Anglo-Norman work, see pp.15–28.

[29] Ibid., p.15.

therefore seems a potentially incongruous location for a romance that does not appear to engage with this concept. In support of this, Ralph Hanna has pointed out that *Kyng Alisaunder*'s 'often substantial and learned historical interests ... stand somewhat outside the usual concerns of the manuscript, with its profusion of later day English heroes'.[30] As I have argued elsewhere, however, the romance's presence in Auchinleck indicates greater variety in its 'continuing thematic meta-narrative' than has previously been recognized.[31] Behind Auchinleck's linguistic status lies the multilingual and transnational literary and cultural world already discussed, an important consideration both for the manuscript and for our understanding of *Kyng Alisaunder*'s *translatio*.

Kyng Alisaunder's Auchinleck text has received little attention, since much of it is lost or damaged. In Auchinleck as it currently stands, a section from the end of *Kyng Alisaunder* survives on fols 278ra and 279rb.[32] Several leaves originally from Auchinleck have been found in two other manuscripts: London, University Library, MS 593 (fols 1ra–2rb) and St Andrews, University Library, MS PR 2065 A. 15 (fols 1ra–vb).[33] The total number of lines found to date of Auchinleck's *Kyng Alisaunder* is thus about 704 (249 in Auchinleck, 307 in London 593, and 148 in St Andrews A. 15),[34] or about 9 per cent of the poem as found in its longest witness, Oxford, Bodleian Library, MS Laud misc. 622.[35] These remnants match lines 6676–8021 of Laud 622, although there are frequent gaps of between six to fifteen lines, mostly through textual loss from the bottoms of pages, and a longer gap of about four hundred lines between lines 7388–760 (between where London 593 ends and Auchinleck begins).[36] In other words, what is preserved is not quite as fragmentary as is

[30] Hanna, *London Literature*, p.105.
[31] Pearsall, 'The Whole Book', p.18. See Venetia Bridges, 'Absent Presence: Auchinleck and *Kyng Alisaunder*', in *The Auchinleck Manuscript*, ed. Fein, pp.88–107. The discussion of *Kyng Alisaunder* in this chapter is based on the analysis in 'Absent Presence'.
[32] See *Kyng Alisaunder*, ed. Smithers, II, pp.4–5. I count 412, however, based on Smithers' edition (he gives 410).
[33] See the discussion by Burnley and Wiggins at <http://auchinleck.nls.uk/mss/alisaunder.html> [accessed 6 March 2017] and the overview of the leaves given in D. Pearsall, 'Literary and Historical Significance of the Manuscript', in *The Auchinleck Manuscript: National Library of Scotland Advocates' MS. 19.2.1*, introd. Derek Pearsall and I. C. Cunningham (London, 1977), pp.vii–xi (p.vii).
[34] This total is based on a count made from the online facsimile checked against Smithers' edition. Burnley and Wiggins, however, count 259 lines in the current Auchinleck.
[35] See Smithers' description of this manuscript in *Kyng Alisaunder*, ed. Smithers, ii, pp.1–3.
[36] The extant lines are as follows (numbering from B which is Oxford, Bodleian Library, MS Laud misc. 622): London 593: lines 6676–711, 6724–61, 6768–805, 6812–50, 7214–52, 7258–63, 7266–91, 7294–300, 7306–44, 7350–88; St Andrews A. 15: lines 6856–81, 6900–24, 6945–68, 6988–7012, 7032–56, 7170–94; Auchinleck: lines 7760–981, 7992–8021. Smithers' edition includes the St Andrews lines but not those in London 593.

often implied,[37] since the extant text is a substantial, more-or-less continuous section of *Kyng Alisaunder*'s narrative that runs from Alexander's letter from Candace (queen of the Amazons) to his poisoning and death, including his conversations with the prophetical trees of the sun and moon and Porus' treachery.[38] It is probable therefore that the Auchinleck text was a complete version of the *Kyng Alisaunder* narrative. A comparison of the other two extant manuscripts, Oxford, Bodleian Library, MS Laud misc. 622 (B), and Lincoln 150 (L), both of which Smithers dates to the late fourteenth century,[39] demonstrates that all three manuscripts share much the same text. Where there are differences (generally of vocabulary), the texts of Auchinleck and B tend to agree against L.[40] Sometimes this agreement is more because L produces a garbled text (like 'God to amours' where both B and Auchinleck have 'honoure', line 6994) rather than because the other two positively agree, but there still appears to be a closer correlation between B and Auchinleck than between B and L. This proposition is supported indirectly by Horobin and Wiggins' idea that L is a revised version of *Kyng Alisaunder*.[41] Although far from a perfect solution, I shall therefore use B where necessary as representative of the text lost from Auchinleck.

Learning and Culture: Kyng Alisaunder *as an Intellectual Romance*

Hanna's observation that *Kyng Alisaunder* differs from other Auchinleck romances in its lack of 'later day English heroes' implicitly poses questions about the work's literary and cultural identity: what are its major concerns and characteristic features? Scholars such as Dieter Mehl and Nancy Mason Bradbury have rightly emphasized the romance's 'instructive character' and its interest in learning, or 'bookness'.[42] Mehl's idea that *Kyng Alisaunder* is 'instructive' views the romance less as an ethically didactic work than as one concerned with 'the passing on of culture and learning',[43] an observation clearly related

---

[37] This is the word used of the text by Hanna, *London Literature*, p. 105.

[38] The gap of about four hundred lines includes Porus' death and Alexander's meeting with Candace as found in the text of B.

[39] *Kyng Alisaunder*, ed. Smithers, ii, p.2, p.3. Horobin and Wiggins consider L to be written in a hand of the first quarter of the fifteenth century, however ('Reconsidering Lincoln's Inn MS 150', p. 31).

[40] For example, both Auchinleck and B preserve the unusual word 'trigoldrye' (line 7006), where L produces 'sygaldrye': see *Kyng Alisaunder*, ed. Smithers, ii, p.13.

[41] Horobin and Wiggins, 'Reconsidering Lincoln's Inn MS 150', p.34, p.43, p.45.

[42] Dieter Mehl, *The Middle English Romances of the Thirteenth and Fourteenth Centuries* (London, 1969), pp. 227–39 (p.228), and Nancy Mason Bradbury, *Writing Aloud: Storytelling in Late Medieval England* (Chicago, IL, 1998), pp.133–4 (p.136). The idea that Auchinleck may have been intended for children also emphasizes its instructive character; see Nicole Clifton, '*Of Arthour and of Merlin* as Medieval Children's Literature', *Arthuriana*, 13.2 (2003), pp.9–22.

[43] Mehl, *The Middle English Romances*, p.232.

to Bradbury's idea of bookness. The nature of *Kyng Alisaunder*'s interest in culture and learning is still mostly unstudied, but I suggest that it can be identified in a variety of contexts that help to define the text's narrative culture and thus its performance of *translatio*: historical writing, language interaction, the text's relationship with its sources, and its unusual headpieces.

Although fictional elements such as Oriental marvels were added to Alexander's stories early in their existence, as we have already seen, the basis for the narratives remains the historical achievements of Alexander the Great.[44] Interest in Alexander from a historical perspective is demonstrated in a passage in *Kyng Alisaunder* that lists and describes Alexander authors:

> Salomon, þat al þe werlde þorouʒ-ʒede,
> Jn sooþ witnesse helde hym myde.
> Ysidre also, þat was so wijs,
> Jn his bokes telleþ þis.
> Maister Eustroge bereþ hym witnesse
> Of þe wondres, more and lesse.
> Seint Jerome, ʒee shullen ywyte,
> Hem haþ also in book ywrite,
> And Magestene þe gode clerk
> Haþ made þerof mychel werk.
> Denys, that was of gode memorie,
> Jt sheweþ al in his book of storie.
> And also Pompie, of Rome lorde,
> Dude it writen euery worde.
> Ne heldeþ me þerof no fynder –
> Her bokes ben my shewer
> And þe ljf of Alisaunder,
> Of whom fleiʒ so riche sklaunder.
> ʒif ʒee willeth ʒiue listnyng,
> Now ʒee shullen here gode thing.[45]

This passage, derived from the *Roman de toute chevalerie* (lines 4604–13), expands freely upon its source, which is one of the characteristics of the poet's *translatio* identified by Smithers. Where the Anglo-Norman text contains brief mentions of 'Solin li alosez' ('Solinus the renowned'), Jerome, and 'li bon Magastenes' ('the skilled Megasthenes') as its 'autoritez', the *Kyng Alisaunder* poet presents a fuller picture, providing not only names of prior authors with their epithets, but also brief descriptions of some of their writings. The English poem concludes by claiming these authors' moral importance as the poet's 'shewer' and thus, by implication, support for his presentation

---

[44] Hanna, *London Literature*, p.105, and, more tellingly, p.118, where he sums up *Kyng Alisaunder* (somewhat unfairly) as 'straightforwardly historical and strikingly uncritical'.

[45] *Kyng Alisaunder*, ed. Smithers, I, 4771–90.

of a 'gode thing'. Such a list of intellectual heavyweights – Aristotle rubs shoulders with Solomon, 'Maister Eustroge', Saint Jerome, 'Magestene the gode clerk', and Pompey – invokes a weighty tradition of broadly historical writing, or 'books of storie' (4782), and thus positions the text as strongly interested in that subject. This tradition also encompasses more fictional writing, since the 'storie' many of these 'gode clerkes' describe is in fact about the 'many wondres' (line 4764) Alexander is soon to encounter in India, which occupy much of the remaining text in B.[46] The text here thus emphasizes the learned nature of every kind of historical writing, both in the diversity of the writers named (Aristotle, Jerome, Magestene) and in those authors' descriptions of, and juxtapositions with, the 'wondres' that follow. We see a conscious intellectualization of Alexander sources developed far beyond the corresponding passage in the *Roman de toute chevalerie*,[47] irrespective of the different sorts of composition involved. The multifaceted story of *Kyng Alisaunder* is presented as learned and intellectual, confirming the idea that the romance author wishes to highlight the importance of culture and learning with reference to historical writing.[48] This *translatio* aligns *Kyng Alisaunder* with the *Alexandreis* in the mutual concern for a historical perspective, and with the *RTC* in its generally learned interests. This is an important reminder that genre does not necessarily define approach, especially in such a multifaceted mode as romance. The interest in learning seen here also highlights *Kyng Alisaunder*'s potentially transnational concept of *translatio*, since the poet calls upon diverse authors drawn from Biblical and classical traditions.

Similarly learned *translatio* is found in *Kyng Alisaunder*'s approach to the languages that as we have already seen are a crucial part of its identity. Baswell's idea about the 'fundamentally French' cultural identity of the text has been countered somewhat by Thea Summerfield, who claims that the French-language moments in Auchinleck texts are often conscious choices that highlight aspects of character or plot, aimed at an audience not proficient in French but able to recognize limited words.[49] In this idea of French, or what she calls 'semi-French'[50] (easily understood stock phrases), Summerfield di-

---

[46] Although *Kyng Alisaunder* does not go to the fictional extremes of the *Roman d'Alexandre*, which contains the famous stories of Alexander's aerial and submarine adventures, these 'wondres' demonstrate that its interest in history reflects more fictional, romance conceptions as well as more factual ones.

[47] Although many of the epithets attached to the authors here may be ascribed to the requirements of the verse form, it is notable that they emphasize knowledge and learning.

[48] Mehl, *The Middle English Romances*, p.232.

[49] Thea Summerfield, '"And she answered in hir language": Aspects of Multilingualism in the Auchinleck Manuscript', in *Multilingualism in Medieval Britain, c.1066–1520*, ed. J. A. Jefferson and A. Putter with A. Hopkins (Turnhout, 2013), pp.241–58.

[50] Ibid., p.249, p.255. In Summerfield's reading, the 'Frenchness' of *Kyng Alisaunder* is part of a general tendency in Auchinleck romances to use 'semi-French' to 'highlight

verges from Baswell's implication that French is an unconscious presence in English texts. Despite these differences, both scholars highlight, to a greater or lesser extent, the inherent multilingualism of *Kyng Alisaunder*'s broad narrative and identity. This multilingualism is discussed in a passage that invokes Latin as well as French material:

> Þis bataile distincted is
> Jn þe Freinsshe, wel iwys.
> Þerefore [I] habbe [hit] to coloure
> Borowed of þe Latyn a nature,
> Hou hiȝtten þe gentyl kniȝttes,
> Hou hii contened hem in fiȝttes,
> On Alisaunders half and Darries also.[51]

The word 'coloure' is reminiscent of the colours of rhetoric, and 'distincted' – here probably meaning 'elucidate, explain' rather than the more common 'separate' – is likewise derived from Latin scholastic terminology.[52] This passage on style and language is an explicit attempt by the narrator to highlight his literary awareness or bookishness, again suggesting his concern to set his poetics in an intellectual context. Like the romance's interest in historical authors, we find a consciously learned approach to *Kyng Alisaunder*'s cultural identity. Once again, this expansive and multilingual *translatio* gestures towards an intellectual world that exists within the British Isles but also beyond it.

Multilingualism and sources are related topics, since the 'Freinsshe' and 'Latyn' mentioned here refer to texts composed in those languages, the *Roman de toute chevalerie* and the *Alexandreis* respectively.[53] Bradbury underlines the importance of French and Latin material for Kyng Alisaunder's poetics, and not just its narrative, in her claim that 'the high quality of the verse seems to derive primarily from the poet's acquaintance with literary tradition in French and Latin'.[54] The poet's enthusiasm for scholarly discussion of languages and sources would appear to support this conclusion, since in these instances *Kyng Alisaunder* defines itself by means of literary traditions derived from these prestigious languages. Although the *Roman de toute chevalerie* is the romance's source, the impact of French material is not confined to this one text nor to French Alexander literature in general. Smithers suggests that the

---

the social standing of legendary aristocratic courts, or typify and ridicule the enemy' (p.256).

[51] *Kyng Alisaunder*, ed. Smithers, I, 2195–201.

[52] *MED*, s.v. *distincten, distincted*, <https://quod.lib.umich.edu/cgi/m/mec/med-idx?-size=First+100&type=headword&q1=distincten&rgxp=constrained> [accessed 14 December 2017] and Bradbury, *Writing Aloud*, p.141.

[53] For brief, tantalizing references to *Kyng Alisaunder*'s use of the *Alexandreis*, see *Kyng Alisaunder*, ed. Smithers, II, p.15, p.22, p.24.

[54] Bradbury, *Writing Aloud*, p.173.

episode in which Alexander destroys the city of Thebes in *Kyng Alisaunder* 'probably implies a knowledge of the [c.1150] *Roman de Thèbes* at least in outline', pointing to similar descriptive passages in both works.[55] A comparison of the texts shows that the *Kyng Alisaunder* poet had greater knowledge of the *Roman de Thèbes* than the word 'outline' suggests. Indeed, the Middle English text reproduces the thematic approach of the Anglo-Norman poem. Both works claim that Thebes' violent Oedipal history, specifically the pride born of incest characteristic of Eteocles and Polynices, is directly responsible for the city's destruction, a moral cause-and-effect connection wholly absent from the *Roman de toute chevalerie* and Statius' *Thebaid* (another likely source for *Kyng Alisaunder*). This correspondence is evident from a comparison of *Kyng Alisaunder* and *Thèbes*:

> *Kyng Alisaunder*:
> Hii hym telden hou Eddipus
> Had yslawe his fader Layus,
> And more woo atte last –
> Hou he wedded his moder Jocast,
> And in hir biȝate twynnes two
> (None wers ne miȝtten go:
> Þe first was Ethiocles,
> Þat oþer was Pollymyces –
> Of pride nas non hir yliche);
> Hou hii stryueden for þe kyngriche,
> Hou for hem were slayn in fiȝttes
> Of Grece alle þe gode kniȝttes …
> [Thebes] Þat was cite of mest werþe,
> Of alle þat weren in erþe.
> For her synne and dede on-hende
> Nou is it brouȝth out of mynde;
> Þus ended Tebes cite.[56]

> *Roman de Thèbes*:
> De deux friers vous dirrai
> et lor gestes acounterai.
> Li uns ot non Ethioclés
> et li autres Polinicés.
> Edypodés lez engendra
> en la reïne Jocasta:
> de sa miere lez ot a tort
> quant son piere le rei ot mort.
> Por le pechié dount sount crié

---

[55] *Kyng Alisaunder*, ed. Smithers, II, p.24, referring to I, lines 2643–53, 2677, 2851–74. He also notes the inclusion of 'a detail proper to Troy as described in the *Roman de Troie*'.

[56] *Kyng Alisaunder*, ed. Smithers, I, 2857–68 and 2887–91.

furent felon et esragié:
Thebes destruistrent lor cite
et en après tout le regné;
destruit en furent lour veisin
et il ambedui en la fin.[57]

*I shall tell you about two brothers and recount their deeds. The name of one
was Eteocles and the other Polynices. Oedipus fathered them with queen
Jocasta: he made them with his mother, a vile deed, when he had killed the
king his father. Through the sin that created them they became cruel and
violent: they destroyed Thebes their city and afterwards the whole kingdom.
Their neighbours were brought down and finally the pair themselves.*

Although a moral interpretation of Thebes' destruction could have been derived independently, the thematic similarities suggest that the Middle English
poet drew on the Anglo-Norman *Roman de Thèbes* not simply for historical
detail but also for inspiration. His engagement with the French poem highlights his scholarly reading of the text, since he not only picks out relevant
and useful details, but also deals with them in an intellectual fashion, ex-
trapolating upon themes. This kind of *amplificatio*, the 'expansionism' noted
by Smithers, suggests the same literary and intellectual approach seen earlier
concerning history, an approach that is not confined to the *Roman de toute
chevalerie* but is also found with reference to a wider range of texts. Once
again, this *translatio* situates *Kyng Alisaunder* in a multilingual and transnational context, although there is an important caveat. It could be argued that
this reference to *Thèbes* locates the poem in an insular context rather than
an international one, given that *Thèbes* is one of the Anglo-Norman *romans
d'antiquité* that are often read as productions of Henry II's court, implicating
them in the politics and literary culture of that time and place.[58] Yet as I have
already argued with reference to the *Roman de Troie*, the *romans d'antiquité*
are difficult to locate politically and have much in common culturally with
continental French and Latin productions as well as with insular texts, making
any insularity hard to define. In addition, their subsequent wide transmission
and circulation histories mean that by the early fourteenth century they are
works with a truly transnational range.[59] The *Kyng Alisaunder* poet's use of

---

[57] *Roman de Thèbes*, ed. G. R. de Lage (Paris, 1966), lines 19–32 (translation my own).
The relevant passage in the *Thebaid* is 1.76–81: see *Thebaid, books 1–7*, ed. and trans.
D. R. Shackleton Bailey, Loeb Classical Library, 207 (Cambridge, MA, 2003). The pas-
sage in the *RTC* is lines 2116–288: see Thomas of Kent, *The Anglo-Norman Alexander*
(Le Roman de Toute Chevalerie), ed. Brian Foster and Ian Short, 2 vols, ANTS, 29–33
(London, 1976 and 1977), I.

[58] See chapter 3, 'Anxious Romance', for discussion of this.

[59] One of the earliest mauscripts of *Troie*, Milan, Biblioteca Ambrosiana, MS D 55, was
potentially copied by a Provençal scribe in the Veneto (see *Le Roman de Troie par*

Thèbes to underline his work's literary and intellectual claims does not make these claims specifically insular, then, but continues to place them on a wider stage.

A similar relationship is found between *Kyng Alisaunder* and the *Alexandreis*, which as mentioned above Smithers claims is a subsidiary source for the English poem. A comparison of the first battle between Alexander and Darius shows that the Middle English poem and the *Alexandreis* share material that is absent from the *Roman de toute chevalerie*, such as the scene of the Persian Negusar's dismemberment and death.[60] The Middle English description is a free adaptation, differing in minor characters and details, but there are lines that are direct translations, demonstrating the English poet's close engagement with the Latin. This close relationship is shown in Philotas' killing of Negusar:

> *Kyng Alisaunder*:
> Philotas sei3 and vnderstood
> Hou Negussar fau3th as he were wood.
> He smoot to hym and dude hym harme,
> For of he carf his ri3th arme.[61]

> *Alexandreis*:
> Hunc ubi multimoda uastantem cede Pelasgos
> Intuitus, stricto celer aduolat ense Phylotas
> … sinistram,
> Quam sibi forte manum frontem pretenderat ante,
> Amputat.

> *But when Philotas beheld him [Negusar] wasting Greeks with varied carnage, he swiftly drew his blade … it cut away the left hand where he [Negusar] held it before his brow.*[62]

The Latin text depicts Negusar's loss of both hands in brutal detail. The English author alters which hand is amputated, but his description is clearly inspired by the Latin work. Smithers' idea that the *Alexandreis* is used 'arbitrarily' as 'material for decoration'[63] misses the point that the *Kyng Alisaunder* poet draws on the Latin text for thematic emphasis, using 'decorative' details to vivify the carnage in a way that, despite its mention of 'le champ hydus'

Benoît de Sainte-Maure, ed. Léopold Constans, 6 vols (Paris, 1904–12), VI, p.5).

[60] The passages are *Kyng Alisaunder*, ed. Smithers, I, lines 2269–314, and *Alexandreis*, ed. Colker, III.90–118.

[61] *Kyng Alisaunder*, ed. Smithers, I, 2287–90.

[62] *Alexandreis*, ed. Colker, III.98–99, 102–4. The translation is by David Townsend, *The Alexandreis of Walter of Châtillon: A Twelfth-Century Epic* (Philadelphia, PA, 1996), p.44 (lines 118–20, 124–5).

[63] *Kyng Alisaunder*, ed. Smithers, II, p.22 and p.15.

(1979), the *Roman de toute chevalerie* does not. This kind of *amplificatio* demonstrates a literary and learned approach to the *Alexandreis* similar to that seen with regard to the *Roman de Thèbes*, and one that once again gestures beyond a local linguistic and cultural context.

The *Kyng Alisaunder* poet's use of French and Latin material, then, is thorough and scholarly, thematically astute and consciously integrated into the learned *translatio* of the narrative performed by the poet. This treatment again emphasizes the poem's characteristics of 'culture and learning' or 'bookness', elements likewise present in the intriguing headpieces, that is, introductory passages, often seasonal, that interrupt the narrative flow.[64] Most of these are either entirely new to *Kyng Alisaunder* or freely developed from odd lines in the *Roman de toute chevalerie*.[65] Many provide gnomic and thematic introductions to subsequent narratives, as John Scattergood and Louise Haywood have demonstrated.[66] For example, the following headpiece describes the sorrow of autumn and the folly of the lover:

> Whan nutte brouneþ on heselrys,
> Þe lefdy is of her lemman chys.
> Þe persone wereþ fow and grys –
> Ofte he setteþ his loue amys.
> Þe ribaude plaieþ at the dys;
> Swiþe selde þe fole is wys.
> Darrie in a verger is,
> Tofore hym many kni3th of prys.[67]

This headpiece precedes a section in which Darius, ashamed of Alexander's previous victory over him, decides to attack the latter once again. Haywood interprets it as a gnomic underlining of Darius' own folly. Other headpieces perform similar roles. In providing gnomic or proverbial interpretations of the action, they emphasize a variety of learning that seems distinct from 'bookness'. However, as they descend ultimately from French and Latin literary traditions, the headpieces are not a Middle English innovation. Smithers identifies them as derived from Old French epics and medieval Latin love lyrics. Bradbury agrees, citing 'the humble minstrel remark' as an additional influence, while Scattergood adduces various kinds of medieval French lyrical

---

[64] For a useful overview see *Kyng Alisaunder*, ed. Smithers, II, pp.35–9.

[65] Bradbury, *Writing Aloud*, p.151.

[66] V. J. Scattergood, 'Validating the High Life in *Of Arthour and of Merlin* and *Kyng Alisaunder*', *Essays in Criticism*, 54 (2004), pp.323–50, and Louise M. Haywood, 'Spring Song and Narrative Organization in the Medieval Alexander Legend', *Troianalexandrina*, 4 (2004), pp.87–105.

[67] *Kyng Alisaunder*, ed. Smithers, I, 3289–96.

genres, such as the *aubade*.[68] The headpieces invoke vernacular and proverbial wisdom, often considered to be orally based, but presented through a poetics derived from literary traditions. So, once again, 'bookness' is prominent,
and, interestingly, it comes from a wide spectrum of texts and genres.

Interpreting the headpieces as both gnomic and based on literary traditions
makes sense of some examples that seem disjunct in their immediate narrative
contexts.[69] One such, not discussed by Haywood or Scattergood, occurs after
Darius' earlier defeat:

> Jn tyme of Maij þe niȝttyngale
> Jn wood makeþ mery gale.
> So don þe foules, grete and smale,
> Summe on hylles and summe in dale.
> Þe day daweþ, the kyng awakeþ;
> He and hise men her armes takeþ.
> Hii wendeþ to þe batailes stede,
> And fyndeþ nouȝth bot bodies dede.[70]

The incongruous juxtaposition of the joys of spring and the battlefield covered with corpses seems designed to point up the pathos of battle. However,
because this lyric passage departs undeniably from the narrative, interrupting
both style and tone, its gnomic wisdom becomes difficult to interpret. Is it
simply to provide brief, contextually bizarre, light relief, or is it there for a
different purpose?[71] In the absence of a clear connection between the passage's sentential observations and the battle narrative, the 'bookness' of the
literary forms behind its poetics comes to the fore as an explanation. Seemingly separate from the 'storie', this passage overtly displays the author's
literary knowledge. It is a moment of poetic preening that briefly dominates
the narrative. 'In tyme of Maij þe niȝttyngale' has close parallels to a medieval
Latin lyric found in the eleventh-century *Cambridge Songs*, demonstrating
the pervasive presence of such lyrics in literary cultures beyond the Latinate.[72]
While there is no suggestion of a direct link between this English text and

---

68   *Kyng Alisaunder*, ed. Smithers, II, pp.35–8; Bradbury, *Writing Aloud*, p.154, and Scat-
     tergood, 'Validating the High Life', esp. pp.342–4. Haywood's focus is on contempo-
     rary medieval French, Spanish, and Middle English rather than on inherited literary
     traditions.
69   Bradbury, *Writing Aloud*, pp.155–6. Scattergood also notes that 'some of them are more
     integrated into the narrative than others' ('Validating the High Life', p.339).
70   *Kyng Alisaunder*, ed. Smithers, I, 2543–50.
71   Scattergood advances the concept of 'pleasure' or 'refreshment' as the purpose of some
     headpieces ('Validating the High Life', p.335, p.339, p.346).
72   The poem 'Carmen aestivum', beginning 'Vestiunt silve tenera ramorum', depicts var-
     ious birds rejoicing at the arrival of summer (lines 9–20), reminiscent of the 'small
     foules' of the Middle English passage (*The Oxford Book of Medieval Latin Verse*, ed. F.
     J. E. Raby (Oxford, 1959), pp.174–5).

a Latin one, the similarity shows that this kind of vernal Latin poetry was so ubiquitous that the romance poet is able to draw on its *topoi* to show off his literary knowledge. Some headpieces in *Kyng Alisaunder* thus function as display verse in which the generally gnomic character of their content is subordinate to the conscious invocation of literary traditions.

By calling on Latin and French texts in these different contexts, the *Kyng Alisaunder* poet proclaims his mastery of a wide range of imaginative literature across both vernacular and Latin spheres, from romance to epic to complex Latin lyrics originally composed in schools. His *translatio* thus consciously invokes a multilingual literary-cultural world, a world that is certainly found in insular contexts but that exists beyond political and geographical boundaries. This transnational literary identity seen so strongly in *Kyng Alisaunder* is supported thematically by Alexander's presentation throughout the text as a chivalric *exemplum*. As well as his performances in battle, in youth he is the noblest in the world (671–2), defends his mother against slander (993–1160), and creates and administers laws (1421–2). All these attributes and achievements create Alexander as a transnational hero, since they are relevant to Western European medieval culture of the period in the widest sense, not just to individual locales and contexts. The wide remit of Alexander's chivalry is underlined further by an explicit authorial comment that creates a broad spiritual interpretation of his behaviour:

> Ac ȝut me þinkeþ wel grete wondre
> Þat he miȝth, wiþ so fewe,
> Al þe werlde hym vnder-þewe,
> And þat he so durst and vnderstood,
> More awondreþ al my blood.
> Ac sooþ it is, cayser ne kyng
> Ne may aȝeins Goddes helpyng.[73]

Here the reader or audience is reminded that Alexander's great achievements, which dominate 'al þe werlde', are nothing without God. This interprets Alexander within the broad framework of the Christian tradition, making him an ethical 'shewer' relevant primarily in this transnational context. The 'instructive character' of *Kyng Alisaunder* observed by Mehl and Bradbury is here almost gnomic, again emphasizing the importance of a timeless realm of learning and culture for the text.

Kyng Alisaunder*: Contexts*

This sense of gnomic timelessness (seen also in the headpieces) means that identifying any political aspect of *Kyng Alisaunder* is difficult, especially when combined with the text's emphasis on a similarly free-floating intellectual

---

[73] *Kyng Alisaunder*, ed. Smithers, I, 1402–8.

context. Its probable London provenance tells us little, although the growing city provides a plausible location for the poem's genesis and composition in terms of the availability of a broad range of literature. Where *Kyng Alisaunder* is political, at least in a modern context, is in its conscious interest in Latin and French texts as vibrant creative forces, not simply as dry source material, and in its lack of concern for 'Englishness'. Yet it may be the case that its presence in Auchinleck and Lincoln 150 provide us with some context that illuminates this *translatio*.

As suggested above, and confirmed by my analysis of the text, *Kyng Alisaunder* seems at odds with Auchinleck in this lack of Englishness and its concomitant multilingual intertextuality. Its emphasis on inherited literary cultures sets it apart from other Auchinleck romances. Part of this is no doubt due to the accumulated weight of Alexander literature. Yet the poet's deliberate invocation of a variety of literary genres and traditions is not fully the result of the looming bulk of his source material. It shows, rather, a conscious desire to create a learned romance drawn from different literary and linguistic traditions. The same cannot be said of a romance like *Horn Childe*, also found in Auchinleck, composed not long after *Kyng Alisaunder*, and probably likewise based on an Anglo-Norman source, the *Roman de Horn*.[74] Judith Weiss describes *Horn Childe* as 'clad in sparer and simpler dress' than the 'ornate' Anglo-Norman romance with its 'vividly realised, complex world and dramatically plausible characters and situations'.[75] The simplification found in the English *Horn Childe* contrasts sharply with the conscious invocation of learned cultures seen in *Kyng Alisaunder*. The difference between the two *Horn* poems in length alone shows this, as the English *Horn* has no space for the kind of non-narrative digressions used in *Kyng Alisaunder* to highlight its poet's literary pretensions.[76] Similarly, Ralph Hanna sees knightly achievement of inheritance and the establishment of royal (national) justice as characteristic of *Sir Orfeo* and *Sir Beues of Hamtoun*,[77] an insular identity (in his analysis) not found in *Kyng Alisaunder* either in terms of narrative or of poetic *translatio*. The Alexander romance thus differs from some of its Auchinleck romance companions in terms of both subject matter and poetic treatment.

---

[74] The nature of the two poems' relationship is 'impossible to unravel totally' according to Judith Weiss; see *The Birth of Romance in England: Four Twelfth-Century Romances in the French of England*, trans. and introd. Judith Weiss, FRETS, 4 (Tempe, AZ, 2009), p.5.

[75] Ibid.

[76] *Horn Childe* is 1,136 lines long in the edition based on Auchinleck: *Horn Childe and Maiden Rimnild*, ed. M. Mills, Middle English Texts, 20 (Heidelberg, 1988), although the loss of two folios means that around 326 lines are missing; see Burnley and Wiggins at <https://auchinleck.nls.uk/mss/horn.html> [accessed 6 March 2017]. In contrast, *The Roman de Horn* in Weiss's edition is 5,240 lines long.

[77] Hanna, *London Literature*, pp.130–1, p.134.

In addition, *Kyng Alisaunder*'s position in Auchinleck sets it apart from other romances physically as well as conceptually. It is in booklet 8 of the manuscript, one of the most damaged, so that care is needed in making claims based on *compilatio*, but it appears that there is a certain thematic unity between *Kyng Alisaunder* and the so-called 'fillers' that occupy the remainder of the booklet. These three texts, *The Thrush and the Nightingale*, *The Sayings of St Bernard*, and *David þe King* (a metrical version of Psalm 50 including Latin quotation), are like *Kyng Alisaunder* variously concerned with inherited intellectual and multilingual traditions, with seasonal description, and with wisdom both gnomic and explicitly Christian.[78] They therefore share several themes that are also prominent in the romance, although they do not create a restrictive thematic unity in this section of Auchinleck; rather, some of their preoccupations overlap with those of *Kyng Alisaunder*, creating a varied narrative that prioritizes different aspects of learning. If we accept that many of Auchinleck's texts, especially the romances, focus on aspects related to English identity, the interests of *Kyng Alisaunder* and booklet 8 represent a departure (or series of departures) from the manuscript's more frequent compilatory preoccupations.

Kyng Alisaunder, then, demonstrates that Auchinleck's compilatory narrative is more varied than its important contribution to English-language literary history might suggest, bringing a wider literary and linguistic perspective to the anthology. The romance's text in Lincoln 150, however, has a different identity. There it is preceded by *Libeaus Desconus* (incomplete) and *AM*, and followed by *SBT* and an A text of *Piers Plowman*, so structurally the manuscript moves from Arthurian material to the historically based narratives of Alexander and Troy and then to *Piers*. As noted above, Horobin and Wiggins have suggested that the Lincoln 150 texts of *AM* and *Kyng Alisaunder* were edited to bring them into line with romance conventions, so that, among other changes, rare vocabulary and the headpieces in both texts have been reduced or removed.[79] These two features are especially important for *Kyng Alisaunder*, where both of these features are more frequent, because reduction in the number of French-derived words and the invocation of inherited literary genres also lessens the 'bookness' of the text. In Lincoln 150, *Kyng Alisaunder* becomes less distinctive and, linguistically at least, more 'English'. This idea is supported by the removal of 1,300 lines dealing with Oriental marvels; with these episodes gone, we are left with a more battle-focused work, which is a more habitual mode of *translatio* in Middle English texts.[80] A full study of the themes of Lincoln 150's texts and the manuscript itself remains to be made, but this brief description emphasizes the manuscript's concern for generic and

[78] See the detailed analysis in Bridges, 'Absent Presence', pp.103–6.
[79] Horobin and Wiggins, 'Reconsidering Lincoln's Inn MS 150', p.43.
[80] Ibid., p.35. See the analyses of *AM* and *SBT* below concerning this form of abbreviation.

linguistic conformity. This seems to distinguish it from *Kyng Alisaunder*'s context in Auchinleck, which despite appearances contains more variety. This may well be due to the chronological separation between the two witnesses; by the early fifteenth century, English romance is firmly established in generic and linguistic terms. In the process, however, *Kyng Alisaunder*'s distinctive *translatio* appears to be lost.

Kyng Alisaunder's altered text in Lincoln 150 serves to highlight the poem's distinctive *translatio* in its earliest witness, a *translatio* that despite the English language of the work is concerned with transnational texts and traditions. Its intellectual interests relate the romance not just to these texts and traditions, but more specifically to the *RTC* and (to a lesser extent) the *Alexandreis*. However, it remains to be seen whether this distinctive *translatio* is an unusual feature of Middle English narratives, or whether it can be paralleled in other works, such as *AM* and *SBT*.

Of Arthour and of Merlin

As mentioned above, *AM* was probably composed at much the same time as *Kyng Alisaunder*, possibly a little earlier.[81] Several critics have addressed the possibility that *Kyng Alisaunder* and *AM* may have been composed by the same author, along with the *Seven Sages of Rome* and *Richard Coeur de Lyon*, in the London area (including Kent and Sussex).[82] The most extensive analysis is made by O. D. Macrae-Gibson in his edition of *AM*, who considers that the two poems display 'extensive similarity in style of composition and in phraseology', make the same kind of modifications to their sources, and show awareness of French epic tradition.[83] Despite these broad similarities, however, Macrae-Gibson accurately concludes that it is 'impossible to distinguish in this way between common authorship and authorship by a "school" whose members knew each other's work', thinking it more likely that these similarities instead suggest 'a group of authors writing in the same area at the same time, using naturally therefore the same sort of language'.[84] John Scattergood develops this idea, claiming that even if the poems are not by the same author, 'they have in common certain dialectical features which

---

[81] *AM*, ed. Macrae-Gibson, ii, p.62: 'the end of the thirteenth century' is the editor's dating suggestion.

[82] See *AM*, ed. Macrae-Gibson, ii, pp.65–75, for an in-depth analysis of the authorship question. The issue of location has been addressed by studies of the poem's dialectical features in manuscripts: Elizabeth S. Sklar considers it to be of Sussex provenance, but Macrae-Gibson disagrees and argues for London more broadly (Sklar, 'The Dialect of *Arthour and Merlin*', *English Language Notes*, 15.2 (1977), pp.88–94; Macrae-Gibson, '*Of Arthour and of Merlin* in Sussex?', *English Language Notes*, 17.1 (1979), pp.7–10).

[83] *AM*, ed. Macrae-Gibson, ii, p.68.

[84] Ibid., ii, p.73, p.67.

demonstrate that they may be from the same area and may represent a local tradition of romance writing'.[85] Scattergood also points out that the poems are interested in history and 'share common narrative procedures and stylistic features' as well as some similarities of phrasing.[86] Whether or not *AM* and *Kyng Alisaunder* are by the same author, it seems that they are connected by broadly similar poetics and provenance, and thus potentially by a shared literary culture at the moment of composition (represented most closely by Auchinleck), as well as in Lincoln 150. This idea of a shared literary culture may indicate that *Kyng Alisaunder*'s *translatio* is also a mutual phenomenon. This in turn suggests that despite the localism inherent in English-language romances, particular approaches to inherited material might still be communal rather than individual, giving texts a wider remit and broader influence. Considering *AM* alongside *Kyng Alisaunder* will therefore help us both to put the Alexander romance's approach in context and also to see if this approach is indicative of a broader intellectual trend.

However, there is one major characteristic of *AM* that appears to distinguish its poetics from those seen in *Kyng Alisaunder*. Elizabeth S. Sklar has observed that the text, in particular the prologue, demonstrates an 'Englishing process' that is 'characterized by a strong nationalistic bias not present in the source, clearly speaking to the interests of the specifically English audience for whom *AM* was intended', and shows a 'linguistic chauvinism' in creating such a bias.[87] Karen Haslanger Vaneman perceives the same process at work in *AM*'s treatment of law, where *AM*'s Englishness is depicted in terms of conflict between different legal traditions in the reigns of Edward I and II.[88] Such a process, and especially 'linguistic chauvinism' regarding English, is the polar opposite of what has been observed about *Kyng Alisaunder*'s identity and language politics. Despite the idea of a shared literary culture at several points in the texts' history, this major divergence indicates that such a culture may not be homogenous.

Like *Kyng Alisaunder*, *AM*'s text differs greatly between Auchinleck and Lincoln 150. Both romances are significantly shorter in Lincoln 150, but unlike the Alexander romance, *AM* in Lincoln 150 is probably a distinct version with a separate transmission history rather than an occasional redaction. Macrae-Gibson designates the Auchinleck version 'AM' and that in Lincoln 150 'AM2', considering them to be related to one another but at several earlier

---

[85] Scattergood, 'High Life', p.323.

[86] Ibid.

[87] Sklar, 'Englishing of Arthur', p.49, p.50, p.51.

[88] Karen Haslanger Vaneman, '*Of Arthour and of Merlin*: Arthour's Story as Arena for the Conflict of Custom and Common Law', *Quondam et Futurus* (*Arthuriana*), 8.2 (1988), pp.8–18.

removes.[89] In Auchinleck, the text falls into two parts, the first concerned with Merlin's birth and *enfances*, and the second with Arthur's reign, which is essentially a series of battles.[90] In Lincoln, however, the text ends with Vortigern's death, without any mention of Arthur; it is only around two thousand lines long, roughly a quarter of the length of the Auchinleck version. Although the focus of my study will be on the longer Auchinleck text, I shall also consider the Lincoln poem to see if it sheds any comparative light upon *AM* in the earlier manuscript.

Language and Identity

As we have seen, a major characteristic of *Kyng Alisaunder*'s poetics is its interest in intellectual engagement with its French and Latin sources, and its strong consciousness of language choice and difference. Even if it is not an English-language text almost by accident, as Baswell's analysis provocatively suggests,[91] it is a work that deliberately highlights its French and Latin inspiration. The prologue to *AM* in Auchinleck, often quoted in discussions of Englishness,[92] seems to support a similar awareness in the Arthurian text:

> Auauntages þai hauen þare
> Freynsch and Latin eueraywhare.
> Of Freynsch no Latin nil y tel more
> Ac on I[n]glisch ichil tel þerfore:
> Riȝt is þat I[n]glische vnderstond
> Þat was born in Inglond.
> Freynsche vse þis gentil man
> Ac euerich Inglische Inglische can,
> Mani noble ich haue yseiȝe
> Þat no Freynsche couþe seye,
> Biginne ichil for her loue
> Bi Ihesus leue þat sitt aboue
> On Inglische tel mi tale –
> God ous sende soule hale.[93]

These lines appear to be a potent combination of language and national identity – 'Riȝt is þat I[n]glische vnderstond/þat was born in Inglond' – with

---

[89] See *AM*, ed. Macrae-Gibson, ii, pp.44–60. William E. Holland thinks that the existing manuscripts are not connected 'by any unbroken chain of written texts' ('Formulaic Diction and the Descent of a Middle English Romance', *Speculum*, 48 (1973), pp.89–105 (p.105)).

[90] For a detailed synopsis of the narrative as it appears in Auchinleck, see Appendix 2.

[91] Baswell, 'Multilingualism on the Page', pp.43–4.

[92] A recent valuable study is Patrick Butler, 'A Failure to Communicate: Multilingualism in the Prologue to *Of Arthour and of Merlin*', in *The Auchinleck Manuscript*, ed. Fein, pp.52–66.

[93] *AM*, ed. Macrae-Gibson, i, lines 17–30.

French and Latin being set aside in preference for 'Inglische', which everyone can understand ('euerich Inglische Inglische can'). It is clear why this passage is of such interest for scholars interested in the development of English as a nationalizing language, since it sets the scene for the Englishness that Sklar and Vaneman perceive in different themes elsewhere in *AM*. Yet there is a crucial factor here that has not been much emphasized. French and Latin are used to underline the ubiquity and comprehensibility of English, but they do so in terms that highlight ignorance: many nobles 'no Freynsche couþe seye', and the narrator himself leaves his linguistic abilities open to question ('Of Freynsch no Latin nil y tel more'). The passage's strong preference for 'Inglische' is based on ignorance of French and Latin, although they are supposedly 'eueraywhare'. The motif of linguistic and scholarly ignorance (genuine or feigned) is of course pervasive in medieval literary culture, especially with reference to vernacular texts,[94] but it is noteworthy that it marks a very different approach to the learned, transnational languages from that seen in *Kyng Alisaunder*, where French and Latin are invoked to demonstrate the intellectual focus of the poet's *translatio*. Here, in contrast, we see ignorance of these languages emphasized as a distinctive feature of the author's approach. This key passage indicates that the Auchinleck *AM*'s relationship with its sources may be very different from that seen in *Kyng Alisaunder*, an intriguing possibility given the two poems' close temporal, geographical, and manuscript relationships.

Sources

AM's material source is the French prose *Lestoire de Merlin*, also known as the *Vulgate Merlin*. Although *AM*'s exact relationship with *Lestoire de Merlin* is a complex issue, it seems that several sources including *Lestoire de Merlin* may have been used in the first part of the Auchinleck tale (Merlin's youth), but that the romance is based on the Merlin text alone in the second part (Arthur's reign).[95] Despite this difference, Macrae-Gibson considers that the poet's treatment of *Lestoire de Merlin* is consistent throughout *AM*, which broadly speaking involves removing digressions to create a more streamlined narrative and emphasizing the many battle scenes, sometimes with expansion.[96] As we have seen, *Kyng Alisaunder*'s relationship to its sources is an intellectual and thematic one, with less emphasis upon simplification (at least

---

[94] See Elizabeth Salter's discussion of the Anglo-Norman and English adaptations of Robert Grosseteste's *Chasteau d'Amour*, in which she comments on this habit (*English and International*, pp.33–4).

[95] For a thorough analysis, see *AM*, ed. Macrae-Gibson, II, pp.2–35. See also the brief overview given in Geraldine Barnes, *Counsel and Strategy in Middle English Romance* (Cambridge, 1993), p.62.

[96] *AM*, ed. Macrae-Gibson, II, pp.7–9, pp.14–17, pp.18–19, pp.32–5.

in the Auchinleck text). *AM*'s relationship with *Lestoire de Merlin* is made more involved by the fact that the French text is prose rather than poetry; linguistically and metrically, there is a greater difference between the two Arthurian works than between *RTC* and *Kyng Alisaunder*, both verse texts. The stylistic differences between prose and poetry to some extent explain *AM*'s tendency to abbreviate material, since *Lestoire de Merlin* can be repetitive. Yet there is a more interesting feature of this *abbreviatio* that appears to have gone unnoticed. *Lestoire de Merlin* makes many references to a written source, claiming 'dist li contes' or 'says the account' at the start of significant sections.[97] In *AM*, phrases such as 'also we finden in þe bok' (467) or in one instance 'so it is written in þe brout' (538) are far less frequent. Instead, we come across phrases such as 'ich ȝou sigge verrament' (589) and 'ich telle more ȝou/of þis romaunce' (625–6). These first-person narratorial comments could be seen as signs of oral delivery, but the point here is that combined with the conscious reduction of source references from *Lestoire de Merlin* they create the impression of a text that is less interested in the niceties of sources and more in dramatic performance. This indicates in turn that the kind of intellectual engagement with literary tradition characteristic of *Kyng Alisaunder* is less of a priority for *AM*. This is supported by the fact that the mentions of 'þe bok', even the more specific one of 'þe brout' (a reference to Layamon's *Brut*), are simple references with no further development, in marked contrast to the discussion of 'storie' in *Kyng Alisaunder*, for example. This lack of interest in inherited literary cultures matches the reading of *AM*'s prologue as unconcerned with linguistic traditions, at least in the explicitly intellectualized sense seen in the Alexander poem. *AM*, despite the possibility that its origins may be shared with *Kyng Alisaunder* and the texts' mutual presence in Auchinleck, appears not to share this aspect of the latter's poetics of *translatio*.

Headpieces

However, there is one feature shared by *AM* and *Kyng Alisaunder* that does potentially highlight shared poetics. This is the presence of unusual seasonal headpieces, which as we have seen in *Kyng Alisaunder* emphasize that poem's 'bookness'. According to Macrae-Gibson, the headpieces indicate a wider knowledge of 'the apparatus of the epic style' and general 'French epic tradition', and as such indicate the influence of French literary traditions in both poems.[98] Such an influence is potentially suggested in *AM*, despite its lack of

---

[97] See for example the beginnings of chapters 1, 2, and 3 in *Le roman de Merlin or the early history of King Arthur*, ed. H. Oskar Sommer (London, 1894), which all start with a version of this phrase. The edition is a transcription of the c. 1316 London, British Library, MS Additional 10292.

[98] *AM*, ed. Macrae-Gibson, II, p.68.

interest in literary tradition observed above, because although the headpieces are present to some extent in *Lestoire de Merlin* they are retained and even developed further in the English romance. The headpieces in *AM*, like in *Kyng Alisaunder*, are therefore important locations for considering the poet's wider *translatio*, since they are places where a less direct but still present relationship with a specific material source allows for *translatio* in both a textually specific and also a broader sense (in terms of wider inspiration from different genres and texts). If these instances shared by the two romances demonstrate similar poetics, then we shall be able to consider *AM*'s poetics not just in terms of its relationship with its material source, *Lestoire de Merlin*, but more usefully in terms of its wider interest in other texts and genres, enabling us to address the question of a shared literary culture in a broader literary context.

Scattergood's analysis of *AM*'s and *Kyng Alisaunder*'s headpieces concludes that the less frequent occurrences in *AM* stay closer to the French source than those in *Kyng Alisaunder*, which are more complex and are sometimes 'accompanied by a gnomic or moralistic statement'.[99] As discussed above, some of those in *Kyng Alisaunder* are used to show off knowledge of French and Latin literary genres and traditions. The headpieces in *AM* may be used for a similar purpose, despite being closer to the French source, and thus may demonstrate similar poetics. One of the most striking differences between the two works, however, is the lack of stylistic variety in *AM*'s headpieces in comparison with those of *Kyng Alisaunder*. Of the eleven occurrences, ten involve the phrase 'mirie time' joined to a month, most often May, and usually accompanied by flowers, damsels, and birds singing, as in this example:[100]

> Miri time it is in May
> Þan wexeþ along þe day
> Floures schewen her borioun
> Miri it is in feld and toun
> Foules miri in wode gredeþ
> Damisels carols ledeþ.
> A baroun com to Fortiger ...

An example (although it occurs at a different point in the narrative) from *Lestoire de Merlin* clearly demonstrates the *AM* poet's abbreviation and simplification of his source:

> Che fu a lentree de mai au tans nouel que cil oisel chantent cler & seri . & toute riens de ioie enflambe & que cil bos & cil uergier sont flori & cil pre rauerdisent derbe nouele & menue & est entremellee de diuerses flors qui

---

99 Scattergood, 'High Life', p.337 and p.338.

100 They occur in the Auchinleck version of *AM* at 259–65, 1709–15, 3059–66, 4199–205, 4675–81, 5349–53, 6596–601, 7397–402, 7619–24, and 8657–62. The example quoted here is 1709–15.

ont douce odour . & ces douces aigues reuienent en lor canel . & les amors
noueles font resbaudir ces valles & ces puceles qui ont les cuers iolis & gais
por la douchor del tans qui renouele . Lors auint que gauaines & agrauains
& guerrehes & gaheries & galessins & cil qui en lor compaignie estoient
uenu furent matin leue par la chaut quil faisoit grant en mi le iour comme
cil qui voloient ceualcier la matinee a la froidour qui estoit bele & li tans
seris & coi .[101]

*It was the beginning of May when the birds sing clearly and pleasantly
again, and joy enflames all creatures, and the woods and the forest come
into leaf and the meadows are enraptured with fresh grass and fruit and
are scattered with all kinds of sweet-smelling flowers. The sweet river flows
back to its channel and new loves gladden the valleys; the young girls have
glad and uplifted hearts for the softness that is renewed. Then it occurred
that Gawain and Agravain and Guerrehes and Gaheris and Galeschin and
those who were part of their company set out early on account of the heat,
which was great in the middle of the day, as they wanted to hunt in the cool-
ness of the morning, which was beautiful, and the area pleasant and quiet.*

What is interesting about *AM*'s *translatio* of these moments is that it removes
their connection with the narrative. The passage in *Lestoire de Merlin*, although prolix in its descriptions of the joys of spring, is structurally present
in order to explain why Gawain and his brothers set out early in the morning,
before the heat of the day begins. In contrast, the *AM* headpiece does not relate
to the events that follow, the announcement of Uther Pendragon's invasion to
Vortigern. We might suppose that this lack of connection aligns it with *Kyng
Alisaunder*'s headpieces that function as display verse, which also tend not to
relate to the narrative, as discussed above. However, the stylistic simplicity
of *AM*'s headpieces contrasts with the more elaborate examples in *Kyng Alisaunder*, as shown here:

> Jn tyme of Maij hoot is in boure.
> D[iuer]s in mede spryngeþ suete floure,
> And the lefdy þe kniȝth honureþ.
> Trewe herte in loue dureþ.
> At gode need coward byhynde coureþ;
> At large ȝift the hungry loureþ.
> Gentyl-man his lemman dooþ honoure
> Jn burgh, in cite, in castel, in toure.
> Darrie þe kyng and Salome
> Habbeþ ydiȝþ her meignee.[102]

---

[101] *Le roman de Merlin*, ed. Sommer, section 64.20–9. This and all subsequent translations
of the text are my own.
[102] *Kyng Alisaunder*, ed. Smithers, I, 2049–58.

In these lines, very similar thematically to those from *AM* quoted above, we see a greater amount of more complicated vocabulary ('diuers', 'meignee'), but most crucially a sense of metaphorical development that is absent from the straightforward description seen in *AM*. Here, in contrast, the season of May is the catalyst for various different kinds of behaviour, especially relating to love; this kind of metaphorical extrapolation distinguishes the poet's poetics from those of *AM*. Instead of the Alexander romance's expansive and intellectual approach, where the headpiece is used as a means of gesturing towards larger and non-English-language literary genres, in *AM* we see a much closer reliance on a literal rendering and simplification of the source. Although there are many more instances of these headpieces in *AM* than in *Lestoire de Merlin*, the *AM* occurrences, with one exception, are straightforward temporal indicators, as Scattergood notes;[103] they simply mark the passage of time, with little thematic relevance or conscious invocation of inherited literary traditions. The single occasion where there appears to be deliberate poetic expansion is as follows:

> In time of winter alange it is
> Þe foules lesen her blis
> Þe leues fallen of þe tre
> Rein alangeþ þe cuntre
> Maidens leseþ here hewe,
> Ac euer hye louieþ þat be trewe.
> Þe kinges þat descomfit ware ...[104]

Scattergood thinks that this description of winter, which becomes a metaphor for loss of love, demonstrates a similar awareness of love lyric tradition to that seen in *Kyng Alisaunder*.[105] Yet the simple acknowledgement that 'maidens leseþ here hewe/Ac euer hye louieþ þat be trewe', an example of minimal thematic expansion, is very different from anything seen in *Kyng Alisaunder*, where more grandiose statements on this theme are standard:

> Whan nutte brouneþ on heselrys,
> þe lefdy is of her lemman chys.
> þe persone wereþ fow and grys –
> Ofte he setteþ his loue amys.
> þe ribaude plaieþ at the dys;
> Swiþe selde þe fole is wys.[106]

---

[103] Scattergood, 'High Life', p.332. I count only three such moments in *Lestoire de Merlin* (in sections 164, 346, and 459, in *Le roman de Merlin*, ed. Sommer).

[104] *AM*, ed. Macrae-Gibson, I, 4199–205.

[105] Scattergood, 'High Life', p.335.

[106] *Kyng Alisaunder*, ed. Smithers, I, 3289–96.

Despite Scattergood's observation of a moment of similarity between the two romances, this example from *Kyng Alisaunder* demonstrates a very different kind of thematic development in its lyric headpiece from the passage from *AM*. It is less concerned with physical description than with the psychological effects of the season, a direct reversal of the emphasis in the *AM* lines, which mostly describe the concrete facts of autumn and winter. In fact, this moment of slight expansion in *AM*'s headpieces, which might seem to align the poem with *Kyng Alisaunder*'s poetics, actually highlights differences between the two works' lyric insertions. Nowhere in *AM* do we see French and Latin lyric consciously invoked to the same extent or with the same effects as in *Kyng Alisaunder*; in the Arthurian poem, the headpieces do not disrupt narrative or provide psychological explanation for characters' actions. The poetic performance of *translatio* between the two romances differs greatly in the headpieces, making it seem less likely that the two were composed by the same author.

As discussed above, the version of *AM* in Lincoln 150 is much shorter and probably only distantly related to Auchinleck's text, making a detailed comparison between the two problematic. However, like *Kyng Alisaunder*, *AM* has been made to look more like a romance and more performative, with marginal marks added probably by the Lincoln 150 scribe to aid in the latter.[107] Although *AM*'s 'bookness' is as we have seen far less pronounced in several contexts than is that of *Kyng Alisaunder*, it too is reduced in Lincoln 150 along the same lines, aligning the two romances more closely in this witness. This greater unanimity again puts the variety between the Auchinleck versions into context and suggests that early fifteenth-century romance culture has become more generically cohesive.

Conclusion

Despite *AM*'s and *Kyng Alisaunder*'s presence in Auchinleck, stylistic similarities, and possible similar origins, then, their poetics of *translatio* are very different when considered at a detailed level. Once again this underlines the fact that Auchinleck's compilation narrative is not homogenous, and emphasizes the variety of literary cultures in the London area in the late thirteenth and early fourteenth centuries. *AM* does, however, put *Kyng Alisaunder*'s *translatio* into context, since the Arthurian romance's closer alignment with other Auchinleck romances like *Sir Beues* and *Sir Orfeo* in its cultural and linguistic Englishness sets the Alexander poem apart. *Kyng Alisaunder*'s approach may be shown to be unusual in the context of Auchinleck, but that makes it all the more interesting.

---

[107] Horobin and Wiggins, 'Reconsidering Lincoln's Inn MS 150', pp.35–40, p.43.

The Seege or Batayle of Troye

The *Seege or Batayle of Troye* (*SBT*) is related to *Kyng Alisaunder* in several extra-textual and extra-thematic ways. As mentioned above, it was probably composed in the late thirteenth or the first part of the fourteenth century, at much the same moment as both the Alexander work and *AM*.[108] It is found in four manuscripts, two from the fourteenth century and two from the fifteenth, in one of which (Lincoln's Inn 150) it immediately follows the Alexander romance.[109] There is thus both a structural and a thematic connection between the two works in that manuscript. In addition, *SBT*, like *Kyng Alisaunder*, survives in different versions across these four witnesses; the latest of its manuscripts, London, British Library, MS Harley 525, preserves a distinctly different text of the Troy romance from the other three copies, a situation paralleled by the version of *Kyng Alisaunder* in Lincoln's Inn 150. *Kyng Alisaunder* and *SBT* are therefore connected in terms of date, witnesses, and textual history as well as by their theme of classical *translatio*, suggesting that, as with *AM*, the Alexander romance and *SBT* may participate in several shared literary contexts. The question that we need to ask is whether these external similarities and connections are mirrored by similar poetic concerns. Does *SBT* resemble *Kyng Alisaunder*, stylistically and/or thematically, in its retelling of the Troy narrative? And what would any resemblance indicate about a shared literary culture?

Like *Kyng Alisaunder*, but perhaps to an even greater extent, *SBT* has experienced scholarly neglect. When it has been read, modern critics have generally taken a negative view of the poem: Derek Pearsall claimed it represents 'third-rate fumbling in an enfeebled tradition', and C. David Benson thought it takes a 'crude unlearned approach' to the story, not fit 'for any serious audience'.[110] Despite such views, the inconvenient fact remains that it was popular enough to be copied at least four times between 1300 and 1500 and significantly altered at least once in that period, suggesting that several different individuals must have had more than a passing interest in it. Recently, however, Nancy Mason Bradbury and Nicola McDonald have begun to address this modern imbalance. Bradbury incorporates the poem into her

---

[108] See n.12.

[109] These are (in probable chronological order): College of Arms, MS Arundel XXII (mid or late fourteenth century), British Library, MS Egerton 2862 (c. 1400), London, Lincoln's Inn, MS 150 (1400–25), and British Library, MS Harley 525 (second half of the fifteenth century). See *SBT*, ed. Barnicle, pp.ix–xviii; Robert A. Caldwell, 'The "History of the Kings of Britain" in College of Arms MS Arundel XXII', *PMLA*, 69.3 (1954), pp.643–54 (p.643); Nicola McDonald, '*The Seege of Troye*: "ffor wham was wakened al this wo?"', in *The Spirit of Medieval English Popular Romance*, ed. Ad Putter and Jane Gilbert (Harlow, 2000), pp.181–99 (p.197 n.5); and Horobin and Wiggins, 'Lincoln's Inn MS 150', p.31.

[110] Both critics' opinions are cited in McDonald, '*The Seege of Troye*', p.181.

continuing interest in the relationship between oral and literate transmission of romance works, concluding that the late version in Harley 525 is a revision made for a more literate audience, whereas the earlier text bears some signs of memorial transmission.[111] Nicola McDonald focuses on the thematic structure of *SBT*'s narrative, arguing that one of its major features is the 'dynamics of the mercantile venture and the ethos of appropriation' and that therefore 'aventure' explicitly becomes a materially acquisitive activity in the poem.[112] Both critics' perspectives, different though they are in focus, are vital in considering *SBT*'s poetics in comparison with those of *Kyng Alisaunder*, since both engage with aspects of *translatio* (stylistic features/alterations and thematic emphasis). However, in contrast to the extra-textual similarities between *SBT* and *Kyng Alisaunder* mentioned above, both views implicitly distinguish the two poems in textual terms. If the *SBT* text found in Harley is a deliberately more literary version (Bradbury's view, supported to some extent by McDonald[113]), this differentiates *SBT*'s later revision from that of *Kyng Alisaunder*, in which the extant version appears to have been simplified stylistically and linguistically.[114] Likewise, McDonald's idea of the more mercantile nature of 'aventure' in *SBT* contrasts implicitly with *Kyng Alisaunder*'s emphasis on traditional forms of chivalry, especially regarding diction.[115] Despite their seeming similarities, then, these important textual contrasts between the poems indicate that their performance of *translatio* may diverge.

An important aspect of the two poems' poetics of *translatio* is their relationships with their respective material sources. As already discussed, *Kyng Alisaunder* consciously intellectualizes the narrative inherited from the *Roman de toute chevalerie*, adding learned discussions about language and genre and gesturing towards external literary traditions. We therefore need to investigate how *SBT* engages with its material sources in order to compare the two romances' *translatio* in more detail.

SBT tells the story of the Trojan War from the first destruction of Troy itself to the returns of the Greeks in just over two thousand lines, following the same outline as the *Ylias* and the *Roman de Troie* but in a far shorter

---

[111] Nancy Mason Bradbury, 'Literacy, Orality, and the Poetics of Middle English Romance', in *Oral Poetics in Middle English Poetry*, ed. Mark C. Amodio and Sarah Gray Miller (New York, 1994), pp.39–69 (pp.48–9).

[112] McDonald, '*Seege of Troye*', p.188.

[113] Ibid., p.196 (citing Pearsall, 'Development of Middle English Romance', p.193).

[114] Horobin and Wiggins ('Lincoln's Inn MS 150') demonstrate that difficult or obscure words are removed and French-inspired aspects (like the seasonal 'headpieces') reduced in the manuscript's text of *Kyng Alisaunder*; see pp.43–5.

[115] The French-language interjections in *Kyng Alisaunder*, especially prominent in battle, invoke chivalry as a tradition inherited from earlier French romance texts, giving it a supposedly timeless feel; see for example Darius' cry to his men 'As armes, as armes!' (*Kyng Alisaunder*, ed. Smithers, I, 4299).

narrative.[116] The issue of which Troy tales the *SBT* poet used has been much debated, but the most plausible consensus is that the poet drew from 'a fluid amalgam' of Troy texts including Dares, the *Roman de Troie, Excidium Troiae*, and *Compendium Historiae Troianae-Romanae*.[117] This of course makes analyzing *SBT*'s relationship with its sources more complicated. However, McDonald has made some useful observations about *SBT*'s structure that shed some light on this complex issue. She comments on the *SBT* poet's drastic shortening of the narrative, claiming that he removes 'extraneous detail' at the same time as 'preserving a sense of the amplitude of Trojan history' and 'condensing and streamlining the twists and turns of a capacious plot'.[118] To put this into perspective, it is worth noting that the *Roman de Troie*, part of *SBT*'s 'fluid amalgam' of sources and itself based on Dares' relatively terse account, is over thirty thousand lines long; *abbreviatio* is not an inevitable consequence of rewriting and adaptation, even if it is a common one in Middle English romance, as seen in detail with reference to *AM* and as has been suggested for *Horn*.[119] *Kyng Alisaunder* demonstrates this point clearly, since the extant versions are around eight thousand lines long, comparable with its narrative source, the *Roman de toute chevalerie*, in length. So the *SBT* poet's decision to create a romance only just over two thousand lines long in all the extant manuscripts is a conscious one, and as such it may have ramifications for other, less structural aspects of his poetics.

Sources and Style

As noted above, *Kyng Alisaunder* is a work deeply conscious of and interested in its literary relationships, and one that engages with these relationships in deliberately intellectual terms. We have seen how the poet discusses his sources in terms of their stylistic contributions to his narrative ('Þis bataile distincted is/In þe Freinsshe, wel iwys', 2195–6), and how he consciously invokes a variety of generic and linguistic traditions within his text. The start of *SBT* seems to suggest a similar interest, since there the poet also explicitly discusses his sources in terms of their language and literary heritage:

---

[116] For a detailed synopsis, see Appendix 2.

[117] This is McDonald's phrase ('*The Seege of Troye*', p.183). See the overview of sources given in *SBT*, ed. Barnicle, pp.lvi–lxxiv and Margaret J. Ehrhart, *The Judgment of the Trojan Prince Paris in Medieval Literature* (Philadelphia, 1987), pp.53–4, and the articles by E. Bagby Atwood ('The Rawlinson *Excidium Troie* – A Study of Source Problems in Medieval Troy Literature', *Speculum*, 9 (1934), pp.379–404; 'The Judgment of Paris in the *Seege of Troye*', *PMLA*, 57 (1942), pp.343–53; and 'The Story of Achilles in the *Seege of Troye*', *Studies in Philology*, 39 (1942), pp.489–501).

[118] McDonald, '*The Seege of Troye*', p.183.

[119] See the discussion of *AM* above and n.76 re *Horn Childe*.

And so sayth a kyng þat þer was,
The huche men kallyd syre adryas;
Al þe doing he knewe, san fayle,
And wrot in grew al the batayle.
And seethe a mayster of sotel engynne
Wrot hyt out of grew into latyne;
And of latyn, wel y wote,
Into englis hit ys wrote.[120]

We see here several features familiar from *Kyng Alisaunder*, namely the use of French or French-derived phrases ('san fayle' and 'sotel engynne') and references to transference from specific languages ('grew' and 'latyne') into 'englis'. Yet their impact and context here is quite different from *Kyng Alisaunder*. There is no discussion of the stylistics of this *translatio* from Greek to Latin to English, in contrast with the Alexander text's interest in using Latin to add rhetorical colour ('Þerefore [I] habbe [hit] to coloure/borowed of þe Latyn a nature', 2197–8). Instead, the translation and rewriting process is described using only the verb 'wrote', a verb that indicates the physical act of writing but little of the mental creativity behind this act.[121]

The first lines of the poem support this lack of interest in the intellectual process of *translatio*, where the poet seems to set historical perspective aside: 'Syth god tyhys worle had wroȝt/... ffele aventures hauet be-falle/we þat now leuyn con noȝt telle alle' (1, 3–4). The sense of dismissal is even stronger in another witness of similar date, the Egerton MS, where the 'Meny Auntres' are not just untellable but actually unknown, 'we ne woot him noȝt alle' (3, 4). The problematics of history suggested here do not seem to affect the story at all, since in both witnesses the narrator jumps straight into the narrative without further ado, setting it in a timeless and ahistorical universe: 'Tyle in grece þer was/a pryns þat hyht pollyas' (Arundel 23–4), 'Lordynges, in Grece sum tyme þer was/a knyȝt þat hiȝt Pallaas' (Egerton 23–4). Unlike in *Kyng Alisaunder*, where discussion of 'storie' and sources is explicit, this passage in *SBT* is uninterested in and even dismissive of classical history; unknown and unnarratable, it is simply cast aside. *SBT*'s lack of interest in history at this point is supported by the Arundel scribe's mangling of Greek names. He gives 'adryas' and 'pollyas' for Egerton's 'sir Daryes' and 'Pallaas', a practical demonstration of the unknown nature of history that the text describes. This perspective aligns *SBT* closely with *AM*, in which a similar lack of interest is

---

[120] *SBT*, ed. Barnicle, 15–22. All the citations from the poem (unless otherwise indicated) are taken from the Arundel MS, since this is probably the earliest witness in date and hence the closest chronologically to *Kyng Alisaunder* as found in its earliest version in Auchinleck.

[121] The physical nature of 'wrote' is made clear in the entries given in the *MED* <http://quod.lib.umich.edu/m/mec/med-idx?type=id&id=MED53686&egs=all&egdisplay=compact> [accessed 9 March 2017].

displayed. The mention of 'englis' in *SBT*'s prologue, although more neutral than *AM*'s insistence upon 'euerich Inglische Inglische can', also indicates that these two romances may share a concern for 'Englishness', linguistically and culturally. Both these facts suggest that *SBT*'s poetics, like those of *AM*, are different from those observed in *Kyng Alisaunder*.

Given this lack of interest in history or any intellectual drivers of *translatio*, the question of the French phrases used here in *SBT* becomes more open. Are they signs of a relatively sophisticated use of French, as seen in *Kyng Alisaunder*, or something more akin to line and rhyme 'fillers'? Their position at the end of lines strongly suggests the latter, a view supported by the grammatical independence of 'san fayle' and its almost proverbial nature by this point in time.[122] 'Sotel engynne', appropriately enough, seems more subtle, but it also occupies a rhyming position and could easily be a direct borrowing from a French romance with little consideration of its linguistics, since it is such a common phrase in romance texts.[123] Neither phrase alone indicates the kind of linguistic analysis seen in *Kyng Alisaunder*'s description of narrative *amplificatio*.

Despite the explicit invocation of history and languages in *SBT*'s Prologue, which might seem to align the poem with *Kyng Alisaunder*, this brief analysis indicates that in fact the Troy text seems to be indifferent to the sort of intellectual approach to its inherited material, or 'bookness', that is so important to the Alexander poem. But what about the rest of *SBT*? Does it display similar attitudes elsewhere, and what are its poetics of *translatio* if they do indeed continue to differ from those seen in *Kyng Alisaunder*?

History and 'Classicism'

A particularly interesting episode in considering these large questions is the Judgement of Paris, a famous classical scene existing in different versions and with various interpretations from antiquity.[124] Intriguingly, although this is such a well-known scene, *SBT*'s version is difficult to locate in terms of its source/s. Bagby Atwood concluded that it draws on Dares and the *Excidium Troiae* but does not derive its narrative primarily from either account; he also claimed that *SBT*'s scene is not 'an original flight of the poet's imagination', since the direct speeches that characterize the scene in *SBT* have parallels in other vernacular Troy narratives, suggesting that there is a lost narrative

[122] See the entry for this phrase in the *AND* <www.anglo-norman.net/gate/index.shtml> [accessed 6 March 2017].
[123] On the frequency of 'engin' in this sense, see *AND* <www.anglo-norman.net/gate/index.shtml> [accessed 6 March 2017].
[124] On the Judgement's antique history, see Ehrhart, *Judgment of the Trojan Prince Paris*, pp.1–34.

lying behind the *SBT* and these other vernacular texts.[125] This fluid situation regarding the sources is, however, an opportunity for poetic creativity, as Margaret J. Ehrhart notes; focusing on the episode's poetics, she claims that 'unhampered by any scholarly impulse, he [the poet] handled his material with almost complete freedom'.[126] Whatever the situation in terms of the sources, now probably indecipherable, the fact remains that in creating the Judgement of Paris scene the poet appears to have had access to several accounts, both late antique and medieval, and to have composed his intriguingly distinctive version drawing on aspects of these sources in a creative fashion. Even if the result is not Bagby Atwood's 'original flight of … imagination' in a modern sense, it is certainly an imaginative and free poetic rendering. The version in *SBT* is therefore a useful place to look for signs of his poetics of *translatio*.

The whole episode is around a hundred lines long in the Arundel, Egerton, and Lincoln's Inn manuscripts (507–616) and around seventy in Harley (400–62, 608–14). One of the first things to strike the reader is the depiction of the female characters, in most accounts of this scene the goddesses Juno, Minerva, and Venus. In Lincoln's Inn, Egerton, and Arundel, however, they are not three goddesses but four 'ladies of eluen londe' named Saturnus, Jubiter, Mercurius, and Venus. This is a conundrum, one that cannot be solved simply by labelling the episode 'prolix and corrupt'.[127] Given that the female characters except for Venus are renamed using the correct names for some of their male counterparts in the classical pantheon, it is difficult to dismiss them as simple indications of ignorance. The addition of Mercury, making four characters not the traditional three, may indeed be a sign of misreading of the *Roman de Troie*, since in the corresponding passage there we are told that Mercury conducts the three goddesses to Paris: 'Mercurion/Juno, Venus e Minerva/ces treis deuesses m'amena' ('Mercury brought those three goddesses to me [Paris], Juno, Venus and Minerva').[128] Yet misreading does not explain the renaming of the other three characters, nor their reduction in status from goddesses to 'ladies of eluen londe'. Whatever the poet's intention, a lessening of classicism is certainly the effect produced, since this renaming

[125] Dares' account of this episode is only a couple of lines long, while the *Excidium Troiae* is around twenty; for these texts, see *The Trojan War: The Chronicles of Dictys of Crete and Dares the Phrygian*, trans. R. M. Frazer (Bloomington, IN, 1966), pp.138–9 (section 7), and *Excidium Troiae*, ed. E. Bagby Atwood and Virgil K. Whitaker (Cambridge, MA, 1944), p.4 (line 23) and p.5 (line 18). On the sources, see Bagby Atwood, 'Judgment of Paris', p.363. It is worth noting that not only vernacular Troy narratives incorporate the goddesses' speeches in the Judgement of Paris scene, since speeches are also a feature of the *Ylias*: see II.237–606 in *Joseph Iscanus: Werke und Briefe*, ed. Ludwig Gompf (Leiden, 1970).

[126] Ehrhart, *Judgment of the Trojan Prince Paris*, pp.53–4.

[127] Bagby Atwood, 'Judgment of Paris', p.344.

[128] *Troie*, ed. Constans, I, 3874–6.

moves the episode away from its antique sources. In addition, their characterization not as goddesses but as ladies from 'eluen londe' (admittedly powerful ones) has the same effect. This possibility, although speculative, brings the Judgement of Paris thematically closer to the poem's general lack of interest in classical history (as demonstrated in the prologue), and hence differentiates it again from *Kyng Alisaunder*'s greater focus on historical perspective. It also sets the scene for McDonald's idea that the poem recreates the narrative with a focus on contemporary mercantile interests, since the goddesses have become 'astute businesswomen' who offer Paris rewards.[129] Lessening the appearance of classical influence, whatever the poetic intention, therefore has the effect of moving the passage's focus away from divine powers and towards Paris' human mercantile decisions. This focus is reinforced by the Greek prince's intriguing reporting of his own decision-making processes, which are wholly based on profit (as McDonald notes): in considering each offer (wealth, strength, beauty, love of women), Paris analyzes whether he needs it or not ('Me þouȝt y was reche/strong/fayre y-now þo'[130]) before deciding to accept Venus' option. Whatever the truth of the renaming of the women and their changed status (and it may after all simply be ignorance), the effect is to concentrate the narrative upon Paris and his decisions, not upon non-human agencies or powers. The traditional classical format of the Judgement of Paris is overwritten, much like a palimpsest, and recast to promote contemporary pragmatic concerns.

Celticism

Another characteristic of the Judgement of Paris episode is its 'atmosphere of romance', which Barnicle describes as 'wholly Celtic and mediaeval',[131] citing the appearance of magic mist and sleep, solitude, and finally the appearance of the elven ladies. Ehrhart suggests that the *SBT* poet draws on the *Roman de Troie* for this Celticization, claiming that the Troy romance's 'aura of a Celtic tale' in the Judgement of Paris is accentuated in *SBT*.[132] Without addressing the issue of Celticism in detail here, these motifs' appearance at this moment in *SBT* is intriguing given the English Troy romance's consistent interest in concrete human concerns, as their otherworldly nature seems incongruous when juxtaposed with Paris' relentless focus on profit in the very same scene. However, if we see these Celtic moments in the light of contemporary romances such as *Sir Orfeo*, in which the supernatural (often seen as definitive of Celticism) plays an important narrative role, it becomes evident that they are broader generic markers rather than specific narrative devices,

---

[129] McDonald, '*The Seege of Troye*', p.193.
[130] *SBT*, ed. Barnicle, 563, 577, 587 (in L, E, and A).
[131] *SBT*, ed. Barnicle, p.xlvi.
[132] Ehrhart, *Judgment of the Trojan Prince Paris*, pp.54–5.

creating an identifiable romance atmosphere without having much impact on the plot.[133] This marks another important difference between *SBT* and *Kyng Alisaunder*, as despite the presence of magic and the supernatural in the Alexander romance, especially in the Nectanebus narrative, such motifs are not used to create atmosphere in this way. The effect of this romance atmosphere in the Judgement of Paris episode is suggestive, since it moves the passage further away from any classically-derived source text and into the realm of contemporary romance composition. The creation of a romance sensibility therefore has the same impact as both the reduction of classical influence discussed above and also the pragmatic and profit-driven focus observed by McDonald: all three features situate the poem primarily in the contemporary medieval world rather than in the historical past, despite its classical *materia*.

SBT *in London, British Library, MS Harley 525*

This synchronic concern sets the *translatio* of *SBT*'s Judgement of Paris apart from *Kyng Alisaunder*'s more diachronic approach to its material. Yet this observation about *SBT*'s *translatio* may only hold true for three of the four *SBT* manuscripts. In Harley, the Judgement of Paris episode is different: there the three (not four) goddesses are described as such, and they have their expected names. This indicates that the scene has been re-classicized to some extent by being brought back in line with expected classical plot motifs. Such a rewriting might suggest an intellectualized approach to sources similar to that found in *Kyng Alisaunder*, in which closer attention is paid to the narrative's relationship with inherited material. Derek Pearsall's view that the Harley version of *SBT* as a whole is a more elaborate and learned version of the romance seems to support this intellectualized approach.[134] However, while this opinion may be accurate in terms of the romance more widely, the Harley Judgement of Paris' narrative is structurally confusing. There are only two goddesses' speeches, and the first one, ascribed to Juno, is potentially that of Pallas;[135] in any event, one speech seems to be missing. Barnicle criticizes the passage for its 'bald, almost anecdotal fashion, which has nothing of the dramatic vitality and emphatic repetition of the

---

[133] For a recent discussion of supernatural phenomena and Celticism, see Aisling Byrne, *Otherworlds: Fantasy and History in Medieval Literature* (Oxford, 2016) especially chapter 3, 'Supernatural Authorities'.

[134] Pearsall, 'Development of Middle English Romance'; see also McDonald, '*The Seege of Troye*', p.196.

[135] Line 430 states 'Juno she went onto Parysse' but after the goddess finishes speaking we are told 'Pallas þe way from him has taken' (439); in addition, the gift offered by 'Juno' here is wisdom (line 436), which seems more appropriate to Pallas, although Juno is described earlier as 'lady of wysenesse' (401). This incongruity is also noted by Ehrhart, *Judgment of the Trojan Prince Paris*, p.56. The Harley text is in *SBT*, ed. Barnicle, appendix A, pp.175–6.

L E A version' and also claims that 'the poetry is irregular and unmusical, stumping along on infirm feet.'[136] Certainly the narrative is harder to follow, since it seems that the Harley rewriting has caused important plot details (such as the number of speeches) to be muddled. In altering the passage to conform in some sense to classical tradition, the adaptor has lost control of the narrative. In addition to this narrative confusion, the idea that the Harley Judgement of Paris is a more intellectually and historically aware adaptation is troubled by Juno's and Venus' anachronistic references to 'Mahound'.[137] A common feature in Middle English romances, especially those involving Saracen–Christian conflicts, it is more striking in this context, especially as Pallas by contrast swears 'be Jubiter and Appolyn', using the historically appropriate classical pantheon.[138] This feature, small though it is, argues against a historically aware re-classicizing *translatio* taking place in the Harley version. This view is supported by the fact that, except for the correct classical names, the Harley Judgement of Paris does not make any obviously classically-inspired alterations. The thematic emphasis here is on timeless chivalric concerns as exemplified in Paris' description as 'þe trewest man' and 'þe trewest knyght' (425 and 443), concerns that are located more obviously in contemporary romance culture than in classically-derived narratives. All this demonstrates that, while the Harley redactor may have wanted to correct his exemplar's strange naming of the goddesses/elven ladies, he does not create a re-classicized narrative in any deeper sense, and neither does he display the kind of consciously intellectual and historical approach characteristic of *Kyng Alisaunder*. Classical learning and historical awareness here is at most skin-deep. The Harley redactor's different practice of *translatio*, which at first glance might have aligned Harley's *SBT* more closely with the Alexander text, in actual fact only serves to point up the differences in approach between the two classically-inspired romances, differences that are broadly maintained across both of *SBT*'s distinctive versions.

Conclusion

SBT's perspective, and its concomitant lack of interest in or ignorance of traditional classical history, is a form of *translatio* very different from that seen in *Kyng Alisaunder*. In that poem, when there is a contemporary focus, it is not created by overwriting an inherited narrative; rather, the poet uses his classical material to insist on the timelessness of values that have medieval resonance, such as chivalry. As mentioned above, the *Kyng Alisaunder* poet is

---

[136] *SBT*, ed. Barnicle, p.xlvii.

[137] *SBT*, ed. Barnicle, appendix A, lines 417 and 442.

[138] *SBT*, ed. Barnicle, appendix A, line 410. The sultan in *The King of Tars* swears 'bi Seyn Mahoun', for example (*The King of Tars*, ed. J. Perryman, Middle English Texts, 12 (Heidelberg, 1980), 102).

deeply interested in the diachronic view, whereas the *SBT* creator is concerned with a synchronic perspective. *AM*'s non-classical narrative makes it harder to analyze its relationship to its *materia* in these terms, but its lack of interest in inherited literary traditions (as represented by its dismissal of French and Latin) and the idea that the poet reflects Englishness by emphasizing themes with contemporary relevance (such as legal conflict)[139] suggests that its perspective too is more synchronic than diachronic.

English and International

Despite the three romances' presence in Lincoln 150, and the editorial desire for generic, thematic, and linguistic continuity displayed in that manuscript that brings *Kyng Alisaunder* closer to *AM* and *SBT*, the three romances do not share approaches to *translatio*. *Kyng Alisaunder*'s intellectual, multilingual, and more diachronic poetics contrast with the other two poems' less learned, more linguistically and culturally English, and synchronic composition. This contrast is not simply a matter of tension between the historical nature of the Alexander *materia* and its contemporary medieval rewriting in *Kyng Alisaunder*, since the Troy legend, seen as equally historical in the Middle Ages, is undoubtedly re-created in an English thematic as well as linguistic context in *SBT*; it would have been entirely possible for the *Kyng Alisaunder* poet to create a thematically as well as linguistically English narrative had he wanted to do so. In other words, the difference in poetic *translatio* between *Kyng Alisaunder* and the other two romances is a conscious choice, not forced by narrative circumstance. This difference in *translatio*, although not as marked as the debate seen between classically-inspired texts at the end of the twelfth century, should still remind us that a local and/or national perspective is not inevitable in English literary texts and manuscripts during this period, especially in the early fourteenth century, the time of Auchinleck's compilation.

Likewise, the idea that texts connected by similar origins and mutual presence in manuscripts necessarily create a shared literary culture identifiable by stylistic similarities is not supported by these three romances; the stylistic similarities in the Auchinleck versions of *Kyng Alisaunder* and *AM* in fact highlight the differences between the two texts' *translatio*, especially in the seasonal headpieces. The edited texts of *Kyng Alisaunder* and *AM* in Lincoln 150, whose increased similarity might be considered to create a more unified literary culture in that later manuscript, bear implicit witness to the diversity of romance poetics in the early fifteenth century, since such close editing would not have been perceived as necessary unless this diversity was a current phenomenon. Lincoln 150's editorial work suggests potential anxiety about

---

[139] Vaneman, 'Arthour's Story as Arena for the Conflict of Custom and Common Law'.

its contents; any reason for this is speculative, but it is tempting to consider the collection as intended to be educative, historically and morally, especially given the presence of *Piers Plowman* at the end.[140] Generic conformity in this light could be said to promote this compilatory narrative. Whatever its intended purpose, the unifying editorial policy of Lincoln 150 ironically highlights literary diversity, diversity we have already perceived in Auchinleck by virtue of *Kyng Alisaunder*.

Whilst it is important not to overstate the case for literary diversity, since my analysis is based solely on *Kyng Alisaunder*, the romance's transnationalism and presence in several manuscripts should remind us that the narrative of Englishness, linguistic and cultural, needs to be nuanced. To compose in English is of course to engage with an insular audience, but this linguistic choice does not mean that poetic interest in issues transcending boundaries of language, geography, and politics is obliterated by local English concerns, as the Alexander text has demonstrated. Unpicking the longstanding yet often unhelpful connections between languages, literatures, and nations in the Middle Ages will enable us not only to contextualize Alexander material with more historical and literary accuracy, but also give insight into other important narratives that help to construct medieval cultures.

---

[140] On a similar phenomenon in the context of manuscripts of Latin poetry, see Venetia Bridges, '"Goliardic" Poetry and the Problem of Historical Perspective: Medieval Adaptations of Walter of Châtillon's Quotation Poems', *Medium Ævum*, 81.2 (2012), pp.249–70, which draws similar conclusions about editorial anxiety.

Conclusion

' In my end is my beginning.'[1] This book ends deliberately at the moment invoked in the introduction, when Alexander narratives are lampooned via Chaucer's Monk as 'commune'. It is surely no coincidence that this Chaucerian witticism occurs at the same moment that such narratives start to be found more frequently in English, some decades after the author of *Of Arthour and of Merlin* is able belligerently to announce 'on Inglisch ichil tel þerfore'.[2] The link between language and 'commune' knowledge is implicit but clear in Chaucer's reference: the Macedonian has become ubiquitous, and in English, which is surely part of Chaucer's Monk's point that 'every man', rich or poor, educated or unlettered, is able to hear of the conqueror, and in his own vernacular. This powerful connection between language and cultural identity, made by the first English-language canonical author, may seem to contradict the complexities of Alexander's *translatio* claimed by this book. Instead of transnational and multilingual perspectives found in both insular and continental texts, we are faced here with the universalizing yet fundamentally local idea of Alexander as vernacular and therefore 'commune'/common. The democratization of Alexander – his *translatio* from the traditional languages of learning and intellectual life to those of everyday exchange, his movement from elite circles to mixed audiences, his journey from transnational conqueror to local *exemplum* – appears to be complete, a movement that leaves little room for other perspectives.

Yet these other perspectives endure. The idea that Alexander has become 'commune' in this movement from learned languages to vernaculars and from elite to wider audiences presupposes a causal relationship between the range of a language and its approach to its subject, one of the key assumptions questioned in this book. In other words, it assumes a shift in focus inextricably linked to the remit, geographical, political, and cultural, of a particular language. The evidence highlighted in this study seems to answer *sic et non* to this assumption, for the thirteenth and early fourteenth centuries at least. The analysis of the *Roman de toute chevalerie (RTC)* and *Horn*, for example, shows that Anglo-Norman romances do not necessarily engage with insular concerns in their *translatio* even if they do so in the historical events of their

---

[1]   T. S. Eliot, 'East Coker', v.38, *Four Quartets* (London, 1944).
[2]   *Of Arthour and of Merlin*, ed. O. D. Macrae-Gibson, 2 vols, EETS, o.s., 268 and 279 (Oxford, 1973 and 1979), I, 20.

narratives; the characteristics of Anglo-Norman as an insular language do not inevitably define the presentation of the stories it tells. However, the study of the Middle English *Kyng Alisaunder* in the context of related Arthurian and Trojan material suggests that the approach demonstrated so clearly by the romance's interest in multilingual material and textual traditions is unusual, as it contrasts with the *translatio* seen in *Of Arthour and of Merlin (AM)* and *The Seege or Batayle of Troye (SBT)*. *Kyng Alisaunder*'s somewhat anomalous approach sets it apart from these other Middle English romances, which do display a form of *translatio* that can perhaps be related to their English language and cultural remit. So it appears that, for these insular works, Alexander *translatio* in a comparative context may reinforce the relationship between location and language, but may also query or trouble such a relationship.

Such a *sic et non* situation brings us back to the earlier Alexander texts, the *Alexandreis* and the *Roman d'Alexandre*, and their comparative companions. The debate over *translatio* seen here is conducted between texts in different languages and in various areas, emphasizing that it is truly a transnational one. Yet both Latin and French are of course themselves transnational languages, so it may be thought that here too the connection between language and cultural remit is reiterated and reinforced, albeit in the opposite sense. However, this transnational *translatio* does not exclude more local issues from involvement and importance; the complex relationship of the *Alexandreis* to Philip Augustus and to concerns of secular and sacred power highly relevant to Reims is a clear example of just such immediate local issues operating with a transnational language and text. Likewise, the anxious ethics of the *Roman d'Alexandre* relates to works from other times and places, both antique and medieval, but also to the specific debate over the *translatio* of inherited material that we have seen is characteristic of the later twelfth century in northern France. For these texts, then, a transnational perspective does not mean the rejection of pressing local concerns; they are aspects of the same literary landscape. Linguistic remit may well indicate the nature of a work's *translatio*, but it does not wholly define it. In this sense, perhaps Chaucer's lugubrious Monk is condemning himself, both as an intellectual snob and also as ignorant, when he seems to decry Alexander's 'commune' nature; to learn of the Macedonian in English is not inevitably to know little of the complexities of his wider 'storie', as its *translatio* in that language may include texts and traditions derived from distant places long ago.

This idea of the multilingual, transnational 'storie' inherent within even apparently local Alexander texts highlights another theme frequently raised in this book, namely history, or, more accurately, historiography. From the beginning of Alexander's literary narratives, especially in the Greek accounts, there is an awareness of Alexander as a historical figure, even if authors choose to focus more on his exemplary value than his historicity (Plutarch being a good ancient example): this awareness is most keenly displayed in the *Alexandreis*, but interest in history of various kinds is also an important feature of the other Alexander texts analyzed. Whilst this textual and critical consciousness of history is vital, I think there is a caveat to be made. The critical debate over the historicity (or otherwise) of the antique accounts in particular has dominated scholarship, potentially to the detriment of analyzing the texts for their literary characteristics, including *translatio*.[3] To some extent, this critical interest in historiography can be paralleled by a similar focus on the relationship between history and fiction in research on medieval romance.[4] Such research is of course both important and useful, but for Alexander texts I think it can be something of a red herring, since it may lead to the idea of different approaches being defined by genre, creating misleading ideas about 'history' and 'romance' Alexanders.[5] The studies in this book highlight rather that from the earliest beginnings Alexander narratives demonstrate a variety of hermeneutic approaches, of which historical accuracy and analysis is only one. And even within what can be broadly termed a 'historical focus', there are many different responses. For example, the *Alexandreis* is concerned about the inappropriate use (in Walter of Châtillon's terms) of history in aligning sacred with secular time periods, whereas the *RTC* and *Kyng Alisaunder* are much more interested in history in terms of texts and traditions and the intellectual processes of historiography. This difference could perhaps be ascribed to genre, the separation of epic from romance (itself of course problematic from a medieval perspective),[6] but within the multivalent discourse of romance too there is a plurality of approaches: the *Alexandre*, for example, is much more interested in exemplary and marvellous *translatio* than the *RTC* and *Kyng Alisaunder*, and far less so in history and historiography. To a large extent, then, the question of Alexander and historiography is most useful as a means of highlighting the variety and multiple approaches of texts of various generic affiliations towards historical narratives.

The concept of variety and multiple approaches in Alexander narratives makes clear another key insight of this book, namely the existence of plural hermeneutic responses to his 'storie'. That such pluralism may operate within

---

[3] On antique Alexander criticism see James Davidson, 'Bonkers about Boys', *London Review of Books*, 1 November 2001, <www.lrb.co.uk/v23/n21/james-davidson/bonkers-about-boys> [accessed 4 January 2017], and the discussion in chapter 1.

[4] Recent examples are D. H. Green, *The Beginnings of Medieval Romance: Fact and Fiction, 1150–1220*, Cambridge Studies in Medieval Literature, 47 (Cambridge, 2002), and Laura Ashe, *History and Fiction in England, 1066–1200*, Cambridge Studies in Medieval Literature, 68 (Cambridge, 2007).

[5] This is the approach taken by Charles Russell Stone, although it is mostly more nuanced than this overview suggests: see his various publications cited in chapter 4, especially '"Many man he shal do woo": Portents and the End of an Empire in *Kyng Alisaunder*', *Medium Ævum*, 81.1 (2012), pp.18–40.

[6] I am thinking particularly of French *chansons de geste* and romances here.

a single text is apparent from all four Alexander works studied in detail, but is perhaps especially evident in the *RTC*'s encyclopaedic approach, which is intertwined with its interest in sources and dialectics, and the *Alexandreis'* *sic et non translatio*.[7] Pluralism is also a feature of manuscript *compilatio*, as the consideration of *Kyng Alisaunder* in Auchinleck indicates; even within a book with such a dominant narrative of Englishness, there is conceptual and compilatory space for a different hermeneutic/s. This insight is not a new one, but it is important to restate it now, since scholarly work on manuscripts in particular is becoming increasingly receptive to the deconstruction, at least in part, of cherished meta-narratives.[8] The idea of networks formed by texts, manuscripts, people, and places has likewise highlighted that narrative *translatio* and textual transmission is far from being a unified, single process, as the complex textual situations of the *RTC*'s manuscripts and the variety of Alexander texts housed at St Albans, only touched on briefly here, clearly illustrates. The copying and circulation of manuscripts of these high medieval texts in later centuries is another intriguing demonstration of this potential variety of responses to inherited texts and narratives, one that this book has also only mentioned briefly, but which is a fascinating area for future study.[9]

Yet this insistence on pluralism should not be interpreted as an interpretative free-for-all lacking in scholarly rigour. There are still dominant hermeneutic tendencies to be seen in Alexander's literary history, as indicated by the works studied here. Alongside interest in various aspects of historiography is a fascination with the exemplary possibilities of Alexander, both the individual and his narratives, which is again found in the earliest accounts. This fascination is especially, even anxiously, strong in the *Alexandre*, in which the marvels of the Orient are frequently used to highlight the eponymous king's ethical possibilities. However, these diachronic tendencies should not conversely suggest that unchanging transcendence defines *translatio studii* any more holistically than does total variety or pluralism. The interest in Alexander's ethical characteristics shown by texts throughout the chronological span covered here may be consistent, but the contexts for it alter markedly, particularly with the advent of Christianity. At this moment his ἔθος is no longer simply a philosophical *exemplum* for a moral life, but becomes part of a wider discourse about the relationship of the pagan past to the Christian present in which the potential exemplarity of a pre-Christian king becomes

---

[7] Arrian's *Anabasis* also displays this combination, again locating this hermeneutic combination in antiquity.

[8] Recent work on Auchinleck in particular indicates this shift, as evidenced by the essays in *The Auchinleck Manuscript: New Perspectives*, ed. Susanna Fein (York, 2016).

[9] I have made a start at such a study by considering the later histories of the *Alexandreis* via its manuscripts: see Venetia Bridges, 'Reading Walter of Châtillon's *Alexandreis* in Medieval Anthologies', *Mediaeval Studies*, 77 (2015), pp.81–101.

more complex, as the *Alexandre*'s plaintive plea reminds us: 'if he had been Christian, such a king would never have existed/who was so courteous and so generous, so wise, so renowned'.[10] So whilst the interest in Alexander as an ethical *exemplum* is maintained, perhaps even increased, through antiquity and into the Middle Ages, the conceptual framework for such an interest gives it a new set of meanings in which continuity is mingled with change.

Finally, this book has demonstrated that Alexander narratives are important participants in both insular and also European literary history, a point that is again not new but that needs to be restated given these narratives' absence from most discussions of the various literary canons.[11] The comparative approach taken here, juxtaposing Alexander material with contemporary works in a variety of languages, enables important contributions and parallels to be highlighted, such as the intriguing interactions between the *Alexandreis* and the romances of Chrétien de Troyes. Just as importantly, reading in this multi-lingual, cross-generic way is perhaps the closest modern scholars can come to experiencing key aspects of medieval literary culture. An accurate historicist approach, it is also a transnational one, refusing to be limited by post-medieval boundaries of language and nation in its desire (as Adam Nicolson puts it) to 'make the [stories of the] distant past as immediate to us as our own lives'.[12] Whether those 'great stories of long ago' are classical or medieval, history or fiction, Christian or pagan, or (as with Alexander) a complex and wonderful combination of all these things, such a pluralist critical approach enables them not to remain tediously ubiquitous, 'commune', in the 'distant past', but rather to come alive, 'beautiful and painful', in our modern present.[13]

---

[10] *Alexandre*, ed. Armstrong, IV.1556–7.
[11] See the introduction's section on 'Alexander Scholarship' for a discussion of critical approaches to Alexander literature.
[12] Adam Nicolson, *The Mighty Dead: Why Homer Matters* (London, 2014), p.xix. For discussion, see the introduction.
[13] Ibid.

Appendix 1

Chronology of main texts and related material (including manuscripts)[1]

From 3rd century BC	*Alexander Romance*
3rd century BC	earliest Greek version (lost: sometimes known as 'Pseudo-Callisthenes')
1st century AD	Greek version of *Epistola Alexandri ad Aristotelem* (*Letter of Alexander to Aristotle*) (lost)
3rd century AD	earliest extant version of Greek *Alexander Romance*
4th century AD	Julius Valerius, *Res gestae Alexandri Magni* (*The Deeds of Alexander the Great*)
5th century AD	Palladius, *De gentibus Indiae et Bragmanibus* (*On the Brahmins*)
7th/10th century AD	Latin versions of *Letter of Alexander to Aristotle*
AD 700	*Collatio Alexandri et Dindimi* (*The Letter-Conversation of Alexander and Dindimus*)
9th century AD	*Epitome* of Julius Valerius, *Res gestae Alexandri Magni*
10th century AD	Leo the Archpriest, *Nativitas et victoria Alexandri Magni regis* (*The Birth and Victories of King Alexander the Great*) (lost)
10th–13th centuries ad	*Historia de preliis*, J1, J2, and J3 versions (*History of Battles*)

[1] For ease of reference I have grouped different textual versions, as well as related material, under a single heading, in particular for the three main texts discussed (the *Alexander Romance*, *RTC*, and *Roman d'Alexandre*). The chronology is taken from the chapters in this book and also from *The Medieval French Alexander*, ed. Donald Maddox and Sara Sturm-Maddox (New York, 2002), pp.17–19.

late 1st century BC	Pompeius Trogus, *Liber Historiarum Philippicarum* (*Philippic Histories*) (lost)
late 1st century BC	Diodorus Siculus, *Historike bibliotheke* (*Historical Library*), book XVII
AD 14–37	Valerius Maximus, *Factorum ac dictorum memorabilium libri IX* (*Memorable Deeds and Sayings in Nine Books*)
	4th century abridged version by Julius Paris
c. 41–79	Quintus Curtius Rufus, *Historiae Alexandri Magni Macedonis* (*Histories of Alexander the Great of Macedon*)
	Supplemented version (books I and II) before 12th century
45–120	Plutarch, *Life of Alexander* (part of the *Bioi Paralleloi* or *Parallel Lives*)
c. 85/90–c. 160	Arrian, *Anabasis Alexandri* (*Campaigns of Alexander*)
late 2nd century– pre-226/7	Justin's *Epitome* of Pompeius Trogus' *Philippic Histories*, books XI and XII
c. 385–after 418	Orosius, *Historiarum adversum paganos libri VII* (*Seven Books of History against the Pagans*), book III.16–20
c. 1150	*Roman de Thèbes*
1159	John of Salisbury, *Policraticus*
c. 1160	*Roman d'Eneas*
c. 1165	Benoît de Sainte-Maure, *Roman de Troie*
c. 1171–72	Master Thomas, *Roman de Horn*
From 1175	*ROMAN DE TOUTE CHEVALERIE*
1175–1200	Thomas of Kent's text is composed
second quarter of 13th century	Cambridge, Trinity College, MS O.9.34 (1446)
start of 14th century	Paris, BnF, MS français 24364
mid-14th century	Durham Cathedral Library, MS C. IV. 27 B

Appendix 1: Chronology

c. 1176	Chrétien de Troyes, *Cligès*
1180	Walter of Châtillon, *Alexandreis* (text written during later 1170s)
From 1110	*ROMAN D'ALEXANDRE*
c. 1110–25	Alberic of Besançon (fragmentary)
1160–70	*Decasyllabic Alexander* (lost in original form)
c. 1170	Eustache, *Fuerre de Gadres* (lost in original form)
c. 1170	Lambert le Tort, *Alexandre en Orient* (lost in original form)
c. 1170	*Mort d'Alexandre* (fragmentary)
after 1180	Alexandre de Paris' version (here known as *Roman d'Alexandre*)
1183–90	Joseph of Exeter, *Ylias*
1184	John of Hauville, *Architrenius*
pre-1189, revised c. 1216	Gerald of Wales, *De instructione principum* (*On the Instruction of Princes*)
late 13th/early 14th century	*Kyng Alisaunder*
late 13th/early 14th century	*Of Arthour and of Merlin*
late 13th/early 14th century	*The Seege or Batayle of Troye*
1331–40	The Auchinleck Manuscript (Edinburgh, NLS, MS Advocates' 19.2.1)
first quarter of 15th century	London, Lincoln's Inn, MS 150
second half of 15th century	London, British Library, MS Harley 525

Appendix 2

Summaries of the principal medieval texts discussed (in order of appearance in this book)

Walter of Châtillon, Alexandreis

The *Alexandreis* is an account of Alexander the Great's life and achievements in ten books, which broadly follows the known historical narrative. It is dedicated to Walter's patron, William of Champagne (also known as 'William of the White Hands') and begins with Alexander as a young man, although it does not include *enfances*. In book I, Alexander is taught wisdom and good governance by Aristotle (unsurprisingly one of the most-copied sections of the poem in medieval manuscripts) before taking up his crown at Corinth after his father's death. After a stand-off with a reluctant Athens is resolved peacefully, Alexander destroys rebellious Thebes, despite the pleadings of the poet Cleades. Since Greece is now subdued, Alexander prepares to head to Persia to attack Darius. A description of Asia follows, including an anachronistically Christian reference to Jerusalem. Alexander visits the site of Troy and makes a sacrifice at Achilles' tomb, wishing for similarly lasting renown. There Alexander recounts a dream in which he is told by a mysterious priest that he will conquer every race, but to spare Jerusalem. After the sack of Tyre, he visits the holy city and enriches it. In book II, Darius, who is portrayed as softened by luxury, hears of Alexander's approach, and sends him deliberately insulting childish gifts in reference to his youth (a harness and a ball). Alexander reinterprets these as signs of his harnessing of the Persians and future domination of the earth. He defeats Darius' troops under Mennon at Granicus, and enters the city of Gordium, where he cuts the Gordian knot. Alexander then advances into Cilicia, sending his subordinate Parmenion to secure Tarsus. Here he swims in the freezing river Cignus in midsummer heat, and becomes seriously ill, finally being cured by his doctor Philip despite letters warning him that Philip intends to poison him. The unfair death of Sisenes, one of Alexander's commanders, at the Macedonian's command, is briefly mentioned. Darius refuses advice to retreat, and makes a stirring speech to his men. Troops on both sides prepare for battle; Alexander likewise makes a speech. Darius' shield is described, on which is pictured the history of the Persians, another frequently copied and commentated on aspect of the poem.

The battle of Issus starts in book III. Individual combats of Greeks and Persians are described in detail. Seeing that the Greeks are winning, Darius flees from the battlefield, and his forces collapse. The Greeks loot and commit rape, but save the women of the Persian royal house, which leads to a brief proleptic aside about Alexander's future fall from virtue. Parmenion takes Damascus. Alexander destroys Tyre and then Gaza before travelling to Ammon's shrine in Libya. He then continues further into Asia, finding towns razed to prevent their conquest. Alexander crosses the Tigris and camps at Arbela, where his troops rebel at their long journey and hardship, but are talked round by ancient Aristander. In book IV, Darius' wife Stateira dies. Darius discovers this and is devastated, suspecting Alexander to have raped and killed her, but is told the Macedonian has treated her with courtesy. He sends an embassy to Alexander offering peace, including marriage with his daughter and control of the lands between the Euphrates and the Hellespont. Alexander summons an assembly to discuss the offer. Parmenion is in favour of accepting it, but Alexander refuses, saying he wants fame and honour, not wealth. Alexander buries Stateira with dignity in a tomb specially carved by the Jew Apelles, which is covered with stories from the Old Testament, another frequently excerpted part of the poem. The Greeks and Persians prepare once more for battle. Alexander passes a sleepless night until the goddess Victory sends Sleep to him. Alexander oversleeps, but his generals are afraid to wake him; eventually, Parmenion does so. Alexander prepares his troops for battle.

Book V begins with the battle of Gaugamela. Individual combats on both sides are described in detail, as is the intervention of the goddess Bellona, who tells Alexander that he will not kill Darius, who has another fate. Alexander ignores her and focuses on Darius anyway. The Persians are routed and Darius flees, pursued by Alexander. Arbela is sacked, and Babylon is handed over to Alexander by the Persians themselves, without Darius' approval. Alexander enters in triumph, compared by the poet apparently favourably to previous Roman heroes. The middle of the poem ends with another anachronistic reference to the possibility of a contemporary king like Alexander, who would create a Christian empire under the guidance of William of Champagne.

Book VI marks a shift in Alexander, as he is depicted as corrupted by Babylonian luxury and beginning a descent from his previous lofty virtue. Initially he makes sensible decisions about conquered towns and goods, however. He takes Susa and marches against the Uxii, but spares the city at Darius' mother Sisigambis' request. Alexander burns Persepolis, partly in vengeance for mutilated captive Macedonians he has encountered en route. He offers these men resettlement in Greece or elsewhere, and there is long debate. Darius hears that Alexander is still chasing him, and he flees to the capital of Media, where he tries to rouse his troops to battle once again. His advisers Bessus and Narbazanes, however, first try unsuccessfully to persuade him to abdicate, and then plot to kill him. Darius is warned, but refuses to believe it. Book VII opens with Darius despairingly wondering what to do, pondering upon Fortune, and he tries to commit suicide but is prevented.

Bessus and Narbazanes hear that Darius is dead, and when they find him alive they take him prisoner. Alexander is horrified at this news, and presses forward harder, aiming to rescue Darius. The two plotters hear Alexander's approach and attack Darius and his household, leaving them for dead. The Greeks arrive and Alexander searches for Darius, whom he finds at the point of death. Darius, not realizing who the Macedonian is, sends a message of thanks to Alexander for his mercy to his family, and asks him to punish his murderers. Alexander weeps at Darius' death, and vows to avenge him. He buries the Persian and marks his grave with a pyramid built by Apelles, on which is balanced a crystal globe with each country described and depicted (another often-copied part of the text). After this, Alexander's men hope to return to Greece; he is horrified and summons the leaders to a council, claiming the need to find and punish Bessus and Narbazanes is paramount. His rhetoric convinces them.

In book VIII, Alexander is visited by Talestris, queen of the Amazons, who demands a son or daughter from him, judging that such a child would be a great ruler. She stays for two weeks and leaves pregnant, in a minimally described episode. Bessus regroups, having usurped the throne; Alexander, furious, mobilizes his sluggish army by burning all the wealth gained from their conquests, including his own, and sets off in pursuit. A plot against Alexander devised by his own men is discovered, and Philotas, son of Parmenion, is accused, one of his finest leaders. Philotas makes a passionate speech declaring his innocence, but is then tortured and confesses. He is thought to be innocent, but is killed anyway; Alexander's role here is left ambiguous. Bessus is captured and tortured before being executed. Alexander moves further east towards Scythia, and meets a Scythian messenger who rebukes him for his hubris, to no effect. Alexander subdues Scythia, inspiring fear in other lands, who submit willingly to him. His mercy is still a major feature. Book IX sees Alexander enter India and seek out its ruler Porus. There are skirmishes around the river Hydaspes as Alexander plans how to cross. Having done so, the Greeks attack the Indians, who have war elephants; despite these, the latter are put to flight, including Porus, although not before killing Bucephalus, Alexander's much-loved horse. Alexander catches up with a badly wounded Porus, who offers to serve him in recognition of his achievements, and is honoured by the Macedonian. Alexander is still not satisfied, however, and pushes further east, subduing yet more peoples and countries. This involves a battle against the city of the Sudracae in which Alexander is cut off from his men, surrounded, and nearly killed. He is badly wounded and yet refuses to allow himself time to recover, even at the request of his men, claiming he wants to conquer the whole world and then the world beyond. He sets off to sail towards the Ocean.

In book X, this desire for dominion alarms Nature, who heads to the underworld to save her creation from Alexander. She goes to Leviathan, who transforms from snake to man as he was before the Fall, and asks him for help against Alexander, who is a threat to his realm also. Leviathan agrees and summons a council, in which Treachery offers to poison Alexander at the hand of Antipater, a Macedonian commander, and all agree. Alexander, having sailed to the Ocean, prepares to return to Babylon and is planning new conquests of Europe. Many countries, including Carthage, Africa, Spain, and Gaul, and German tribes, submit to him to avoid battle. In Babylon their embassies arrive, and he decides to attack Rome, which has turned away from allegiance to him. Portents suggest imminent disaster, and Alexander is poisoned. His army troops past him as he lies dying, and he claims to be summoned now to rule the heavens. He leaves his kingdom to the best of them, and gives his ring to Perdicas as he dies. There is great mourning. The poem ends with a reflection on the mutability of fortune and the pointlessness of worldly glory, with Alexander as the ultimate example, and a valediction to William of Champagne.

Joseph of Exeter, Ylias

The *Ylias* tells the story of the Trojan War and its immediate aftermath in six books, mainly based on Dares Phrygius. The Prologue asks for divine aid and repudiates Homer and Virgil as inappropriate poetic models in a Christian age before praising Joseph's patron, Baldwin, Archbishop of Canterbury. The first book begins with the Argonauts, led by Jason and including Hercules, sailing to Colchis to seek the Golden Fleece. En route they stop at Troy, and are seen as a threat by the Trojans under their king Laomedon, and are sent away. Angrily, the Greeks leave and plot revenge. Jason gains the Golden Fleece and returns to the Peloponnese. King Pelias, who sent him to fetch it hoping he would die in the attempt, is angry at his return. Meanwhile, Hercules broods on the perceived insult offered to him by Troy, and resolves to attack the country. A Greek fleet sails to Troy and the Greeks and Trojans fight. The Greeks gain the city as Laomedon attacks their ships; he is killed by Hercules. The city is destroyed, and many of the king's women, including his daughter Hesione, are taken as slaves to Greece. Priam, his son, is away, however, and returns to lamenting and destruction. He rebuilds the city, which is described at some length, along with the surrounding countryside.

Book II opens with Priam prospering materially, but, tormented by Allecto, he cannot rest until Hesione is regained. He sends Antenor as a messenger to the Greeks asking for her return. Hesione's wedding to Telamon is described, which she views as rape. Antenor arrives and asks for her return, but Telamon refuses. Antenor returns to Troy, where Paris insists on setting out to rescue Hesione, claiming that as the gods have already shown him favour he will succeed. In support of this, he tells the story of the Judgement of Paris, which he depicts as a dream. Venus offered him a Spartan bride as his prize for choosing her, so Paris claims that this journey to Greece is part of his divine destiny. Book III sees Priam and the Trojans sacrificing to Venus, asking for Hesione's return. Helenus, another of Priam's sons, prophesies disaster for Troy as a result of Paris' journey, but he is overruled by Aeneas. Panthus also predicts disaster, more convincingly, but Priam insists on Paris' mission to rescue Hesione, encouraged by Antenor. The Trojan fleet sets sail, even as Cassandra also prophesies doom. Priam instructs Paris to reclaim Hesione only. Paris arrives at Mycenae to find Helen alone, as Menelaus is away. The two fall in love, aided by Paris' wealth, and leave Mycenae that night, Helen a willing participant, whilst the Greeks rob the city. Paris and Helen sail for Troy, where they are greeted rapturously, and Priam hopes to exchange Helen for Hesione. Cassandra screams that Helen will bring doom to Troy, but is imprisoned. The Greeks, outraged at Helen's kidnap, gather and prepare for war. Castor and Pollux, Helen's brothers, are drowned en route, enabling Joseph to append a short discussion of the futility of pagan beliefs about divinity, comparing this to the Britons' hope for Arthur's return.

Book IV begins with the Trojans gathering allies against the Greek threat. Troilus and Hector are the leading lights on the Trojan side. The leaders and main characters of both sides are described in detail, ending with Helen. Achilles and Patroclus seek the Delphic oracle, with a disapproving authorial excursus, and are told the Greeks will win in the tenth year. Calchas also receives the same oracle, and joins forces with the other two. The Greeks set sail, but the weather is against them, so on Calchas' advice they stop at Aulis and make sacrifices. The weather turns fair, and they sail to Troy. The Greeks destroy Tenedos and send an embassy of Ulysses and Diomedes to the Trojans to demand reparations and Helen's return. Meanwhile, Achilles plunders the nearby land of Mysia, fights its king, Teuthras, and kills him. His richly decorated tomb is described. Ulysses returns and tells the Greeks that the Trojans have refused their demands.

In book V the fighting begins. The Greeks, sailing close to Troy at night, attack at dawn, after a rousing speech from Agamemnon. The Trojans, led by Hector, rush out of the city's gates to join battle. Many on both sides are killed, including Patroclus. A truce of two years is agreed while each side recovers, but during this time the Greek leaders begin to disagree amongst themselves. The fighting resumes, and the Greeks are hard pressed by Hector. Paris and Menelaus fight, but the former is rescued by Hector, amidst great general bloodshed. Another three-year truce is agreed, against Hector's will, and once again the fighting restarts. Andromache dreams of blood and death, and begs Hector not to fight, bringing their baby son Astyanax to help persuade him. Hector pauses, but the Greeks gain courage in his absence, so he takes the field. Juno and Minerva lend Achilles strength to attack Hector, and Achilles kills him. He is compared to Henry the Young King, who also died young.

Book VI begins with the Trojans mourning Hector's loss. Infighting amongst the Greeks sees Palamedes in charge, with which Agamemnon is content, but which makes Achilles angry. The fighting resumes, but is followed by a year's truce. Achilles sees the Trojan women mourning and falls in love with Polyxena, Priam's daughter. He secretly offers to withdraw from the battle if he can marry her. Priam makes a bargain that Achilles can marry Polyxena if open war ends. Achilles tries to persuade the Greeks to stop fighting and to return home; they prepare to do so, but then more supplies arrive and morale is boosted. Battle is rejoined, without Achilles. Palamedes is killed, and the Greeks are pushed back to their ships, which the Trojans burn. Still Achilles refuses to fight. Troilus' prowess causes even more destruction. Ulysses, Nestor, and Diomedes try to persuade Achilles to join the conflict, unsuccessfully. The Greeks debate a truce, but Menelaus refuses to countenance it. Troilus continues to slaughter Greeks mercilessly, so Achilles allows his Myrmidons into the fight. The battle reaches Achilles' tent, and he is wounded by Troilus but kills him in return. Achilles rages throughout the battle and chases the Trojans back to the city.

Hecuba mourns Troilus and plots her revenge. She arranges to meet Achilles in secret to arrange his marriage to Polyxena, but he is ambushed by Paris at Hecuba's command and killed after a fierce fight. The Greeks, distraught, debate whether to leave or stay. Calchas tells them that Achilles' son Pyrrhus will win the war, so the fighting continues, and Paris and Ajax kill one another. Helen contemplates suicide. Penthesilea aids the Trojans, but is ultimately killed by newly arrived Pyrrhus, and the Trojans flee. They debate returning Helen to the Greeks in order to gain peace, strongly pressed by Antenor and Aeneas, but Priam is suspicious of these two and plans to continue. Antenor and Aeneas plot to betray Troy and inform the Greeks, who are suspicious in turn, but finally believe them. At night the Greeks, led by Pyrrhus, are let into the city, and slaughter its inhabitants, burning it as they go. Priam is killed and Hecuba laments over his body. The Greeks sack the town and prepare to sail home, but Pyrrhus realizes that Polyxena has not been found; she has been hidden by Aeneas. The latter is exiled as punishment, but Antenor is made king. Aeneas tries to find allies to oppose this, but ultimately wanders in exile before founding what will become Rome. The Greeks' various returns are described, several killed by their wives, and Ulysses' wanderings are briefly mentioned until he is killed by Circe's son. Helen is returned to Mycenae, and all Europe visits her as an infamous marvel. The work ends with an announcement that Joseph will now compose a poem about the Crusades, specifically the battle for Antioch.

Alexandre de Paris, Roman d'Alexandre

The *Roman d'Alexandre* was compiled around 1180 from extant French texts that were reworked into a different form (see appendix 1). It is usually divided into four branches for ease, since it is extremely long. Branch ɪ covers Alexander's *enfances*, Branch ɪɪ describes his victories against Darius, king of the Persians, Branch ɪɪɪ depicts his adventures in India and the East, and Branch ɪᴠ narrates his death and burial.

Branch ɪ (157 *laisses*) begins with a prologue in which Alexandre de Paris discusses the importance of telling stories for the benefit of the laity, and decries envious poets. It then describes Alexander's birth, surrounded by celestial omens, and his youthful prowess and tutoring by Aristotle. Alexander kills the sage Nectanebus for claiming he is Alexander's father. He tames and rides Bucephalus, and is dubbed a knight. He defeats king Nicholas of Caesarea and chooses twelve favoured companions, or 'peers'. Meanwhile, his father Philip has cast off Olympias, Alexander's mother, and is intending to remarry; Alexander is furious at the perceived slight on his honour and puts a stop to it. Darius, king of the Persians, sends insulting letters and toys to Alexander in anger at Nicholas' defeat, and Alexander resolves to defeat him. Alexander's tent is described at length. The Greeks set out and conquer La Roche Orgueilleuse, a kingdom on a high mountain. Alexander swims in a cold river and becomes ill, but recovers. He discovers an enchanted mountain that induces cowardice as it is climbed. Alexander besieges Tarsus and destroys it, but then is so pleased by a musician's playing that he gives him the town and helps to restore it. He then besieges Tyre, building a castle in the sea in front of the city to blockade it.

Branch II (149 *laisses*) begins with Alexander sending troops under the peer Emenidus to attack the army of Betis de Gadres, which is destroyed after hard fighting. The castle in front of Tyre is also destroyed, but Alexander manages to build another tower on a bridge, and ultimately takes the city and kills its duke. He then conquers the city of Gadres before crossing Syria and reaching Jerusalem, which he intends to destroy but is so impressed with the humility of the people and the power of the priests, who provide him with the Jewish Law given to Moses, that he spares the city and guarantees its future status and safety. He continues his pursuit of Darius, who sends him more insulting presents and letters before offering him a peace deal, which Alexander haughtily refuses against the peer Perdicas' advice. The Greeks and Persians fight a bloody, long battle. Darius is badly wounded and flees, leaving his family and treasure behind. Alexander treats Darius' family with great courtesy, but soon afterwards the latter's wife dies, to Alexander's great grief as well as Darius' own. Darius is so impressed with Alexander's magnanimity that he wishes the two were not enemies. Alexander prepares to follow Darius once more.

Branch III is the longest branch, with 457 *laisses*. It starts with Aristotle giving Alexander much wise advice. Darius, abandoned by his men, is killed by treacherous servants, but as he is dying he summons Alexander and offers him his daughter as wife. Alexander weeps at Darius' death and buries him with honour before capturing and executing his killers. Alexander lists his achievements so far, and says that he wishes to travel under the sea, building a glass submarine in which to do so against his men's wishes, who are terrified he will die. He watches the fish and draws morals from their habits. He then attacks the Indian king Porus and defeats him for the first time. Alexander then enters Porus' city and is amazed by its wealth and marvels. After this, he sets out across the vast Indian deserts, which causes his men great suffering. The army suffers terrible thirst, and Alexander in solidarity refuses water. En route they are attacked numerous times by various savage animals, including hippopotami, snakes, lions, rhinoceros, and other fantastical creatures, before they finally reach the end of the desert. Alexander, still in pursuit of Porus, plays a trick on him by disguising himself as a messenger and telling Porus that Alexander is an old man. The two sides fight again, and Porus is defeated; he surrenders, and Alexander grants him his territories back, entering into an alliance with him. Alexander then builds a wall to enclose Gog and Magog in the mountains of Tus. He lectures Porus about the qualities of a good king. The army then travels to the bounds of Hercules before losing its way and encountering a valley which to enter is death. Alexander insists upon exploring it himself, braving earthquakes and dragons. He reaches the end but cannot find a way out until he enters a cave and helps a demon, who shows him the exit. The army is overjoyed. After this, they reach the Ocean, where they encounter mermaids. Alexander is then led towards three fountains, one giving youth, one immortality, and one resurrection. Only the first person to bathe can benefit from these gifts, so Alexander forbids anyone to do so; however, when the fountain of immortality is reached, a lord called Enoch does so, and Alexander shuts him up in a pillar as punishment. Travelling on, the army suffers from the heat, and is attacked by dog-headed men, finally reaching the Ocean at the edge of the world. Terrible extremes of weather are attributed to divine anger. Alexander meets two ancient Indians who offer to show him the way to the prophetic Trees of the Sun and Moon. En route, the army reaches a forest full of beautiful women who can take the form of flowers. They reach the Fountain of Youth, which comes from one of the rivers of Paradise, and the ancient Antigonus is rejuvenated. Alexander reaches the Trees, and at dawn and dusk they speak, telling Alexander that he will never return to his home, dying instead in Babylon, but that he will never be defeated nor overcome. He returns to India, where he finds that Porus has rebelled against him. They fight in single combat, and Porus kills Bucephalus before himself being killed by Alexander.

Divinuspater and Antipater are summoned to Babylon and begin to plot Alexander's death by poison. Meanwhile, Alexander's fame reaches queen Candace, who falls madly in love with him, sending rich gifts; Alexander assures her of his affection. Candace sends an artist to paint Alexander on the sly. Her son, mistaking Ptolemy for Alexander, asks for help to rescue his kidnapped wife; Alexander, posing as Antigonus, does so, and goes to meet Candace. She realizes that 'Antigonus' is Alexander because of the secret portrait, but keeps quiet until they are alone, when she shows him the picture and charges him with being Alexander. She tells him of her love and desire for an heir from him, and swears to keep his secret. The two swear oaths to one another despite the realization of Candace's youngest son that 'Antigonus' is Alexander. Alexander takes his leave and heads to Babylon, where he will die. On the way, he passes through a country full of griffons, and decides to harness some to a special box so he can ascend into the sky and see the world, the planets, the zodiac, and the whole universe, which he wants to dominate. He flies so high that the sun's heat begins to burn him before returning to earth. He then calls his barons and says he has conquered the whole world except for Babylon, which is his next goal. He travels to the city, which defies him, and fights a first long and bloody battle with the emir of Babylon's army (similar in detail to the Gadres episode in Branch II). A second lengthy battle begins, which describes the feats of leaders on both sides before Alexander kills the emir. He buries the Babylonian in a beautiful tomb, which is described at length. Alexander takes the city but assures its inhabitants of safety. He visits the Tower of Babel and plans his coronation as master of the entire world, but it is pointed out to him that he has not yet conquered the Amazons. Alexander sets off for their land. Meanwhile, the queen of the Amazons dreams of an approaching eagle that will snatch her own peacocks; she consults with a diviner, who interprets this as a military threat from a great king, and advises her to place her country under his rule to avoid its destruction. The queen agrees, and hears of Alexander's arrival. She sends messengers to him with gifts to assure him of tribute, but Alexander is so impressed with their beauty and mien that he renounces it. He returns to Babylon, where envoys from all countries await him. Olympias warns him of Divinuspater's and Antipater's plotting, and he summons them to Babylon to answer the charge. They are angry and afraid and decide definitely to poison him, arriving in the city the night before Alexander's coronation.

Branch IV opens with a prodigious birth of a monster, which signifies Alexander's imminent death. Divinuspater and Antipater offer the tribute they have brought as a sign of good faith and Alexander gives them gifts in return. The celebrations begin, with Roxane, Alexander's wife, also present. Alexander, feasting, drinks the poison; he realizes something is wrong and asks for a feather to make him sick. The feather, however, is also poisoned. Alexander knows he is dying and is grieved by the cries of his men. Roxane begs him to live for her sake and that of her unborn child. He speaks to the men, saying he will give them a lord of their own choice; they ask for Perdicas. Alexander then divides his empire among the twelve peers. Feeling death approaching, he asks to be buried at Alexandria, and dies. The laments of Roxane and the twelve peers are described individually. Alexander's body is embalmed and Aristotle pronounces a eulogy before the body is taken to Alexandria, not without argument among the peers, and placed in a wondrous tomb. The work ends with moral reflections on Alexander as an *exemplum* for noble knights, ladies, and wise clerks as well as kings, and with the observation that Fortune is fickle, at least for the poet himself.

Benoît de Sainte-Maure, Roman de Troie

This is another extremely long text, which follows the same narrative as the *Ylias*, based on Dares Phrygius. After a long prologue in which Benoît describes the importance of passing on learning and the intellectual and historical importance of his source, the narrative begins with the story of the Golden Fleece, including an extensive section on the love of Jason and Medea, and the first destruction of Troy. The reconstruction of the city is an opportunity for a long description of its wonders. Priam sends Paris to Greece to seek the return of Hesione, enslaved in the city's first destruction; in the discussion of this mission, Paris tells the story of the Judgement he made between the goddesses Juno, Minerva, and Venus. He reaches Greece and meets Helen, then attacks the Greeks and sails away with her. The pair arrive back at Troy, where Priam marries them, whilst the Greeks summon their forces. Helen's brothers, Castor and Pollux, disappear at sea. Agamemnon is chosen as head of the Greek army. There follow descriptions of each of the main Greek and Trojan protagonists and a list of the Greek ships. Oracles are sought by both Greeks and Trojans from Delphi, and Achilles and Calchas learn that the Greeks will win; the oracle orders Calchas to aid the Greeks. The Greek army sails to Troy after sacrificing to Diana at Aulis. Ulysses and Diomedes are sent to the Trojan city as ambassadors, which allows another description of the city's wonders. Priam rejects the embassy. Achilles ravages Mysia, killing its king, and gaining its future food resources for the Greeks. Hector is placed in charge of the Trojan forces.

The fighting begins, which occupies much of the remaining narrative (twenty-three individual battles in all). Hector kills Patroclus in the second battle; Achilles is devastated. There is a truce whilst both sides bury their dead. Patroclus is placed in a sumptuous tomb. Cassandra prophesies disaster for Troy, which unnerves the Trojans. The third to seventh battles occur, with terrible losses on each side, leading to despondency in both camps, and another truce. Calchas reclaims his daughter Briseida from Troy, who is in love with Troilus. Hector suggests a single combat with Achilles, but is refused. The lovers lament their impending separation, which is followed by a misogynistic discourse and praise of a 'noble dame' thought to be Eleanor of Aquitaine. Briseida goes to the Greek camp and Diomedes declares his love for her; she returns a non-committal answer. Diomedes unhorses Troilus in battle and sends Briseida the latter's horse. Hector is wounded in the eighth battle and during the subsequent truce is sent to recover in the Chamber of Beauties, a visual and sensory marvel that is described at length. Meanwhile, Diomedes' and Briseida's relationship develops; he is in torment for love of her, whilst she toys with him, finally giving him her sleeve as a favour. The ninth and tenth battles take place. Hector's wife Andromache dreams of disaster and tries to persuade Hector not to fight, but he repulses her. Priam forbids him to take part and Hecuba also intervenes. As a last resort, Andromache brings their son with her to plead, to no avail; she begs Priam to help, who forces Hector to stay behind. Troilus and Diomedes fight; Troilus performs great deeds before Achilles intervenes and routs the Trojans. Seeing the panic in the city, Hector rejoins the fighting. He rallies the Trojans and kills several Greeks before Achilles in turn kills him. During another truce, Hector's funeral is marked by the individual laments of Paris, Hecuba, Andromache, and Helen before he is buried in an extraordinary tomb. Agamemnon hands over leadership of the Greek army to Palamedes, which makes Achilles angry. Priam himself takes part in the eleventh battle.

Meanwhile, a year after Hector's death, Achilles sees Polyxena, Hector's sister, at the anniversary memorial and falls desperately in love with her. He sends a message to Hecuba offering to cease fighting and return to Greece if he can marry her. Hecuba speaks to Priam, who agrees despite his doubts. The messenger returns to Achilles saying that if he can get the Greeks to leave Troy, he can marry Polyxena. He summons the Greek leaders and they debate withdrawal but decide to continue. Achilles forbids his men to fight. The twelfth battle sees the death of Palamedes, and the fourteenth the wounding of Diomedes by Troilus, which forces Briseida to realize she loves the former. Achilles is still in agonies of love for Polyxena, but takes part in the eighteenth battle, at which Priam swears Achilles will never marry his daughter. Achilles focuses his agony and hatred upon Troilus, whom he kills in the nineteenth battle. Hecuba, grief-stricken, resolves to be revenged on Achilles, and arranges to meet him secretly at the temple of Apollo to discuss his marriage to Polyxena. There, Paris ambushes him and Antigonus; they resist bravely and kill many Trojans, but are finally killed. The Greeks are devastated and hold a huge funeral, building Achilles an elaborate monument. Polyxena mourns for his loss in secret. The Greeks send Menelaus to search for Achilles' son, Pyrrhus, and the twentieth battle begins, in which Ajax and Paris kill one another. Helen laments despairingly and Paris' tomb is described. The city of Troy is besieged. Here the narrative breaks off to include a description of the world and the country and customs of the Amazons in order to introduce the arrival of Penthesilea, their queen, at Troy. Along with her Amazons she fights in the twenty-first battle, doing great deeds. Pyrrhus arrives and is wounded by Penthesilea in the twenty-second battle before he kills her in the twenty-third and final fight. At this point Benoît discusses Dictys Cretensis, whom he uses as a source for the final part of the tale. The Trojans debate the possibility of peace. Priam is furious with Antenor's and Aeneas' suggestions and plots to kill them; they discover this and increase their own plots to hand over the city to the Greeks. Antenor goes as ambassador to the Greeks and secretly arranges terms to betray Troy; he then persuades the Trojans to hand over goods and treasures to the Greeks supposedly to secure peace. Penthesilea is buried, and Ulysses and Diomedes arrive in the city to conclude peace. Meanwhile Antenor steals the Palladion from the temple of Minerva, the sacred relic that protects Troy, and hands it over to Ulysses. Calchas tells the Greeks to build a wooden horse and to take it to the temple of Minerva, to which Priam, encouraged by Antenor and Aeneas, agrees. Both Greeks and Trojans swear oaths of peace and there is much rejoicing.

The Greeks pretend to depart from Troy. At night, however, they enter the city from the horse and from outside; they massacre the inhabitants and destroy it. Hecuba accuses Aeneas of treachery. Menelaus searches for Helen; Andromache and Cassandra are taken alive by the Greeks and guarded, unhurt. Discussions about Helen's fate go on for three days, but finally she is restored to Menelaus rather than being executed. Agamemnon is desperate for Cassandra. Antenor begs for mercy for Andromache and Helenus, both of whom opposed the war, which is granted. A storm prevents the Greeks from leaving, which Calchas interprets as the unquiet soul of Achilles demanding vengeance. Polyxena, as the reason for his death, is sought out and sacrificed to appease him. Hecuba is stoned to death. The Greeks argue over possession of the Palladion, which is finally given to Ulysses. The Greek leaders' various returns are narrated, including Ulysses' death at the hands of his son by Circe, Telegonus. The work ends with a short epilogue warning against its denigration by envious and inferior poets.

Chrétien de Troyes, Cligès

Cligès is set in an Arthurian world. It begins with a well-known prologue in which the poet lists his previous works, claims his source is a book found in a church at Beauvais, and describes the movement of learning over time. The narrative proper starts with the two sons of the emperor of Greece and Constantinople, the elder called Alexander and the younger Alis. Alexander travels to Britain to win renown and knighthood at Arthur's court. With a group of noble companions he travels to Winchester and impresses the king and his court with his bearing. Alexander asks to serve king Arthur and ultimately to be knighted by him. He does well and is extremely generous. He travels to Brittany with the king and falls in love with the queen's maiden Sordamour, Gawain's sister, who, unbeknownst to him, has fallen for him too. Their mutual yet unshared anguish lasts for months until Arthur hears of the treachery of his regent, count Angrès, and returns to London. Alexander is given a shirt sewn by Sordamour with a golden hair from her head on it instead of thread, but is unaware of this. Arthur attacks the count's forces by the Thames, and Alexander does the best in the battle. He is rewarded by Arthur with more men under his command and a kingdom in Wales. The queen realizes Alexander is wearing the shirt with Sordamour's hair embroidered on it, and realizes at the pair's reactions to this information that they are in love. Meanwhile, the rebels make a foray into Arthur's camp but are thrown back. Alexander sees the count fleeing back to the castle by a secret way, and tells his companions to switch armour with the dead rebels in order to trick their way in. The stratagem works, and the Greeks gain the castle and start to attack. Alexander fights the count and defeats him, taking him prisoner; he sends him and the other rebels to Arthur, who rewards him with a precious cup. Alexander wants to ask for Sordamour's hand, but is afraid that she will be angry even though he knows Arthur will grant it. He visits the queen as usual, who reveals to each that the other loves them, and tells them to marry. The marriage takes place at Windsor, and Sordamour is soon pregnant. She gives birth to a son, Cligès.

During this time, the emperor of Greece and Constantinople has died. Messengers are sent to Britain to recall Alexander, but they are all drowned in a shipwreck save one, who wishes the younger son Alis to be the new ruler. The messenger returns, saying that Alexander has been drowned, so that Alis takes the throne. Alexander learns of this and sets out for his home, leaving his wife and son behind, to reclaim his crown, but by choice without a great army. The brothers agree that Alis will keep the title and crown, but that Alexander will rule; the latter is not wholly pleased, but consents on condition that Alis never marries and that after him all will go to Cligès. The arrangement prospers.

Some years later, Alexander realizes that he is dying, and tells his son to test himself under a different name at Arthur's court, particularly against his uncle, Gawain. Alexander and Sordamour both die, and to begin with Alis keeps his promise not to marry. However, he is constantly pressured by his counsellors to do so, and eventually he agrees to seek to marry the emperor of Germany's daughter, Fenice. The marriage is arranged, but as the girl is already promised to the duke of Saxony the German emperor asks Alis to send an army to escort her. Cligès goes with the army, and when Fenice sees him, they exchange loving looks by which they effectively make vows to be true to one another. Meanwhile, the duke of Saxony sends his nephew to demand Fenice. The young man challenges Cligès to combat, and the Greeks win the day, with Cligès performing extraordinary feats. Fenice's nurse Thessala realizes the girl is in love. Fenice is anguished that she cannot marry Cligès but is promised to his uncle Alis, and, whilst refusing to be like Iseult, is determined not to give her body to Alis even if they marry, particularly in order not to bear a child that would cheat Cligès of his future throne. Thessala, who is skilled in magic, promises to make a potion for Alis, so that he will not be able to sleep with her but will dream that he has done so. The marriage between Alis and Fenice takes place, and Thessala prepares the potion. She asks Cligès to serve it to Alis, hinting that it may do Cligès himself some future good. Alis drinks it and sleeps soundly all night, convinced that he is making love to Fenice.

In the meantime, the spurned duke of Saxony assembles an army and mans his borders, determined to prevent Alis from taking Fenice back to his kingdom. The Germans and Greeks camp by the Danube near the Black Forest. The Saxons are close by keeping watch; they see Cligès riding out hunting and the duke of Saxony's nephew ambushes him, wounding Cligès slightly. Cligès, however, kills the young man and chases after the Saxons alone back to their camp, where the duke has just learned of his nephew's death and offers a rich reward for Cligès' head. Cligès, seeing the army, turns back to seek his companions, who have gone to mobilize the army, when he is overtaken by a Saxon; they fight and the Saxon is killed. Cligès puts on his armour as a disguise. He then sees both armies on the move and heads for the Saxons, followed by the Germans and Greeks, carrying the dead Saxon's head on his spear. Both sides assume that the head belongs to Cligès, and rush towards him. Cligès shouts defiance at the Saxons, who are stunned to see him alive; Alis rejoices. Cligès fights the Saxon duke and unhorses him. A Saxon spy then realizes that the Greek/German camp has been left unguarded, and offers to go and snatch Fenice, which is achieved. However, she is single-handedly rescued by Cligès. Both Cligès and Fenice are tongue-tied and remain silent despite their feelings. The enraged duke of Saxony challenges Cligès to combat. In a fierce fight Cligès triumphs, and the duke, shamed, leaves with his army.

The Greeks travel to Constantinople, and Cligès requests permission to visit Britain. Alis denies him initially, but then agrees and sends him away with many treasures. When Cligès goes to bid Fenice farewell, she weeps copiously and he turns pale and also sheds tears. Fenice torments herself, debating whether he loves her or not. Meanwhile Cligès arrives at Wallingford, where he fights in a tournament, each day wearing differently coloured armour so that no-one knows who he is. He defeats Sagremor, Lancelot, and Perceval in turn, and people realize that a single knight is behind this. Gawain is particularly keen to know who the mystery knight is, and the next day the two fight in a fierce but well-matched battle until Arthur calls a halt. Cligès goes to Arthur's court and Arthur asks who he is; the truth is received with much joy, especially by Gawain. Cligès stays with Arthur for a while, but his love for Fenice calls him back to Greece. Alis and Fenice are both thrilled to see him. After a while Fenice plucks up courage to ask if he fell in love with anyone in Britain; he replies that he could not, since he had left his heart in Constantinople. She replies that hers travelled to Britain, and they both realize the truth. Fenice explains the effects of Thessala's potion, and they discuss what they should do. Fenice is desperate not to be like Iseult, so she rejects Cligès' suggestion of exile in Britain in favour of her plan of faking death with Thessala's help and living in a secret place with Cligès. Cligès asks a builder, John, to construct a secret place for them. Thessala agrees to help and mixes a potion that gives the appearance of death. Fenice pretends to be ill, refusing doctors, and ultimately seems to die. Unfortunately for her, three doctors from Salerno are suspicious, and subject her to torture to try and prove that she is alive. The women of Constantinople, however, charge the palace and throw the doctors to their deaths out of the window. Fenice is buried in the tomb that Cligès conveniently has had built, and at night he comes to rescue her. The potion's effects wear off, but she is still weak from the torture. Thessala cures her, however, and the two live in secluded bliss for over a year.

One day, a Thracian knight called Bertrand wanders close to the tower in search of a lost hawk, and sees Fenice and Cligès asleep in the orchard, naked. Fenice wakes up, sees Bertrand, and screams, confirming that she is indeed the empress. Cligès attacks him, but Bertrand escapes and tells Alis. Alis goes to the tower, but the couple have fled; he threatens John the builder, who defiantly retorts that although Cligès may have wronged the emperor, Alis himself has broken his promise not to marry, and that he has never actually slept with Fenice but has been enchanted. Alis sends out search parties, but Cligès and Fenice escape and reach Arthur in Britain. At Cligès' complaint of Alis' broken promise, Arthur sends him to Constantinople with an army to take the throne by force if necessary. On the way, however, Cligès encounters messengers who report that his uncle Alis has died of grief. Fenice and Cligès return to Greece and are married and crowned. However, Chrétien ends by claiming that Fenice's behaviour in deceiving Alis is the reason that later empresses are kept in close confinement.

Thomas of Kent, Roman de toute chevalerie

This Alexander romance, initially composed in the same period as the *Roman d'Alexandre*, is half the latter's considerable length but follows the same basic narrative structure. Despite this overall similarity, the poem spends more time describing Alexander's *enfances* and contains fewer fantastical adventures. It begins with a prologue describing the world as a place of suffering and the narrative in contrast as one of life's few pleasures, cheering the good-hearted and making the envious feel pain. The story proper begins with the magician Nectanebus' exile in Macedonia and his desire for the beautiful queen Olympias, whom he deceives into sleeping with him in the belief that he is the god Amon in the form of a dragon, and with whom he conceives Alexander. He also sends the king, Philip, a dream in which a dragon makes Olympias pregnant with a future powerful emperor who will avenge Philip's own death. Omens and portents accompany Alexander's birth. He is brought up and educated as befits a prince. He kills Nectanebus by pushing him into a ditch, on the grounds that he ought to have foreseen his own death; Nectanebus, dying, tells Alexander he is his real father, and Alexander, after telling Olympias the truth, buries the magician with honour. At this time, Philip, worried about who will inherit his kingdom, is told by the gods that the one who can ride Bucephalus, the man-eating horse, will be his heir. Alexander, now fourteen, does so, and Philip publically acknowledges him as a king.

At fifteen, Alexander is knighted. He is insulted by Nicholas, king of Elim, and Alexander fights against the latter's forces, destroying his city. Back in Greece, Philip repudiates Olympias and marries Cleopatra, but Alexander, arriving, starts a fight and sends Cleopatra and her retinue away, exhorting Philip to be reconciled with Olympias. After defeating the city of Mathona, Alexander receives a message from Darius, king of the Persians, asking for tribute and submission; Alexander angrily defies him. Meanwhile, Pausanias, a young Trojan, falls in love with Olympias and kidnaps her, mortally wounding Philip, who manages nonetheless to kill Pausanias in his turn, being given a sword by the newly arrived Alexander. As Philip dies, he reminds Alexander of the prophecy at his birth indicating he would avenge his father, saying he now knows it was true. Alexander buries him in a sumptuous monument. As king, Alexander immediately sends messages to tributary kings as far as Assyria, claiming overlordship; all are wise enough to accept him. He travels to Tarsus and Sicily and receives their submission before taking Lombardy and Egypt. He is crowned on his birthday at Tripoli, and finds a statue of Nectanebus, which he honours. Alexander founds cities named after himself in Egypt and Syria, and then besieges Tyre, whilst receiving a message of non-intervention from Jerusalem, which angers him greatly. [The taking of Tyre itself is not in any extant manuscript, and has probably been lost during copying.] The narrator then provides an excursus on the proper way to write history.

After this, Darius, king of Persia, receives Alexander's defiant answer to his earlier request for tribute and submission and sends insulting presents in reply. Alexander interprets them in response as signs of his future domination, and sets out to find the Persian king. Darius, furious at Alexander's answer, sends a third angry message, and holds a council, as does Alexander. The Greeks and Persians take the battlefield, and the fighting begins, with several individual combats described. The Persians have the worst of it, and Darius takes flight, with Alexander in pursuit. Alexander takes many prisoners and goods from the Persians. In following Darius, he arrives at Thebes, which resists him; after a long and bitter siege, he takes the city and razes it to the ground, killing the inhabitants. Alexander then sends messages to Athens and gains its submission after a long debate, afterwards taking Lacedaemon (Sparta). Meanwhile, Darius is tormented by desire for revenge, and plans military action. Alexander enters Silicia, where he becomes ill after swimming in the river Tigris. His doctor Philip is accused of trying to poison him by Parmenion, but Alexander takes his prescriptions confidently and executes the latter. The Greeks cross the river and battle against the Persians once more, after a skirmish by Ptolemy; Darius flees, leaving his mother, wife, and daughters behind, and takes refuge in a castle. Alexander, pretending to be a messenger, gains entry and meets Darius, seeing the wealth of his court. A third battle between Greeks and Persians takes place, with the same result. Darius, in despair, writes to Alexander offering him vast territories in exchange for his family, and saying he will go into exile. Alexander considers his answer, and Darius in desperation asks Porus of India for help. It is too late, however, as before either can reply, Darius is mortally wounded by treacherous servants. Alexander finds him dying, and Darius begs him for honourable burial and to marry his wife. The Macedonian mourns for him, and takes his embalmed body to Assyria to be buried there. Alexander humiliates and executes Besas and Barzanes, Darius' killers, before he travels to Jerusalem. There he is so impressed with the panoply of Jewish religion that he worships God and spares the city, describing a previous dream of Jewish prophecies about him that have now come true.

Another excursus summarizes Alexander's achievements so far and discusses the narrative's sources before announcing the major remaining points in the story: the travels in India and Alexander's death by poison. Porus and Alexander exchange angry messages and the latter travels east. The Greeks and Indians fight a terrible battle, with war elephants, in which Bucephalus is killed, causing Alexander to leave the battle out of grief and shame. He buries the horse with honour and founds a city in his memory. A truce between the two sides expires, after an episode involving the king of Albania's hunting dogs failing to catch anything, enraging Alexander; the second battle begins. Alexander has the best of it and Porus flees. Alexander captures the city of Faacen, and Porus' palace is described. He then travels deeper into India after hearing of a desert containing many wild beasts, wanting to see marvels as well as to capture Porus. He passes the Caspian Gates and sets out across the desert. Another excursus discusses the sources for this part of the story. A long section describing the various peoples of India follows. The army suffers terrible thirst, and Alexander in solidarity refuses water. They travel on, finding a castle guarded by hippopotami, who attack and eat some of the men; encounters with murderous snakes, dragons, lions, tigers, rhinoceros, and huge mice follow. Finally they reach Baghdad, where Porus has taken refuge. Alexander pretends to be a messenger and talks to Porus himself;

the latter defies Alexander in a letter. The two sides fight once more, and Porus, defeated, surrenders to Alexander, who restores his lands to him.

Alexander then heads further east towards the borders of Hercules, and learns of other strange peoples from an old man. He is keen to reach and conquer the Earthly Paradise, but is eventually dissuaded, since it is ruled not by a man but by God. He turns back and conquers more of India, but at great cost; in a dream an angel shows him a herb that will heal wounds. The army then encounters a variety of strange animals and peoples before experiencing terrible storms that they interpret as divine anger, although they pass once the men pray. Alexander conquers another city, fighting alone and having a narrow escape. After he has thus explored all of India and met the Brahmins, he meets a strange one-footed messenger who tells him about other Indian marvels. The Greek army then heads for Taragonce and Alexander distributes wealth to his followers. The queens of Scythia and the Amazons visit Alexander. He fights his way towards Gog and Magog and besieges them without success. He is distracted from his grief at this failure by an expedition under the sea, where he watches the fish, from which he derives new military ideas. He then dreams that God tells him to wall up Gog and Magog and other hostile people, and he builds a huge wall to do so.

An authorial discussion of the highest mountains of the world follows before Alexander enters Ethiopia, which he conquers in its entirety. Descriptions of its peoples and marvels, especially animals, precede Alexander's visit to a burning mountain, where, after he makes a sacrifice to the gods, a voice tells him he will never return home; he is upset and afraid. Alexander then approaches Albania, where he is met by messengers from its queen Candace offering presents and tokens of love. She commissions a portrait of him. He travels into a dark land, where he learns of the Trees of the Sun and Moon, who reveal the future. Alexander consults them, aided by a high priest, and learns that he will conquer all realms but will never return to Macedonia, instead dying by poison in Babylon the following year. He comforts his companions and swears them to silence. He returns to Faacen and enters Jordan. Porus learns the prophecy of Alexander's death and decides to rebel against him. Alexander meets yet more extraordinary peoples and monsters, and then receives a defiant message of rebellion from Porus; Alexander challenges him to single combat, and after a dramatic battle kills him. The Indians pay him homage. Alexander is now master of Asia, Europe, and a large part of Africa.

Meanwhile, Candace's son Candeulus asks Alexander for help in retrieving his kidnapped wife. Alexander disguises himself as Antigonus and helps Candeulus regain her, and then visits his mother Candace. An authorial discussion of the evils of love follows. Alexander and Candace meet, and she realizes he is not Antigonus but Alexander; she shows him her portrait of him, claiming to be craftier than Alexander himself. The two go to bed. Another of Candace's sons, Caregarus, realizes who Alexander really is and wants to kill him to avenge Porus, but Candace protects him. Alexander takes his leave of her and travels to Babylon, which is described at some length. The king sends out messengers to the whole world summoning its kings to pay tribute. Olympias warns him that Antipater, governor of Greece, intends him harm. Antipater prepares poison and arrives at Babylon. Alexander drinks the poison unknowingly and immediately realizes that his death is imminent. He divides his goods and kingdoms amongst his companions after making a resigned speech, and dies. There are debates and quarrels over where Alexander should be buried, and so they ask the gods, who ordain that Alexandria in Egypt should be his resting place. His body is taken there in a grand procession, and philosophers gather in front of his tomb, contrasting his past glories with his present state and lamenting greatly. The poem ends with a brief mention of the conflicts amongst Alexander's successors and the destruction of more than fifteen kingdoms and their peoples.

Thomas, Roman de Horn

The *Roman de Horn* begins with a prologue naming its author as 'Master Thomas'. The young prince Horn, Aalof's son, is found hidden in a garden with his companions by a Saracen called Malbroin, and is taken to his king Rodmund, who pities them, yet is afraid of their future prowess as he has killed their families. He sets them adrift in a boat, but they are looked after by God and come ashore in Brittany. Herland, seneschal to king Hunlaf, finds them and, learning of their plight, takes them to the king, who greets them kindly. Horn recounts his lineage and his adventures, and the king orders for all the boys to be fostered to his lords, Horn and his friend Haderof living with Herland.

Horn grows up and becomes extremely accomplished, so that the king's daughter Rigmel hears about him. When Horn is sixteen, king Hunlaf holds a feast at Pentecost, which Horn attends, and where he is admired for his beauty. Horn serves as cup-bearer for the king and all talk about him. Rigmel, in her chamber, is intrigued by the conversation and plans to meet Horn. She sends her companion Herselot to ask Herland to visit her, and when he arrives she offers him several gifts, including a cup, horse, and hawk, and in return asks to meet Horn. Herland agrees to bring him the next day, but is worried that Rigmel may have fallen in love with Horn and that Herland will be accused of disloyalty to the king. He resolves to take Haderof instead. Meanwhile, Rigmel cannot sleep, but tosses and turns, realizing she is in love with Horn. Herselot reassures her, saying she has had a dream that Rigmel and Horn will be married, which comforts her. The next day, Herland comes to Rigmel with Haderof, who realizes that she thinks he is Horn but does not wish to expose Herland's trick; fortunately, Rigmel's lady Godswith arrives and greets Haderof by name. Rigmel realizes Herland's plan and is furious, but before she can express this Herland apologizes and says he will bring Horn tomorrow, being too afraid of the king to do so before. The following day, Herselot reports Horn's beauty to Rigmel, who sends her to hasten Herland. The latter arrives with Horn, who sits with Rigmel and hears of her love for him;

he says he is too poor for her, but she counters saying he is of noble birth and that he will regain his inheritance. She gives him a ring, but he refuses to wear it until he is knighted and worthy of her; similarly, he refuses to exchange love promises for the same reason. He leaves, and she wonders if his rejection of her offers is out of pride; Herselot answers that no man has more humility.

Meanwhile, messengers come from two powerful African kings, brothers of Rodmund, called Gudlof and Egolf, who threaten Hunlaf with destruction unless he converts. Horn advocates refusal, and Hunlaf agrees, giving Horn his own armour. A Canaanite, Marmorin, challenges anyone to single combat, and he and Horn fight to defend their respective faiths. Horn kills Marmorin and is made constable by Hunlaf. They prepare for war. Rigmel sends Horn a banner for the forthcoming battle. Horn rides out with the young men only, leaving the older ones on guard, and a fierce fight begins. Horn and Haderof fight valiantly, and the former rescues Herland before winning the entire battle. Horn strips the Saracens' ships of their goods and distributes them fairly before returning in triumph to Hunlaf, who makes him his deputy. Horn challenges those who resist the king's rule, destroying Anjou and strengthening the king's remit throughout his domains.

Rigmel hears of Horn's prowess and summons him, saying that now he is a knight he may wear her ring, which he does. He asks Rigmel to encourage her father to help Horn regain his own kingdom, and then if Hunlaf agrees he will marry her; they swear to be true to one another. However, they are soon separated by treachery, as Horn is traduced by his companion Wikele, who tells Hunlaf that Horn boasted of sleeping with Rigmel and planning never to marry her, and to seize the realm from Hunlaf. The king is sad and angry, and accuses Horn of sleeping with his daughter, demanding an oath to the contrary. Horn offers to prove this false in single combat, saying that such oaths are not the custom in his country; the king insists that Horn must swear or be exiled. Horn takes leave of Herland and goes to Rigmel for the same reason, asking her to wait for seven years for him but no longer. They exchange rings. Horn bids Hunlaf farewell, saying that despite the calumny he will come to his aid if he ever needs it.

Horn, alone, travels to Westir (Ireland), and calls himself Gudmod. He seeks the court of king Gudreche, and en route meets the king's two sons, Egfer and Guffer, hawking. Horn takes service as Egfer's knight and goes to court, where the king asks him his background, which Horn describes, but claims to be a poor noble-man's son. Gudreche thinks he is Aalof's son, however, as he resembles him so closely; Horn denies it. The king's daughter Lenburc notices Horn, and sends him a cup as an indication of love. Horn says she is too hasty, and should wait to see if he is virtuous or not, and that sudden love does not last. Lenburc is embarrassed and loves Horn all the more. She summons a messenger and sends him to Horn's lodgings with offers of greater gifts and her love in return for his; Horn makes the same reply. Lenburc is miserable.

Meanwhile, there are no battles to engage in, but Horn surpasses all others in every sport without being boastful or revealing his own superior skill or knowledge in conversation. After three years of this, Horn is asked to take part in a stone-throwing context with a braggart called Eglaf to defend his lord Egfer's honour; he beats him roundly, and Lenburc sends him more promises of land, which Horn also kindly rejects. A similar competition happens in Lenburc's chamber, playing chess; Horn ends up playing Lenburc and defeating her. She then plays some lays on the harp, ending with one composed for Rigmel by her brother of which she only knows half; Horn, who knows the whole, is asked to perform, and plays the complete work. Lenburc realizes that 'Gudmod' is so skilled that he can in fact only be Horn, who is so renowned. She is in despair and tormented by her love.

Horn is frustrated at the lack of military action in which he can win renown and defend his faith, but then Hildebrant and Herebrant, two more Saracen brothers of the king Rodmund, arrive in Westir with their nephew Rollac, who killed Aalof, Horn's father. Rollac arrives at Dublin and threatens king Gudreche on their behalf, demanding his conversion and tribute, or a single combat against two men. Horn is furious and demands that he fight Rollac. There is a fierce and lengthy battle, in which Horn kills Rollac; he then leads an army to attack the enemy and defeats them, although the king's sons are both killed in the process. Gudreche, having lost both his sons, is distraught and summons his brother-in-law, the king of Orkney. Gudreche wants Horn to marry Lenburc, and consults the king of Orkney, who agrees. They suggest this to Horn, who says he is too low-born to marry a king's daughter, and explains he is promised to a nobleman's daughter in Brittany. At this point a pilgrim arrives who turns out to be lord Herland's son; he is seeking Horn because Wikele has become Hunlaf's seneschal and has expelled Herland, and is also seeking to marry Rigmel to the king of Fenenie, Modin, in a month's time. Horn, pretending to be Gudmod still, says that Rigmel surely would not do such a thing; the pilgrim agrees, but says she is hard pressed. He then admits he is Horn and swears revenge on Wikele. Gudreche, who has heard the whole conversation, tries again to give Horn his kingdom and Lenburc, but Horn again refuses, explaining he has a sweetheart elsewhere. He says he will always protect Gudreche, however. Lenburc hears that Gudmod is Horn, and resolves to become a nun; Gudreche determines to become a monk and leave his kingdom to Horn. Horn advises him not to do so until he returns from his journey to recover his inheritance and gain his revenge upon Wikele.

Horn arrives in Brittany and exchanges clothes with a pilgrim as a disguise. Wikele and the king of Fenenie ride past, talking of Rigmel's great beauty; Horn angrily says they are drunk, and Wikele, thinking he is a poor pilgrim, insults him, although the king suspects he is better born. Horn arrives at the city and is refused entry, but forces his way in. The nobles attend mass and Rigmel's wedding, and then begin to feast; the poor, including Horn, are also present. Rigmel is miserable, thinking of Horn and her broken faith (under compulsion). Following the usual custom, Rigmel herself serves her new husband wine out of a bejewelled horn cup, and then everyone else; on the fifth circuit, Horn stops her and accuses her of missing out the poor. She offers him a drink in a valuable cup, but he does not drink it. She looks at him more closely, and realizes that he does not look like a pilgrim, and then asks him why he does not drink. Horn replies that he will do so if she offers him a drink out of the horned cup she brought to her husband, but says he doubts she will, as she has no love for the man on whose behalf he asks this. Rigmel nearly faints, thinking he is a messenger from Horn, but returns with the horn, into which he puts the ring she gave him on his departure. He drinks, and gives the cup to her; she also drinks from it, and finds the ring. Rigmel recognizes the ring and asks Horn for news about himself, saying she would never leave Horn for the man she has married. Horn replies that he grew up in this land and won a goshawk, which he left safe seven years ago, and he has now returned to see whether it is still valuable and obedient; if so, he promises it will be his. Rigmel laughs joyfully and says she knows who he is, and that the goshawk is safe. Horn says that he is a poor outcast, however, which would be hard for her; she says she does not care, which proves to Horn she is faithful. Horn is conscious that Wikele is watching them, however, and asks her to tell her husband to go out to joust, as is the custom, and Horn will claim her. Horn returns to his ships and his men and prepares for the tournament. Rigmel tells her husband Modin to go out to joust, and calls Haderof, telling him Horn has returned; he, rejoicing, promises to gather Horn's companions and prepare for a fight.

Horn defeats Modin (who is unharmed), and returns to the city with Rigmel and his troops, intending to besiege it if necessary. But Hunlaf, hearing of his return, realizes his own foolishness, and that Horn has both his daughter and Modin. He sends an embassy to Horn, telling him he will do as the latter requests, and that Rigmel's marriage will be dissolved. Horn agrees, and is received back into the city by Hunlaf. Herland is reinstated as seneschal, and Wikele is due to be punished as a traitor, but the barons intercede for him and Horn issues a pardon. Horn and Rigmel marry and there is a great feast.

[Horn then probably gathers his forces and sails back to his birthplace of Suddene, meeting his father's seneschal Hardré, but these *laisses* are missing.] Hardré offers to help Horn, and returns to king Rodmund saying that some strange ships have arrived. Rodmund says he is still afraid of Horn, as he knows now he did not drown, and recently had a dream that he himself was killed by a boar. Hardré dismisses this, so Rodmund reluctantly goes to meet the strangers. Horn ambushes Rodmund's forces, and Rodmund realizes his dream is about to come true. The fighting is fierce, but finally Horn kills him and retakes his own lands, restoring the Christian faith. His mother Samburc, who has been hiding in the forest of Arden and then by the sea, hears of this, and travels to the court, where despite her poor clothing she is recognized by Hardré and reunited with Horn.

Meanwhile, Horn dreams that Rigmel is being drowned by Wikele, and wakes worried that he will try to harm her whilst Horn is away. He leaves for Brittany the next morning, with Suddene in Hardré's care. He finds that Wikele has betrayed his trust again, spending Horn's money and goods, and plotting to marry Rigmel by force. Wikele's brother Wothere, however, warns him against this plan, and, escaping his murderous sibling, warns king Hunlaf, who makes preparations for a siege. Wikele arrives and besieges the city, demanding that Hunlaf release Rigmel to him within a certain time or he will starve the citizens to death. Hunlaf wonders what to do, but the day arrives and he has no choice but to hand over his daughter. Rigmel laments, sure that Horn is not dead, as Wikele claims, but is married to Wikele anyway against her will. Horn arrives during the feasting with his men, who pretend to be songsters and ask to entertain the revellers. Instead, they kill all the traitors, saving Hunlaf's men, and Horn himself kills Wikele. Horn then tells his whole story and feasts for a fortnight. After this, he visits Westir and marries Lenburc to Modin, and Haderof to Lenburc's sister. He then returns to Brittany and has a son, Hadermod, with Rigmel, who is to conquer Africa in future, and then Horn returns to Suddene with his wife, living there for the rest of his days.

Kyng Alisaunder

The text begins with a prologue describing the variety and pain of human experience, and the profit and pleasure that one may gain in hearing about remarkable events. There follows a brief overview of Alexander's narrative before the story proper begins with Nectanebus the skilled astrologer fleeing to Macedonia after learning of a pending attack upon him by Philip of Macedon, and plotting revenge. Nectanebus sees Olympias, Philip's wife, riding through the city, and is amazed by her beauty. She notices him and asks about his origins, at which he indicates he has something to tell her. Later, in her chamber, Olympias asks if it is true that Philip will abandon her for another wife, as she has been warned in a prophecy, and Nectanebus confirms this. He also says that she will bear an extraordinary son by Jupiter Amon who will avenge her and conquer the world. Nectanebus causes Olympias to dream of a dragon who leaves her pregnant; she believes the astrologer's claims entirely, and he tells her that Amon will come to her that night. Nectanebus transforms himself into a dragon and spends the night with Olympias, conceiving Alexander.

Philip, away, is warned that his wife is pregnant, but Nectanebus reassures Olympias that Amon will protect her. He causes Philip to dream that the child will conquer the world and die by poison. When Alexander is born, with help from Nectanebus in determining the perfect moment, signs and wonders appear, which Philip interprets as evil. Alexander grows up and is trained in courtly and military habits, the only one who can ride the horse Bulciphal. One day Alexander, hearing about astrology from Nectanebus, pushes the astrologer into a hole and breaks his neck, because of rumours that Nectanebus is his real father. Nectanebus, dying, assures him this is true, and Alexander sees to his burial.

Philip asks an oracle which of his two sons will be his heir, and is told that it will be the one who can ride Bulciphal, namely Alexander. Philip then dubs him knight and crowns him as his heir. Alexander makes a punitive expedition against king Nicholas of Carthage, and destroys the town. In his absence, Olympias is accused of adultery and imprisoned, and Philip arranges to marry Cleopatra of Assyria. Alexander returns during the marital feast, and is initially quiet, but an insult to his mother causes him to overthrow the banquet and make peace between his mother and Philip.

Alexander is deputed by Philip to subdue the rebellious city of Mantona, which he does. Meanwhile Darius sends messages to Philip demanding tribute, which Alexander rejects on his father's behalf before marching against a city in the East. Whilst he is away Olympias is seduced by Pausanias, who plans revenge against Philip, which results in the latter being mortally wounded. Alexander returns in the middle of this and kills Pausanias as Philip dies. He formally assumes the crown, summons his vassals, and prepares for war. He subdues Thrace and Sicily before travelling victoriously through Italy and receiving tribute from Rome. He conquers Libya, where in Tripoli he discovers that Nectanebus was its king before his flight; the idol Nectanebus set up in honour of Jupiter Amon speaks to him, saying his father is Philip. Afterwards Alexander besieges Tyre. During this, Darius learns of his refusal to pay tribute, and replies with insulting gifts, which Alexander interprets as signs of his future dominance. In response, Darius demands Alexander's submission; instead, Alexander heads to Arabia to attack him, crushing opposition en route. The two sides meet in a huge battle, in which Darius is routed; he flees to Babylon, pursued by Alexander, who in the meantime shares out booty and treats Darius' womenfolk kindly. On the way, Alexander destroys Thebes with all its inhabitants, and gains tribute (after an initial refusal) from Athens. The city of Macedoyne submits to him.

Darius takes up position by the river Tigris as Alexander approaches. The latter tries to swim the river in full armour and becomes ill, being healed by his doctor Philip, whom Parmenion accuses falsely of wanting to poison the king. The two sides fight again, with Darius offering half his kingdom and his daughter to anyone killing Alexander. After the battle ends at nightfall, Alexander plays a trick on Darius by visiting his court pretending to be a messenger and taking a cup; he is finally recognized and chased away, but escapes. In a final battle, Alexander is victorious and Darius flees to the castle of Melonare. He writes to Alexander suing for peace, but Alexander delays his reply and Darius in despair asks Porus of India for help. Meanwhile the Persian traitors Besas and Besanas mortally wound Darius, who is found dying by Alexander. The Macedonian mourns him and, apprehending the murderers, hangs them.

Alexander then heads to India, making for Facen in pursuit of Porus. Some of the nine thousand peoples of India are described. The army suffers from terrible thirst, and is attacked by wild beasts. Alexander heads to Baudas, where he tricks Porus by visiting him claiming to be a Greek merchant; he tells Porus that Alexander is old and frail, inducing the Indian king to write to Alexander offering battle. Alexander defeats Porus, who submits to him and leads him through India, reaching the Pillars of Hercules by the sea. Alexander then heads north into upper

India, where he crushes any resistance and experiences marvels including people who live in water and those who stand on one foot staring at the sky all day. He attacks a city, gets into trouble, and is saved by Perdicas; the city is destroyed. Alexander then meets the Brahmins and learns about their way of life. Intending to invade France, England, and Germany, Alexander hears of Gog and Magog and resolves to destroy them and their city Taracun. He learns from an oracle how to destroy them, and builds a wall of bitumen that encloses Gog and Magog entirely. Alexander travels to Ethiopia; its inhabitants and fauna are described. He then returns to India, where he receives a love letter from queen Candace, and visits the prophetic Trees of the Sun and Moon, learning of his imminent death by treason in Babylon the next year. Porus also learns of this and rebels. Alexander reaches the Caspian Gates and is attacked by wild beasts, founding a city named after himself. Porus defies him and Alexander suggests single combat. At Facen they fight, and Porus is killed by Alexander, who assumes dominion over all India.

Meanwhile Canulek, Candace's son, asks Alexander for help in recovering his abducted wife. Alexander pretends to be Antigonus and regains her before meeting Candace. She realizes he is in fact Alexander, and shows him the portrait she has of him to prove it. She asks him to be her lover, and he agrees. When his identity becomes known, he returns to India and leads his army to Babylon. Antipater, a justice deposed by Alexander, sends him poisoned wine, which the king drinks. Realizing he is doomed, he divides his lands amongst his captains before he dies. His body is taken to Alexandria and buried. The captains fight over Alexander's territory.

Of Arthour and of Merlin

The romance tells the story of Merlin and Arthur from the reign of Vortigern, covering both Merlin and Arthur's conceptions and births before moving to long descriptions of Arthur's battles in which Merlin's role is crucial. It begins with a well-known preface in the Auchinleck version describing the need to tell the tale in English. The narrative itself starts with the three brothers Constantine, Aurilis Brosias, and Uther Pendragon, the king of England's sons. Constantine, the eldest, has become a monk, but on his father's death is forced to become king, to the chagrin of his father's steward Fortiger (Vortigern). King Angus of Denmark invades England and overcomes 'King Monk', taking over many castles and towns. Fortiger takes advantage of anger at king Constantine to arrange the latter's death at the hand of his barons, and then to become king despite Aurilis and Uther, who are too young to rule. Some barons loyal to Constantine take his two sons across the sea to Brittany. Meanwhile, Fortiger defeats Angus and the Danes, but loses the goodwill of the barons by murdering those who killed Constantine on his behalf, and conflict between king and barons results. Fortiger asks Angus for help and makes an agreement to share the land with him, marrying Angus' daughter. He is afraid of Aurilis and Uther, and so decides to build a castle at Salisbury to defend against attack. However, its walls keep falling down once they reach a certain height, and no learned man can help until astronomers tell Fortiger that he needs to find a child born of no man and smear his blood on the castle walls. The king searches for the child.

The story then describes Merlin's conception, birth, and childhood. The devil rapes a virtuous girl who has unfortunately forgotten to cross herself before sleeping one night; the girl is advised by a local hermit, Blaise, to do penance and trust in God, and he manages to save her from immediate death at the hands of a local justice. She is shut in a tower to give birth and to be kept there until the child is old enough to speak, when she will be buried alive. When he is born, Blaise christens him Merlin; he has miraculous powers but is not demonic. The boy is able to talk from soon after his birth and promises to save his mother's life, which he does as he is able to know the past, present, and future, and sees that the justice himself was conceived in adultery. Merlin asks Blaise to write down all his deeds. When Merlin is five years old his mother becomes a nun.

At this point the king's searchers arrive in the town and hear of a child with no human father. Merlin realizes who they are and tells them his blood will not solve the problem of the walls. He offers to help the king. En route he demonstrates his powers of knowledge, and when he meets Fortiger he explains that the reason the castle walls will not stand is that underneath the ground two dragons, one red and one white, fight every night, knocking down the walls. The ground is dug up and the dragons discovered, who then fight to the death, with the red dragon winning. The castle is built strongly. Merlin explains, once Fortiger has promised not to harm him, that the white and red dragons represent Fortiger and the true heir to the throne respectively, and that the red dragon will ultimately defeat Fortiger. Merlin then disappears.

Meanwhile, Fortiger learns that Aurilis Brosias and Uther Pendragon have invaded and are nearly at Winchester. Fortiger asks Angus of Denmark for help, but many of his barons desert him for the brothers and Winchester opens its gates to them. Battle is joined, and both sides fight bravely, but in the end Fortiger's troops are driven away and he flees to his castle at Salisbury. Uther burns the castle down, with Fortiger in it. Uther learns about Merlin and seeks him to discover how he may defeat Angus, who has taken refuge in another castle, which Uther leaves to Aurilis to besiege. When Aurilis meets Merlin, the boy warns him of Angus' future battle plans, and Aurilis kills Angus as a result.

Uther is crowned king of England at Winchester. Merlin warns him of another Danish invasion force, and the brothers defeat it, but Aurilis is killed, in line with a prophecy from Merlin. Uther's reign is marked by military victories and the establishment of the Round Table. At a gathering for Pentecost Uther sees Ygerne, wife of Heol duke of Cornwall, and falls in love with her. Heol takes her to Tintagel to protect her, and Uther, besieging the castle, begs Merlin for help. Merlin disguises Uther as Heol using magic, and Uther makes Ygerne pregnant with Arthur the same night that Heol himself is killed. Uther and Ygerne marry.

When Arthur is born, Merlin takes him to Sir Antour to be fostered in secret with the latter's own son Kay, to keep Arthur safe on account of his dubious parentage. Arthur grows up strong and noble, ignorant of his descent. Meanwhile, Uther becomes ill and dies. A parliament of all the nobles is convened to discuss who should be the next king. After they pray for a sign, a sword is found thrust into a stone by a nearby church, with an inscription claiming that the man who can pull out the sword is the true king of England. No one is able to until Arthur, seeking a sword for his foster-brother Kay in a tournament, sees the sword and retrieves it. Antour and Merlin reveal Arthur's parentage, and Arthur pulls out the sword again in front of all the nobles, who accept him as king. Merlin tells the whole story. Arthur is crowned with great rejoicing, but king Lot and king Nanters dispute his right to the throne. Arthur puts them to flight, with Merlin's aid. Merlin then advises him to head to London and ask king Ban and king Bors, his father's allies, for help in defeating the rebels. They help him fight a fierce battle in which the rebels are again pushed back. Merlin prophesies much fighting ahead, and advises Arthur to help Leodegan of Carmalide against his enemy king Rioun.

After Arthur leaves, the Danes return and cause more havoc. The sons of the rebel kings, Galaheit, Gawain, Agravain, Gaheris, and Gareth, realize that Arthur is in fact their uncle, as their mothers are Ygerne's daughters, and wish to be knighted by him, which makes peace between Arthur and their families. The young knights learn of attacks on London, and that Arthur is away, and so they lead the fight against the invaders, which they win. Meanwhile, Arthur and his closest companions arrive at Carmalide, and, keeping their identities secret, they join Leodegan in several long battles. Leodegan has preserved Uther's Round Table. Arthur falls in love with Guinevere, Leodegan's daughter.

During his absence, the Danes yet again harass England, but under Gawain and with Merlin's help the different kingdoms band together against the invaders. They are joined by more knights, including Ywain. Leodegan is deeply impressed by Arthur and his men, and when Merlin arrives suggesting that Arthur seeks a noble wife, Leodegan is happy to betroth the pair; when Arthur's true identity is revealed, Leodegan is delighted and does him homage. After even more battles, and with the aid of Merlin's magic, Leodegan and Arthur finally defeat king Rioun.

Seege or Batayle of Troye

For discussion of the different manuscript versions, see chapter 5. This Middle English version of the Troy story uses Dares and the *Roman de Troie* as its major sources, and follows the same narrative structure, although it is far shorter and condenses the fighting into ten battles. It begins with a short introduction describing the conflict as the greatest war ever known before introducing 'Sir Daryes' as an eye-witness and the poet's ultimate source. The narrative proper starts with Jason seeking the Golden Fleece, but from Troy not Crete. Jason and Hercules arrive at Troy but are turned away by Laomedon. They return angrily to Greece, where they gather troops to attack the Trojan city. The Greeks destroy Troy and kill Laomedon, kidnapping Hesione before sailing home. Priam is introduced with his sons Hector, Troilus, and Paris. Paris' upbringing as a child of a pig-herder far away from chivalric pursuits on account of his mother Hecuba's dream of giving birth to a fire-brand is told, with his return to Troy as a young man. Priam rebuilds the city and sends Antenor to Greece to investigate if Hesione may be returned; the request is denied by Hercules. Priam is furious and prepares an army to take to Greece. Paris, asking to be sent instead of Hector, recounts his dream of the Judgement of Paris (here between ladies of 'elven land') and Venus' promise of his future journey to Greece to snatch Helen. Priam allows Paris to go despite the misgivings of Hector and other knights.

Paris sails to Greece and finally arrives at Menelaus' court, where he meets Helen; the two fall in love, and Paris attacks Menelaus' city, taking Helen to Troy. Helen weeps and mourns despite her love for Paris, who marries her. Meanwhile, Menelaus also mourns for her loss, and summons all his lords and men to prepare to set sail for Troy. The poet lists the main Greek leaders and their number of ships. Menelaus sends gifts to the shrine of Apollo, asking for an oracle; he is told the Greeks will destroy Troy. Agamemnon is put in charge of the army, which travels to Troy. Messengers are exchanged, but neither side will back down, so fighting begins. Various battles occur in quick textual succession, passing over such events as Patroclus' death in a few lines, before a truce is agreed. Agamemnon asks the Greeks to focus on killing Hector, but is told the only man who can is Achilles; there follows the tale of Achilles' conception by a witch ('Tithes', Thetis) and a centaur, bathing at birth in enchanted water to make him invulnerable, followed by his disguise as a girl and subsequent discovery through his love of weapons. He arrives at Troy to much joy from the Greeks and swears to kill Hector. His protection through enchanted water 'of helle' is retold, and he is described as wholly black with flint-hard skin.

Meanwhile, Andromache, Hector's wife, pleads Priam not to let Hector fight on account of a dream she has had that he will be killed; Priam agrees. Achilles causes great loss to the Trojans, so Hector finally takes the field; the two fight and Hector is killed. Another truce is agreed, and Hector is buried with great mourning. Achilles sees Hector's sister Polyxena at the funeral and falls in love with her; he offers to end the war if he may marry her. Priam, persuaded by Hecuba, agrees, but Agamemnon refuses to let Achilles make peace in this way; the latter, furious, will not fight. In Achilles' absence, Troilus inflicts great loss on the Greeks and burns their ships. Menelaus begs Achilles to rejoin the battle, and the latter does so, killing Troilus. Another truce follows, in which Hecuba, grieving for her sons' loss, plots with Paris to avenge them by betraying Achilles. Paris sets an ambush for Achilles in a temple, where the Greek is lured by being told his wedding to Polyxena will take place; despite Achilles defending himself bravely, Paris eventually kills him. Menelaus and the Greeks are devastated, but take vengeance on the Trojans for Achilles' death, with Ajax killing Paris before his own demise. The

Greeks besiege the city, and Antenor and Aeneas plot to betray it to them, making a secret bargain with Menelaus. The two Trojans let the Greeks into Troy, and it is destroyed and its people slaughtered, including Priam and Hecuba. Achilles' son kills Polyxena in vengeance for his father. Helen is brought to Menelaus, and both are happy to see one another. The Greeks return home to great feasting and rejoicing, without any of the deaths and tragedies characteristic of accounts derived from Dictys.

Bibliography

Manuscripts

Cambridge, Corpus Christi College, MS 219
Cambridge, Gonville and Caius, MS 154/204
Cambridge, Trinity College, MS O.9.34 (1446)
Cambridge, University Library, Dd. 10. 24
Dublin, Trinity College, MS 177
Durham Cathedral Library, MS C. IV. 27 B
Edinburgh, National Library of Scotland, MS Advocates' 19.2.1
Geneva, Bibliothèque publique et universitaire, MS Latin 98
London, British Library, MS Additional 10292
London, British Library, MS Additional 20009
London, British Library, MS Additional 34114
London, British Library, MS Cotton Caligula A. IX
London, British Library, MS Egerton 2862
London, British Library, MS Harley 525
London, British Library, MS Harley 527
London, British Library, MS Royal 13. A. I
London, British Library, MS Royal 20 B. XX
London, College of Arms, MS Arundel XXII
London, Lincoln's Inn, MS 150
London, University Library, MS 593
Milan, Biblioteca Ambrosiana, MS D 55
Montpellier, Bibliothèque de l'École de médecine, MS 251
Oxford, Bodleian Library, MS Bodley 264
Oxford, Bodleian Library, MS Bodley 603
Oxford, Bodleian Library, MS Digby 32 (part 2)
Oxford, Bodleian Library, MS Laud misc. 622
Paris, Bibliothèque de l'Arsenal, MS 3472
Paris, BnF, MS français 60
Paris, BnF, MS français 375
Paris, BnF, MS français 784
Paris, BnF, MS français 1450
Paris, BnF, MS français 24364
St Andrews, University Library, MS PR 2065 A. 15
Venice, Museo Civico Correr, MS VI.665
Vienna, Österreichische Nationalbibliothek, MS 568

Primary Texts

Abelard, Peter, *Historia calamitatum*, ed. J. Monfrin (Paris, 1967)

Alan of Lille, *Anticlaudianus*, ed. R. Bossuat (Paris, 1955)

Alexander A: *The Romance of Alisaunder*, ed. W.W. Skeat, EETS, e.s., 1 (London, 1867)

Alexander B: *Alexander and Dindimus*, ed. W. W. Skeat, EETS, e.s., 31 (London, 1878)

Alexander C: *The Wars of Alexander*, ed. Hoyt N. Duggan and Thorlac Turville-Petre, EETS, s.s., 10 (Oxford, 1989)

Alexander's Letter to Aristotle about India, trans. Lloyd L. Gunderson (Meisenheim am Glan, 1980), pp.140–56

Der Alexanderroman des Archipresbyters Leo, ed. Friedrich Pfister (Heidelberg, 1913)

Arrian, *Anabasis*, in *The Campaigns of Alexander*, trans. Aubrey de Selincourt and introd. J. R. Hamilton, rev. ed. (London, 1971)

Of Arthour and of Merlin, ed. O. D. Macrae-Gibson, 2 vols, EETS, o.s., 268 and o.s. 279 (Oxford, 1973 and 1979)

The Auchinleck Manuscript: National Library of Scotland Advocates' MS. 19.2.1, introd. Derek Pearsall and I. C. Cunningham (London, 1977)

Béroul, *The Romance of Tristan by Béroul*, ed. Stewart Gregory (Amsterdam, 1992)

The Buik of Alexander, ed. R. L. Graeme Ritchie, 4 vols, STS, n.s., 12, 17, 21, and 25 (Edinburgh, 1921–29)

The Buik of King Alexander the Conquerour, ed. John Cartwright, 3 vols (2 published to date), STS, n.s., 16, 18 (Edinburgh, 1986 and 1990)

'Carmen aestivum', in *The Oxford Book of Medieval Latin Verse*, ed. F. J. E. Raby (Oxford, 1959), pp.174–5

La Chanson de Roland, ed. Louis Cortés and trans. Paulette Gabaudan (Paris, 1994)

Chaucer, Geoffrey, *The Riverside Chaucer*, gen. ed. Larry D. Benson, 3rd edn (Boston, MA, 1987)

Chrétien de Troyes, *Lancelot* or *Le Chevalier de la charrette*, in *Oeuvres complètes*, ed. Daniel Poirion (Paris, 1994)

—, *Cligès*, ed. Claude Luttrell and Stewart Gregory, Arthurian Studies, 28 (Cambridge, 1993)

—, *Cligès*, trans. Ruth Harwood Cline (Athens, GA, 2000)

Cligès: Chrétien de Troyes, trans. Burton Raffel (New Haven, NJ, 1997)

Dares Phrygius and Dictys Cretensis, *The Trojan War: The Chronicles of Dictys of Crete and Dares the Phrygian*, trans. R. M. Frazer (Bloomington, IN, 1966)

Diodorus Siculus, *VIII: Books XVI.66–XVII*, trans. C. B. Welles, Loeb Classical Library, 422 (Harvard, MA, 1963)

Eneas, roman du XIIᵉ siècle, ed. J.-J. Salverda de Grave, 2 vols, Classiques français du moyen âge, 44 and 62 (Paris, 1925 and 1929)

An Epitome of Biblical History: Glosses on Walter of Châtillon's Alexandreis

4.176–274, ed. David Townsend, Toronto Medieval Latin Texts, 30 (Toronto, 2008)

Excidium Troiae, ed. E. Bagby Atwood and Virgil K. Whitaker (Cambridge, MA, 1944)

Flavii Arriani Anabasis Alexandri, ed. A. G. Roos (Leipzig, 1907)

Geoffrey of Monmouth, *The History of the Kings of Britain*, trans. Lewis Thorpe (London, 1966)

Gerald of Wales, *Concerning the Instruction of Princes*, trans. J. Stevenson (London, 1858: repr. 1991)

Gervase, *Bestiary*, 'Le *Bestiaire* de Gervase', ed. Paul Meyer, *Romania*, 1 (1872), pp.420–43

The Greek Alexander Romance, trans. and introd. Richard Stoneman (London, 1991)

Henry of Huntingdon, *Historia Anglorum: The History of the English People*, ed. and trans. Diana Greenway, Oxford Medieval Texts (Oxford, 1996)

Historia Alexandri Magni (Historia de Preliis) Rezension J1, ed. Alfons Hilka and Karl Steffens (Meisenheim am Glan, 1979)

Historia Alexandri Magni (Historia de Preliis) Rezension J2 (Orosius-Rezension), ed. Alfons Hilka, 2 vols (Meisenheim am Glan, 1976 and 1977)

Die Historia de preliis Alexandri Magni *Rezension J3*, ed. Karl Steffens (Meisenheim am Glan, 1975)

The Historia regum Britannie *of Geoffrey of Monmouth*, ed. Neil Wright and Julia Crick, 5 vols (Cambridge, 1985–91)

The History of Alexander's Battles: Historia de preliis – The J1 Version, trans. and introd. R. Telfryn Pritchard, Medieval Sources in Translation, 34 (Toronto, 1992)

Horn Childe and Maiden Rimnild, ed. M. Mills, Middle English Texts, 20 (Heidelberg, 1988)

L'Iliade: épopée du XIIᵉ siècle sur la guerre de Troie, trad. and notes under direction of Francine Mora, introd. Jean-Yves Tilliette, Miroir du Moyen Âge (Turnhout, 2003)

John of Hauville, *Architrenius*, trans. and introd. Winthrop Wetherbee, Cambridge Medieval Classics, 3 (Cambridge, 1994)

John of Salisbury, Letters 136 and 167, in *The Letters of John of Salisbury*, ed. W. J. Millor and H. E. Butler, rev. C. N. L. Brooke, 2 vols (Oxford, 1955 and 1979), ii: *The Later Letters (1163–1180)* (1979), pp.2–15, 94–95

—, *Policraticus*, i–iv, ed. K. S. B. Keats-Rohan, CCCM, 118 (Turnhout, 1993)

—, *Policraticus*, ed. and trans. C. J. Nederman, Cambridge Texts in the History of Political Thought (Cambridge, 1990)

Joseph of Exeter: Iliad, trans. A. G. Rigg (Toronto, 2005)

—, *The* Iliad *of Dares Phrygius*, trans. and introd. Gildas Roberts (Cape Town, 1970)

—, *Joseph Iscanus: Werke und Briefe*, ed. Ludwig Gompf (Leiden, 1970)

Julii Valerii Epitome, ed. Julius Zacher (Halle, 1867)

Julius Valère, Roman d'Alexandre, trans. and comm. Jean-Pierre Callu (Turnhout, 2010)

Justin: Epitome *of the* Philippic History *of Pompeius Trogus*, vol. 1: *Books 11–12: Alexander the Great*, trans. and introd. J. C. Yardley and Waldemar Heckel (Oxford, 1997)

Justini Historiae Philippicae ex editione Abrahami Gronovii, 2 vols (London, 1822)

Juvencus, *Evangeliorum libri quattuor*, ed. John Hümer, CSEL, 24 (Vienna, 1891)

Juvencus' Four Books of the Gospels: Evangeliorum Libri Quattuor, trans. Scott McGill (London, 2016)

Kyng Alisaunder, ed. G. V. Smithers, 2 vols, EETS, o.s., 227 and 237 (London, 1952 and 1957)

The King of Tars, ed. J. Perryman, Middle English Texts, 12 (Heidelberg, 1980)

Layamon, *Brut*, ed. by G. L. Brook and R. F. Leslie, 2 vols, EETS, n.s., 209 and 277 (Oxford, 1963 and 1978)

Libro de Alexandre, ed. Francisco Marcos Marín (Madrid, 1987)

Matthew Paris, *The Life of Saint Alban by Matthew Paris*, trans. and introd. Jocelyn Wogan-Browne and Thelma S. Fenster, FRETS, 2 (Tempe, AZ, 2010)

Matthew of Vendôme, *Opera*, ed. Franco Munari, 3 vols, Storia e letteratura, 144, 152, and 171 (Roma, 1977–88), III: *Ars versificatoria* (1988)

The Medieval French Roman d'Alexandre, II: *Version of Alexandre de Paris*, ed. E. C. Armstrong et al., Elliott Monographs, 37 (Princeton, NJ, 1937)

The Medieval French Roman d'Alexandre, III: *Version of Alexandre de Paris, Variants and Notes to Branch I*, introd. Alfred Foulet, Elliott Monographs, 38 (Princeton, NJ, 1949)

The Medieval French Roman d'Alexandre, IV: *Le Roman du fuerre de Gadres* d'Eustache, introd. E. C. Armstrong and Alfred Foulet, Elliott Monographs, 39 (Princeton, NJ, 1942)

The Medieval French Roman d'Alexandre, VI: *Version of Alexandre de Paris: Introduction and Notes to Branch III,* introd. Alfred Foulet, Elliott Monographs, 42 (Princeton, NJ, 1976)

The Medieval French Roman d'Alexandre, VII: *Version of Alexandre de Paris: Variants and Notes to Branch IV*, introd. Bateman Edwards and Alfred Foulet, Elliott Monographs, 41 (Princeton, NJ, 1955)

Orderic Vitalis, *The Ecclesiastical History of Orderic Vitalis*, ed. and trans. Marjorie Chibnall, 4 vols (Oxford, 1969–80)

Orose, Histoires (Contre Les Païens), ed. and trans. Marie-Pierre Arnaud-Lindet, 3 vols (Paris, 1990 and 1991)

Orosius: Seven Books of History Against the Pagans, trans. and introd. A. Fear (Liverpool, 2010)

Ovid, *Metamorphoses*, ed. William S. Anderson, Bibliotheca Scriptorum Graecorum et Romanorum Teubneriana (Leipzig, 1991)

Parker, Matthew, *De antiquitate Britannicae ecclesiae* (London, 1572)

Plutarch, *Life of Alexander*, in *The Age of Alexander: Ten Greek Lives by Plutarch*, ed. and trans. Ian Scott-Kilvert and Timothy E. Duff, rev. ed. (London, 2011)

Plutarch's Lives, trans. Bernadotte Perrin, 11 vols, Loeb Classical Library (Cambridge, MA, 1914–26), VII: *Demosthenes and Cicero: Alexander and Caesar* (1919)

Bibliography

The Prose Life of Alexander, ed. J. S. Westlake, EETS, o.s., 143 (London, 1913 for 1911)

Quintus Curtius Rufus, *Historiae Alexandri Magni*, ed. Carlo M. Lucarini, Bibliotheca Scriptorum Graecorum et Romanorum Teubneriana (Berlin, 2009)

Quintus Curtius Rufus, History of Alexander, ed. and trans. John C. Rolfe, 2 vols, Loeb Classical Library, 368 and 369 (Cambridge, MA, 1946)

Quintus Curtius Rufus, *The History of Alexander*, trans. John Yardley and introd. Waldemar Heckel, rev. edn (London, 2001)

Richer of Saint-Rémi, *Historiae*, ed. and trans. Justin Lake, Dumbarton Oaks Medieval Library, 2 vols (Cambridge, MA, 2011)

Rigord of St Denis, *Gesta Philippi Augusti*, in *Oeuvres de Rigord et de Guillaume le Breton*, ed. H. François Delaborde, 3 vols (Paris, 1882–5), I

Le Roman d'Alexandre, trans. and introd. L. Harf-Lancner, Lettres Gothiques (Paris, 1994)

Le Roman d'Alexandre ou le roman de toute chevalerie, trans. and introd. Catherine Gaullier-Bougassas and Laurence Harf-Lancner (Paris, 2003)

Le Roman d'Eneas, introd. and trans. Aimé Petit, Lettres gothiques (Paris, 1997)

Le roman de Merlin or the early history of King Arthur, ed. H. Oskar Sommer (London, 1894)

Roman de Thèbes, ed. G. R. de Lage (Paris, 1966)

Le Roman de Troie par Benoît de Sainte-Maure, ed. Léopold Constans, 6 vols (Paris, 1904–12)

The Romance of Horn, ed. M. K. Pope with T. B. W. Reid, 2 vols, ANTS, 9–10, 12–13 (Oxford, 1955 and 1964)

The Romance of Horn, in *The Birth of Romance in England: Four Twelfth-Century Romances in the French of England*, trans. and introd. Judith Weiss, FRETS, 4 (Tempe, AZ, 2009), pp.45–137

Scott, Sir Walter, *Ivanhoe* (Edinburgh, 1820)

The Seege or Batayle of Troye, ed. Mary Elizabeth Barnicle, EETS, o.s., 172 (London, 1927)

Statius, *Thebaid, books 1–7*, ed. and trans. D. R. Shackleton Bailey, Loeb Classical Library, 207 (Cambridge, MA, 2003)

Thomas of Britain, *Les Fragments du Roman de Tristan, poème du XIIᵉ siècle*, ed. Bertina H. Wind, 2nd edn (Paris, 1960)

Thomas of Kent, *The Anglo-Norman Alexander* (Le Roman de Toute Chevalerie), ed. Brian Foster and Ian Short, 2 vols, ANTS, 29–33 (London, 1976 and 1977)

Valerius Maximus, *Memorable Deeds and Sayings: One Thousand Tales from Ancient Rome*, trans. and introd. Henry John Walker (Indianapolis, IN, 2004)

—, *Memorable Doings and Sayings*, ed. and trans. D. R. Shackleton Bailey, 2 vols, Loeb Classical Library, 492 and 493 (Cambridge, MA, 2000)

Venantius Fortunatus, 'Vexilla regis prodeunt', in *The Oxford Book of Medieval Latin Verse*, ed. and trans. F. J. E. Raby, 2nd edn (Oxford, 1974), p.75

La Vie de seint Auban, ed. A. R. Harden, ANTS, 19 (Oxford, 1968)

Virgil, *Opera*, ed. R. A. B. Mynors, Scriptorum Classicroum Bibliotheca Oxoniensis (Oxford, 1969; repr. 1972)

Walter of Châtillon, *The* Alexandreis *of Walter of Châtillon: A Twelfth-Century Epic*, trans. David Townsend (Philadelphia, PA, 1996)

—, *Galteri de Castellione* Alexandreis, ed. M. L. Colker (Padua, 1978)

—, *Moralisch-satirische Gedichte Walters von Châtillon*, ed. Karl Strecker (Heidelberg, 1929)

Walter of Châtillon: The Shorter Poems: Christmas Hymns, Love Lyrics, and Moral-Satirical Verse, ed. and trans. David A. Traill, Oxford Medieval Texts (Oxford, 2013)

William the Breton, *Philippidos*, in *Oeuvres de Rigord et de Guillaume le Breton*, ed. H.-F. Delaborde, 3 vols (Paris, 1885), ii: *Philippide de Guillaume le Breton*

Secondary Works

Adkin, Neil, 'The Date of Walter of Châtillon's *Alexandreis* Again', *Bollettino di studi latini*, 23:2 (1993), pp.359–64

—, 'The Date of Walter of Châtillon's *Alexandreis* Once Again', *Classica et mediaevalia*, 59 (2008), pp.201–11

—, 'The Proem of Walter of Châtillon's *Alexandreis*: "Si … nostros uixisset in annos"', *Medium Ævum*, 60 (1991), pp.207–15

—, 'Walter of Châtillon: "Alexandreis" IV 206–207', *MJ*, 32:1 (1997), pp.29–36

Atwood, E. Bagby, 'The Judgment of Paris in the *Seege of Troye*', *PMLA*, 57 (1942), pp.343–53

—, 'The Rawlinson *Excidium Troie* – A Study of Source Problems in Medieval Troy Literature', *Speculum*, 9 (1934), pp.379–404

—, 'The Story of Achilles in the *Seege of Troye*', *Studies in Philology*, 39 (1942), pp.489–501

Agapitos, Panagiotis A., 'Contesting Conceptual Boundaries: Byzantine Literature and Its History', *Interfaces: A Journal of Medieval European Literatures*, 1 (2015), pp.62–91

Akbari, Suzanne Conklin, 'Alexander in the Orient: Boundaries and Bodies in the *Roman de toute chevalerie*', in *Postcolonial Approaches to the European Middle Ages*, ed. Ananya Jahanara Kabir and Deanne Williams (Cambridge, 2005), pp.105–26

Allen, J. B., *The Ethical Poetic of the Later Middle Ages* (Toronto, 1982)

Anderson, Benedict, *Imagined Communities: Reflections on the Origin and Spread of Nationalism*, 2nd edn (London, 1991)

Anson, Edward M., 'The *Ephemerides* of Alexander the Great', *Historia: Zeitschrift für Alte Geschichte*, 45.4 (1996), pp.501–54

Archibald, Elizabeth, 'Ancient Romance', in *A Companion to Romance: From Classical to Contemporary*, ed. Corinne Saunders, Blackwell Companions to Literature and Culture, 27 (Oxford, 2014), pp.10–25

Ashe, Laura, 'The Hero and His Realm', in *Boundaries in Medieval Romance*, ed. Neil Cartlidge (Cambridge, 2008), pp.129–47

—, *History and Fiction in England, 1066–1200*, Cambridge Studies in Medieval Literature, 68 (Cambridge, 2007)

Barnes, Geraldine, *Counsel and Strategy in Middle English Romance* (Cambridge, 1993)

Baswell, Christopher, 'The Manuscript Context', in *The Life of Saint Alban by Matthew Paris*, trans. and introd. Jocelyn Wogan-Browne and Thelma S. Fenster, FRETS, 2 (Tempe, AZ, 2010), pp.169–94

—, 'Men in the *Roman d'Eneas*: The Construction of Empire', in *Medieval Masculinities: Regarding Men in the Middle Ages*, ed. Clare A. Lees (Minneapolis, MN, 1994), pp.149–68

—, 'Multilingualism on the Page', in *Middle English*, ed. Paul Strohm (Oxford, 2007), pp.38–50

Batany, Jean, 'Benoît, auteur anticlerical? De Troïlus à Guillaume Longue-Épée', in *Le Roman Antique au Moyen Âge*, ed. Danielle Buschinger (Göppingen, 1992), pp.7–22

Baumgartner, Emmanuèle, *Histoire de la litterature française*, vol. I: *Moyen Âge* (Paris, 1987)

—, 'L'Image royale dans le roman antique: le *Roman d'Alexandre* et le *Roman de Troie*', in *Cours princières et châteaux: Pouvoir et culture du IXᵉ au XIIIᵉ siècle en France du Nord, en Angleterre et en Allemagne. Actes du Colloque de Soissons (28–30 septembre 1987)*, ed. Danielle Buschinger (Greifswald, 1993), pp.25–44

—, 'Tombeaux pour guerriers et amazones: sur un motif descriptif de l'*Eneas* et du *Roman de Troie*', in *Contemporary Readings of Medieval Literature*, ed. G. Mermier, Michigan Romance Studies, 9 (Ann Arbor, MI, 1989), pp.37–50

Baynham, Elizabeth J., *Alexander the Great: The Unique History of Quintus Curtius Rufus* (Ann Arbor, MI, 1998)

—, 'Who Put the "Romance" in the Alexander Romance? The Alexander Romances within Alexander Historiography', *Ancient History Bulletin*, 9 (1995), pp.1–13

Beartot, Cinzia, 'Royal Autobiography in the Hellenistic Age', in *Political Autobiographies and Memoirs in Antiquity*, ed. Gabriele Marasco (Leiden, 2011), pp.37–85

Bellis, Joanna, *The Hundred Years War in Literature, 1337–1600* (Cambridge, 2016)

Benton, John F., 'The Court of Champagne as a Literary Center', *Speculum*, 36.4 (1961), pp.551–91

Berg, B. J. B., 'An Early Source of the Alexander Romance', *Greek, Roman and Byzantine Studies*, 14 (1973), pp.381–7

Billows, Richard, 'Polybius and Alexander Historiography', in *Alexander the Great in Fact and Fiction*, ed. A. B. Bosworth and E. J. Baynham (Oxford, 2000), pp.286–306

Boffey, Julia, 'Short Texts in Manuscript Anthologies: The Minor Poems of John Lydgate in Two Fifteenth-Century Collections', in *The Whole Book: Cultural Perspectives on the Medieval Miscellany*, ed. S. G. Nichols and S. Wenzel (Ann Arbor, MI, 1996), pp.69–82

Bond, Gerald A., *The Loving Subject: Desire, Eloquence and Power in Romanesque France* (Philadelphia, PA, 1995)

Borsa, Paolo, Christian Høgel, Lars Boje Mortensen, and Elizabeth M. Tyler, 'What is Medieval European Literature?', *Interfaces: A Journal of Medieval European Literatures*, 1 (2015), pp.7–24

Borza, Eugene N., 'The Nature of the Evidence', in *The Impact of Alexander the Great: Civilizer or Destroyer?*, ed. Eugene N. Borza, European Problem series (Hinsdale, IL, 1974), pp.21–5

Bossuat, Robert, *Histoire de la littérature française*, gen. ed. Jean Calvet, 10 vols (Paris, 1955), I: *Le Moyen Âge*

Bowersock, Graham, *Greek Sophists in the Roman Empire* (Oxford, 1969)

—, *Hellenism in Late Antiquity* (Cambridge, 1990)

Bradbury, J., *The Capetians: Kings of France, 987–1328* (London, 2007)

Bradbury, Nancy Mason, 'Literacy, Orality, and the Poetics of Middle English Romance', in *Oral Poetics in Middle English Poetry*, ed. Mark C. Amodio and Sarah Gray Miller (New York, 1994), pp.39–69

—, *Writing Aloud: Storytelling in Late Medieval England* (Chicago, IL, 1998)

Breckenridge, Carol A., Homi K. Bhabha, Sheldon Pollock, and Dipesh Chakrabarty (eds), *Cosmopolitanism* (Durham and London, 2002)

Bridges, Venetia, 'Absent Presence: Auchinleck and *Kyng Alisaunder*', in *The Auchinleck Manuscript: New Perspectives*, ed. Susanna Fein (York, 2016), pp.88–107

—, '"L'estoire d'Alixandre vos veul par vers traitier [...]": Passions and Polemics in Latin and Vernacular Alexander Literature of the Later Twelfth Century', *Nottingham Medieval Studies*, 58 (2014), pp.87–113

—, '"Goliardic" Poetry and the Problem of Historical Perspective: Medieval Adaptations of Walter of Châtillon's Quotation Poems', *Medium Ævum*, 81.2 (2012), pp.249–70

—, 'Reading Walter of Châtillon's *Alexandreis* in Medieval Anthologies', *Mediaeval Studies*, 77 (2015), pp.81–101

—, 'Writing the Past: The "Classical Tradition" in the Poetry of Walter of Châtillon and Contemporary Literature, 1160–1200' (unpublished PhD thesis, University of Cambridge, 2012)

Broadhurst, Karen, 'Henry II of England and Eleanor of Aquitaine: Patrons of Literature in French?', *Viator*, 27 (1996), pp.53–84

Bunt, Gerrit H. V., *Alexander the Great in the Literature of Medieval Britain*, Mediaevalia Groningana, 14 (Groningen, 1994)

Burnley, J. D., 'The *Roman de Horn*: Its Hero and Ethos', *French Studies*, 32 (1978), pp.385–97

Busby, Keith, '"Codices manuscriptos nudos tenemus": Alexander and the New Codicology', in *The Medieval French Alexander*, ed. Donald Maddox and Sara Sturm-Maddox (Albany, NY, 2002), pp.259–73

Buszard, B., 'Caesar's Ambition: A Combined Reading of Plutarch's *Alexander–Caesar and Pyrrhus–Marius*', *Transactions of the American Philological Association*, 138 (2008), pp.185–215

—, 'A Plutarchan Parallel to Arrian *Anabasis* 7.1', *Greek, Roman and Byzantine Studies*, 50.4 (2010), pp.565–85

Butler, Patrick, 'A Failure to Communicate: Multilingualism in the Prologue to *Of*

Arthour and of Merlin', in *The Auchinleck Manuscript: New Perspectives*, ed. Susanna Fein (York, 2016), pp.52–66

Buttenweiser, Hilda, 'Popular Authors of the Middle Ages', *Speculum*, 17.1 (1942), pp.50–5

Butterfield, Ardis, *The Familiar Enemy: Chaucer, Language, and Nation in the Hundred Years War* (Oxford, 2009)

Byrne, Aisling, *Otherworlds: Fantasy and History in Medieval Literature* (Oxford, 2016)

Cadilhac-Rouchon, Muriel, 'Revealing Otherness: A Comparative Examination of French and English Medieval Hagiographical Romance' (unpublished PhD thesis, University of Cambridge, 2009)

Caldwell, Robert A., 'The "History of the Kings of Britain" in College of Arms MS Arundel XXII', *PMLA*, 69.3 (1954), pp.643–54

Cary, George, *The Medieval Alexander*, ed. D. J. A. Ross (Cambridge, 1956)

de Cesare, R., *Glosse latine e antico-francesi all'*Alexandreis *di Gautier de Châtillon*, Pubblicazioni della Università Cattolica del Sacro Cuore, n.s. 39 (Milan, 1951)

Chaplain, Jane D., 'Conversations in History: Arrian and Herodotus, Parmenio and Alexander', *Greek, Roman and Byzantine Studies*, 51.4 (2011), pp.613–33

Chesnut, Glenn F., 'Eusebius, Augustine, Orosius, and the Later Patristic and Medieval Christian Historians', in *Eusebius, Christianity and Judaism*, ed. Harold W. Attridge and Gohei Hata (Leiden, 1992), pp.687–713

Christensen, Heinrich, *Das Alexanderlied Walters von Châtillon* (Halle, 1905)

Church, Stephen D., *King John: England, Magna Carta and the Making of a Tyrant* (London, 2015)

Clark, James, *A Monastic Renaissance at St Albans: Thomas Walsingham and his Circle, c.1350–1440* (Oxford, 2004)

Clauss, James J., and Martine Cuypers, 'Introduction', in *A Companion to Hellenistic Literature*, ed. James J. Clauss and Martine Cuypers, Blackwell Companions to the Ancient World (Oxford, 2010), pp.1–14

Clifton, Nicole, '*Of Arthour and of Merlin* as Medieval Children's Literature', *Arthuriana*, 13.2 (2003), pp.9–22

Cohen, Jeffrey Jerome (ed.), *The Postcolonial Middle Ages* (New York, 2001)

Cooper, Helen, 'Lancelot, Roger Mortimer and the Date of the Auchinleck Manuscript', in *Studies in Late Medieval and Early Renaissance Texts in Honour of John Scattergood*, ed. Anne Marie d'Arcy and Alan J. Fletcher (Dublin, 2005), pp.91–9

Cornish, Alison, *Vernacular Translation in Dante's Italy: Illiterate Literature*, Cambridge Studies in Medieval Literature, 83 (Cambridge, 2011)

Cotts, John D., 'Peter of Blois and the Problem of the "Court" in the Late Twelfth Century', *Anglo-Norman Studies*, 27 (2005), pp.68–84

Crane, Susan, *Insular Romance: Politics, Faith, and Culture in Anglo-Norman and Middle English Literature* (Berkeley, CA, 1986)

Crick, Julia, 'St Albans, Westminster, and Some Twelfth-Century Views of the Anglo-Saxon Past', *Anglo-Norman Studies*, 25 (2003), pp.65–83

Crofts, Thomas H., and Robert Rouse, 'Middle English Popular Romance and

National Identity', in *A Companion to Medieval Popular Romance*, ed. Raluca Radulescu and Cory Rushton (Cambridge, 2009), pp.79–95

Cruse, Mark, *Illuminating the* Roman d'Alexandre *(Oxford, Bodleian Library, MS Bodley 264): The Manuscript as Monument*, Gallica, 22 (Cambridge, 2011)

Currie, Harry MacLeod, 'Quintus Curtius Rufus: The Historian as Novelist?', in *Groningen Colloquia on the Novel*, III, ed. Heinz Hofmann (Groningen, 1990), pp.63–77

Davidson, James, 'Bonkers about Boys', *London Review of Books*, 1 November 2001

Demouy, Patrick, *Genèse d'une cathédrale: les archevêques de Reims et leur Église aux XIe et XIIe siècles* (Langres, 2005)

Desportes, Pierre, *Reims et les Rémois aux XIIIe et XIVe siècles* (Paris, 1979)

Dosson, S., *Étude sur Quinte-Curce, sa vie et son œuvre* (Paris, 1887)

Dronke, Peter, *Medieval Latin and the Rise of European Love-Lyric*, 2 vols (Oxford, 1965 and 1966)

—, 'New Approaches to the School of Chartres', in *Intellectuals and Poets in Medieval Europe*, Storia e letteratura: raccolta di studi e testi, 183 (Rome, 1992), pp.15–40

—, 'Peter of Blois and Poetry at the Court of Henry II', *Mediaeval Studies*, 38 (1976), pp.185–235

Duggan, Joseph D., 'Afterword', in *Cligès: Chrétien de Troyes*, trans. Burton Raffel (New Haven, NJ, 1997), pp.215–26

Dukat, Z., 'The Romance of Alexander: A Specimen of the Ancient Popular Literature', *Ziva antika*, 26 (1976), pp.463–86

Dunkle, J. Roger, 'Satirical Themes in Joseph of Exeter *De bello troiano*', *Classica et mediaevalia*, 38 (1987), pp.203–13

Duval, Frédéric, *Le français médiéval* (Turnhout, 2009)

Ehrhart, Margaret J., *The Judgment of the Trojan Prince Paris in Medieval Literature* (Philadelphia, 1987)

Eliot, T. S., *Four Quartets* (London, 1944)

Falkenstein, Ludwig, 'Guillaume aux Blanches Mains, archevêque de Reims et légat du siège apostolique (1176–1202)', *Revue d'histoire de l'église de France*, 91:226 (2005), pp.5–25

Faral, Edmond, *Recherches sur les sources latines des contes et romans courtois du moyen âge* (Paris, 1913)

Fears, J. Rufus, 'The Stoic View of the Career and Character of Alexander the Great', *Philologus*, 118 (1974), pp.113–30

Fein, Susanna (ed.), *The Auchinleck Manuscript: New Perspectives* (York, 2016)

Field, Rosalind, 'Children of Anarchy: Anglo-Norman Romance in the Twelfth Century', in *Writers of the Reign of Henry II: Twelve Essays*, ed. Simon Meecham-Jones and Ruth Kennedy (Basingstoke, 2006), pp.249–62

—, 'Patterns of Availability and Demand in Middle English Translations *de romanz*', in *The Exploitations of Medieval Romance*, ed. Laura Ashe, Ivana Djordjević, and Judith Weiss (Cambridge, 2010), pp.73–89

Foster, Brian, 'The *Roman de toute chevalerie*: Its Date and Author', *French Studies*, 9 (1955), pp.154–8

Foulet, Alfred, 'La date du *Roman de toute chevalerie*', in *Mélanges offerts à Rita Lejeune*, ed. F. Dethier, 2 vols (Gembloux, 1969), ii, pp.1205–10

Fourrier, A., *Le Courant réaliste dans le roman courtois en France au moyen âge* (Paris, 1960)

Fraker, Charles F., *The* Libro del Alexandre*: Medieval Epic and Silver Latin*, North Carolina Studies in the Romance Languages and Literatures, 245 (Chapel Hill, NC, 1993)

Freeman, Michelle A., *The Poetics of* Translatio Studii *and* Conjointure: *Chrétien de Troyes's* Cligés (Lexington, KY, 1979)

Furrows, Melissa, '*Chanson de Geste* as Romance in England', in *The Exploitations of Medieval Romance*, ed. Laura Ashe, Ivana Djordjevíc, and Judith Weiss (Cambridge, 2010), pp.57–72

Ganin, John M., and Shayne Aaron Legassie (eds), *Cosmopolitanism and the Middle Ages*, The New Middle Ages series (Basingstoke, 2013)

Gaullier-Bougassas, Catherine (ed.), *Alexandre le Grand à la lumière des manuscrits et des premiers imprimés en Europe (XIIᵉ–XVIᵉ siècle)* (Turnhout, 2015)

—, 'L'altérité de l'Alexandre du *Roman d'Alexandre*, et en contrepoint, l'intégration à l'univers arthurien de l'Alexandre de *Cligès*', *Cahiers de recherches médiévales et humanistes*, 4 (1997), pp.1–7

— (ed.), *L'historiographie médiévale d'Alexandre le Grand* (Turnhout, 2011)

—, *Les Romans d'Alexandre: aux frontières de l'épique et du romanesque* (Paris, 1998)

Gaunt, Simon, 'French Literature Abroad: Towards an Alternative History of French Literature', *Interfaces: A Journal of Medieval European Literatures*, 1 (2015), pp.25–66

Godman, Peter, *The Archpoet and Medieval Culture* (Oxford, 2014)

Le Goff, Jacques, *Saint Louis* (Paris, 1996)

Goldhill, Simon, *Who Needs Greek? Contests in the Cultural History of Hellenism* (Cambridge, 2002)

Gosman, Martin, 'Alexandre le Grand: les avatars d'un héros français', in *Polyphonia Byzantina: Studies in Honour of Willem J. Aerts*, ed. Hero Hokwerda, Edmé R. Smits, and Marinus M. Woesthuis, Mediaevalia Groningana, 13 (Groningen, 1993), pp.179–88

—, 'Le *Roman de toute chevalerie* et le public visé: la légende au service de la royauté', *Neophilologus*, 72.3 (1988), pp.335–43

—, 'Le Roman d'Alexandre et ses versions du XIIᵉ siècle: une réécriture permanente', *Bien Dire et Bien Aprandre*, 13 (1996), pp.7–23

Graham, Timothy, and Andrew G. Watson, *The Recovery of the Past in Early Elizabethan England: Documents by John Bale and John Goscelin from the Circle of Matthew Parker*, Cambridge Bibliographical Society, 13 (Cambridge, 1998)

Gransden, Antonia, *Historical Writing in England*, 2 vols (London, 1974)

—, *A History of the Abbey of Bury St Edmunds*, 2 vols (Woodbridge, 2007 and 2015)

Gray, V. J., 'The Value of Diodorus Siculus for the Years 411–386 BC', *Hermes*, 115 (1987), pp.72–89

Green, D. H., *The Beginnings of Medieval Romance: Fact and Fiction, 1150–1220*, Cambridge Studies in Medieval Literature, 47 (Cambridge, 2002)

Grimbert, Joan Tasker, '*Cligés* and the Chansons: A Slave to Love', in *A Companion to Chrétien de Troyes*, ed. Norris J. Lacy and Joan Tasker Grimbert, Arthurian Studies, 63 (Cambridge, 2005), pp.120–36

Hahn, Cynthia, 'Proper Behavior for Knights and Kings: The Hagiography of Matthew Paris, Monk of St. Albans', *Haskins Society Journal*, 2 (1990), pp.237–48

Hamilton, G. L., 'Quelques notes sur l'histoire de la légende d'Alexandre le Grand en Angleterre au moyen âge', in *Mélanges de philologie et d'histoire offerts à M. Antoine Thomas par ses élèves et ses amis* (Paris, 1927), pp.195–202

Hamilton, G. R., 'The Date of Quintus Curtius Rufus', *Historia*, 37 (1988), pp.445–56

Hammond, N. G. L., *Three Historians of Alexander the Great: The So-Called Vulgate Authors, Diodorus, Justin and Curtius* (Cambridge, 1983)

—, *Sources for Alexander the Great: An Analysis of Plutarch's* Life *and Arrian's* Anabasis Alexandrou (Cambridge, 1993)

Hanna III, Ralph, 'Reconsidering the Auchinleck Manuscript', in *New Directions in Later Medieval Manuscript Studies*, ed. Derek Pearsall (York, 2000), pp.91–102

—, *London Literature, 1300–1380*, Cambridge Studies in Medieval Literature, 57 (Cambridge, 2005)

Hardie, Philip R., *Ovid's Poetics of Illusion* (Cambridge, 2002)

Harf-Lancner, Laurence, 'Alexandre le Grand dans les romans français du moyen âge: un héros de la démesure', *Mélanges de l'école française de Rome: Moyen Âge*, 112.1 (2000), pp.51–63

—, 'De la biographie au roman d'Alexandre: Alexandre de Paris et l'art de la conjointure', in *The Medieval Opus: Imitation, Rewriting and Transmission in the French Tradition*, ed. Douglas Kelly (Amsterdam, 1996), pp.59–74

—, 'From Alexander to Marco Polo, from Text to Image: The Marvels of India', in *The Medieval French Alexander*, ed. David Maddox and Sara Sturm-Maddox (Albany, NY, 2002), pp.235–57

—, 'Medieval French Alexander Romance I', in *A Companion to Alexander Literature in the Middle Ages*, ed. Z. David Zuwiyya, Brill's Companions to the Christian Tradition, 29 (Leiden, 2011), pp.201–30

Hasty, Will (ed.), *German Literature of the High Middle Ages* (Rochester, 2006)

Haywood, Louise M., 'Spring Song and Narrative Organization in the Medieval Alexander Legend', *Troianalexandrina*, 4 (2004), pp.87–105

Haywood, Paul A., 'The Cult of St. Alban, *Anglorum Protomartyr*, in Anglo-Saxon and Anglo-Norman England', in *More than a Memory: The Discourse of Martyrdom and the Construction of Christian Identity in the History of Christianity*, ed. Johan Leemans (Leuven, 2005), pp.169–200

—, 'Sanctity and Lordship in Twelfth-Century England: Saint Albans, Durham, and the Cult of Saint Oswine, King and Martyr', *Viator*, 30 (1999), pp.105–44

Henderson, Ernest F., *Select Historical Documents of the Middle Ages* (London, 1896; repr. 1921)

Heng, Geraldine, 'The Romance of England: *Richard Coeur de Lyon*, Saracens, Jews and the Politics of Race and Nation', in *The Postcolonial Middle Ages*, ed. Jeffrey Jerome Cohen (Basingstoke, 2000), pp.135–71

Holland, William E., 'Formulaic Diction and the Descent of a Middle English Romance', *Speculum*, 48 (1973), pp.89–105

Horobin, Simon, and Alison Wiggins, 'Reconsidering Lincoln's Inn MS 150', *Medium Ævum*, 77.1 (2008), pp.30–53

Howlett, D. R., *The English Origins of Old French Literature* (Dublin, 1996)

Hunt, Richard W., 'The Library of the Abbey of St. Albans', in *Medieval Scribes, Manuscripts and Libraries: Essays Presented to N. R. Ker*, ed. M. B. Parkes and Andrew G. Watson (London, 1978), pp.251–77

James, M. R., *The Western Manuscripts in the Library of Trinity College, Cambridge: A Descriptive Catalogue*, 4 vols (Cambridge, 1904)

Jordan, William Chester, '"Quando fuit natus": Interpreting the Birth of Philip Augustus', in *The Work of Jacques le Goff and the Challenge of Medieval History*, ed. M. Rubin (Woodbridge, 1997), pp.171–88

Jung, Marc-René, *La Légende de Troie en France au moyen âge: analyse des versions françaises et bibliographie raisonée des manuscrits* (Basle, 1996)

Karla, Grammatiki A., 'Folk Narrative Techniques in the "Alexander Romance"', *Mnemosyne*, series 4, 65 (4–5) (2012), pp.636–55

Kay, Sarah, *The Chansons de Geste in the Age of Romance: Political Fictions* (Oxford, 1995)

Kelly, Douglas, 'Honor, Debate, and *Translatio imperii* in *Cligés*', *Arthuriana*, 18.3 (2008), pp.33–47

—, 'The Invention of Briseida's Story in Benoît de Sainte-Maure's *Troie*', *Romance Philology*, 48 (1995), pp.221–41

—, 'Troy in Latin and French: Joseph of Exeter's *Ylias* and Benoît de Sainte-Maure's *Roman de Troie*', in *The Conspiracy of Allusion: Description, Rewriting, and Authorship from Macrobius to Medieval Romance,* Studies in the History of Christian Thought, 47 (Leiden, 1999), pp.121–70

Kerr, Julie, *Monastic Hospitality: The Benedictines in England, c. 1070–c. 1250* (Woodbridge, 2007)

Kinoshita, Sharon, 'Chrétien de Troyes's *Cligès* in the Medieval Mediterranean', *Arthuriana*, 18.3 (2008), pp.48–61

—, 'The Poetics of Translatio: French-Byzantine Relations in Chrétien de Troyes's *Cligès*', *Exemplaria*, 8.2 (1996), pp.315–54

Konstan, David, 'The "Alexander Romance": The Cunning of the Open Text', *Lexis*, 16 (1998), pp.123–38

Kratz, Dennis, *Mocking Epic: Waltharius, Alexandreis, and the Problem of Christian Heroism*, Studia Humanitatis (Milan, 1980)

Lafferty, Maura K., 'Mapping Human Limitations: The Tomb Ecphrases in Walter of Châtillon's *Alexandreis*', *Journal of Medieval Latin*, 4 (1994), pp.64–81

—, 'Walter of Châtillon's *Alexandreis*', in *A Companion to Alexander Literature in the Middle Ages*, ed. Z. David Zuwiyya, Brill's Companions to the Christian Tradition, 29 (Leiden, 2011), pp.177–99

—, *Walter of Châtillon's* Alexandreis: *Epic and the Problem of Historical*

Understanding, Publications of the Journal of Medieval Latin, 2 (Turnhout, 1998)

Lane Fox, Robin J., 'The "Itinerary of Alexander": Constantius to Julian', *Classical Quarterly*, n.s. 47 (1997), pp.239–52

Legge, M. Dominica, *Anglo-Norman in the Cloisters: The Influence of the Orders on Anglo-Norman Literature* (Edinburgh, 1950)

—, *Anglo-Norman Literature and Its Background* (Oxford, 1963)

—, 'La Précocité de la littérature anglo-normande', *Cahiers de civilisation médiévale*, 8 (1965), pp.327–49

—, and D. J. A. Ross, 'Discussions: Thomas of Kent', *French Studies*, 9.4 (1955), pp.348–51

Liebeschütz, H., 'John of Salisbury and Pseudo-Plutarch', *Journal of the Warburg and Courtauld Institutes*, 6 (1943), pp.33–9

Loomis, Laura Hibbard, 'The Auchinleck Manuscript and a Possible London Bookshop of 1330–1340', *PMLA*, 57.3 (1942), pp.595–627

Lusignan, Serge, '*Translatio studii* and the Emergence of French as a Language of Letters in the Middle Ages', *New Medieval Literatures*, 14 (2012), pp.1–19

Macfie, A. L., *Orientalism* (London, 2002)

Macrae-Gibson, O. D., '*Of Arthour and of Merlin* in Sussex?', *English Language Notes*, 17.1 (1979), pp.7–10

Maddox, David, and Sara Sturm-Maddox (eds), *The Medieval French Alexander* (Albany, NY, 2002)

Mallette, Karla, 'Cosmopolitan Philology', *Postmedieval*, 5.4 (2014), pp.414–27

Martin, Janet, 'Classicism and Style in Latin Literature', in *Renaissance and Renewal in the Twelfth Century*, ed. Robert L. Benson, Giles Constable, and Carol D. Lanham (Oxford, 1982), pp.537–68

—, 'John of Salisbury as Classical Scholar', in *The World of John of Salisbury*, ed. Michael Wilkes, Studies in Church History, Subsidia, 3 (Oxford, 1984), pp.179–201

Mathorez, J., *Guillaume aux Blanches-Mains, évêque de Chartres* (Chartres, 1911)

Matthew, Donald, 'The Incongruities of the St Albans Psalter', *Journal of Medieval History*, 34.4 (2008), pp.396–416

McCash, June Hall, 'The Cultural Patronage of Medieval Women: An Overview', in *The Cultural Patronage of Medieval Women*, ed. June Hall McCash (Athens, GA, 1996), pp.1–49

McCracken, Peggy, 'Love and War in *Cligés*', *Arthuriana*, 18.3 (2008), pp.6–18

McCulloch, Florence, 'Saints Alban and Amphibalus in the Works of Matthew Paris: Dublin, Trinity College, MS 177', *Speculum*, 56.4 (1981), pp.761–85

McDonald, Nicola, '*The Seege of Troye*: "ffor wham was wakened al this wo?"', in *The Spirit of Medieval English Popular Romance*, ed. Ad Putter and Jane Gilbert (Harlow, 2000), pp.181–99

McInerney, Jeremy, 'Arrian and the Greek Alexander Romance', *The Classical World*, 100.4 (2007), pp.424–30

McLeod, W., 'Alban and Amphibal: Some Extant Lives and a Lost Life', *Mediaeval Studies*, 42 (1980), pp.407–30

Mehl, Dieter, *The Middle English Romances of the Thirteenth and Fourteenth Centuries* (London, 1969)

Mews, Constant J., and John N. Crossley (eds), *Communities of Learning: Networks and the Shaping of Intellectual Identity in Europe, 1100–1500*, Europa Sacra series, 11 (Turnhout, 2011)

Meyer, Paul, 'Étude sur les manuscrits du *Roman d'Alexandre*', *Romania*, 11 (1892), pp.213–332

Mickel, E., 'Writing the Record: The Old French Crusade Cycle', in *Epic and Crusade: Proceedings of the Colloquium of the Société Rencesvals British Branch*, ed. P. Bennett, A. Cobby, and J. Everson, British Rencesvals Publications, 4 (Edinburgh, 2006), pp.39–64

Minnis, A. J., and A. B. Scott (eds) with David Wallace, *Medieval Literary Theory and Criticism c. 1100–c. 1375: The Commentary Tradition*, rev. edn (Oxford, 1998)

Mooney, Linne R., and Estelle Stubbs, *Scribes and the City: London Guildhall Clerks and the Dissemination of Middle English Literature, 1375–1425* (York, 2013)

Mora-Lebrun, Francine, 'D'une esthétique à l'autre: la parole féminine dans l'*Iliade* de Joseph d'Exeter et le *Roman de Troie* de Benoît de Sainte-Maure', in *Conter de Troie et d'Alexandre: pour Emmanuèle Baumgartner*, ed. Laurence Harf-Lancner, Laurence Mathey-Maille, and Michelle Szkilnik (Paris, 2006), pp.31–50

——, 'De l' *Énéide* à l' *Énéas*: le traducteur médiéval à la recherche d'une nouvelle stylistique', *Bien Dire et Bien Aprandre*, 13–14 (1996), pp.21–40

——, 'L'*Ylias* de Joseph d'Exeter: une réaction cléricale au *Roman de Troie* de Benoît de Saint-Maure', in *Progrès, réaction, décadence dans l'occident médiéval*, ed. E. Baumgartner and L. Harf-Lancner, Publications Romanes et Françaises, 231 (Geneva, 2003), pp.199–213

——, 'Y a-t-il des circonstances atténuantes dans l'*Iliade* de Joseph d'Exeter et dans le *Waltharius*?', in *La Faute dans l'épopée médiévale: Ambiguïté de jugement*, ed. Bernard Ribémont (Rennes, 2012), pp.205–18

Morey, Dom Adrian, *Bartholomew of Exeter, Bishop and Canonist: A Study in the Twelfth Century* (Cambridge, 1937)

Morris, C., *The Papal Monarchy: The Western Church from 1050 to 1250*, Oxford History of the Christian Church (Oxford, 1989; repr. 1991)

Mortensen, Lars Boje, 'The Diffusion of Roman Histories in the Middle Ages: A List of Orosius, Eutropius, Paulus Diaconus, and Landolfus Sagax Manuscripts', *Filologia mediolatina*, 6–7 (1999–2000), pp.101–200

——, 'Orosius and Justinus in One Volume: Postconquest Books Across the Channel', *Cahiers de l'Institut du moyen âge grec et latin*, 60 (1990), pp.389–99

Moser Jr, Thomas C., *A Cosmos of Desire: The Medieval Latin Erotic Lyric in English Manuscripts* (Ann Arbor, MI, 2004)

Mossman, J. M., 'Tragedy and Epic in Plutarch's *Alexander*', *Journal of Hellenic Studies*, 108 (1988), pp.83–93

Munk Olsen, Birger, 'Quintus Curtius Rufus', in *L'étude des auteurs classiques latins aux XIe et XIIe siècles*, I: *Catalogue des manuscrits classiques latins copiés du IXe au XIIe siècles: Apicius–Juvénal* (Paris, 1982), pp.355–62

Munz, Peter, *Frederick Barbarossa: A Study in Medieval Politics* (London, 1969)

Nicolson, Adam, *The Mighty Dead: Why Homer Matters* (London, 2014)

Nolan, Barbara, *Chaucer and the Tradition of the Roman Antique* (Cambridge, 1992)

O'Callaghan, Tamara, 'Tempering Scandal: Eleanor of Aquitaine and Benoît de Sainte-Maure's *Roman de Troie*', in *Eleanor of Aquitaine: Lord and Lady*, ed. Bonnie Wheeler and John Carmi Parsons (Basingstoke, 2002), pp.301–17

Orchard, Andy, *Pride and Prodigies: Studies in the Monsters of the* Beowulf-*Manuscript* (Cambridge, 1995)

Otter, Monika, '"New Werke": *St. Erkenwald*, St. Albans, and the Medieval Sense of the Past', *Journal of Medieval and Renaissance* [Early Modern] *Studies*, 24.3 (1994), pp.387–414

Pade, Marianne, 'The Reception of Plutarch from Antiquity to the Italian Renaissance', in *A Companion to Plutarch*, ed. Mark Beck, Blackwell Companions to the Ancient World (Oxford, 2014), pp.531–43

Parker, H. C., 'The Pagan Gods in Joseph of Exeter *De bello Troiano*', *Medium Ævum*, 64.2 (1995), pp.273–8

Pearsall, Derek, 'The Development of Middle English Romance', *Mediaeval Studies*, 27 (1965), pp.91–116

—, 'The Whole Book: Late Medieval English Manuscript Miscellanies and Their Modern Interpreters', in *Imagining the Book*, ed. S. Kelly and J. J. Thompson (Turnhout, 2005), pp.17–29

Pearson, Lionel, *The Lost Histories of Alexander the Great* (London, 1960)

Pelling, C. B. R., 'Plutarch, *Alexander* and *Caesar*: Two New Fragments', *Classical Quarterly*, n.s. 23 (1973), pp.343–4

Petit, Aimé, *L'Anachronisme dans les romans antiques*, Nouvelle bibliothèque du Moyen Âge (Villeneuve d'Ascq, 1985; repr. Paris, 2002)

—, *Naissances du roman: les techniques littéraires dans les romans antiques du XIIe siècle*, 2 vols (Paris, 1985)

Phillips, Jonathan, *The Second Crusade: Extending the Frontiers of Christendom* (New Haven, NJ, 2007)

Polak, Lucie, *Chrétien de Troyes* Cligés, Critical Guides to French Texts, 23 (London, 1982)

Pollock, Sheldon, *The Language of the Gods in the World of Men* (Berkeley, CA, 2006)

Pope, M. K., 'Notes on the Vocabulary of the Romance of Horn and Rimel', in *Mélanges de philologie romane et de littérature médiévale offerts à Ernest Hoepffner* (Paris, 1949), pp.63–70

Putter, Ad, and Keith Busby, 'Introduction: Medieval Francophonia', in *Medieval Multilingualism: The Francophone World and its Neighbours*, ed. Christopher Kleinhenz and Keith Busby, Medieval Texts and Cultures of Northern Europe, 20 (Turnhout, 2010), pp.1–13

Putter, Ad, 'Knights and Clerics at the Court of Champagne: Chrétien de Troyes's Romances in Context', in *Medieval Knighthood V: Papers from the Sixth*

Strawberry Hill Conference, 1994, ed. Stephen Church and Ruth Harvey (Woodbridge, 1995), pp.243–66

Ratkowitsch, Christine, *Descriptio picturae: Die literarische Funktion der Beschreibung von Kunstwerken in der lateinischen Grossdichtung des 12. Jahrhunderts* (Vienna, 1991)

Reynolds, L. D. (ed.), *Texts and Transmission: A Survey of the Latin Classics* (Oxford, 1982)

Riddehough, Geoffrey Blundell, 'The Text of Joseph of Exeter's *Bellum Troianum*' (unpublished doctoral dissertation, Harvard University, 1951)

Rigg, A. G., 'Joseph of Exeter: Pagan Gods Again', *Medium Ævum*, 70.1 (2001), pp.19–28

Ross, D. J. A., *Alexander historiatus: A Guide to Medieval Illustrated Alexander Literature*, 2nd edn (Frankfurt am Main, 1988)

——, 'A Check-List of Manuscripts of Three Alexander Texts: The *Julius Valerius Epitome*, the *Epistola ad Aristotelem* and the *Collatio cum Dindimo*', *Scriptorium*, 10.1 (1956), pp.127–32

——, 'A Thirteenth-Century Anglo-Norman Workshop Illustrating Secular Literary Manuscripts?', in *Mélanges offerts à Rita Lejeune*, 2 vols (Gembloux, 1969), I, pp.689–94

——, *Studies in the Alexander Romance* (London, 1985)

Rouse, R. H., '*Florilegia* and Latin Classical Authors in Twelfth- and Thirteenth-Century Orléans', *Viator*, 10 (1979), pp.131–60

Rubincam, Catherine, 'Did Diodorus Siculus Take Over Cross-References from his Sources?', *American Journal of Philology*, 119.1 (1998), pp.67–87

——, 'How Many Books Did Diodorus Siculus Originally Intend to Write?', *Classical Quarterly*, n.s., 48.1 (1998), pp.229–33

Rychterová, Pavlína, 'Genealogies of Czech Literary History', *Interfaces: A Journal of Medieval European Literatures*, 1 (2015), pp.110–41

Sacks, K. S., *Diodorus Siculus and the First Century* (Princeton, NJ, 1991)

Said, Edward, *Orientalism* (London, 1978)

Salter, Elizabeth, *English and International: Studies in the Literature, Art and Patronage of Medieval England*, ed. Derek Pearsall and Nicolette Zeeman (Cambridge, 1988)

Saunders, Corinne (ed.), *A Companion to Romance: From Classical to Contemporary*, Blackwell Companions to Literature and Culture, 27 (Oxford, 2014)

Saunier, Pierre-Yves, *Transnational History*, Theory and History series (Basingstoke, 2013)

Scardigli, B. (ed.), *Essays on Plutarch's Lives* (Oxford, 1995)

Scattergood, V. J., 'Validating the High Life in *Of Arthour and of Merlin* and *Kyng Alisaunder*', *Essays in Criticism*, 54 (2004), pp.323–50

Schmidt, Paul Gerhard, 'The Quotation in Goliardic Poetry', in *Latin Poetry and the Classical Tradition*, ed. P. Godman and O. Murray (Oxford, 1990), pp.39–55

Selden, Daniel L., 'Mapping the Alexander Romance', in *The Alexander Romance in Persia and the East*, ed. Richard Stoneman, Kyle Erickson, and Ian Netton (Eelde, 2012), pp.19–59

Shipley, Graham, *The Greek World after Alexander 323–30 BC*, Routledge History of the Ancient World (London, 2000)

Short, Ian, 'Literary Culture at the Court of Henry II', in *Henry II: New Interpretations*, ed. Christopher Harper-Bill and Nicholas Vincent (Woodbridge, 2007), pp.335–61

—, *Manual of Anglo-Norman*, 2nd edn (Oxford, 2013)

Simons, Penny, 'Theme and Variations: The Education of the Hero in the *Roman d'Alexandre*', *Neophilologus*, 78 (1994), pp.195–208

Sklar, Elizabeth S., '*Arthour and Merlin*: The Englishing of Arthur', *Michigan Academician*, 8.1 (1975), pp.49–57

—, 'The Dialect of *Arthour and Merlin*', *English Language Notes*, 15.2 (1977), pp.88–94

Smalley, Beryl, *The Becket Conflict and the Schools: A Study of Intellectuals in Politics* (Oxford, 1973)

Smits, Edmé R., 'A Medieval Supplement to the Beginning of Curtius Rufus' *Historia Alexandri*: An Edition with Introduction', *Viator*, 18 (1987), pp.89–124

Southern, Richard, 'The Necessity for Two Peters of Blois', in *Intellectual Life in the Middle Ages: Essays Presented to Margaret Gibson*, ed. Lesley Smith and Benedicta Ward (London, 1991), p.103–18

—, *Platonism, Scholastic Method, and the School of Chartres*, Stenton Lecture 1978 (Reading, 1979)

—, 'The Schools of Paris and the School of Chartres', in *Renaissance and Renewal in the Twelfth Century*, ed. Robert L. Benson, Giles Constable, and Carol D. Lanham (Oxford, 1982), pp.113–37

Steele, R. B., 'Quintus Curtius Rufus', *American Journal of Philology*, 36 (1915), pp.402–23

Stein, Robert M., *Reality Fictions: Romance, History, and Governmental Authority, 1025–1180* (Notre Dame, IN, 2006)

Still, Michelle, *The Abbot and the Rule: Religious Life at St Albans, 1290–1349* (Aldershot, 2002)

Stock, Markus (ed.), *Alexander the Great in the Middle Ages: Transcultural Perspectives* (Toronto, 2016)

Stone, Charles Russell, *From Tyrant to Philosopher King: A Literary History of Alexander the Great in Medieval and Early Modern England* (Turnhout, 2013)

—, 'Investigating Macedon in Medieval England: The *St Albans Compilation*, the *Philippic Histories*, and the Reception of Alexander the Great', *Viator*, 42.1 (2011), pp.75–111

—, '"Many man he shal do woo": Portents and the End of an Empire in *Kyng Alisaunder*', *Medium Ævum*, 81.1 (2012), pp.18–40

—, *Roman de toute chevalerie* (forthcoming, Toronto)

Stoneman, Richard, *Alexander the Great* (London, 1997)

—, 'The Latin Alexander', in *Latin Fiction: The Latin Novel in Context*, ed. Heinz Hofmann (London, 1999), pp.167–86

—, *Legends of Alexander the Great*, 2nd edn (London, 2012)

Summerfield, Thea, '"And she answered in hir language": Aspects of Multilingualism in the Auchinleck Manuscript', in *Multilingualism in Medieval*

Britain, c.1066–1520, ed. J. A. Jefferson and A. Putter with A. Hopkins (Turnhout, 2013), pp.241–58

Swain, Simon, *Hellenism and Empire* (Oxford, 1996)

Telfryn Pritchard, R., 'Gautier de Châtillon's *Alexandreis* as an Historical Epic', *Bien Dire et Bien Aprandre*, 7 (1989), pp.35–49

Thomson, R. M., *Manuscripts from St Albans Abbey 1066–1235*, 2 vols (Cambridge, 1982)

Townsend, David, '"Michi barbaries incognita linguae": Other Voices and Other Visions in Walter of Châtillon's *Alexandreis*', *Allegorica*, 13 (1992), pp.21–37

—, 'Paratext, Ambiguity, and Interpretative Foreclosure in Manuscripts of Walter of Châtillon's *Alexandreis*', *New Medieval Literatures*, 14 (2012), pp.21–61

Traube, Ludwig, *Vorlesungen und Abhandlungen*, ed. Franz Boll, Paul Lehmann, and Samuel Brandt, 3 vols (Munich, 1909–20; repr. 1965), II: *Einleitung in die lateinische Philologie des Mittelalters*, ed. Paul Lehmann (1911)

Turville-Petre, Thorlac, *England the Nation: Language, Literature, and National Identity, 1290–1340* (Oxford, 1996)

Tyler, Elizabeth M., *Conceptualizing Multilingualism in Medieval England, c. 800–c. 1250*, ed. Elizabeth M. Tyler, Studies in the Early Middle Ages, 27 (Turnhout, 2012), pp.1–13

Uitti, Karl D., 'Chrétien de Troyes's *Cligès*: Romance *Translatio* and History', in *Conjunctures: Medieval Studies in Honor of Douglas Kelly*, ed. Keith Busby and Norris J. Lacy (Amsterdam, 1994), pp.545–57

Vaneman, Karen Haslanger, '*Of Arthour and of Merlin*: Arthour's Story as Arena for the Conflict of Custom and Common Law', *Quondam et Futurus* (*Arthuriana*), 8.2 (1988), pp.8–18

Vaughan, Richard, *Matthew Paris* (Cambridge, 1958)

Wallace, David (ed.), *Europe: A Literary History, 1348–1415*, 2 vols (Oxford, 2016)

Weiss, Judith, 'Insular Beginnings: Anglo-Norman Romance', in *A Companion to Romance: From Classical to Contemporary*, ed. Corinne Saunders, Blackwell Companions to Literature and Culture, 27 (Oxford, 2004), pp.26–44

—, 'Thomas and the Earl: Literary and Historical Contexts for the *Romance of Horn*', in *Tradition and Transformation in Medieval Romance*, ed. Rosalind Field (Cambridge, 1999), pp.1–13

Weynand, Johanna, *Der Roman de toute Chevalerie des Thomas von Kent in seinem Verhältnis zu seinen Quellen* (Bonn, 1911)

Whitmarsh, Tim, 'Addressing Power: Fictional Letters between Alexander and Darius', in *Epistolary Narratives in Ancient Greek Literature*, ed. Owen Hodkinson, Patricia A. Rosenmeyer, and Evelien M. J. Bracke (Leiden, 2013), pp.169–86

—, 'Alexander's Hellenism and Plutarch's Textualism', *Classical Quarterly*, n.s., 52 (2002), pp.174–92

—, *Greek Literature and the Roman Empire: The Politics of Imitation* (Oxford, 2001)

—, 'Prose Fiction', in *A Companion to Hellenistic Literature*, ed. James J. Clauss and Martine Cuypers, Blackwell Companions to the Ancient World (Oxford, 2010), pp.394–411

—, *The Second Sophistic*, New Surveys in the Classics, 35 (Oxford, 2005)

Wiener, Claudia, *Proles vaesana Philippi totius malleus orbis: Die Alexandreis des Walter von Châtillon und ihre Neudeutung von Lucans Pharsalia im Sinne des typologischen Geschichtsverständnisses* (Munich, 2001)

Williams, John R., 'The Cathedral School of Reims in the Eleventh Century', *Speculum*, 29 (1954), pp.661–77

—, 'The Quest for the Author of the *Moralium dogma philosophorum*, 1931–1956', *Speculum*, 32.4 (1957), pp.736–47

—, 'William of the White Hands and Men of Letters', in *Anniversary Essays in Medieval History by Students of Charles Homer Haskins*, ed. C. H. Taylor (Boston, 1929), pp.365–87

Witke, Charles, review of Peter Dronke, *Medieval Latin and the Rise of European Love-Lyric*, *Modern Philology*, 64.4 (1967), pp.326–31

Wogan-Browne, Jocelyn, et al. (eds), *Language and Culture in Medieval Britain: The French of England, c.1100–c.1500* (York, 2009)

—, 'What's in a Name? The French of England', in *Language and Culture in Medieval Britain: The French of England, c.1100–c.1500*, ed. Jocelyn Wogan-Browne et al. (York, 2009), pp.1–13

Yardley, J. C., *Justin and Pompeius Trogus: A Study of the Language of Justin's Epitome of Trogus* (Toronto, 2003)

Zecchini, G., 'Latin Historiography: Jerome, Orosius and the Western Chronicles', in *Greek and Roman Historiography in Late Antiquity: Fourth to Sixth Century A.D.*, ed. Gabriele Marasco (Leiden, 2003), pp.317–45

Zuwiyya, Z. David, 'The Arabic Alexander Tradition', in *A Companion to Alexander Literature in the Middle Ages*, ed. Z. David Zuwiyya, Brill's Companions to the Christian Tradition, 29 (Leiden, 2011), pp.73–112

— (ed.), *A Companion to Alexander Literature in the Middle Ages*, Brill's Companions to the Christian Tradition, 29 (Leiden, 2011)

Online Resources

Anglo-Norman Dictionary < www.anglo-norman.net/>
Auchinleck Manuscript <http://auchinleck.nls.uk/editorial/importance.html>
Global Chaucers < https://globalchaucers.wordpress.com/resources/translations-and-adaptations-listed-by-country/>
Middle English Dictionary < https://quod.lib.umich.edu/m/med/>
Medieval Francophone Literary Culture Outside France project <www.medievalfrancophone.ac.uk/textual-traditions-and-segments/alexandre/manuscripts-and-periods-of-production/>
St Albans Psalter < www.abdn.ac.uk/stalbanspsalter>

Index

Abelard, Peter 70n, 78n

Achilles: Alexander's attitude to 27, 45, 84, 247; in *Roman de Troie*, 256–7; in *SBT*, 273–4; in *Ylias*, 251–2

Adkin, Neil 74n, 77n, 78n

Adrian IV, Pope 191

Aeneas 23n

Akbari, Suzanne Conklin 150n

Alan of Lille 83n, 104n

Alban, St 186–8

Alberic of Besançon 114

Alcuin 57, 149

Alexander A 196

Alexander and Dindimus 196

Alexander B 196

Alexander C 196

Alexander literature: discontinuities in literary history 5–6; and genres, 29–31; lost works, 28–31; medieval overview, 4–5; philosophical works, 23n; portrayal of Alexander, 167n; scholarship overview, 12–15

Alexander Romance: ethics and exemplarity 118; historical context, 24–7; overview, 32–7; popularity, 120; as source, 152; textual history, 32–3, 34–5

Alexander the Great: and Athens 166, 247, 262, 269; and Babylon, 75–9, 248, 264; cultural identity, 27–8; death, 45, 53n, 62, 250, 255, 264, 270; and Homer, 27, 45, 84, 247; paternity and bloodline, 33, 38–9, 159–61, 163, 252, 261,

268–9; royal diaries, 29; submarine adventure, 116–18; and Thebes, 79n, 166, 208, 247, 262; treatment of Darius' family, 39, 54–5, 61, 248, 253, 269

Alexander III, Pope 96

Alexandre de Paris: life 122–3

    ROMAN D'ALEXANDRE: approach to historiography 122, 127–8, 143, 239; Christian themes, 89n, 119–20; dating, 110n; ethics and exemplarity, 115–20, 122, 143, 240; and fiction, 122; influence, 192n; manuscripts, 154n; narrative summary, 252–5; Oriental marvels, 120–2, 169, 253–4; overview, 114–24; political dimension, 122–4; popularity, 113n; relationship to *Alexandreis*, 111–14, 119–20, 122; relationship to *Cligès*, 133, 140; relationship to *Roman de Troie*, 124–32; relationship to *RTC*, 19, 152, 153–4; sources, 112–13, 114–15; spread of manuscripts, 196; and transnationalism, 122–4, 238

Alexandre en Orient 120n, 134n

Alexandreis see Walter of Châtillon

Amazons: in *Alexandreis* 99, 249; in early Alexander literature, 34, 36; in *Roman d'Alexandre*, 255; in *Roman de Troie*, 257; in *RTC*, 263

ambivalence *see sic et non* concept

Volumes Already Published